War and Conflict in the Modern World

War and Conflict Through the Ages

Jeremy Black, *War in the Nineteenth Century*
Brian Sandberg, *War and Conflict in the Early Modern World*

War and Conflict in the Early Modern World

1500–1700

Brian Sandberg

polity

First published in 2016 by Polity Press

Polity Press
65 Bridge Street
Cambridge CB2 1UR, UK

Polity Press
350 Main Street
Malden, MA 02148, USA

ISBN-13: 978-0-7456-4602-2
ISBN-13: 978-0-7456-4603-9(pb)

A catalogue record for this book is available from the British Library.

Library of Congress Cataloging-in-Publication Data

Names: Sandberg, Brian, 1968- author.
Title: War and conflict in the early modern world : 1500–1700 / Brian
    Sandberg.
Description: Malden, MA : Polity Press, 2016. | Series: War and conflict
    through the ages | Includes bibliographical references and index.
Identifiers: LCCN 2015035482| ISBN 9780745646022 (hardback) |
    ISBN 9780745646039 (pbk.) | ISBN 9781509503018 (mobi) |
    ISBN 9781509503025 (epub)
Subjects: LCSH: War–History–16th century. | War–History–17th century. |
    War and society–History–16th century. | War and society–History–17th
    century.
Classification: LCC U39 .S26 2016 | DDC 355.0209/031–dc23 LC record available at
http://lccn.loc.gov/2015035482

Typeset in 10.5 on 12 pt Times
by Toppan Best-set Premedia Limited
Printed and bound in the UK by Clays Ltd. St Ives PLC

For further information on Polity, visit our website: politybooks.com

For John A. Lynn, mentor and friend

Contents

Preface

This book presents a global examination of the dynamics of war, culture, and society in the early modern period. Studying warfare and its incredibly complex history on a global scale presents a truly daunting task, however. *War and Conflict in the Early Modern World* is situated at the intersection of several competing approaches to the study of war, violence, and conflict in current and historical contexts.

The interrelated fields of military history and diplomatic history have long focused on the history of warfare through the study of states, their military systems, and their international relations. These "traditional" fields, shaped by the writings of Antoine-Henri Jomini and Carl von Clausewitz in the mid-nineteenth century, have tended to focus on major international wars fought between nation-states, narrating military operations, battles, and peace treaties. Military history and international relations history have continued to evolve, but a number of other approaches have greatly broadened notions of warfare and the study of its practices.

Historians of war and society began to incorporate social history methods in the late 1960s and 1970s, considering the social composition of armies and the relationships between military institutions and their political systems. John Keegan's *The Face of Battle* (1976) provided a powerful example of how historians could consider the experience of combat for ordinary soldiers in past wars.[1] Throughout the 1970s and 1980s, historians such as André Corvisier, John Shy, Michael Howard, John A. Lynn, Geoffrey Parker, Denis Showalter, and Brian McAllister Linn constructed a "New Military History" by embracing social history approaches as a way of uncovering broader realities of warfare beyond the conventional battlefield accounts and campaign narratives of previous military histories.[2] In the same period, social historians examined peasant revolts, revolutions, civil wars, crowd conflicts, bread riots, religious riots, and other forms of social conflict and organized violence – significantly stretching the academic study of war and conflict.

In the 1980s and 1990s, cultural history transformed the study of warfare and conflict even further. Cultural historians have examined rhetoric, language, and political culture in the context of revolutions, civil conflicts, and major wars. Cultural histories of war have expanded the historical "actors" in conflicts to consider reservists, logistical personnel, military wives, camp followers, refugees, indigenous peoples, and civilian victims of war. Historians such as Christopher Browning, Jeremy Black, Drew Gilpin Faust, Isabel V. Hull, Hervé Drévillon, and Wayne E. Lee have explored diverse aspects of war and culture within specific societies or in broader global and imperial contexts.[3]

Alongside these histories of warfare, a broader history of violence has been developed by anthropologists, sociologists, and historians who examine diverse manifestations of violence – often outside conventional wartime situations. Physical aggression remains important for violence studies, but some of these scholars explore psychological, economic, legal, gendered, and emotional dimensions of warfare. Elaine Scarry's pioneering work, *The Body in Pain*, contemplates bodily dimensions of violence, insisting that the primary purpose of war is to inflict injury on human beings.[4] Julius Ruff, Neil L. Whitehead, Veena Das, Arthur Kleinman, Paul Virilio, and others have examined mass rape, dueling cultures, militarization, mechanization, and suffering in warfare.

Peace and conflict studies (or war and peace studies) have developed on a markedly different trajectory since the 1960s. This interdisciplinary field examines conflict resolution and peace implementation and has often been focused on contemporary cases, rather than historical analysis. Scholars such as Johan Galtung, Johannes Botes, Francis A. Beer, Larry J. Fisk, and Douglas P. Fry have pushed beyond diplomatic histories of ambassadors and international treaties to consider broader peacemaking processes. Historians are taking insights from peace and reconciliation processes in Ireland and South Africa to re-examine the dynamics of peacemaking in the past.

Serious tensions exist between these various methods of examining warfare. Proponents of each of these approaches sponsor their own conferences, journals, and publications – often producing divergent lines of research and fragmented debates. This book will confront these tensions through an exploration of early modern warfare, recognizing that specialists in different fields of study will undoubtedly challenge some of my methodological and coverage choices. This study cannot consider all the possible manifestations of violence, conflict, and warfare in the early modern world, however.

I will instead concentrate on *organized armed violence*, examining specific forms of violence that were prevalent during the early modern period. By *organized armed violence*, I mean physical violence and coercion organized by clans, communities, militant groups, military elites, organizations, and institutions at the civic, regional, or state level in order to wage armed conflict internally or externally. This approach emphasizes the importance of warfare and social conflict over interpersonal violence or economic conflict, but allows for a broad examination of diverse forms of violence within and between societies.

Despite my aspiration to compose a global history of warfare and my training as a comparative historian, I must acknowledge the difficulties and limitations that I have encountered in attempting to write a history of warfare in the early modern world. My own historical research focuses on early modern France, Italy, and the Mediterranean in the late sixteenth and early seventeenth centuries. My language skills confine my archival research to English, French, and Italian manuscripts, supported by broader reading of printed sources in these languages, as well as some Spanish and German sources. This book required me to stretch well beyond my research specialization to consider historical developments around the world across almost three centuries. The book thus necessarily relies heavily on the research and writing of other scholars across a range of specialized fields in early modern history.

Parts of chapters 6 and 9 are adapted from my article, "Beyond Encounters: Religion, Ethnicity, and Violence in the Early Modern Atlantic World, 1450–1700," *Journal of World History* 17 (March 2006): 1–25. Portions of several chapters are adapted from my reviews of books by Maurizio Arfaioli, Stuart Carroll, Darryl Dee, Pablo E. Pérez-Mallaína, Jonathan Spangler, B. Ann Tlusty, and Matthew Vester.

My teaching of global and comparative courses, entitled "The Mediterranean World," "The Renaissance," "Religion in Early Modern Europe," "The European Wars of Religion," "Religious Violence in Global Perspective," "Religious Politics and Sectarian Violence," and "Western Civilization (1500–1815)," significantly shaped my understanding of war and conflict in the early modern world. I wish to thank the undergraduate and graduate students who attended my courses at Northern Illinois University for their excellent questions and comments. Graduate students and colleagues at the Université de Paris I (Panthéon-Sorbonne) and the Université de Paris IV (Paris-Sorbonne) provided invaluable reactions to my ideas and approaches during seminar and workshop sessions.

I thank my colleagues and audiences at numerous historical and interdisciplinary conferences for raising issues and providing crucial feedback that allowed me to write and revise this book. Research support and collaboration as a residential fellow at the Institut d'études avancées de Paris, as a Fulbright Research Scholar in France, and as a Solmsen Postdoctoral Fellow at the Institute for Research in the Humanities of the University of Wisconsin at Madison shaped this project. A Franklin Grant from the American Philosophical Society, a Summer Research and Artistry Award from Northern Illinois University, sabbatical leave from Northern Illinois University, and assistance from the Medici Archive Project all provided crucial research support. I especially wish to thank the readers for Polity who offered detailed commentaries and constructive criticism on earlier drafts of this book.

This book was inspired by my studies on war and society with professors John Lamphear, Geoffrey Parker, and John A. Lynn. I thank them profusely, as well as my family and friends in Texas, Illinois, and Europe, who remained curious and inquisitive about the book as it gradually coalesced. I want to express my deepest appreciation to Laura Kramer, who read the first draft of the manuscript and provided vital feedback on it. Finally, I want to thank David Krugler, my good friend and writing collaborator, for all his support and encouragement throughout the long process of researching and writing this book.

Introduction

War and Conquest in the Yucatán

Francisco de Montejo and his *conquistadores* landed in the Yucatán peninsula in 1527 to conquer the Maya and establish Spanish imperial rule. The cover image of this book depicts the amphibious landing of Montejo's expeditionary force at Cozumel, as horses are unloaded from one ship, while Montejo and his officers are rowed from another in a small launch. The gunports of the powerful carracks are open, allowing the shipboard artillery to cover the troops as they land. Near the shoreline, cavalrymen are forming up and reviewing an infantry unit composed of pikemen and arquebusiers. In another narrative sequence in the center of the composition, Montejo and his bodyguard of arquebusiers greet the local Maya, who are shown naked. A final sequence in the foreground centers on Montejo as he draws his sword against a threatening Maya warrior who has seized a scimitar from an African slave in order to attack Montejo, while other Maya flee from the conflict.[1]

This dramatic representation of Francisco de Montejo's amphibious landing is part of a large series of prints of the Americas published by the Flemish engraver and printer Theodore de Bry in the late sixteenth century.[2] De Bry, whose prints of Christopher Columbus's landing in Hispaniola and of Brazilian cannibals are much better known, based this composition on a vivid account in Girolamo Benzoni's *History of the New World*.[3] The image of Montejo's landing offers a curious entry point to the problems of war and conflict in the sixteenth century. New technologies such as carracks, shipborne cannon, and firearms are prominently displayed, alongside older weapons such as swords and halberds. The Spanish cavalry uses horses equipped with saddles and stirrups to provide balance and control, facilitating their military use. The Spanish infantry is depicted using a mixed-arms formation and infantry drill, even though Montejo's actual troops probably did not utilize these techniques. These technologies and weapons systems were all unknown to the Maya before their sudden contact with the Spanish *conquistadores*.

The print hardly presents a triumphal account of Spanish conquest and European technological superiority, however. Montejo and his son led a series of military expeditions in the Yucatán peninsula between 1527 and 1547, but ultimately failed to subjugate the Maya. Montejo's campaigns usually receive less attention than Hernán Cortés's stunning conquest of central Mexico, but these "ambivalent conquests" in the Yucatán reveal important aspects of colonial warfare.[4] Spanish imperial authority gradually expanded in the peninsula later in the century as the Maya perished from epidemics, retreated into the rainforest, or assented nominally to Spanish rule. The Maya continued to resist assimilation, however, even as they traded with the Spanish and embraced Christianity. De Bry, a Protestant printer, worked in the Spanish Netherlands during the Dutch Revolt, before fleeing to Germany and England. He visually juxtaposes Montejo's violence against Maya innocence as one component in a monumental polemical campaign against the Spanish Empire and Catholicism, helping to shape a lasting Black Legend of Spanish imperial domination and cruelties against Amerindians.[5]

War in World History

This book takes a global approach to the history of war and conflict in the early modern period, when new military technologies and practices transformed armies and societies around the world. Beginning around 1500, growing trans-oceanic contacts and cross-cultural exchanges produced maritime empires that spanned the globe. Economic development, population growth, religious reform, and political conflict all resulted in extensive social disruption and civil warfare during the sixteenth and seventeenth centuries. The increasing military and financial demands of sustained warfare and empire-building produced powerful territorial states by 1700.

Early modern warfare is sometimes described as the "sport of kings," since dynastic states routinely fought over precedence, privileges, territories, and succession claims. Wars between royal states were hardly the only forms of conflict, however; civil wars, noble revolts, religious conflicts, and peasant revolts also erupted frequently during the sixteenth and seventeenth centuries. Urban populations witnessed periodic protests, riots, and massacres during chaotic civil conflicts and sometimes during peacetime. Armies extracted financial and material resources from urban and rural populations, while soldiers routinely plundered peasants living in war zones. Law courts and special tribunals sometimes operated in war zones and conquered lands, prosecuting rebels and conducting inquisitorial campaigns against heretics. Maritime expeditions, imperial conquests, and colonial conflicts occurred throughout the period. Piracy and raiding warfare plagued coastlines, colonial outposts, and borderlands. Bandits dominated forests and sparsely populated regions, preying on travelers and raiding isolated villages. Military and social elites engaged in feuding and other forms of familial violence that sometimes produced broader social conflicts. War and conflict were seemingly ubiquitous in the early modern period.

We must reconsider Clausewitzian notions of war in order to examine these diverse dimensions of early modern warfare. Carl von Clausewitz, the most important theorist of modern warfare, famously argues that "war is not a mere act of policy but a true political instrument, a continuation of political activity by other means....The political object is the goal, war is the means of reaching it, and means can never be considered in isolation from their purpose."[6] Writing in the aftermath of the French Revolutionary and Napoleonic Wars (1792–1815), Clausewitz considered nation-states, their armies, and their generals as the principal protagonists in his theory of war. None of the city-states, republics, or princely states of the early modern period constituted nation-states, however, making Clausewitz's theory problematic for considering conventional warfare between states prior to the Napoleonic period. Although Clausewitz did contemplate guerrilla warfare in a limited fashion, nationalism and wars of national liberation remain central to his thinking on low-intensity conflicts. His state-centered political approach to war cannot fully grasp the dynamics of colonial conquests, religious conflicts, civil wars, and mercantile struggles in the early modern period, when various non-state actors and organizations played significant roles in waging war.

Instead of viewing war merely as an instrument of state policies, this book will examine early modern war and conflict as constituting *organized armed violence*, which could assume many forms. A stunning array of individuals and organizations orchestrated military activity during the early modern period, using armed forces to inflict physical violence on enemies and to dominate civilian populations. Rulers and their advisors directed the war efforts of major princely or city-states, but military and administrative officers mobilized troops at the regional and local levels – often on their own initiative and with their own agendas. Field armies assembled infantry regiments, cavalry companies, and artillery batteries composed of soldiers from diverse "nations," sometimes organized in stipendiary contingents. Nobles, military entrepreneurs, municipal leaders, commercial associations, religious organizations, clans, and village councils were all capable of organizing and directing armed forces to defend themselves or to join broader militant causes. Meanwhile, individuals joined "national" military units, civic guards, artisanal groups, warrior monks, warships, corsairs, colonial militias, nomadic horsemen, and peasant bands that engaged in combat using culturally specific military practices and tactics.

The methods of organizing armed violence responded to changing political, economic, and social contexts in the early modern period. Military systems around the world adapted, diffused, exchanged, and appropriated weapons technologies and military techniques. At the same time, global contacts and exchanges allowed some armies to impose political and social change through military conquest and outright subjugation. Certain military systems operated in conjunction with elaborate imperial structures and colonial configurations over distant territories. Other military organizations employed complex overland and maritime communication networks to contest imperial power using alternative forms of violence. Finally, state development processes created new institutions to manage military administration, logistical, and information services. I will argue that these overlapping processes transformed the nature of war and conflict in the early modern world.

Interpreting Early Modern War and Conflict

Several competing historical approaches offer pathways for exploring the complex dynamics of early modern warfare. The concept of a *Military Revolution* focuses on the development and diffusion of military technologies and techniques in the sixteenth and seventeenth centuries. In contrast, the notion of *Encounters* emphasizes global contacts, suggesting that biological exchanges, human migrations, and environmental changes shaped early modern warfare. *New Imperial Histories* stress the significance of imperial systems and colonial enterprises in generating conflicts over trading routes, ports, and terrains. *Connected Histories* envision the world as linked through transnational economic, social, and communication networks, highlighting borderlands and maritime spaces as zones of conflict. *State*

Development studies examine changing administrative and financial techniques that governments used to organize early modern warfare, as well as conflicts produced by state formation processes.

Each of these methodologies emphasizes a different historical explanation for the changing relationships between war and society in the sixteenth and seventeenth centuries. We need to examine these methodologies in some detail, since each approach will play a role in analyzing aspects of early modern warfare throughout the book. No single methodology will be privileged, but combining elements of these competing approaches will allow us to consider how the transformations of military practices in the early modern period were closely linked to new forms of warfare.

The Military Revolution and early modern warfare

For four decades, scholarship on early modern warfare has revolved around the concept of a Military Revolution. Michael Roberts, a historian of early modern Sweden, first enunciated the notion of revolution in military systems in a 1955 lecture, arguing that sweeping changes transformed European militaries between 1560 and 1660 and created modern warfare.[7] According to Roberts, a series of "tactical innovations" – especially the development of infantry firearms drill and discipline in the early seventeenth century – increased the size of armies and greatly expanded the scale of warfare, prompting states to create standing armies and expansive new powers to wage war. Roberts later wove his interpretation of a Military Revolution into his studies of the Swedish army and state during the seventeenth century, while other historians popularized the concept or adopted parallel formulations.[8]

The staying power of the Military Revolution concept is largely due to its modification by Geoffrey Parker, a historian of sixteenth-century Spain and the Dutch Revolt. In a short epilogue to his detailed study of the Spanish Army of Flanders, Parker questioned Roberts's emphasis on the Dutch and Swedish tactical developments and later expanded his ideas in a 1976 article.[9] Over the following decade, Parker gradually developed a new definition of the concept.[10] Parker concurs with Roberts that tactical innovations transformed warfare, but he argues that the naval developments and *trace italienne* fortifications (bastioned artillery fortresses) were crucial technological aspects of the revolution, in addition to the new infantry drill and discipline. This emphasis shifts the chronology of the Military Revolution solidly to the sixteenth century, allowing for later refinements and transmissions of the new technologies and tactics. Like Roberts, Parker presents the Military Revolution as a primarily European development, but his analysis of the global diffusion of the military transformations links the concept to the narratives of the Rise of the West and modernization. He concludes that "only military resilience and technological innovation – especially the capital ship, infantry firepower and the artillery fortress: the three vital components of the military revolution of the sixteenth century – allowed the West to make the most of its smaller resources in order to resist and, eventually, to expand to global dominance."[11]

Parker's *The Military Revolution* generated a sustained debate over the definition of the concept itself, as well as the chronology, technological nature, and geographic diffusion of the military changes associated with it. Many historians question the timing of key military developments or the revolutionary nature of early modern warfare, seeing changes as more incremental and evolutionary. Jeremy Black and other scholars criticize the concept as reductionist, arguing that economic, political, social, and environmental factors also contributed to changes in warfare and imperialism in the period.[12] Clifford J. Rogers's *The Military Revolution Debate* assembles many of the most important contributions in a useful collective volume, which includes a response essay by Geoffrey Parker.[13]

Although the Military Revolution concept involves broad institutional, organizational, and social aspects, much of the debate has unfortunately focused too narrowly on technological or technical issues of *trace italienne* fortification designs, infantry volley-fire systems, shipboard gunports, and socket bayonets. Some critics have accused Michael Roberts and Geoffrey Parker of technological determinism. Often, proponents and critics of the Military Revolution implicitly assume that battlefield victories necessarily signify the superiority of victorious military systems, misinterpreting the complexities of technological transformations and diffusions.

The conceptual debates over the Military Revolution have largely consisted of appropriations, expansions, or redefinitions of the concept. Ancient and medieval historians discern a series of "military revolutions" preceding the developments of the sixteenth and seventeenth centuries. Meanwhile, modern historians argue that later developments of the eighteenth or nineteenth centuries produced more significant transformations of warfare. Proponents of the related concept of Revolutions in Military Affairs (RMA) insist that revolutionary military changes have not only occurred in the past, but can be actively fostered by military policymakers in the present.

The Military Revolution debate continues to fuel new research on early modern military systems, but the concept has been also heavily criticized for its Eurocentric perspective on world history. Indeed, in a number of aspects, the Military Revolution concept reinforces classic interpretations of early European imperialism, such as Carlo M. Cipolla's *Guns, Sails, and Empires* and William McNeill's *The Rise of the West*.[14] The Military Revolution concept is flexible enough to contemplate cross-cultural exchanges and military acculturation, but many histories of early modern military technologies and warfare have merely applied European historical categories and periodizations to world history.[15] Eurocentric histories of warfare thus tend to employ narratives of modernization that privilege the role of the European states and militaries in creating the modern world. Jeremy Black has critiqued such Eurocentric approaches, calling on military historians to examine warfare around the world, lamenting:

> The study of war, especially prior to the modern period, is a subject that has received insufficient attention in academic circles over the past four decades. Furthermore, most of that attention has been devoted to warfare in Europe. When the rest of the world has been considered, it has generally been with reference to the expansion of European military power.[16]

The Military Revolution concept remains useful, but it best explains technical and organizational developments in European military systems that gradually spread worldwide as European soldiers and colonizers exported them to colonial territories. Recent research on sixteenth- and seventeenth-century European naval power, colonization, arms trade, technical training, and military treatises has enhanced our understanding of early modern warfare on a global scale. Proponents of the Military Revolution may be correct in their belief that European models of warfare had become globally exportable by 1700, as permanent professional armies, artillery fortifications, barracks, and infantry drill became signs of centralized state power throughout the world.[17] However, the Military Revolution cannot effectively explain other dynamics of war and conflict that originated in non-European contexts or that developed along alternative global trajectories.

Encounters in the early modern world

Soldiers and sailors often confronted unexpected opponents in the early modern period, as maritime expeditions brought radically diverse military and social systems into contact. The shock of cross-cultural contacts in the late fifteenth and early sixteenth centuries in the Americas, Africa, and the Indian Ocean shattered some political systems and upset social and cultural cohesion. However, these violent "first contacts" were not determined purely by military technologies and tactics, as we saw in the Yucatán. Alfred W. Crosby's classic *The Columbian Exchange* provides a vital perspective for an analysis of war and conflict in the early modern world because it examines conflict in the context of diverse human, animal, plant, and material exchanges around the world in the wake of Columbus's voyages.[18]

The Americas had been divided from the rest of the world for thousands of years, almost completely isolated from biological and cultural exchanges elsewhere. When Columbus's first expedition landed in the Bahamas in October 1492, "the two worlds...were reunited, and the two worlds, which were so very different, began on that day to become alike. That trend toward biological homogeneity is one of the most important aspects of the history of life on this planet since the retreat of the continental glaciers."[19] This dramatic description highlights the momentous transformations of human, animal, and plant life that were unleashed by Columbus's trans-Atlantic voyages and by those that followed.

Crosby describes the complex biological interactions and migrations across the Atlantic Ocean during the sixteenth and seventeenth centuries as a set of interlinked processes that he calls the Columbian Exchange. Biological and environmental exchanges – such as the spread (and exchange) of epidemic diseases, agricultural crops, food products, grasses, horses, and livestock – produced long-term economic, cultural, and social transformations around the world. Although the concept of the Columbian Exchange tends to privilege specifically trans-Atlantic exchanges, many of the encounters, exchanges, and transformations were global in nature, allowing historians to analyze cross-cultural contacts and exchanges that occurred around the world during the sixteenth and seventeenth centuries. The concept of "encounters" has been popular since the 1992 quincentennial commemorations of Columbus's initial voyage, but scholars have largely ignored its implications for the history of warfare.

Environmental historians and historians of science have nonetheless studied various aspects of global encounters, greatly expanding our understandings of biological dimensions of early modern conflicts. Eurasian diseases such as smallpox decimated Amerindian populations, facilitating European colonial expansion in the Americas. Meanwhile, tropical diseases plagued colonizing soldiers and sailors, arguably preventing European colonial expansion in Africa and parts of the Americas until the nineteenth century.[20] Anthony Pagden examines the scientific and intellectual implications of trans-Atlantic exchanges in forming European rationales for conquest, colonization, and assimilation of indigenous peoples.[21] The spread of horses and draft animals allowed certain armies to develop cavalry forces and transport services, even as global exchanges of food crops, medicinal plants, and intoxicants transformed logistical systems and military culture elsewhere.

Global climate changes in the early modern period forced military systems to adapt to altered agricultural conditions and severe weather events. Historians and scientists have discovered massive evidence for a period of global cooling during the seventeenth century, which produced particularly harsh winters and shorter campaigning seasons. This Little Ice Age shortened growing seasons in many parts of the world, triggering agricultural disruptions, lengthy famines, massive floods, and social conflicts. Many scholars argue that these conflicts also produced or worsened political conflicts and wars, resulting in a global Crisis of the Seventeenth Century.[22]

Creating a more nuanced history of encounters requires inserting a comprehensive examination of warfare into histories of the early modern world.[23] The notion of encounters sometimes obscures agency in the production of violence and deflects attention from the horrendous consequences of armed conflict. Too often, historians have emphasized the creative aspects of cross-cultural exchanges without fully contemplating the killing, destruction, and brutality of early modern contacts and encounters. Crosby's own depiction of the processes of trans-Atlantic exchange actually emphasizes the violent, destructive clashes of conquering germs, plants, animals, and humans – indeed, his subsequent book explores "biological imperialism."[24] Historians have begun to construct studies of violent aspects of early modern encounters, integrating human migration and biological factors into histories of conflict. Wayne E. Lee rightly argues that "new cultures of power and cultures of war were born in the many crucibles of encounter around the globe."[25]

Cross-cultural encounters often occurred in the context of colonial conflicts, maritime expeditions, and raiding warfare. The French explorer Samuel de Champlain employed violence in the beaver pelt trade in North America, even though French colonization in Québec has often been seen as less aggressive than English colonization along the Atlantic coast. Chinese military forces reacted harshly to encroachments by foreigners – in one case killing many of the survivors of a Portuguese shipwreck who were stranded on the soil of mainland China.[26] In the Mediterranean, pirates and privateers engaged in perpetual slave-taking operations, often later ransoming captives. The developing history of encounters allows us to place warfare at the center of early modern world history during the period when sustained global contacts and exchanges were first occurring.

New Imperial Histories

New empires and novel forms of imperialism transformed war and conflict in the early modern period. Curiously, historians of imperialism have tended to focus on nineteenth-century imperialism, and in particular on the British and French colonial empires in Africa and South Asia. Marxist histories of imperialism have long portrayed nineteenth-century European empires as forging a distinct stage of capitalism that involved colonial domination, concentration of capital, and bourgeois appropriation of state power. Other modernization narratives have portrayed European imperialism and colonialism as natural outgrowths of nationalism and industrialization. European nation-states indeed constructed vast colonial empires in the nineteenth and early twentieth centuries, often employing imperialist discourses of a "civilizing mission" to justify conquest and occupation of distant colonies around the world. J.M. Blaut criticizes such imperialist rhetoric, emphasizing that Eurocentrism has served as "the colonizer's model of the world."[27] Postcolonial scholars have exposed the racism, coercion, and brutality of European imperialism in the modern period, dismantling Eurocentric models of modernization. Since the late twentieth century, postcolonial criticism and archival research on modern empires has produced New Imperial Histories that investigate race, class, gender, and violence as intimately interconnected.

Imperialism has a much longer history, however, spanning much of world history, including the early modern period. Immanuel Wallerstein has influentially argued that the modern world system emerged in sixteenth century through a combination of global capitalism, sovereign states, and colonial empires.[28] The methods of the New Imperial History are now being applied to study early modern empires around the world comparatively. According to Jane Burbank and Frederick Cooper, "Empires are large political units, expansionist or with a memory of power extended over space, polities that maintain distinction and hierarchy as they incorporate new people."[29] Comparative definitions, such as this one, have encouraged historians to examine early modern empires as imperial states that waged war and deployed power to dominate ethnically diverse populations. Many of these empires engaged in complex multidirectional exchanges and circulations of military technologies, techniques, and practices with adjacent peoples and states.

Historians also need to reconceptualize Europeans' roles in the production of global violence in the early modern world in order to disrupt Eurocentric historiographical narratives even further.[30] New Imperial History approaches are now being applied to the study of early modern empires, but challenges remain in examining the many diverse forms of imperialism in the sixteenth and seventeenth centuries.[31] New Imperial Histories break down the binary focus on imperial metropoles and colonial peripheries in order to consider the different historical actors and groups who forged imperial structures and societies. Comparative methodologies also are being used to examine empires, their military systems, and their ways of warfare.[32] Nonetheless, the sheer diversity of early modern empires presents challenges to analyzing imperial armies and their military practices in the sixteenth and seventeenth centuries.

Immense agricultural empires ruled diverse peoples in much of Eurasia and Africa throughout the early modern period. The Ming emperors of China employed sophisticated administrative, tributary, and taxation systems to rule over a vast territorial empire. The Ottoman, Safavid, and Mughal Empires have often been referred to as "gunpowder empires," yet their authority rested on complex political structures and agricultural systems. The Uzbeks and other Timurid successor states competed to control Afghanistan and other regions of the former Mongol Empire in Central Asia. Meanwhile, the Russian Empire was expanding its authority in Ukraine. Songhay armies conquered much of West Africa, establishing an extensive empire in the grasslands and savannas south of the Sahara. Smaller imperial states asserted control over areas of Central and South Africa during this period.

Imperial ideologies and discourses molded these early modern territorial empires and encouraged expansionist warfare. In Central Asia, the dream of reviving Genghis Khan's Mongol Empire remained powerful for Timurid and Safavid princes. Ancient Rome remained the principal model of empire for rulers in Europe and the Mediterranean. Following its conquest of the old Byzantine Empire, Ottoman emperors presented their new capital as a Third Rome and claimed the legacy of ancient Roman ideals of empire. Meanwhile, the Habsburg rulers of the Holy Roman Empire increasingly articulated claims to universal monarchy, potentially offending other European kings and princes.

New maritime empires emerged in the late fifteenth and early sixteenth centuries. Portuguese kings launched aggressive maritime expeditions to establish trading posts and control the Indian Ocean spice trade. The newly united monarchy of Spain forged an "accidental" empire through military conquests in the Caribbean islands, Central America, and South America. Amerindian empires crumbled as Spanish *conquistadores* destabilized the Mexican and Incan political systems and imposed military and political control. During the sixteenth century, the Spanish and Portuguese gradually developed colonial empires with settler colonies and slave plantations.

These colonial empires relied on local defenses composed of fortifications, garrisons, and militias that employed irregular tactics. The Spanish and Portuguese Empires constructed bastioned fortifications and organized colonial military forces to consolidate their authority over indigenous peoples and to defend their maritime empires from new competitors. Pirates, privateers, and fleets increasingly preyed on Portuguese and Spanish merchant ships in the Atlantic and Indian Oceans. Dutch, English, and French maritime empires emerged by the early seventeenth century, competing over global trade routes and trans-oceanic economies.

The earliest and perhaps fullest combination of aggressive trans-oceanic imperialism, settler colonies, racial slavery, and mercantile warfare developed in the Atlantic World. The dramatic growth of the trans-Atlantic slave trade in the seventeenth century provided labor for the colonial plantations producing crops for a booming global commerce in sugar, tobacco, and chocolate. John Elliott describes the "framework" of colonial empires by comparing the Spanish and English Atlantic empires in the early modern period.[33] The performances of violence in the Atlantic World arguably served as models for the development of the slave trade, the plantation complex, and mercantile war throughout the world in the seventeenth century. However, the forms of ethnic conflict and colonial violence produced in the Atlantic World were also connected to ongoing or contemporaneous imperial structures in the Mediterranean and Indian Ocean Worlds. New research on all these forms of imperialism reveals the complexities of colonial warfare and ethnic conflict in the early modern world.

Connected histories of early modern warfare

Another approach examines war and conflict in the borderlands and maritime spaces beyond empires and states, focusing on interactions along commercial routes and communication networks in the early modern world. Scholars using economic history, cultural history, and area studies approaches are increasingly considering vast territorial supra-regions (and even entire continents) as zones of commercial exchanges and cultural interactions. Eurasian, African, and Latin American studies are providing new perspectives to challenge or complement national or local histories. Bridging these area or supra-regional studies is a series of "connected histories," or histories of connectivity, that examine the human and material linkages between different communities and cultures across vast distances. Sanjay Subrahmanyam and Victor Lieberman have forged methodologies for interpreting such connected histories across territories, borderlands, and maritime worlds.[34] These methods can effectively be applied to construct connected histories of warfare in the early modern world.

Borderlands studies offer important new perspectives on the pervasive conflict that plagued the contested zones between colonial empires and autonomous cultures. Richard White's groundbreaking *The Middle Ground* demonstrates how conflict and accommodation between Amerindians and European colonists operated in the borderlands of the Great Lakes region in North America. Although mutual cooperation and social interactions could occur in the "middle ground" between societies, White emphasizes that "this world was not an Eden, and it should not be romanticized. Indeed, it could be a violent and sometimes horrifying place."[35] Borderlands studies have proliferated, allowing for comparisons of conflicts involving colonizers, intermediaries, and indigenous peoples around the world.

Anthropologists R. Brian Ferguson and Neil L. Whitehead have theorized the "violent edge of empire" as a dynamic space of ethnic conflict and social reorganization. "That area continuously affected by the proximity of a state, but not under state administration, we call the 'tribal zone'," they explain. "Within the tribal zone, the wider consequence of the presence of the state is the radical transformation of extant sociopolitical formations, often resulting in 'tribalization,' the genesis of new tribes."[36] Ferguson and Whitehead's useful conceptualization of imperial and colonial frontiers as "tribal zones" allows a rethinking of ethnicity and conflict in the early modern world.

Envisioning the steppes, mountains, rainforests, and woodlands that lay beyond effective state authority as borderlands or "tribal zones" exposes ethnic dimensions of war and conflict. Historians have long debated whether or not cannibalism was actually practiced in the early modern period, but it is evident that various combatants did engage in torture, bodily mutilation, and massacre. John K. Thornton traces the connections between African warfare, the European slave trade, and the brutal plantation complex in the Atlantic World.[37]

Wayne E. Lee demonstrates how ethnic conceptions of "barbarians" broke down restraints among combatants, producing atrocities in conflicts involving Amerindians, Irish, and English in the early modern period.[38] Examining non-state military organizations, military migrants, and cultural intermediaries reveals how borderlands warfare potentially redefined ethnic categories and identities.

Trans-oceanic or "waterborne" histories consider the links between port cities and coastal communities bordering immense bodies of water as constitutive of broader maritime "worlds" that are understood as hybrid cultures. Histories of the Mediterranean and Atlantic Worlds have forged this new approach, replacing older naval and maritime histories. Trans-oceanic histories are now being attempted on the Indian Ocean and Pacific Ocean Worlds, as well as on smaller bodies of water such as the Baltic, South China, and Black seas.[39] During the sixteenth and seventeenth centuries, trans-oceanic trading connections that increasingly linked Europe, Africa, Asia, and the Americas began to construct hybrid cultures and colonial empires. Although these trans-oceanic connections were largely created by European navigation and maritime routes that broke down the pre-existing isolation of various societies ringing the oceans, the human interactions and migrations should not be seen as either Eurocentric or peaceful.[40]

Growing connectivity across the maritime worlds, steppes, and borderlands stimulated early forms of globalization, but also led to extensive conflict. Rather than considering unidirectional diffusions or bilateral exchanges between states and bounded cultures, connected histories of violence examine collaborations and appropriations within and between militaries and societies. Connected histories thus propose an array of cultural intermediaries and powerbrokers who organized raids and mercantile warfare in borderlands and maritime worlds. Nobles, military officers, soldiers, pirates, crowds, peasants, and criminals used force and coercion in various forms of low-intensity conflict. Julius Ruff's survey of violence in early modern Europe emphasizes the diverse forms of violence in the period and traces the gradual growth of state institutions and judicial power, which may have gradually reduced criminality and social violence.[41] Some cultural studies of conflict that use more global perspectives point to increasing, rather than declining, levels of violence in the early modern period.

State development and conflict

States, armies, and warfare intersected in new ways in the early modern period. Administrative institutions and military organizations expanded in tandem during the sixteenth and seventeenth centuries, as some princely states and republics built up permanent armies. In this context, certain monarchies began to articulate new ideologies of royal sovereignty, authority, and power. State development theorists and historians have examined early modern European states in order to chart the formation of nation-states and the modern international system during the course of the seventeenth century. Charles Tilly, one of the most influential theorists of state development, argues that "war made the state, and the state made war" in the early modern period.[42]

Louis XIV's France has long served as a key example in theoretical definitions of the state and in studies of state development processes. The sociologist Max Weber famously defined states through their relationship to violence: "A state is that human community which (successfully) lays claim to the *monopoly of legitimate physical violence* within a certain territory, this 'territory' being another of the defining characteristics of the state."[43] Weber's definition of the state has been incredibly influential for state development studies, which often view the royal state of Louis XIV as the epitome of an early modern "absolutist" state.

Scholars of state development and warfare have both extended Weber's model and challenged its applicability to early modern states. The Weberian model of state formation and bureaucratic development strongly influenced Norbert Elias's model of a "civilizing process" that supposedly tamed nobles and centralized warfare in the late seventeenth century.[44] John A. Lynn demonstrates the rapid growth of the permanent army and military administration in Louis XIV's France, partially confirming Weber's insights.[45] The state's ability to assert a monopoly over violence and control its exercise seems to have been much more problematic in the early modern period than Weber and his followers realized, however.[46] Critics of the concept of "absolutism" have demonstrated the limitations on royal power and discovered numerous forms of "social collaboration" between the king and his military officers, judges, and municipal officials.[47]

If Louis XIV's royal state was never as "absolute" as once imagined, it also represented an atypical example of an early modern state. Monarchies, republics, and city-states raised multiethnic "polyglot" armies and often engaged in dynastic wars and civil conflicts throughout the sixteenth and early seventeenth centuries. Historians have sometimes described these states as "Renaissance monarchies" in order to distinguish them from modern nation-states. Yet, theorists of state development have rarely analyzed these states and their military systems, since they do not fit well with their definitions and models. John Elliott has proposed investigating these Renaissance states as "composite monarchies," emphasizing their complicated institutional structures and clientage networks.[48] Historians have extended this concept to study a variety of composite states in the early modern world, often stressing the continued vitality of municipal defenses and civic guards in many societies.[49] David Parrott demonstrates the crucial role that military enterprisers played in early modern European warfare, as they combined public and private finances and authority to mobilize armies and orchestrate warfare – both for and against composite states.[50] Such findings confirm the importance of a mixed organization of violence by civic, regional, and princely authorities during the early modern period. Although the linked notions of composite monarchies and the Renaissance were originally developed to analyze European principalities of the late fifteenth and sixteenth centuries, Jack Goody and other scholars have now extended these concepts to consider Renaissances and composite states in various early modern societies around the world.[51]

Transformations in early modern states created new types of civil violence. Even if we do not accept Weberian or absolutist theories of state development, changing articulations of state authority and power in the seventeenth century seem to have provoked significant conflict. Historians formerly portrayed peasant revolts and noble revolts as "resistance" to "absolutism," but such explanations often mask the overlapping dynamics of various forms of civil conflict. Comparative revolutionary studies have developed different approaches for examining early modern civil conflicts. Charles Tilly distinguishes various forms of early modern civil conflict by comparing the severity of "revolutionary situations" with the significance of "revolutionary outcomes."[52] Jack A. Goldstone contends that state breakdowns, rather than revolutions, characterized early modern civil conflicts: "State breakdown occurs when a state crisis leads to widespread overt conflict, including a combination of elite revolts, intra-elite struggles, and popular uprisings."[53] Stathis N. Kalyvas's theoretical study of civil war asserts that "political actors draw from a limitless variety of cultural repertoires and models of violence."[54]

Early modern societies experienced many lengthy wars, which sometimes lasted for decades – blurring the boundaries between war and peace. The rhythms of warmaking and peacemaking were closely intertwined, making peace often seem illusory. Nonetheless, some early modern peacemaking initiatives – such as the Peace of Augsburg, the Edict of Nantes, and the Peace of Westphalia – aimed at terminating religious conflicts and building coexistence.[55] Historians are increasingly examining early modern negotiating strategies of indigenous peoples, travelers, merchants, consuls, diplomats, and other intermediaries who arranged truces and implemented peace agreements. Early modern war and society can thus be considered within these newer frameworks of state development, peacemaking, and conflict resolution, in addition to more conventional diplomatic histories of relations between states.

A Global History of Early Modern Warfare

These diverse approaches to the history of warfare together lay the groundwork for this study of war and conflict in the early modern world. Making sense of all this organized violence on a global scale is no easy task, especially in a period of complex cultural contacts, colonial conflicts, and maritime wars. Anthropologist Eric R. Wolf presents the central problem in contemplating world history: "The world of humankind constitutes a manifold, a totality of interconnected processes, and inquiries that disassemble this totality into bits and then fail to reassemble it falsify reality."[56] Constructing a global history of warfare then requires examining the myriad social and military dynamics of waging war, which may be the most intense and expansive of all human activities.

Periodization

This book's analysis begins around 1500 precisely because of the global ramifications of the maritime expeditions of the late fifteenth century and the ensuing interchanges. The voyages of Christopher Columbus and Vasco da Gama in the 1490s highlight the sailing warships, trans-oceanic contacts, maritime violence, and colonial empires that grew out of those expeditions. Many armies were experimenting with new weapons systems and tactics at the beginning of the sixteenth century, integrating artillery, firearms infantry, and cavalry forces. The global scale and diverse nature of war in the sixteenth and seventeenth centuries make this period a vital stage in the long-term historical development of war and conflict in world history.

The notion of an "early modern" period is useful in analyzing the global developments in warfare in the sixteenth and seventeenth centuries. Although the term "early modern" originally developed in European historiography to replace the older designation of a Renaissance and Reformation period, the concept has now been expanded and globalized to refer to the period of world history from approximately 1500 to 1800.[57] This book will utilize the notion of an early modern period, recognizing that its definitions are imprecise and contested. Individual rulers' reigns will be indicated by dates in parentheses.

The book will conclude around 1700 because of important transitions in states and military systems in the early eighteenth century. A new stage of warfare was emerging in which religious and social movements were no longer as central to conflicts as they had once been. Fiscal-military states were increasingly maintaining permanent armies, composed of professional officers and soldiers who were recruited for long periods of service and supported by administrative institutions and logistical services. Few major technological and tactical developments occurred around the turn of the eighteenth century, but the structures of states and imperial power were changing significantly. The Mughal Empire began to collapse in the early eighteenth century, destabilizing South Asia. The Habsburg and Russian Empires expanded against the Ottoman Empire in the Balkans and the Caucuses. The Dutch maritime empire was severely strained by perpetual naval warfare in the late seventeenth century, allowing Britain to emerge as the dominant maritime and colonial empire during the War of the Spanish Succession (1700–14). Britain, the Netherlands, France, Spain, and other European states formalized their colonial relationships and promoted mass migration by settlers and indentured servants. The global slave trade grew enormously in the early eighteenth century as plantation agricultural economies expanded. All these changes suggest that states and their military systems were changing in the early eighteenth century, requiring different historical approaches to understand the emerging practices of war.

Sources

Historians have recently taken up the challenge of examining early modern warfare using world history approaches. Jeremy Black rightly insists that "conflict is central to human history" in a collective volume, *War in the Early Modern World, 1450–1815*, which fashioned one of the first attempts at a global history of early modern warfare.[58] Black went on to publish his own comparative study of war in the early modern world, providing an "emphasis on non-Western powers."[59] Collective volumes have developed global analyses of empire-building, colonial warfare, naval warfare, and other aspects of war in the early modern period.[60] Meanwhile, the early modern period is now treated as a significant stage of military development in general studies of warfare throughout human history.[61] These global studies of early modern warfare often adopt a comparative approach, examining the military systems of various princely states and empires.

The main sources for this study are scholarly monographs, academic journal articles, and historiographical essays on war and society in the early modern period. The works of Geoffrey Parker, John A. Lynn, Jeremy Black, Jan Glete, and David Parrott have reshaped the field of early modern war and society, stimulating a growing body of new research. The book also relies heavily on specialized studies of particular military systems and individual wars between 1500 and 1700. My analysis places these works of military history into dialogue with sources from diverse historical fields: maritime history, history of technology, history of science, climate history, history of the book, Renaissance studies, early modern history, trans-oceanic history, ethnohistory, imperial history, violence studies, and peace and conflict studies. These distinct lines of inquiry allow us to compose a mosaic of the practices of warfare in the early modern world.

Organization

The book employs an intricate organization of thematic chapters, episodic sequences, and nonlinear chronological structures to construct a global history of early modern war and conflict. This multi-layered architecture allows for a historical analysis of warfare both diachronically (over time) and synchronically (at a specific time).

Each chapter focuses on a particular form of organized armed violence during a specific time frame. The chronological period associated with each theme has been chosen based on when that form of organized violence was most emblematic. Thematic chapters thus advance the overarching analysis in overlapping chronological sequences as they examine different aspects of early modern warfare.

Episodes within chapters deal with individual wars, particular conflicts, and specific military developments. Specific wars and conflicts have been selected to illustrate the dynamics of the various forms of violence treated in each chapter. In a global history of war and conflict over 200 years, no pretense of exhaustive coverage is possible. I have deliberately chosen certain episodes to provide case studies or illustrations of key changes in warfare during the time frames of the successive chapters. I attempt to provide balance in selecting episodes from different societies and military systems around the world, but the available sources and the short length of the book have limited my choices.

A segmented and circuitous chronological progression from 1500 to 1700 structures the book. The episodes and chapters create overlapping chronologies that advance this history of war and conflict gradually from the late fifteenth century to the early eighteenth century. The traversing sequences allow for competing narratives of historical developments and transformations, rather than a single overarching storyline.

This organizational method provides several distinct advantages: it disrupts any single narrative of historical change; it challenges the metanarratives of modernization that have driven previous histories of warfare; it decenters Europe and encourages global perspectives; it allows for diverse vantage points on early modern warfare. The book will thus present readers with a multifaceted approach to distinct problems in the history of early modern warfare, rather than an oversimplified narrative.

1

Innovative Warfare, 1450s–1520s

An Ottoman army led by Sultan Mehmed II (1444–46 and 1451–81) initiated a siege of Constantinople in 1453, aiming to complete the conquest of the Byzantine Empire. An Ottoman fleet controlled the Sea of Marmara and the Bosphorus, attacking Byzantine ships and blockading Constantinople. The besieging Ottoman army deployed dozens of artillery pieces, many of which were large bombards that had been cast on site by experienced gun founders. The artillery was manned by Hungarian gunners and other specialists, who directed their fire at Byzantine defensive artillery and ships. The great bombards then began to hurl massive stone projectiles, which were specifically carved to fit their barrels, at the walls of Constantinople. George Sphrantzes, a Byzantine Greek chronicler, described the effects of the Ottoman artillery: "The sultan directed a violent bombardment against our walls, day and night. Their war engines, bombardment, assaults, and strong attacks alarmed us greatly."[1]

Ottoman gunners seem to have used mortars and other artillery innovatively, and their sustained two-month bombardment created a breach in the walls of Constantinople.[2] The Byzantines had appealed to Latin Christian rulers for military aid, but none responded effectively, leaving the approximately 8,500 Greek Orthodox defenders to their fate as they scrambled to repair their walls and fortify the defenses of the beleaguered city. The Ottoman janissary infantry finally launched a major assault on one of the breaches on May 29, 1453, breaking into the city and plundering its palaces and residences. A Venetian doctor named Niccolò Barbaro described blood running through the streets of Constantinople, corpses floating in the sea, and Ottomans ransacking Orthodox churches. The last Byzantine Emperor had been killed and Constantinople was "desolate, lying dead, naked, soundless, having neither form nor beauty."[3]

News of the fall of Constantinople shocked many contemporaries and the siege is generally remembered for its impressive use of artillery. The siege can indeed be viewed as one of the first in a series of "cannon conquests" in the fifteenth century that radically changed warfare and ushered in the early modern period. Yet, the experimental use of siege artillery was only part of the story. The conquest of Constantinople signaled a new pattern of imperial expansion, based on multiethnic armed forces employing artillery and firearms, but also using new organizational techniques. This chapter will examine how new weapons, organizational techniques, military experiments, war news, and naval innovations all transformed the practices of warfare around 1500.

Experimental Weapons and Tactics

Military organizations increasingly engaged in deliberate experimentation with weaponry and tactics in the fifteenth century. Rulers often sought to attract artisans and experts in experimental weapons design and manufacture. Some states and empires began to invest in weapons development and production in a dedicated pursuit of military advantage.

Siege artillery

The most stunning examples of new weapons were the massive cannons used in siege warfare. Gunpowder technologies, first developed in medieval China, had spread throughout Eurasia by the fifteenth century. Metallurgical developments and casting techniques allowed for the production of iron cannons, known as bombards, and these "large stone-shooting cannon became the military fashion of the early fifteenth century." Foundries produced enormous iron bombards, with reinforcing iron hoops to prevent their barrels from exploding. Princely and municipal governments invested immense funds in founding these massive bombards, which were often given names ("Mons Meg," "Dulle Griet," or "Messenger," for example) and decorated as expressions of dynastic or civic pride. Wide-bored great bombards capable of firing massive stone shot that weighed 700–900 pounds became common, and a few great bombards such as the "Pumhart von Steyr" could hurl a carved stone shot of more than

1,500 pounds into castle and city walls.[4] These massive bombards struck fear into the residents of cities that faced their bombardments, but they were difficult to maneuver and some were actually founded at the sites of sieges.

The production of lighter iron and bronze artillery pieces gradually allowed for an enhanced mobility of siege artillery. Indian, Ottoman, and European foundries manufactured bronze and brass artillery that could be mounted on rolled wooden carriages. Some of the medium-weight siege artillery pieces, called cannons or culverins, used iron shot, or cannonballs. Various types of lightweight artillery were increasingly utilized in field armies, in defensive fortifications, and onboard ships. Despite the Ottomans' use of some massive bombards in sieges, their conquest of Constantinople probably stemmed largely from their flexible deployment of more mobile siege guns and light artillery. Although some mechanical siege engines would continue to be used, by 1500 armies across Eurasia consistently employed gunpowder artillery pieces to conduct siege warfare, and they soon began to be used on battlefields.

Infantry units

The infantry was playing a more prominent role in warfare by the mid-fifteenth century, in part because of expanding populations and growing urbanization. Foot soldiers had accompanied many cavalry-dominant armies in the medieval world, but they were mostly seen as auxiliaries – perhaps more because of their perceived social inferiority rather than any lack of military effectiveness. Chinese banner armies employed large infantry formations, while the armies of the Delhi sultanate mobilized Indian peasants of diverse ethnic and caste groups. West African forest kingdoms and Amerindian empires organized effective all-infantry armies, in which soldiers utilized mixed armaments of swords, clubs, spears, javelins, and bows-and-arrows.

Infantry units became increasingly specialized, adopting specific weaponry and tactics. English yeoman longbowmen and Genoese crossbowmen had already accrued noted reputations based on their refined weapons and formidable military skills. In many other societies, specialized infantry companies emerged with particular identities and distinct armaments, often based on their captain's preferences or their local origins. Many cities organized civic guards and militias, composed largely of foot soldiers who practiced together in local archery or crossbow competitions. For example, Flemish cities maintained infantry companies that could display civic pride as well as defend civic privileges.

Nowhere was the increasing prominence of infantry more visible than in the Swiss Confederation, where member cantons (city-states) each mobilized infantry bands in mutual defense. The Swiss infantry fought in cantonal infantry units, or *Haufen*, composed primarily of pikemen. In battle, each cantonal unit formed a dense block hedgehog formation, bristling with multiple ranks of pikes and able to withstand cavalry charges. Because pikes were only useful in coherent block formations, the Swiss *Haufen* had to maintain strict discipline to maneuver and fight successfully.

The effectiveness of the Swiss pike blocks was demonstrated in successive victories over Burgundian armies at the battles of Grandson and Morat in 1476 – even though the Burgundians fielded numerous *gendarmes*, some of the best heavy cavalry in Europe. Then, the Swiss inflicted a final disastrous defeat on the Burgundians at the battle of Nancy in 1477, killing Charles the Bold, Duke of Burgundy. While some military historians have touted these victories as proof of a decisive "rise of infantry" and the antiquated character of *gendarmes*, all three of these battles were fought in peculiar circumstances that advantaged the Swiss infantry. Despite the "rise of infantry," cavalry could still be decisive, as in the rapid conquest of Lorraine by the Burgundians in 1475. The Swiss victories did solidify the fearsome reputation of the Swiss pikemen, though, leading many governments to experiment with new infantry units.

Swiss infantry organization and tactics gradually influenced their opponents' military practices. The Holy Roman Emperor and individual German princes sometimes recruited Swiss infantry for military campaigns, but they also began to form their own infantry units of *Landsknechts*, patterned after the Swiss infantry organizations and tactics. When pike units faced each other in combat, specialist halberdiers and two-handed swordsmen would weave between pikemen, attempting to smash their enemies' pikes. French kings began to recruit Swiss infantry to join their armies. Italians began to refer to the pike-based infantry tactics as warfare *alla moderna* (modern warfare) as they became acquainted with Swiss and German infantry tactics and organizations during decades of war in northern Italy in the early sixteenth century.[5]

Firearms began to influence infantry tactics, as individual personnel, and then specialized infantry units, were increasingly equipped with gunpowder-propelled projectile weapons. Early handguns, which resembled small culverins, were used by city garrisons and besieging armies in the 1410s–40s; however, these weapons were essentially employed as small artillery pieces to support infantry formations. As a result, crossbows and bows-and-arrows continued to be employed by many soldiers.

The arquebus, the first hand-held firearm, reshaped infantry warfare beginning in the 1450s. Arquebuses were smooth-barreled firearms that used a long-burning match, held in a mechanical match-lock, to ignite its powder charge and fire a lead bullet. Specialist foot soldiers initially seem to have used arquebuses as defensive firearms from fortifications, wagon laagers, or entrenched positions, but mobile bands of arquebusiers soon began to appear in composite armies across Eurasia. Arquebusiers gradually developed articulated maneuvers and disciplined firing techniques in order to maximize their firepower and to reload their weapons safely. By the early sixteenth century, many infantry companies employed a mixture of arquebus-iers and pikemen to have both firepower and solidity on battlefields and in sieges.

Cavalry forces

Despite the growing importance of firearms and specialized infantry units, cavalry forces were still vitally important for many early modern armies. Armored heavy cavalry, mounted on specially bred war horses and often composed of military elites, continued to be a crucial com-ponent of many armies – contrary to some historians' claims that infantry had made heavy cavalry obsolete by the sixteenth century. The French and Burgundian *gendarmes*, fully armored men-at-arms bearing couched lances, provided tremendous shock value on Euro-pean battlefields. French kings maintained *compagnies d'ordonnance* (regular companies) of *gendarmes* as permanent contingents paid directly by the royal treasury. The Spanish, Milanese, and Venetian armies continued to use their own men-at-arms effectively, especially in the broad plains of northern Italy.[6] Ottoman sultans raised heavy cavalry, known as *sipahis*, to strengthen the offensive power of their field armies. Contingents of heavily armored cavalry also served in Mamluk, Indian, and some African armies, occasionally accompanied by elephant corps that provided additional shock value.

New tactics of supporting heavy cavalry emerged in the late fif-teenth century as commanders combined different mounted forces. Medium-sized horses, which cost much less than the great war horses, could be used to mount cavalrymen wearing partial armor and utiliz-ing swords rather than lances. Medium cavalry companies, often made up of provincial nobles and non-nobles, could support heavy cavalry in combat, but were more mobile and maneuverable than the heavy men-at-arms companies. Some of these medium cavalry forces began to adopt pistols and arquebuses in the early sixteenth century, offering mobile firepower.

Light cavalry forces performed reconnaissance, raiding, and combat duties for many armies in Eurasia and Africa. Eastern European and North African armies relied heavily on highly mobile light cavalry forces, such as *hussars* and *stradariots*, that were armed with sabers or light lances. Turco-Mongol armies in West and Central Asia continued to use numerous horse archers, but these light cavalry forces were now supported by infantry and artillery contingents. The limited dispersal of horses prevented some societies from developing even light cavalry, however, and the complete lack of horses in the Americas meant that Amerindians simply had no cavalry forces.

Effective cavalry organization drove the dramatic rise of the Songhay Empire in West Africa in the late fifteenth century. The Songhay elite cavalrymen wielded lances or swords, riding into battle wearing armor and hide shields, while mounted on saddled horses and using stirrups. Songhay cavalry used javelins and bows-and-arrows for their initial attacks, while infantry soldiers carried shields and diverse weapons. Sunni Ali (1464–92) led Songhay armies in campaigns of imperial conquest almost every year of his reign. His successor, Askiya Muhammad (1492–1529), "took over an army composed in large measure of levies from allied or conquered provinces, and developed a permanent guard army."[7] The innovative cavalry tactics of Songhay armies influenced the military practices of other African kingdoms and empires, suggesting the advantages of mixed composition armies in the early modern world.

Contracted Armies

Princely states and large territorial empires experimented with military organization, developing new ways of assembling field armies in the fifteenth century. Individual captains recruited infantry and cavalry companies, negotiating contracts with rulers to serve in their field armies. John A. Lynn has described this method of recruitment and mobilization as forming "aggregate-contract armies" in fifteenth- and sixteenth-century Europe. Although the term "aggregate-contract armies" has so far been used primarily to describe European armies, a number of non-European military systems seem to have utilized similar methods of recruitment in this period.[8]

Recruitment and army formation

The field armies of the late fifteenth century drew on the earlier recruitment practices developed by the Italian *condottieri*, or contracted captains, who commanded stipendiary contingents, which were often described as mercenaries. Individual captains signed a *condotta* (contract) to recruit troops and serve a government for a specified period of time. A few *condottieri* successfully obtained open-ended contracts for long-term service with a particular state.

Some of the *condottieri* companies had become permanent military organizations by the mid-fourteenth century, when Sir John Hawkwood led the White Company in multiple campaigns in Renaissance Italy. A century later, Italian nobles were acting as *condottieri*, but they had limited employment within Italy because of the peace of Lodi (1454). Nobles in other regions of Europe adopted the organizational techniques of the *condottieri* and acted as military entrepreneurs. Some states relied on specialist units and bodyguards that gradually became permanent contingents, retained with regular appointments and wages. These specialist units would eventually become the nuclei of permanent armies.

Infantry and cavalry companies were usually recruited in specific geographic regions and identified by their "nation" of origin, which mostly referred to the language of command that the unit employed. Captains and their subordinate officers instilled discipline in their companies through infantry drill that coordinated the movements of individual soldiers so that they could act cohesively. The use of pikes and arquebuses necessitated close coordination of infantry companies, which could not fight effectively if their soldiers did not perform bodily movements synchronously. Infantry drill would become progressively more elaborate and regulated during the course of the sixteenth century.

Soldiers often developed close relationships with their captains. Nobles had long commanded cavalry companies, but many nobles now became captains of infantry companies and commanders of larger infantry formations in expanding military systems. Noble officers carried out much of the recruitment process, often advancing their own money to pay recruiting bounties to new infantry recruits, who tended to come from the urban poor and rural peasantry.

Army composition

Field armies varied widely in their composition, assembling diverse infantry, cavalry, and artillery forces. Aggregate-contract recruitment practices produced field armies that were "assemblages of diverse hired, often foreign, units temporarily combined....Mercenary bands could be purchased 'off the shelf' for a particular campaign and then dismissed as soon as they were no longer needed."[9] Individual field armies gathered as temporary constructions, rather than as institutional organizations. Each winter, field armies normally demobilized entirely, releasing the vast majority of the units that had been recruited during the campaigning season and dispersing a few permanent units into garrisons or to perform other duties. Aggregate-contract army formation thus allowed for a rich diversity of military systems in the late fifteenth century.

The Hungarian armies of King Mátyás Hunyadi, or Matthias Corvinus (1458–90), employed contingents of various "nations" as they battled Ottoman forces and central European foes. The Hungarian army successfully defended Belgrade in 1456, but the Ottomans overran Serbia in 1459 and Bosnia in 1463 – leaving Hungary with no buffer states between its borders and the expanding Ottoman Empire. The Hungarian king maintained a defensive system of garrisoned castles and a core of permanent troops, around which to assemble Hungarian noble cavalry, allied forces, and hired contingents. This military system, which has been described as "a strange mixture of paid army and the traditional feudal levy," won victories in 1479 and established a wary peace with the Ottomans between the 1480s and the 1520s. The Hungarian army also waged wars of conquest in Silesia and Moravia.[10]

Large territorial empires dominated central Europe and western Eurasia through their diverse armies. Poland-Lithuania was a vast, but sparsely inhabited kingdom with an elective monarchy that was nonetheless led by the Jagiellon dynasty throughout the fifteenth century, in part because of its ability to raise contracted armies. Kazimierz IV (1447–92) solidified the Polish-Lithuanian Union and waged a war against the crusading Teutonic Knights in Prussia from 1454 to 1466, using contracted military forces.

Muscovite princes established a territorial empire using contracted multiethnic armies. Ivan III (1462–1505) seized Novgorod in 1478 and then refused to pay tribute to the Khan of the Golden Horde in 1480, organizing a new military system to defend his expanded Grand Principality of Moscow. Ivan III created a new recruitment system for raising *pomestie* cavalry through land grants to a new landholding service elite, the *pomeshchiki*. Muscovite field armies deployed infantry contingents and artillery to support these cavalry forces.[11]

The Chinese Empire could deploy massive field armies using the *wei-so* recruitment and command system, and Ming emperors had periodically launched campaigns of imperial expansion in the fourteenth and early fifteenth centuries. Each *wei* (guard) consisted of about 5,600 soldiers, arrayed in several *so* (battalions), allowing a total of perhaps 500,000 soldiers to be mobilized across the vast empire. The Chinese military faced continuing threats of invasion by Mongol cavalry, and the capture of the Zhengtong Emperor in 1449 seems to have led to a major reorganization of the Ming military system and a more defensive posture.[12]

In the 1450s, Ming emperors began improvements to the fortifications that guarded the mountain passes along the steppe in northwestern China, altering Chinese army composition. Bombards, handguns, and incendiary devices were installed in these fortresses to enhance their defenses. Two sections of walls with watchtowers were completed in the 1470s, creating a system that would eventually become the Great Wall.[13] Military reforms in the 1460s involved integrating infantry, cavalry, and artillery using a divisional structure and a training program. A specialized frontier defense organization of the Nine Defense Areas, each with heavily garrisoned fortresses, was also created for the crucial northwestern border of the empire.[14] In addition to its defensive roles along the northwest frontier, the Chinese military was responsible for suppressing internal rebels and bandits, as well as enforcing a complex tribute trade system with Mongols, Tibetans, Vietnamese, Koreans, and other peoples. By the 1490s, Ming military commanders seem to have been relying on local militias and auxiliary forces to assist in facing its many tasks. The Ming experimentation with innovative defensive systems had thus produced a very different process of forming field armies.[15]

The growing use of contracted units, the increasing size of field armies, and the maintenance of additional permanent forces forced governments to spend more money to feed, lodge, and equip their soldiers. Military systems resorted to increased taxation and new forms of resource mobilization to meet the growing logistical demands.

Contracted armies in the Reconquista

Spanish military forces provide an excellent example of the new aggregate-contract armies of the late fifteenth century. The marriage of King Ferdinand I of Aragon and Queen Isabella of Castille in 1469 had united their two kingdoms, forming the new kingdom of Spain. The aggressive policies of the new kingdom threatened the *convivencia* (coexistence) between Christians, Jews, and Muslims in Iberia, if it ever fully existed. Spain created a new military system and initiated a renewed war of *Reconquista* against the Muslim kingdom of Granada in 1481.

The Granada War (1481–92) began with a series of raids and retaliations, but the newly united kingdoms of Castile and Aragon, under Ferdinand and Isabella, escalated the conflict into an aggressive war to complete the *Reconquista*. The Christian–Muslim frontier in Iberia had seen primarily raiding warfare and sporadic sieges over the previous century, so the Nasrid rulers of Granada suddenly had to respond to a new style of warfare. The Nasrid dynasty raised military forces composed of cavalry, artillery, and *renegados* (converts to Islam), drawn from a diverse population of Muslims, Jews, and some Christians. Granada's position was isolated as the only Muslim polity remaining in Iberia, but the Nasrids maintained diplomatic relations with Muslim states in nearby North Africa and hoped for military aid.

The Spanish armies employed large artillery trains in a series of major sieges, leading one historian to refer to the "cannon conquest" of Granada.[16] A chronicler described the Spanish siege of the Granadan city of Ronda in 1485:

> The bombardment was so heavy and continuous that the Moors on sentry duty could hear one another with great difficulty. [The Muslim defenders] did not have the opportunity to sleep, nor did they know which sector needed support,…and if they tried to repair the damage wrought by the cannon they could not, for the continuous hail of fire from the smaller weapons…prevented the repairs and killed anybody on the wall.[17]

Spain's *Reconquista* involved much more than just cannon, however, and the new Spanish military system that the Nasrids faced was formidable. The Castilian *guardas reales* (royal bodyguards composed of noble cavalry) formed the core of royal field armies, supported by additional cavalry, militia, and siege guns provided by Castilian nobles and towns. Ferdinand I enhanced the royal artillery establishment, creating three arsenals and a gunpowder works by 1482, then organizing a sustained campaign of sieges of Granadan towns in 1484, beginning with Alora. Ferdinand I "set up all his artillery in three days. Immediately, the horrific firing of the *bombardas* tore up parts of the walls, and there arose the most extraordinary clamor, howls and laments from the women, the weeping of children, raising the panic of defenders already overwhelmed with other fears."[18] Ronda surrendered quickly after being encircled in 1485, but two years later the port city of Málaga sustained a lengthy siege and a bombardment by the "Seven Sisters of Ximenes," as some of the Spanish guns were known. In 1489, the Spanish king formed a permanent royal artillery train and organized another lengthy siege of Baza.

After a year of preparation, a large Spanish royal army began to encircle the city of Granada itself in April 1491. Tightening siege lines and months of skirmishing finally led to Granada's capitulation and a triumphal entry to the city by Ferdinand and Isabella on January 2, 1492. The Spanish polemicists explained the victory as a miraculous event accomplished by the hand of God, but modern historians have seen the fall of Nasrid Granada as a "cannon conquest." Weston F. Cook, Jr., argues that "by moving artillery from a supporting to primary role, Ferdinand and Isabella transformed the style of Spanish warfare from a static choreography of plunder raids and border adjustments into a total war of annexation. The Granadans were not 'gunless' but they were outgunned."[19]

Although artillery played a prominent role in the Granada War, the contracted army recruitment and military organization of the unified Spanish kingdom were probably more decisive. Ferdinand and Isabella crafted a religious and cultural program to forge a new Spanish identity by celebrating the common Castilian and Aragonese heritage of crusading and *Reconquista*. Royal patronage supported the emerging dominance of Castilian language through works such as Antonio de Nebrija's *Gramática de la lengua castellana* (1492). The monarchs promoted Christian immigration to Granada in an effort to Christianize Granada and convert its many remaining Muslim inhabitants. An estimated 35,000–40,000 Castilians resettled in Granadan communities in the 1490s, even if Christianization proceeded slowly. The village that had served as the site of the Spanish army's camp during the final siege of Granada became the new Christian town of Santa Fe.[20] The Spanish monarchy quickly began planning for new campaigns of military expansion against Muslims in North Africa, creating an extraordinary tax called the *cruzada* in 1494 in order to finance the effort.

The *Reconquista* was complete and Spanish imperial expansion was just beginning. Ferdinand and Isabella promoted religious unity through identification with the king, intensive religious patronage, and the institution of the Spanish Inquisition. In the *anno mirabilis* (year of miracles) of 1492, the Spanish monarchs completed the conquest of Granada, issued legislation forcing Spanish Jews to convert or face expulsion, and launched the Columbian oceanic expedition.

Military Experimentation in the Italian Wars

When King Ferrante I of Naples died in January 1494, King Charles VIII of France decided to pursue the Valois dynasty's claim to the kingdom of Naples, leading an impressive army across the Alps in September. Charles VIII's invasion of Italy caused panic all along the Italian peninsula and upset diplomatic relationships between the various principalities and city-states. The 1494 invasion disrupted the established norms of warfare in Italy, producing rapid innovation in artillery production, fortification design, and army formation as the small Italian states struggled to respond to the crisis. The Italian Wars (1494–1559) constitute an important case of military experimentation and innovation that reshaped the practices of war far beyond Italy.

The invasion of Italy

Charles VIII invaded Italy at the head of a French army composed of *gendarmes*, infantry, and an artillery train of large iron bombards and lighter bronze cannons. Francesco Guicciardini later commented on the maneuverability of the new bronze cannon, which "almost always marched right along with the armies and were led right up to the walls and set into position there with incredible speed." Guicciardini claimed that "so little time elapsed between one shot and another and the shots were so frequent and so violent was their battering that in a few hours they could accomplish what previously in Italy used to require many days."[21]

The French army successfully intimidated the duchy of Milan into joining the French cause, and then advanced rapidly down the Italian peninsula. Piero de' Medici, who supported Aragonese claims to Naples, fled from Florence in advance of the French arrival, prompting the Florentine Republic to form a new government and open its gates to the French king. The Sienese Republic and the Papal States allowed the French army passage southward toward the kingdom of Naples. King Alfonso II of Naples now abdicated, leaving his son, Ferrante II, in power. French artillery quickly breached the walls of the fortress of Monte San Giovanni, allowing Charles VIII to continue his advance and to enter triumphally into the city of Naples in February 1495.

Emperor Maximilian I (1486–1519) of the Holy Roman Empire staunchly opposed Charles VIII's claims to the kingdom of Naples, however, and his ambassadors scrambled to negotiate an anti-French league including Venice, Milan, the Papal States, and Spain to oppose

Valois control of Naples. Spanish troops landed in southern Italy, while Imperial forces gathered in northern Italy. Charles VIII's army left garrisons in Naples and several other Neapolitan fortresses, then marched northward to avoid entrapment. The main French army fought its way through a League army near Parma at the battle of Fornovo on July 6, 1495, permitting Charles VIII to escape from Italy, but leaving his forces in Naples isolated.

The 1494–95 Naples campaign demonstrated the effectiveness of armies with mobile siege artillery and the fragility of principalities that were diplomatically isolated. Princely rulers and republican councils all along the Italian peninsula frantically sought new defensive schemes as the region descended into chaos. Fighting continued in the kingdom of Naples in 1496, but the French garrison in Naples capitulated and Valois forces were never able to consolidate control over the kingdom. The succession crisis in the kingdom of Naples worsened after Ferrante II died in 1496, leaving his uncle Federigo to contest the throne, which both French and Spanish kings still claimed. But Charles VIII suddenly died from an accidental head injury in April 1498, before he could organize another military expedition to Naples. The French king's bid to seize Naples had ended in failure, but the conflict that he had instigated outlived him, widening into a series of Italian Wars that would last until 1559.

The struggle for Naples

Charles VIII's cousin, Louis d'Orléans, succeeded him as Louis XII (1498–1515) and soon determined to pursue the Valois claim to the kingdom of Naples. After securing an annulment of his first marriage, Louis XII negotiated a new marriage pact with Anne of Brittany, whose wealth and titles reinforced the Valois claim to Naples and other Italian territories. An attempt to partition the kingdom of Naples with the Aragonese King Federigo failed, leading to renewed warfare over Naples.

Louis XII sent a new royal army under Béraut Stuart, seigneur d'Aubigny, to secure the kingdom of Naples in 1501. The French initially had success, occupying the city of Naples and defeating Spanish forces at the battle of Terranovo in December 1502. The next year, Spanish commander Gonzalo Fernández de Córdoba led a combined fleet and army from Spain to contest Naples. Spanish troops used entrenchments and defensive arquebus fire to repel French assaults at the battle of Cerignola in April 1503. Córdoba's army besieged Naples in May 1503, bombarding the hasty earthwork fortifications that the French had built around Naples, especially on the San Martino hill. Spanish engineer Pedro Navarro exploded a gunpowder mine under one of the outworks surrounding the Castel dell'Ovo, leading the French garrison to capitulate. Córdoba's Spanish troops later outflanked French defenses along the Garigliano River in December 1503 and then reduced the remaining French garrisons in southern Italy. Córdoba became known as *El Gran Capitán* (the Great Captain) for his victories in the kingdom of Naples, which now was incorporated into the growing Spanish empire.[22]

The early phases of the Italian Wars had showcased new weapons, tactics, and military techniques. Army commanders employed arquebus firepower, cavalry coordination, and entrenchment on battlefields in Italy. Artillerists deployed a wide variety of artillery pieces in increasingly large siege trains. Francesco Guicciardini famously claimed that "after King Charles [VIII] had come to Italy, the terror of unknown nations, the ferocity of infantry organized in waging war in another way, but above all, the fury of the artillery, filled all of Italy with so much dread that no hope of defending oneself remained for those not powerful enough to resist in the countryside." Military engineers directed batteries of cannons and exploded gunpowder mines during sieges. Guicciardini concluded that "men who were unskilled in defending their towns, surrendered as soon as the enemy approached, and even if some put up resistance, they were taken within a very few days."[23]

Diplomatic realignment and the war for Milan

If the struggle for Naples was now over, the Italian Wars were already spreading, since Louis XII not only reaffirmed Valois claims to the kingdom of Naples, but also articulated new claims to the duchy of Milan. Louis XII led a French army into northern Italy in 1499, occupying Milan and Genoa. Ludovico Sforza, who also claimed the title of Duke of Milan, was able to retake the city of Milan in 1500, but French forces continued to contest control of the duchy throughout the 1500s and 1510s. Northern Italy became the site of sustained warfare for two generations, prompting intensive military experimentation and diplomatic innovation.

The rapidly changing military contexts of the Italian Wars produced shifting diplomatic relations and political realignments. A powerful new alliance coalesced, as France joined together with its previous enemies – the Papal States, Spain, and the Holy Roman Empire – to form the League of Cambrai against the Republic of

Venice, whose growing *terraferma* (land) empire in northern Italy seemed threatening. A League army destroyed the main Venetian army at Agnadello in May 1509, creating a severe political crisis in Venice as the entire Republic seemed poised to collapse. Francesco Guicciardini lamented the decline of Venice, claiming that many Italians, "realizing how wretched and calamitous it would be for all of Italy to be entirely subjugated under the foreign yoke, heard the news with incredulity and displeasure that such a city, the fixed seat of liberty, the glory of the name of Italy throughout the world, should have fallen to such extremity."[24] Venetian diplomats gave up major portions of the Republic's *terraferma* empire, but convinced the Pope and King Ferdinand to abandon the League of Cambrai and instead join a new alliance against France.

The French forces, suddenly isolated, now had to organize the defense of the duchy of Milan against multiple foes. The Spanish and Papal forces marched to relieve the town of Ravenna, which had been besieged by a French and Ferrarese army under Gaston de Foix. The Spanish and Papal troops entrenched along a river near the French siege lines, prompting Gaston de Foix to launch an attack on the Spanish–Papal positions at the battle of Ravenna on April 11, 1512. Following a sustained artillery duel, Gaston de Foix's *gendarmes* swept the Spanish and Papal heavy cavalry from the field and then returned to outflank and rout the Spanish infantry. The French won a stunning victory, but Gaston de Foix was killed toward the end of the battle, leaving the drastically reduced French army in confusion and unable to take advantage of its victory. In 1513, another French field army crossed the Alps to defend the duchy of Milan, but it was defeated at the battle of Novara in June 1513. The French forces garrisoning Milan had to abandon the city to Swiss forces.

The Italian Wars were now expanding into a series of Habsburg–Valois Wars that would be waged simultaneously in multiple theaters. Emperor Maximilian I had abandoned the short-lived League of Cambrai in 1512 and launched an invasion of northern France. King Henry VIII of England allied with Maximilian, leading an expeditionary force to Calais in June 1513. French ambassadors successfully negotiated separate truces with England and the Holy Roman Empire, but Louis XII died in January 1515, leaving the status of the Valois claims in Italy ambiguous.

François I (1515–47) succeeded Louis XII and soon led a new invasion of Italy in August 1515, aiming to re-establish French control over the duchy of Milan. French negotiators offered Swiss captains massive monetary payments and succeeded in convincing a number of them to defect and return to their cantons. In September, the remaining Swiss infantrymen marched out of their garrison in Milan to challenge François I's army southeast of the city. An intense battle developed at Marignano as the French artillery battered the Swiss pike blocks, allowing the *gendarmes* to charge the disorganized Swiss infantry. The defeated Swiss retreated, allowing the French army to consolidate its positions in the duchy of Milan. King François I held a triumphal entry into the city of Milan in October 1515, celebrating his conquest.

Habsburg and French diplomats negotiated a truce in 1516, which left the French masters of the duchy of Milan and the Spanish in control of the kingdom of Naples. The Italian Wars were far from over, however. The swirling combats over the duchy of Milan showed the potential for localized dynastic struggles to escalate into much broader conflicts that involved many different states. The large field armies fighting in Italy employed diverse unit types, which forced tactical changes and organizational developments.

Military engineering and fortification design

The Italian Wars prompted rapid innovations in weapon designs, fortification plans, and siege tactics. Military engineers working in Italy utilized powerful new techniques of mechanical drawing that revolutionized ways of viewing and reproducing images. Complex mathematical techniques of visual representation had emerged in Renaissance Italy, influenced by ancient geometry texts and by medieval Arabic studies of optics. Artists and architects trained in Italy drew on this mathematics to create intricate systems of linear perspective using a wide variety of drawing machines and mechanical instruments, such as the *camera obscura.*

The new systems of linear perspective and mechanical drawing were immediately applied to military architecture and engineering. Artists and military engineers such as Albrecht Dürer and Baldassarre Lanci created specialized observation instruments that could be easily carried on military campaigns for use in calculating distances and mapping fortifications during sieges.[25] Renaissance artists often engaged in surveying, drafting, design, engineering, and construction on architectural projects. Leonardo da Vinci, Michelangelo Buonarroti, Hans Holbein, and other artists who were working in Italy depicted idealized fortification systems and imaginary sieges. Architects and military engineers also played important roles in urban planning and civic renewal schemes based on Renaissance notions of the ideal city. Artists celebrated these urban projects with prints depicting panoramas and city views, often prominently displaying new fortifications.[26]

Italian military engineers drew on previous experimentations with fortification design. Late medieval castle-building had involved shared Arabic and European influences, stemming from crusading warfare. As the Ottomans had tightened their grip on Constantinople, they successfully used new fortifications at Anadolu Hisar and Rumeli Hisar to mount artillery in positions to threaten shipping in the Bosphorus.[27] Architectural projections incorporated new rings of sunken walls, artillery platforms, and outworks. Impressive additional fortifications were added to existing castles, such as the Castello Nuovo in Naples.[28] Portuguese engineers experimented with defensive works in the conquered enclaves along the coasts of Morocco, reinforcing existing Muslim fortifications with artillery towers, angled bastions, and outworks.[29]

These diverse experiments with fortification design gradually led to the development of more complex bastioned fortification systems, as military architects in Italy employed careful mathematical calculations to design projections of fortification works that could use artillery more effectively. New designs emerged during the early stages of the Italian Wars, as artists and architects such as Francesco di Giorgio Martini, Giuliano da Sangallo, and Leonardo da Vinci altered castle-building practices by applying geometrical principles to fortress construction.[30] Fortification designs increasingly envisioned lower and broader towers, which would be capable of mounting artillery pieces and creating interlocking fields of fire.

Mechanical drawing and mathematical projections fueled experimental weapons development during the Italian Wars. Leonardo da Vinci's famous drawings of experimental weapons and siege engines suggest the importance of artists' involvement in military engineering. Studies of ballistics began to apply mathematics to the problem of the motion of artillery projectiles. Experiments in cannon founding produced more reliable bronze and iron casting techniques by the early sixteenth century. Italian city-states invested in defensive artillery pieces, while French, Spanish, and Imperial armies founded siege guns to besiege cities. Firearms manufacturers developed a range of arquebuses for use as infantry, cavalry, and hunting weapons. Artisans crafted specialty weapons, such as hybrid pistols and multibarrel firearms. Defensive shields, barricades, and gunpowder mines were increasingly used in siege warfare. Engineers experimented with new designs for pontoon bridges, amphibious craft, and gunboats for use in coastal warfare and sieges.[31] Some armies utilized improvised weapons systems such as war wagons. The weaponry developed or refined by the belligerents in the Italian Wars quickly spread beyond the peninsula.

Circulation of War Knowledge

Military information and war news circulated widely, borne by print media and travelers along expanding commercial routes. Manuscript and printed documents shared war news and technical information well beyond war zones, diffusing war knowledge to distant audiences eager to hear about the latest combats and military innovations.

Print media and war news

Printing presses created new forms of war news and political propaganda. European print media cultivated fear of the "Turkish peril" through terrifying depictions of Ottoman cruelty in the wake of the fall of Constantinople. In 1455, the Gutenberg press produced a short pamphlet, *A Warning to Christendom against the Turk*, warning of the Turkish threat to Europe. Gutenberg and other early printers eagerly printed indulgences in an effort to raise money to support crusading efforts against the Ottomans. According to a recent study of early printing, "indulgences in support of the Turkish war effort make up the single largest group of printed indulgences published during the fifteenth century."[32] Short printed pamphlets in quarto format reported the news of the second siege of Rhodes by Ottoman forces in 1522. After Rhodes capitulated, accounts written by some of the Knights of Saint John of Jerusalem who survived the siege were published.

The rapid Ottoman expansion through Greece, the Balkans, and the Dalmatian coast in the late fifteenth century was viewed with horror by Europeans. Shocking news pamphlets reported the disastrous battle of Mohács in Hungary in 1526 and the death of King Louis II Jagiellon in the ensuing rout. This defeat stunned many observers, who had considered the Hungarian army to be innovative and effective because of its gunmen and artillery, in addition to its light and heavy cavalry.[33] Victorious Ottoman armies overran the country and the kingdom of Hungary rapidly collapsed. Many of the news publications reporting on the Ottoman expansion were short, inexpensive pamphlets in quarto or ottavo format that were accessible to a broad reading public in urban centers across Europe.

Printed war news drew from older forms of chronicles, as continuing intersections of oral and textual sources suggest. The griots in West Africa recounted war tales along with religious stories in long lyrical poems. Oral recitations of epic poems in Morocco kept alive the memory of battles and sieges, sometimes even hundreds of years after the events occurred. Many Muslims memorized the entire text of the Quran, allowing for oral transmission to illiterate believers in their communities. The Quran and the collections of *hadiths*, or sayings of the Prophet, spread ideas on warmaking and peacemaking across the Muslim world. Illuminated manuscripts produced by copyists and artists often blended oral, visual, and textual techniques. In North Africa, manuscripts called *taqayid* provided short accounts of battles and skirmishes. Italian manuscript *avvisi* (handwritten newsletters) continued to circulate diplomatic and military news long after printing had been adopted. Despite these continuities with oral and manuscript accounts of war news, printing offered new forms of communication and more rapid dissemination of information.

Printed pamphlets soon reported the latest news of the fighting in the Italian Wars for eager audiences in the Italian city-states, as well as in the warring states of France, Spain, and the Holy Roman Empire. Battles such as Fornovo in 1495, Ravenna in 1512, and Marignano in 1515 were almost immediately reported in print publications and depicted in woodcuts and engravings. Perhaps no battle of this period attracted more interest than the dramatic battle of Pavia in 1525, when King François I and his sons were captured on the battlefield.[34] Pamphlets often incorporated woodcut illustrations, which frequently presented generic battle scenes that could be easily reused in subsequent pamphlets. Northern and central Italy had a high concentration of printing presses by the late fifteenth century. Lengthy sieges of Italian cities with bastioned fortifications attracted great interest. The Habsburg and Valois dynasties both used pamphlets to promote their victories during the Italian Wars, and printers published numerous news pamphlets during each round of intensive fighting.

Military experts and military treatises

Military experts traveled between territorial empires and princely courts, offering diverse technical services to rulers. Military engineers, artists, and draftsmen with experience in Italy, the Balkans, and other persistent war zones could work simultaneously as military architects, surveyors, and mapmakers. Military engineers directed siege operations using geometrical principles and mechanical instruments to gauge distances, lay out approach trenches, and site batteries. Artists accompanied armies, making sketches of battlefield formations and siege fortifications using perspective drawings made using on-site observations. Ottoman armies employed military engineers from diverse ethnic backgrounds, who developed technical approaches to amphibious landings and siegecraft in the eastern Mediterranean. Armorers constructed personalized armor and specialty weapons for noble courtiers, while fencing masters offered them training in personal weapons.

Military treatises diffused the experimental techniques of army composition, fortification design, and military engineering used in the Balkans and Italy far beyond these war zones. Manuscript copies of ancient military treatises were already circulating widely before the spread of mechanical printing technologies. The Ming empire instituted military examinations for its military officers in 1464, emphasizing the learning of classic military treatises.[35] Nobles and military experts in Europe and the Mediterranean valued manuscript copies of Roman military treatises. The precision and exactness of printing progressively assisted the diffusion of mathematical, scientific, and military knowledge by the early sixteenth century.

Printed military treatises included complex diagrams, projections, and illustrations that were reproduced using woodcuts or copper plate engravings. Complex mathematical calculations and geometric projections could now be reproduced rapidly, with exacting accuracy, in dedicated treatises on war. Military treatises increasingly incorporated mathematical tables and engraved illustrations. Presses in Florence, Venice, Paris, Lyon, and Nuremberg published a dizzying array of treatises on fortification design, cannon founding, siege warfare, fencing practices, and military techniques.

Printed editions of ancient texts by Livy, Caesar, Sallust, and Tacitus circulated ancient knowledge of the art of war. Multiple editions and translations of Vegetius's *De Re militari* popularized Roman ideas on military discipline and the practice of warfare in the early sixteenth century. The writings of Vegetius inspired numerous commentaries and new military treatises, which often borrowed heavily from – or even plagiarized – Vegetius's classic text. Niccolò Machiavelli and other humanists refined the concepts of just war, legitimate defense, and military organization. Machiavelli had served as chancellor for the Florentine Republic, and then wrote his controversial works on political and military theory in exile. Many Renaissance scholars and artists were fascinated by Roman military systems, engineering projects, and architectural remains.

Military propaganda

Rulers and military commanders could use illustrated pamphlets to celebrate their conquests of cities and territories. The rapid spread of printing presses through major European and Mediterranean urban centers allowed for a broad diffusion of information in wartime. Hastily printed pamphlets, which typically numbered a mere eight to twelve pages, could be published cheaply and distributed by wandering street vendors in urban spaces. European elites sent pamphlets, prints, and drawings along with their manuscript correspondence in multimedia packets that could be delivered by postal couriers over great distances. Broadsheets and periodicals would gradually emerge to communicate war news to interested readers across great distances.

Pamphlets celebrated triumphal entries by rulers and nobles into conquered or subjugated cities. Such entries often involved a grand parade through triumphal arches, accompanied by ceremonial music, poetry, speeches, and festivities. These festive celebrations generally used elaborate ephemeral art and music to celebrate rulers' power before mass audiences of city inhabitants. Emperor Maximilian I commissioned the renowned artist Albrecht Dürer to compose a massive woodcut triumphal arch, publicizing his power through a print edition of 700 copies that were distributed throughout Europe. This dramatic artwork involved assembling 192 separate prints into an intricate triple arch covered with illustrated scenes of Habsburg power and Imperial authority.[36] Printed pamphlets could commemorate actual civic entries, such as the entry by Prince Charles von Habsburg (the future Charles V) into the city of Bruges in 1515.[37] Accounts of royal entries could also be used to subordinate cities following rebellions or territorial conquests.

Pamphlets and printed books popularized military imagery, encouraging popular identification with soldiers and military causes. Works of chivalric literature, such as Ludovico Ariosto's *Orlando furioso* (1516) and *Amadis de Gaule* (1533), celebrated the heroic deeds of Carolingian warriors and crusading knights. Images of Landsknecht soldiers circulated in woodcut prints and illustrated books throughout Germany and beyond. Such prints could present military ideals to a broad viewing public, since prints were hung in taverns and other public spaces.[38] Some historians have interpreted pamphlet authors as engaging in "pamphlet wars" that were confined to intellectual elites, but clearly prints and pamphlets were part of much broader multimedia communications that could be read by diverse audiences.

Pamphlets helped create public opinion about warfare, requiring authors to make elaborate arguments to justify military action not only to rulers, but also to literate elites and urban audiences. Although the mechanical printing technologies were developed in Europe, the print and hybrid media rapidly transformed war news and communication across the Mediterranean, West Africa, and beyond.

Naval Innovation

Some empires and city-states were already investing in dedicated shipbuilding and naval infrastructure, even if modern notions of standing navies had not yet developed. Although fleets could not establish control of the seas, they did fight for access to major shipping lanes, especially through narrow straits. Naval forces sometimes employed amphibious warfare to launch attacks on strategic ports and islands along shipping routes. Intense commercial conflict grew up around already existing patterns of long-distance trade in several supra-regions, producing new commercial conflicts and maritime expeditions.

Commercial conflict

Silk, porcelain, and spice trade in East Asia stimulated commercial development, competition, and conflict. China produced highly valued silk and porcelain, but also constituted a vast market for spices, natural resources, and artisanal products from the rest of Asia. Ming emperors had sponsored the immense tribute fleets of Admiral Zheng He in the early fifteenth century, but had already abandoned their long-distance expeditions by the 1430s. Chinese vessels nonetheless continued to conduct maritime trade and to exact tribute in the South China Sea. Japanese, Vietnamese, Malay, and other ships plied the waters of East and Southeast Asia, but usually in small groups.

Zheng He's political and commercial voyages stimulated a sustained period of economic growth across the Indian Ocean World that was fueled by long-distance commerce in spices. Anthony Reid argues that a "take-off" occurred around 1400, producing an "age of commerce" in Southeast Asia and the Indian Ocean.[39] After the great Chinese tribute voyages ended, Muslim merchants dominated the Indian Ocean spice trade. Muslim merchant ships may have sometimes operated together in clusters of vessels along seasonal routes, but convoys and naval expeditions seem to have been relatively rare in the Indian Ocean World during the late fifteenth century. Localized conflicts along the African, Arabian, and Indian coasts only occasionally disrupted Indian Ocean commerce in this period.

In the Mediterranean World, commercial conflict increasingly took on naval dimensions. Venice's Arsenale, or naval arsenal, outfitted and maintained the galley fleets for the Venetian maritime empire, known as the *stato da mar*. By the fifteenth century, the Arsenale had developed from a small artisanal galley manufactory into a massive state-sponsored proto-industrial facility – complete with dry docks, slips, cannon foundries, warehouses, and thousands of skilled workers. The impressive galley fleets allowed the Venetians to organize *muda* convoys throughout the Adriatic, eastern Mediterranean, and Aegean seas. Venice periodically launched maritime expeditions to assist merchant shipping in the Adriatic and to protect its island possessions in the eastern Mediterranean. The Venetian fleets increasingly relied on shipboard artillery and amphibious warfare to control its maritime communications. Venetian *galee grosse* (large galleys), began to mount large bow guns in the late fifteenth century. By this time, naval battles between the Venetians and the Ottomans were revealing the weakness of the Venetian fleet and its *stato da mar* in the face of growing Ottoman naval power.

The Ottoman victory over the Byzantine Empire had relied on the construction of fleets and fortifications to blockade and besiege Byzantine cities. After the Ottoman conquest of Constantinople, Mehmed II consolidated his imperial authority by transforming the city into his new capital of Istanbul, complete with bases for building and maintaining galley fleets. The Ottomans launched major maritime expeditions during the Ottoman–Venetian war of 1463–79. Ottoman forces employed naval and amphibious warfare to besiege and take port cities in the Aegean and Black Seas during this war. An Ottoman expedition conquered the island of Negroponte in the Aegean in 1470. Another fleet landed at Otranto in 1480, massacring many of the city's inhabitants and stirring fear across southern Italy. Despite successive conflicts with their Venetian rivals in the eastern Mediterranean, the Ottomans often let the *muda* convoys continue, since the Venetians were also their main trading partners.

The Ottoman–Venetian war of 1499–1502 brought a new level of Ottoman naval projection in the eastern Mediterranean, as an Ottoman fleet seized Lepanto on the western coast of Greece in 1499. Venice and its allies retaliated by seizing the Ionian islands of Corfu, Cephalonia, and Zante. Sultan Bayezid II (1481–1512) authorized a massive shipbuilding and refitting campaign during the winter of 1500–01, which produced a naval force of perhaps 400 warships. A peace treaty ended the war in 1503, but the Ottomans had clearly demonstrated their naval strength in the Mediterranean.[40]

The Ottoman Empire's increasing control of the eastern Mediterranean Sea led many Italian and Iberian merchants to seek alternative ways of accessing luxury goods from East Asia. Ottoman fleets threatened the fleets of the Knights of Rhodes and the Mamluk Empire in Egypt, which had previously conducted spice trade in the Indian Ocean. Genoese military and merchant elites invested in shipbuilding and maritime expeditions westward into the Atlantic Ocean, instead of eastward toward the Levant. In Genoa and other Italian city-states, public–private partnerships underwrote small maritime expeditions involving several merchant vessels.

Maritime expeditions

Navigators organized maritime and oceanic expeditions to seek new long-distance commercial routes. Maritime expeditions by the Mamluks, Ottomans, Portuguese, and Spanish began to generate new forms of conflict over the harbors, port cities, and islands that were located at strategic points relative to the prevailing winds that were crucial for oceanic sailing. Maritime expeditions included military personnel, who could control these key sites and potentially establish control of sea lanes.

The organization of maritime expeditions required significant financing and extensive planning. Princely rulers in Portugal and Spain sponsored expeditions into the Atlantic Ocean, drawing on major banking firms such as the Fuggers to provided loans to finance shipbuilding, equipment, and supplies. Ships were often built expressly for major expeditions. Iberian shipbuilders developed caravels by the 1440s as larger and sturdier ships for long-distance voyages in the Atlantic Ocean. Caravels were built with carvel planking construction, which strengthened the hulls and allowed them to be up to 70 feet long with 50 tons of cargo space. A Sicilian described caravels as "rather small ships, but strong enough for long, rough sailing."[41] Some larger caravels could sport three masts with multiple lateen sails and more ample rigging. Craftsmen also designed *naus*, three-masted ships with forecastles, as a response to the demands of long-distance voyages being conducted by the Portuguese by the 1480s. The *naus* employed many of the design features of the earlier caravels, but had larger cargo holds and a full rigging of square sails and lateen sails. The Spanish quickly began building their own *nãos*, as they referred to the new ship designs, and shipbuilders along the entire Atlantic coast of Europe followed suit.

Shipborne artillery had been used since the mid-fifteenth century, but these guns were often small anti-personnel weapons. A wide variety of artillery (including baselisks, falcons, culverins, demi-cannons, and cannons) was increasingly mounted on ships in the 1470s and 1480s, first on the decks and later below decks, using gunports. Caravels and *naus* continued to evolve, adopting new features and leading to considerable confusion between these ship types and the new carracks that were emerging in the late fifteenth century. Caravels and *naus* became the workhorses of the maritime expeditions launched by Portugal and Spain in the late fifteenth century.

Launching a maritime expedition required managing a diverse body of shipboard personnel. Ship captains hired pilots, doctors, carpenters, and other specialists. Experienced sailors could be found in major port cities and fishing ports. Soldiers and ordinary crewmembers had to be recruited in port cities, often from the urban poor. The logistics of assembling food and supplies sufficient for the entire crew during an entire voyage proved daunting.

A maritime expedition set out from port amid hopes and fears, due to the incredible risks of open sea navigation. Earlier navigation had relied mostly on tramping from port to port within sight of coastlines and islands. By the fifteenth century, however, Mediterranean navigation techniques involved ships' masters using portolan charts and compasses to cross open bodies of water to arrive at a distant coast near a desired port. Then, local pilots could be brought on board to navigate shoals, river mouths, and harbor entrances. As maritime expeditions ventured into the Atlantic Ocean, a new specialized group of ocean pilots developed techniques of sailing westward into the Atlantic, then turning north or south toward the western coasts of Europe or Africa. These ocean pilots relied on learning a battery of local knowledge and keeping their navigational information secret.

Portuguese navigators organized numerous maritime expeditions. Dom Henrique of Portugal, generally known as Prince Henry the Navigator, built up Portuguese naval forces in an extended campaign at trade and crusading along the coast of West Africa and the islands off its coast. Portuguese forces landed and occupied the uninhabited island of Madeira, then took the Azores and the Cape Verde Islands. Portuguese voyages reached Sierra Leone in 1460. Another Portuguese expedition sailed into the Gulf of Guinea and scouted the Gold Coast.

Portuguese began to use the verb *descobrir*, "to discover," to refer to their new geographical findings, emphasizing the imperial claims of their maritime expeditions. The notion of "discovery" made sense from the perspective of Portuguese mariners and their financial backers, but as a historiographical concept, "discovery" distorts the contexts of fifteenth-century maritime expeditions. After all, Portuguese "discovery" involved mariners mapping islands and coasts, claiming territories and rights, and seizing ports and strategic points from indigenous peoples. Portuguese seized islands such as São Tomé, in the Gulf of Guinea, subjugating its population. Portuguese expeditions engaged in aggressive naval and amphibious warfare in order to extend their maritime communications down the coast of Africa, reaching the Kongo River in 1485. Portuguese soldiers constructed walled fortresses along the western coast of Africa, using the term *feitoría* (trading post) to refer to their fortified trading compounds in foreign territories.

By the 1490s, Portuguese mariners were able to navigate almost to the southern tip of Africa, but other competitors were attempting long-distance maritime expeditions of their own. Ambitious maritime expeditions scouted distant coastlines and ports, producing new forms of colonial conflict with naval dimensions. Maritime and commercial innovation gradually expanded the spatial dimensions of warfare to a global scale.

Conclusion

Military and naval experimentation quickened the pace of innovations in military technologies, techniques, and practices in the early sixteenth century. New artillery and firearms technologies were being developed and employed in warfare on land and at sea. Contracted armies employed diverse contingents of infantry, cavalry, and artillery, including a few permanent military forces. The increasing size of field armies broadened the scale of warfare and the logistical requirements of supplying troops. All these technological, organizational, and social developments prompted military systems in diverse regions to experiment with new weaponry, equipment, formations, and tactics.

Rulers sought arms experts and military engineers as military advisors and artisans of war. Leonardo da Vinci famously offered his services to the Duke of Milan by stressing his ability to produce new artillery, siege engines, and military inventions. Rulers across Eurasia and North Africa sponsored artillery founders, gunsmiths, alchemists, and other artisans who could craft experimental weapons. Military engineers traveled widely in the early sixteenth century, offering their services and expertise to different princely courts in Europe, the Levant, and Asia. Niccolò Machiavelli's *The Art of War* (1521) and other treatises on warfare contributed significantly to the growing field of military knowledge, which emphasized inventive concepts, organizational theories, and practical applications.[42]

Sustained warfare in major war zones such as the Balkans, Iberia, West Africa, western China, and Italy produced rapid military innovation. The practices of warfare became explicitly experimental and innovative as princely states adapted their military systems to face diverse rivals and opponents. Growing global contacts and long-distance exchanges allowed military engineers and advisors to observe diverse military organizations, and then to report on them through expanding correspondence networks and print media, creating a broad diffusion of military ideas and war knowledge. Certain areas of the globe – such as the Americas, Australia, and the interior highlands of Eurasia and Africa – remained isolated from these patterns of military innovation and exchange around 1500. Maritime expeditions and global maritime conflict soon began to break down this isolation and force new military innovations on disparate populations.

2

Maritime Conflict and Colonial Expansion, 1490s–1530s

By the late fifteenth century, some merchants, sea captains, and geographers were discussing the theoretical possibilities of global navigation. Martin Behaim constructed a detailed globe for the Imperial city of Nuremberg in 1492, providing an elaborate world map with inscriptions detailing local and regional information of interest to navigators and merchants. Behaim's globe "unequivocally renders Europe as little more than the northwestern neighbor to a huge inhabited world that was now heavily weighted toward the seemingly interminable littorals of the tropics."[1] Henricus Martellus's *mappa mundi* (world map), drawn up around 1489, presented a similar global vision using a two-dimensional projection of the earth. Both of these cartographic works and other period world maps depended on vast collections of geographic and navigational information gathered by previous Portuguese and Spanish maritime expeditions, but world maps rapidly diffused this knowledge more broadly.

The cartographers who produced world maps in the 1490s were actively imagining global communication, trade, and conflict. Globes and world maps presented traversable oceans, navigable coastlines, and habitable landscapes – offering enticing visualizations of a world ready for conquest and colonization. The concept of "discovery," developed by the Portuguese in the late fifteenth century, now became operational on a global scale. This chapter examines how the rise of global navigation, maritime imperialism, and naval warfare fundamentally altered maritime conflict.

Global Navigation

Columbus's "Enterprise of the Indies"

Christopher Columbus, a Genoese navigator, sought patronage for an oceanic project that he referred to as the "Enterprise of the Indies." Columbus developed or adapted theories about the possibilities of a westward oceanic crossing from Europe to Asia, which included several important misconceptions: an underestimation of the size of the globe, an overestimation of the size of Asia, and a misunderstanding of the proportion of the earth's surface covered by water. Despite, or because of, these mistaken apprehensions, Columbus boldly planned to find a southwestward route through the tropics to Asia, notwithstanding the common belief that the "torrid zone" was uninhabitable and treacherous. The ultimate aim of the voyage would be to accomplish a westward crossing to Asia and establish trading relations with Indonesia, Japan, and China, but Columbus may also have intended to claim possession of intervening islands in the western ocean.

In the 1480s, Columbus and his family members proposed the "Enterprise of the Indies" to various potential patrons – including João II of Portugal, Henry VII of England, and Charles VIII of France. Columbus lobbied Ferdinand and Isabella, co-monarchs of Spain, for support for his projected voyage several times before they finally agreed to the plan in April 1492. The Capitulation of Santa Fe of April 1492 awarded Columbus the title of Admiral and granted him control over lands that he would "discover."[2] The Pinzón family in the port of Palos de la Frontera provided Columbus with the *Niña*, *Pinta*, and *Santa María* (two caravels and a *não*). Genoese merchants supplied credit and local residents in the port assisted with outfitting the 1492 oceanic expedition.

Columbus's expedition finally departed from Palos de la Frontera on August 3, 1492, sailing southwest to the Canary Islands to resupply before launching westward on 6 September from the island of Gomera into the oceanic expanses. The small flotilla endured the crossing, before striking land in the Bahamas on October 12, 1492. Columbus portrayed the Taíno inhabitants of San Salvador as "naked" with "very handsome bodies." In his journal, Columbus claimed that the inhabitants would "make good servants" and that "they will easily be made Christians."[3] He decided to take several Taínos captive to use as guides, and later as human specimens to display to his royal sponsors in Spain. He also noted potential sites for fortifications that could be built to control San Salvador. From this first momentous European encounter with Amerindians, the rationales of colonization and conversion were thus intertwined.

Since Columbus believed that his flotilla had reached an archipelago in the Indies, the expedition ventured southward through the Bahamas, searching for mainland Asia. The flotilla instead found the massive islands of Cuba and Hispaniola in October and November, leading Columbus to focus on searching for gold and spices by sailing southeast. He carefully described each island he encountered, noting ethnographical and geographical details about the inhabitants, natural resources, and trading goods. These strategies reflect the military and colonial nature of Columbus's expedition: "While Columbus the *explorer* had contributed to proving the ancients wrong by inventing a vastly temperate, fertile, and inhabitable expanse to the west and to the south of Mediterranean Europe, Columbus the *colonizer* continued to regard this expanse as the sweltering wasteland whose peoples were nature's subjects or slaves."[4] Columbus emphasized the tameness of the Taínos and the cruelty of the Caribes in his descriptions, both providing imperatives for future colonization by Spanish forces. The *Santa María* ran aground off Hispaniola on December 25, leading Columbus to establish a fort built from the wreckage of the flagship. The fort, named La Navidad, was the first European settlement in the Americas. The flotilla departed from Hispaniola in January and successfully made the trans-Atlantic crossing to Spain, arriving in Palos de la Frontera in March. The admiral traveled to Barcelona to report his triumphal voyage to the Spanish royal court and to display the curiosities that he brought from the Indies.

The "discovery" of the Americas

The admiral's dramatic success set the stage for his second voyage of 1493–96, which would employ an armada of 17 ships and 1,300 men, led by Columbus and members of his household. Several royal officials, notaries, priests, and Franciscan friars joined the expedition, as well as 20 *hidalgos* (minor noblemen) and a company of *escuderos* (armed horsemen). This expedition departed from Cádiz in September 1493, aiming to claim territory and establish permanent Spanish colonial holdings in the Indies. Columbus plotted a southwestern course, arriving in the Lesser Antilles, and then sailing northwestward to Hispaniola. The expedition arrived at La Navidad on November 28, to discover that the fort and the adjacent Taíno settlement had been burned and all the Spanish settlers had been killed. Columbus searched for a better location and then founded the fort and *factoría* (trading post) of La Isabela in December 1493, before scouting the southern coast of Cuba, the island of Jamaica, and the southern coast of Hispaniola. While building the new *factoría* at La Isabela, Columbus sent a small fleet under Antonio de Torres back to Spain to report on the fledgling colony and to seek additional supplies. During Torres's absence, Columbus mapped the coastlines of Cuba and Jamaica, while his brother, Diego Colón, expanded the Spanish colonial foothold on Hispaniola. After additional reinforcements under Torres and Bartolomé Colón (another of Columbus's brothers) arrived at La Isabela, Christopher Columbus finally departed for Spain in April 1496 to report on his colonizing mission.

Columbus's third voyage of 1498–1500 sailed from Seville and again searched for the *terra firma* of mainland Asia, finding instead the coast of Venezuela, which Columbus described as "an enormous land, to be found in the south, of which until the present time nothing has been known....the earthly Paradise." The admiral claimed to his royal patrons that "your Highnesses have here a new world, where our Holy Faith can be greatly increased, and whence such great profits can be derived."[5] In addition to making these sweeping imperial claims, the expedition also attempted to salvage the difficult situation of the fledgling colonial enterprise in Hispaniola. Troubled relations with the local Taínos and divisions among the Spanish settlers led to conflicts and the abandonment of La Isabela in 1497, as a new *factoría* was constructed at Santo Domingo. A royal commissioner sent to investigate the administration of the colony arrested Columbus and his brothers, sending them back to Spain in chains to be tried.

Ferdinand and Isabella removed Columbus as governor of Hispaniola, replacing him with Don Nicolás de Ovando, who led a new expedition to Hispaniola in February 1502 with 30 ships and 2,500 crew and personnel. Columbus, who had been exonerated, led a final trans-Atlantic expedition in 1502–03, which bypassed Hispaniola and scouted the coast of Central America, which the admiral still apparently believed lay near the Indian Ocean.

The voyages of Christopher Columbus, and of other oceanic navigators who followed him, have often been hailed as epic "voyages of discovery." Samuel Eliot Morison famously celebrated the triumphal voyages of Columbus as amazing feats of seamanship that yielded dramatic discoveries.[6] This Eurocentric conception of "discovery" has rightly been criticized for its problematic presentation of trans-oceanic voyages as entrepreneurial adventures that were beneficial to human progress. More recent historians present late fifteenth- and sixteenth-century voyages as instigating cross-cultural contacts, military conquests, and sustained colonization.

The dramatic news of Columbus's voyages excited audiences across Europe and beyond. An illustrated edition of Columbus's letter recounting his first voyage was published as *De Insulis inventis* (1493). The news of Columbus's oceanic route, which was still assumed to lead to Asia, prompted other navigators to organize westward maritime expeditions. Alonso de Ojeda and Peralonso Niño led a new voyage for Spain in 1499, arriving off the coast of Venezuela. Venetian mariner Zuan Cabotto (John Cabot) received the backing of King Henry VII of England to plan a westward oceanic voyage. Cabotto led an English expedition across the North Atlantic in 1497, landing in Newfoundland. The Florentine noble, Amerigo Vespucci, led a series of expeditions across the Atlantic to the Caribbean and the Gulf of Mexico. Vespucci would popularize the phrase *mundus novus*, or New World, to describe the landmass that would later bear his name. Martin Waldseemüller's printed map of 1507 emblazoned the name America on the new continent in celebration of Amerigo Vespucci's voyages. The "discovery" of the Americas encouraged new attempts at global navigation and broader assertions of commercial privilege and territorial possession.

Contacts and claims

Navigators and rulers increasingly advanced territorial claims and legal confirmations. Portuguese kings had repeatedly sought papal bulls to ratify their seizures of territories in their *Reconquista* against Muslims in Iberia and the Mediterranean. Portuguese and Spanish forces expanded crusading warfare along the Moroccan coast and nearby islands in the Atlantic, resulting in competition and negotiations between these two kingdoms in the 1470s over their rival claims to ports and islands. The Treaty of Alcáçovas (1480) recognized Spain's claim to the Canary Islands and Portugal's possession of the Azores, Madeira, the Cape Verde Islands, and unspecified territories in Africa. The long-distance maritime expeditions that the Portuguese and Spanish launched to the West African coast and into the Atlantic Ocean depended on the possession of islands and coastal bases for resupply and refitting of ships.

Columbus's expeditions to the Caribbean in 1492 and 1493 then radically transformed global conceptions of oceanic space and territorial possession. The famous Treaty of Tordesillas of 1494 drew a line of demarcation running through the eastern Atlantic Ocean in order to disentangle the competing Spanish and Portuguese imperial claims. The treaty thus split the entire oceanic world into two hemispheres, each conceived of as an imperial sphere of dominion.

The Portuguese mariner Vasco da Gama assembled a small flotilla of two *nãos* and two caravels, departing Lisbon in 1497. Da Gama's fleet navigated south along the coast of Africa, then rounded the Cape of Good Hope and sailed into the Indian Ocean. The expedition, relying on a Muslim pilot, reached the western coast of India, and da Gama was able to negotiate trading relations with Calicut (Kozhikode). When he finally arrived back in Lisbon in 1499, his ships' cargoes of rare and precious spices excited Portuguese merchants and investors. Reports of da Gama's expedition would prompt other efforts to navigate the Indian Ocean and develop commercial ties with India, China, Japan, and Southeast Asia.

The success of the epic voyages of Columbus and da Gama is often attributed to the brilliance of navigators or to the technological possibilities of compasses. Yet, local knowledge and cooperation of indigenous peoples were also crucial in forging global navigation. When Spanish and Portuguese ships arrived at a new island or coast, their crews desperately sought out local assistance in navigating unknown waters, entering harbors, and obtaining fresh water and supplies. Amerindian, African, and Asian coastal peoples often initially welcomed contacts with European mariners, fostering potential connections despite linguistic barriers. Port cities in West Africa, East Africa, and South Asia were sometimes eager to negotiate trading agreements with the newly arrived mariners. Muslims who had had dealings with Italians in Istanbul or the Mediterranean could serve as translators or associates.

Global Maritime Imperialism

Da Gama's 1497–99 expedition into the Indian Ocean accelerated expectations for establishing regular long-distance maritime links between Europe, Africa, India, and Southeast Asia. Aspirations for truly global navigation became linked with ambitions for world empire.

Portuguese ventures

Following the fabulous success of da Gama's voyage across the Indian Ocean, Portuguese mariners began to construct the first global maritime empire. King Manuel I of Portugal organized a second expedition to India under Pedro Alvares Cabral, a Portuguese noble. Cabral's fleet sailed southwest from Lisbon in March 1500 and stumbled into the Brazilian coast in May. Cabral claimed this territory for his king before sailing on to the Cape of Good Hope and into the Indian Ocean. The fleet suffered losses during the difficult passage, but the surviving ships arrived in India in September, almost six months faster than da Gama's fleet. Cabral successfully negotiated with Samudri Raja, ruler of Calicut, to found a trading post in the city. Calicut–Portuguese relations soon soured, however, and Portuguese seizure of a merchant ship led to armed conflict. Cabral's fleet bombarded Calicut, then sailed to nearby ports of Cochin and Cannanur to acquire merchandise for the return voyage to Portugal. Although Cabral arrived in Lisbon in 1501 with lucrative cargo, he had failed to establish a *feitoría* and had disrupted Portuguese relations with Calicut. Even before his return, a smaller fleet under João da Nova had departed for India. Da Nova exacerbated the strained relations with Calicut by attacking several of its ships and trading with its rivals, Cochin and Cannanur.

A new Portuguese expedition sailed to India in March 1502 under Vasco da Gama's command, followed by a second squadron that departed a few months later and joined da Gama's ships along the western coast of India. The united Portuguese fleet consisted of six carracks, five caravels, and four *nãos*. The Portuguese caravels and carracks carried heavy guns, mounted below decks, as well as light artillery pieces above decks. Da Gama's fleet began a blockade of Calicut, aiming to cut the spice trade between Calicut and the Mediterranean via Mameluk Egpyt. The Mameluk sultan, Qansuh al-Ghauri (1501–16), launched a fleet to assist Calicut in breaking the Portuguese blockade. The joint Mameluk-Calicut fleet, composed of 20 *dhows* (lateen-rigged sailing vessels) and about 60 *prahus* and small craft, attacked da Gama's vastly outnumbered fleet of 15 ships in February 1503 along the Malabar coast near Calicut. As the fleets met, da Gama directed "the caravels to come one astern of the other in line...firing their guns as much as they could, and he did the same with the carracks to their rear."[7] Da Gama's ships seem to have remained in line, using their broadside artillery to smash the *dhows* and local craft, while avoiding boarding attempts. Da Gama's victory at this battle destroyed the Mameluk-Calicut fleet, allowing him to continue the blockade of Calicut and to establish trading factories at Cochin and Cannanore.

Francisco de Albuquerque and his brother Afonso led another voyage to India in 1503, paving the way for regular maritime expeditions and colonial expansion in the Indian Ocean. Portuguese *fidalgos*, or minor nobles, joined some of these voyages in the hope of gaining military experience and riches. Their participation in imperial projects may have contributed to the growing levels of violence in the Indian Ocean. Portuguese ships sailed into Muslim harbors, threatening communities and ships along the coasts of the Arabian Peninsula and India in the early sixteenth century. In 1505, Portuguese forces raided merchant shipping and seized the port of Colombo.

King Manuel I began to institutionalize the Portuguese Empire, sending Dom Francisco de Almeida in 1505 as his viceroy to establish an *Estado da Índia* (state of India). Almeida was given sweeping powers over Portuguese naval, maritime, commercial, military, and diplomatic affairs in the Indian Ocean in a detailed set of royal instructions, known as a *regimento*. Viceroy Almeida built fortresses and *feitorías* on the Indian coast, negotiating tributary relationships with local rulers. The Portuguese quickly developed the *carreira da Índia*, a system of regular maritime voyages between Portugal and India. Despite Manuel I's attempts to assert direct royal control over the fledgling *Estado da Índia*, Portuguese maritime commanders often acted on their own authority, as when Afonso de Albuquerque's fleet plundered ports and merchant ships in the Persian Gulf in 1507.

The creation of the *Estado da Índia* and the Portuguese global maritime empire called for new ships and naval technologies. Carracks were designed as three-masted warships that sported tall forecastles and sterncastles, which could be used as firing platforms for artillery and small arms. Although carracks could be built using a variety of designs and construction methods, they were generally larger than *nãos* or caravels, allowing more cannons to be mounted. Their reinforced hulls could sustain the recoil of many cannons being fired simultaneously. Carracks were bulky, with large cargo holds that enabled them to fulfill supply or commercial roles within the growing global maritime empires. By around 1500, carracks were large enough and sturdy enough to mount waterline broadside artillery using watertight gunports. Ship designs would continue to evolve, but carracks – with their heavy armament and sturdy construction – provided the prototype for naval ships for the next 300 years.

The Portuguese issued *cartaz*, or licenses, to ships trading in the Indian Ocean. Merchant vessels that were caught sailing without a *cartaz* were confiscated. The Portuguese system has been described as "a vast protection racket,"[8] but Portuguese officers justified their attacks using laws of the sea and concepts of sovereignty. Portuguese interdiction of rival commerce relied on the effectiveness of their shipboard artillery and the defensibility of their carracks and caravels. Initially, Venetian merchants worried that "the Portuguese caravels have interrupted everything," believing that the Portuguese warships would completely interdict the flow of pepper and spices through the Red Sea and Persian Gulf to their traders in the Levant.[9]

However, Portuguese fleets experienced serious difficulties in maintaining global maritime links and enforcing their *cartaz* system. Vincenzo Quirini, a Venetian ambassador, reported in 1506 on the limited successes of the Portuguese expeditions to the Indian Ocean: "From 114 ships which have been on this voyage between 1497 and 1506, only 55 have returned, and 19 are lost for certain, almost all of them laden with spices, and of another 40 nothing is known as of now."[10] Despite these losses, the Portuguese *Estado da Índia* was beginning to assert its control over maritime commerce and to reroute the spice trade from India and East Asia.

When Almeida's viceroyalty ended in 1509, Afonso de Albuquerque replaced him as governor of an increasingly powerful *Estado da Índia*. Albuquerque commanded a 400-ton flagship as he directed an amphibious landing to take the port of Goa in February 1510, but the sultan of Bijapur and his Turkish allies quickly retook the city. The Portuguese had to return to besiege Goa, which finally fell in December 1510 as Albuquerque's soldiers massacred the Muslim garrison and inhabitants. Goa was fortified and would eventually become the central base for the *Estado da Índia*.

Under Albuquerque's leadership, the Portuguese expanded the *Estado da Índia* ever eastward into Indonesian waters. In early 1511, Albuquerque organized an expedition of 18 ships and 800 men to conquer the important port of Melaka, which dominated the Melaka Straits between Malaysia and Sumatra. Albuquerque employed amphibious landings to conduct a siege of Melaka, taking it in July 1511. Having established the *Estado da Índia's* control over key ports and straits in the central and eastern Indian Ocean, Albuquerque now worked to extend Portuguese control over commerce in the Red Sea and Persian Gulf. The governor's fleet attacked Aden in 1513, but could not take the well-fortified port. Albuquerque soon seized Hormuz, imposing Portuguese control over the local ruler and fortifying the port in 1515. Although Albuquerque died later that year, he had succeeded in solidifying the *Estado da Índia* as a vast maritime empire stretching across the Indian Ocean.

The Portuguese employed local populations significantly in the construction of their maritime empire. Portuguese ships relied on local pilots to navigate shoals and enter ports along the coasts of Africa, India, and Southeast Asia. Arab merchants from the

Mediterranean and Levant could act as interpreters and business associates. At least a few Christian, Jewish, and Muslim converts of European origin were already living in South and Southeast Asia, possessing useful linguistic skills and specialized knowledge. Portuguese colonizers used indigenous laborers and soldiers to construct and maintain their trading posts.

The Portuguese method of combining naval power and artillery fortresses stemmed in part from certain technical and technological advantages. Duarte Pereira Pacheco, a Portuguese commander in the *Estado da Índia*, claimed in a 1508 text that in "fortresses surrounded by walls...Europe excels Asia and Africa; and she also excels them in her larger and better fleets, better equipped and armed than those of all other areas."[11] Despite the military advantages of European artillery fortresses, technological determinism fails to explain Portuguese military and colonial expansion.

Coastal fortresses gradually became a crucial tool of empire as the Portuguese established military and naval control of ports and constructed their *feitorías*, creating a global trading-post empire. The Portuguese continued to consolidate their control of the Moroccan coast through the construction of forts at Arzila and other towns. Portuguese forces built additional fortresses with trading compounds along the western and eastern coasts of Africa at Mozambique and Mombasa. Along the Arabian Sea and Persian Gulf, the Portuguese constructed fortifications at Muscat and Hormuz. Key cities in India, such as Goa, Calicut, and Colombo, were all fortified. Many of the coastal fortifications built in the 1490s–1530s were hastily constructed under the direction of Portuguese engineers who had limited experience with the fortifications *alla moderna* that had developed in the Italian Wars.

Beginning in the 1540s, however, Portugal launched a second wave of fortification building. Portuguese officials began to employ Italian engineers to construct elaborate bastioned artillery fortresses at key strategic points across the vast empire. Enormous bastions were built at Mazagão and Ceuta (Morocco). New bastions sprung up around the key port city of Salvador (Brazil). In 1558–60, bastioned fortifications were built at Hormuz, ringing the older walls that had been built by Albuquerque. Artillery emplacements were installed in the 1560s at the key port of Melaka (Southeast Asia), to protect the vital commercial route through the Melaka Straits. The reconstruction of Mombasa's Fort Jesus (East Africa) in the 1590s involved a regular geometrical design. The forces of the *Estado da Índia* gradually built artillery fortresses at Goa, Diu, Beçaim, Chaul, Damão, and São Tomé.

Despite Portuguese efforts to modernize and strengthen fortifications, financial difficulties often prevented the completion of bastions and the installation of sufficient guns. Major port cities such as Goa also held naval dockyards and maritime construction facilities. When naval expeditions were organized, artillery pieces were sometimes taken from fortifications and placed onboard warships. Even the viceregal seat of Goa apparently suffered from severe artillery shortages. Despite the difficulties in building and maintaining fortifications, Geoffrey Parker argues that "the artillery fortress constituted the crucial link between the Europeans' naval mastery and their ability to attract and exploit local allies."[12]

Successive kings of Portugal issued charters for the establishment of new cities in Brazil, Africa, and the *Estado da Índia*. Portuguese settlements were often situated within conquered indigenous cities or adjacent to already existing city sites. King Manuel I selected Goa as a key administrative center within the *Estado da Índia*, designating it as a royal city with special privileges for Portuguese nobles and merchants who settled there. By the 1540s, some 4,800 households resided in the Portuguese quarters of "Golden" Goa. Portuguese fortress governors and military officers reorganized urban space in conquered cities, creating ethnically distinct districts. Manuel I appointed governors to command his empire's far-flung fortifications, each holding authority for a three-year term. The new imperial cities and their promise of fabulous wealth attracted an estimated 280,000 Portuguese migrants between 1500 and 1580. The Portuguese monarchy had succeeded in constructing the first global maritime empire, but the *Estado da Índia* soon faced increasing competition in the Indian Ocean.

Ottoman ambitions

Although the Ottoman Empire tends to be remembered primarily as a land-based empire, Mehmed II and later sultans built powerful galley fleets after their conquest of Constantinople. A naval rivalry developed with Venice, as the Ottomans attempted to expand their influence in the Aegean and eastern Mediterranean. The massive amphibious force that took Negroponte in 1470 reportedly consisted of 300–450 ships and 70,000 soldiers. The Ottomans built diverse types of vessels for their fleets and began to mount artillery pieces on some of them. The Ottomans were able to wage sustained naval warfare during the Ottoman–Venetian War of 1499–1502. The naval combat at Zonchio in 1499 was inconclusive, but the Ottoman fleet

succeeded in intimidating the Venetian garrison at Lepanto to surrender. Kemal Reis emerged as one of the principal naval commanders for the Ottomans against the Venetian fleets.

Ottoman expansion in the eastern Mediterranean also involved
periodic naval campaigns against the vessels of the Knights of Saint
John of Jerusalem, a crusading order based in Rhodes that often waged
piracy against Muslim shipping. Kemal Reis led an Ottoman fleet to
conduct an antipiracy campaign against the Knights' galleys in 1505.

The Ottomans competed with the Portuguese in the Red Sea,
Persian Gulf, and Indian Ocean, making a bid to construct their own
global maritime empire. Ottoman fleets began to operate in the Red
Sea by 1505, using galleys and other ships with shipboard artillery.
The Ottomans also seem to have been supplying their commercial
rivals, the Mamluks, with artillery, ships, and naval expertise in the
1500s and 1510s in order to assist the Mamluk naval campaigns
against the Portuguese in the Indian Ocean. The Portuguese defeated
several successive Mamluk fleets, however, leading to an expansion
of Ottoman power in the Levant and Red Sea. Ottoman admiral
Selman Reis built a powerful Red Sea fleet at Suez in 1515, which
"signified the arming of Ottoman ambitions to oust the Portuguese
from the Indian Ocean."[13]

The Ottomans steadily developed formidable galley fleets and
specialized techniques of amphibious warfare. Ottoman naval power
supported the landward expansion of the Ottoman Empire throughout Greece and the Balkans in the late fifteenth and early sixteenth
centuries. Ottoman fleets also supported Sultan Selim I's rapid conquest of Syria, Egypt, and portions of the Arabian peninsula in 1516–
17. On the basis of these conquests, Selim I became protector of the
Muslim holy sites of Mecca and Medina, allowing him to claim the
title of caliph. Ottoman fleets were crucial in facilitating the dramatic
Ottoman expansion in the eastern Mediterranean islands, as well as
the Ottoman drive down the Levant to Egypt and then westward
along the North African coast.

Sultan Süleyman came to power in 1520 and quickly instigated new
campaigns of expansion, both in Hungary and in the eastern Mediterranean. He organized a major amphibious force of around 300 ships
and perhaps 100,000 crew and soldiers to besiege Rhodes in 1522.
The epic siege involved naval blockade, extensive entrenchments,
massive bombardments, and successive janissary assaults on the city's
defenses. The Knights of Saint John finally capitulated after a five-
month siege, submitting to a complete evacuation of the island of
Rhodes. Süleyman's conquest of Rhodes confirmed the tremendous
power of Ottoman amphibious warfare in the Mediterranean.

The consolidation of Ottoman rule in Egypt and the Arabian peninsula allowed Süleyman's strategic planners to contemplate imperial expansion in the Indian Ocean. Ibrahim Pasha, who became grand vizier (first minister) in 1523, led a military campaign to subdue a rebellion by Ahmed Pasha, the newly appointed governor of Egypt. While in Egypt, Ibrahim Pasha commissioned the Ottoman navigator Piri Reis to assemble an atlas and maritime navigational guide. The grand vizier's patronage allowed Piri Reis to complete his carto-graphical masterpiece, *Book of the Sea*, which he presented to the sultan in 1526. The atlas included detailed maps of the Mediterra-nean, but also broader geographical information drawn from Spanish and Portuguese navigations in the Atlantic and Indian Oceans. Selman Reis, a captain who had served in the Mamluk fleets against the Por-tuguese, drew up a report for Ibrahim Pasha on maritime expansion in the Indian Ocean. The Ottomans rebuilt a galley fleet at Suez, which became the base for Selman Reis's expeditions on the Red Sea in the 1520s. Ibrahim Pasha "had successfully built a platform for protecting Ottoman power abroad" into the Indian Ocean by the time of his death in 1536, when a jealous Sultan Süleyman suddenly ordered his execution.[14] Hadim Süleyman Pasha, who became the new grand vizier, negotiated an anti-Portuguese alliance in the Indian Ocean and waged aggressive maritime warfare against the Portu-guese in the Red Sea and Persian Gulf in the 1530s and 1540s.

Meanwhile, Sultan Süleyman named the North African corsair captain Khaireddin Barbarossa admiral of the Ottoman fleet at Istan-bul in 1533. Barbarossa, named for his red beard, seized Tunis in 1534, only to lose it to a Spanish counteroffensive the next year. A new Ottoman maritime expedition was organized in 1537 to besiege the Venetian base of Corfu, which protected the mouth of the Adriatic, during the Ottoman–Venetian War of 1537–39. Süleyman planned to launch an invasion of southern Italy once Corfu was taken, but the Venetian garrison held out. Despite this failure, Barbarossa's fleets consolidated Ottoman control of the eastern Mediterranean, with the notable exception of the islands of Corfu, Cyprus, and Crete, which remained under Venetian control. Barbarossa continued to threaten Spanish and Italian ports throughout the central Mediterranean, con-ducting major maritime raids on Reggio Calabria and Nice in 1543. Ottoman fleets raided the Italian coast in the 1550s and supported a campaign in North Africa to conquer Tripoli, one of the new bases of the Knights of Saint John.

The Ottomans' successes in the Mediterranean may paradoxically have prevented them from building a global maritime empire. Ottoman seapower was increasingly diverted toward amphibious warfare in the central Mediterranean instead of organizing commercial convoys in the eastern Mediterranean, the Red Sea, or the Indian Ocean. Ottoman–Habsburg rivalry in southeastern Europe and the Mediterranean seems to have prevented Ottoman military and naval leaders from focusing on broader strategic aims and ambitions in Central Asia and the Indian Ocean. In addition, the Ottoman Empire had different aims in the Indian Ocean: "Where the Portuguese intended to monopolize the sea trade and gain naval supremacy on the open sea, the Ottomans sought to conquer territories and tax agricultural lands."[15]

Spanish Conquests

Columbus had left an ambiguous legacy in the Caribbean, but Spanish forces tentatively began to forge a maritime empire in the early sixteenth century. Nicolás Ovando, the first governor of Hispaniola, arrived in 1502 with 2,500 men to colonize the island and several Franciscan friars to convert the indigenous Taíno population. Gold was discovered on Hispaniola and Santo Domingo quickly became the principal Spanish port in the Caribbean, attracting Spanish, Italian, Flemish, and German immigrants.

During the first two decades of the sixteenth century, Spanish mariners scouted the Caribbean Sea, charting islands and finding Florida. Juan Ponce de León led colonizing efforts on Puerto Rico beginning in 1507 and Diego Velázquez de Cuéllar led an expedition of *conquistadores* to Cuba in 1511, conquering the island. Vaso Núñez de Balboa made an excursion across the isthmus of Panama in 1513, claiming to have found another ocean. Spanish soldiers subjugated indigenous peoples on all of these islands, allowing settlers to establish towns and *encomiendas* (tributary land grants) that were patterned on the already existing settlements in the Canary Islands. Spanish forces enslaved Taínos and Arawaks on the islands they occupied and conducted slave raids in the Bahamas. Francisco Hernández de Córdoba's 1517 expedition detected the Yucatán peninsula, sighting large cities and clashing with well-armed Maya warriors. The same year, another expedition under Juan de Grijalva scouted the coast of the Yucatán and Central American mainland.

Hernán Cortés, a Spanish adventurer, organized an expedition to Mesoamerica in 1519 that would greatly alter the Spanish Empire. Cortés, worried that he would be relieved of command, departed prematurely, picking up additional men and supplies in Cuba on his voyage toward the mainland. Cortés's 11 ships and 450 men arrived on the coast of Mesoamerica and established a settlement named Vila Rica de la Vera Cruz. Cortés sent one ship to Spain to report on his colonizing efforts, then burned the remaining ten ships to silence dissension among members of his expedition.

Cortés's arrival created opportunities for Amerindian city-states in Mesoamerica that were dissatisfied with their status as tributary states within the Mexican (Aztec) Empire, under Mexica rule. The Totonacs and Tlaxcaltecs forged political alliances with Cortés in order to check the power of the Mexica, who were based at their capital city of Tenochtitlán. Large numbers of indigenous warriors eventually joined in a broad alliance against the Mexica, but it was probably the Amerindians, and especially the Tlaxcaltecs, who guided the military campaign, rather than Cortés. The Spanish-Tlaxcaltec forces conducted a riverine advance toward Tenochtitlán and orchestrated a brutal massacre of Chololtec nobles, punishing their rivals and terrorizing other cities.

The Mexica responses to foreign military forces and to growing civil warfare across the empire seem confused and hesitant, indicating serious political divisions within the Mexica nobility and the broader Aztec elite in the Valley of Mexico. Emperor Moctezoma (1502–20) decided to meet with Cortés, inviting the Spanish contingent into Tenochtitlán. The Spanish seized Moctezoma and held him hostage, however, further destabilizing the imperial regime. While Cortés was away from the capital city, his lieutenant, Pedro de Alvarado, carried out a brutal massacre of Mexica nobles in the courtyard of the Great Temple, probably following Cortés's orders. When Cortés returned to the capital, Mexica crowds rose up against him and surrounded Spanish forces. Cortés's attempt to use his imperial hostage to calm the Mexica backfired, and Moctezoma was killed either by Spanish soldiers or outraged Aztecs. Cortés and his Spanish soldiers barely managed to escape from Tenochtitlán.

The Tlaxcaltecs received the Spanish refugees and determined to continue their alliance with Cortés. With Cortés's assistance, they pressured other nearby cities to join their alliance. Meanwhile, the Mexica attempted to restore imperial order in Tenochtitlán, establishing Cuitlahua as successor to the fallen Moctezoma. Diseases ravaged Tenochtitlán, however, and the new emperor died after only 80 days of rule, leading to further political disruption of the Mexica Empire. The Spanish-Tlaxcaltec army then marched to Tetzcoco, a city-state that had been a key ally of the Mexica but that was experiencing a succession crisis. Cortés and his Tlaxcaltec allies successfully supported one of the royal claimants to the Tetzcocan throne, winning an important new defection from the beleaguered Mexica imperial system. With Tetzcocan support, Cortés and his Amerindian allies could launch the conquest of Tenochtitlán.

The siege of the Mexica capital of Tenochtitlán demonstrates the significant amphibious and naval dimensions of the Spanish conquest of Mexico. Tenochtitlán was a major city built on an island in a lake, with multiple causeways connecting the city with the shore. The Spanish constructed 13 brigantines, each mounting artillery, near Tetzcoco especially for the siege. Cortés's Amerindian allies used canoes. Cortés directed his Spanish and allied forces to cut the causeways and blockade the capital, and he periodically launched assaults on the Mexica positions at the causeways, eroding their defenses. Spanish forces used arquebuses and artillery during the siege, as famine gripped the isolated city. After three months of sustained siege, Tenochtitlán surrendered. Spanish infantry and thousands of Amerindian allies occupied the devastated city.

The meaning and significance of the conquest of Mexico has been debated ever since. Although the defeat of the Mexica is often labeled as the "Spanish Conquest," Ross Hassig rightly points out that "Spanish weapons made the conquest of Mexico feasible, not because they defeated the Mexica, but because the Indians recognized the potential of these arms for multiplying their own effectiveness and allowing tens and even hundreds of thousands of Indian soldiers and auxiliaries to execute the conquest."[16] Spanish *conquistadores* thus were not principally responsible for the conquest of Mexico, but they would soon capitalize on the collapse of the Mexica Empire to forge a Spanish Empire across Central and South America.

Colonial Development

Imperial claims and conquests began to produce novel conceptions of maritime empire and new patterns of colonization in the early sixteenth century. Maritime expeditions and imperial mapping efforts progressively constructed trans-oceanic transportation networks, allowing enhanced connectivity and sustained exchange around the world. Ships carried humans, plants, animals, and goods to distant lands in elaborate efforts to develop colonies, but often with unexpected results.

The Columbian Exchange

New global maritime links carried germs across oceans, transmitting diseases between disparate human and animal population groups.

People all around the world, including European mariners, African coastal dwellers, Arab merchants, and Hindu pepper cultivators, confronted new diseases. But the peoples of the Americas were especially affected, since Amerindians had been epidemiologically isolated from germ exchanges that had been occurring for thousands of years between Eurasian and African peoples. This isolation meant that Amerindians' immune systems were completely unprepared to encounter diseases that had become endemic in Eurasian and African populations. "When the isolation of the New World was broken," Alfred Crosby relates, "the American Indian met for the first time his most hideous enemy...the invisible killers which those men brought in their blood and breath."[17] The germs that Spanish mariners and their animals brought with them to the Americas ravaged Amerindian bodies, which had never before been exposed to them. Childhood diseases that had become relatively benign in Eurasia – such as mumps, measles, and chicken pox – produced epidemics among Amerindians. Smallpox apparently first arrived in the Americas in 1518 and caused devastation among the Amerindians in Santo Domingo, before spreading throughout the Caribbean islands and to the Yucatán peninsula. This deadly smallpox pandemic may have been accompanied by influenza, pneumonia, and other diseases that were previously unknown in the Americas. Epidemic diseases progressed throughout the Amerindian populations of Central America, then ranged into North and South America.

The impact of Eurasian and African epidemic diseases on Amerindians was devastating, resulting in massive depopulation. According to one account of epidemics in New Spain, "more than one half of the population died [in some provinces]; in others the proportion was little less....They died in heaps, like bedbugs."[18] Epidemic diseases also swept through the Incan Empire in Peru, killing the emperor, Huayna Capac, and decimating the Incan elites. The death of the emperor and numerous political and military leaders destabilized the entire Incan Empire, allowing Spanish forces to conquer it. Pedro Pizarro commented that had "this Huayna Capac been alive when we Spaniards entered this land, it would have been impossible for us to win it, for he was much beloved by all his vassals."[19]

The severe depopulation of the Americas had global implications. The new Spanish and Portuguese colonies in the Americas suffered from severe labor shortages that limited their economic development. Spanish colonizers enslaved surviving Amerindian populations in the Caribbean and Mexico, forcing them to work as agricultural laborers. Portuguese landholders soon began to import enslaved Africans as farmworkers, creating a global demand for African slave labor. The depopulation of the Americas also had military and strategic implications, allowing Spanish and Portuguese military forces to establish port cities and coastal fortifications that would operate as strategic bases for maritime communications and fleet operations.

Eurasian plants quickly began to transform the Americas. Spanish and Portuguese colonizers brought seeds with them to plant key food crops in their newly conquered territories. Early experiments with planting wheat, grape vines, and olive trees on Caribbean islands and along the South American coast utterly failed. Spanish colonizers also planted greens, banana trees, and orange trees, however, which thrived in the tropical climate. As the Spanish expanded deeper into Central and South America, settlers found more temperate regions that could grow European wheat, vegetables, and staple crops for human and animal consumption on their *encomiendas*. Global maritime communications promoted plant exchanges well beyond the Americas, producing an "ecological imperialism," as plants favored by humans and by climates colonized new territories, overrunning indigenous plant species.[20] Spanish and Portuguese colonists not only imported crops native to their own countries, but also Asian and African plants such as bananas, oranges, lemons, rice, and sugarcane. Indigenous American food plants such as maize, sweet potatoes, tomatoes, cassava, beans, chili peppers, and peanuts gradually entered African, European, and Asian cuisines during the sixteenth century.

Columbus's second expedition and successive colonizing missions brought domesticated animals and livestock to the Americas. Pigs, sheep, dogs, and cattle spread across Caribbean islands. A Spanish colonizer in Cuba claimed in 1514 that his pigs had reproduced dramatically and that there were "more pigs than I ever saw before in my life."[21] Some Spanish nobles on Hispaniola developed herds of hundreds, or even thousands, of cattle. Cortés's expedition brought cattle ranching to Mexico in the 1520s, disrupting indigenous environments and spreading diseases – prompting the first viceroy of New Spain, Antonio de Mendoza, to report that "if cattle are allowed, the Indians will be destroyed."[22] Nonetheless, cattle ranching rapidly expanded across Central America in the 1520s, and soon developed in Spanish territories in Colombia and Portuguese Brazil in the 1530s. Spanish cattle ranchers imported Eurasian grasses, which spread rapidly, as "Europeans followed and extended the Indian practice of burning over grasslands, and European livestock overgrazed large areas, opening the way for the heartier immigrant grasses and weeds."[23] Spanish *conquistadores* brought numerous

Eurasian horses to the Americas, initially providing them with a great military advantage against Amerindians. Stray horses would later transform Amerindian warfare across the great plains of North America.

The Columbian Exchange also involved human migration and biological mixing. Some Spanish *conquistadores* reportedly raped Amerindian women during their conquests in the Caribbean and the Valley of Mexico. As Spanish forces established imperial control, many *conquistadores* had consensual sexual relations with Amerindian women, sometimes leading to marriages and *mestizo* (mixed) offspring. Initially, Spanish colonies experienced difficulty in attracting settlers, leading colonial officials to seek banished subjects and prisoners as settlers. News of the discovery of gold in the Caribbean islands and Mesoamerica excited a fresh wave of migration to New Spain. A severe shortage of European women in early Portuguese and Spanish colonies in the Americas led to mixed marriages between European men and Amerindian women.

Often overlooked are the military dimensions of the Columbian Exchange. Global navigation accelerated military technology transfers worldwide. Many armies encountered diverse weapons systems, organizational methods, and military practices, prompting them to adapt rapidly through military acculturation. Military and naval specialists with technical expertise – such as shipmasters, pilots, mapmakers, founders, artillerists, engineers, and architects – could seek employment at princely courts and city-states around the world.

A global arms trade was born. Firearms and artillery were among the most desirable manufactured export goods in emerging global markets. Early maritime empires guarded their artillery pieces and arquebuses, but even these advanced military technologies could be traded as gifts or sold. Other military and naval equipment was exchanged in large quantities. Europeans were not the only purveyors of arms and military technologies, however. Ottoman officials used Arabian horses as princely gifts, which were highly valued as elite cavalry mounts. Arab merchants also sold the prized horses to wealthy buyers in the Mediterranean Sea and Indian Ocean. Artillery and firearms produced in the Ottoman Empire seem to have been traded across the Indian Ocean and throughout Central Asia. Iron and bronze, used in founding artillery, took on enhanced military significance, altering trading patterns in these metals. Global markets also developed for the main components in manufacturing gunpowder: charcoal, sulfur, and saltpeter. Naturally occurring saltpeter had been used for centuries in producing gunpowder locally in China, the Levant, and Europe, but now large saltpeter deposits in the Ganges

River valley began to serve the growing global arms trade. Corned gunpowder, a refined and relatively stable gunpowder mixture, was transported and exchanged globally.

Mapping maritime empires

The transformations of the Columbian Exchange created great confusion in scientific and intellectual communities around the globe, forcing adjustments or wholesale revisions of well-established biological, geographical, and cosmological theories. New techniques of information collection and management were gradually developed to assess the changing understandings of the earth. The emergence of global imperial claims in the late fifteenth century demanded new geographical approaches to mapping empires. Some historians have described the resulting changes in the fields of geography and cartography as a "geographical revolution," but other scholars have challenged this notion as claiming too sweeping a departure from older techniques of mapping.

Navigators who conducted maritime expeditions greatly expanded knowledge of global geography, but usually kept their precise navigational charts and data secret. Portuguese cartographers produced world maps and navigational guides tracing the routes of the da Gama, Cabral, and da Nova expeditions, assembling navigational and geographic knowledge to assist future Portuguese mariners in making the voyages across the Indian Ocean. Maps and logbooks containing such geographic information, often produced under royal patronage, could be considered classified state documents. Nonetheless, manuscript copies of navigators' maps and logbooks circulated in Mediterranean and European courts, where they could fetch astronomical prices. Ottoman cartographer Piri Reis was able to produce world maps based closely on Portuguese and Spanish voyages to the Americas as early as 1513.

The techniques of mapping navigational routes on portolan charts had long included details about ports, their inhabitants, and available trading goods. Territories were sometimes indicated on portolan charts using flags and illustrations of enthroned rulers. By the early sixteenth century *mappae mundi* and globes increasingly incorporated additional information on interior territories and entire landmasses. Rulers began to commission globes depicting their maritime empires in three dimensions, including ethnographic descriptions of inhabitants in their colonized territories. Broader audiences could view printed world maps, which began to circulate in a rapidly expanding market for geographical information. Johannes Ruysch produced a printed world map around 1507 that incorporated Amerigo Vespucci's designation of the Americas as the *mundus novus*, or New World. Martin Waldseemüller labeled South America as *terra nova*, or new land, on his 1513 map of the emerging Spanish Empire in the Americas, adding depictions of cannibals and a monstrous animal. Waldseemüller also communicated Spanish claims of territorial empire by planting a Spanish flag prominently on the island of Cuba in the map.

Geographic texts and world maps aimed at mapping imperial territories and bounding expansive spaces. As Walter D. Mignolo points out, early modern attempts to map the Americas can be considered "as social and semiotic interactions and territorial control instead of as representations of an ontological space."[24] Thus, early maps of the Americas should not be understood as quaint sketches filled with inaccuracies, but as powerful documents that shaped patterns of colonization and global conflict.

Localized maps of specific regions delimited local territorial claims, surveying administrative boundaries, plantation limits, and settlers' landholdings. Books of city views portrayed urban centers in New Spain, such as Mexico and Cuzco, as well as new colonial settlements. Mapping colonial cities and roads provided coordinates for understanding imperial space, as well as establishing population control and commercial power in the Americas and the Indian Ocean. As cartographers worked to map the growing maritime empires of the Portuguese, Spanish, and Ottomans, they also had to grapple with how to consider other competing maritime powers.[25]

Several regional maritime empires in Eurasia and Africa seem to have had the potential to become global maritime empires around 1500. Gujarati merchants had extensive Indian Ocean networks, but their city-state ports lacked centralized political authority. Mameluk Egypt, as discussed above, controlled much of the spice trade in the Indian Ocean in the early sixteenth century, but fell to Ottoman conquest in 1517. The sultanate of Aceh on the northern tip of the island of Sumatra developed a formidable fleet in the sixteenth century, allowing it to compete with the Portuguese for control of trade in the eastern Indian Ocean. The Acehans constructed walled fortifications to defend their cities from the Portuguese threat in Indonesia. Japanese mariners maintained significant maritime trading networks between Honshu, Shikoku, Kyushu, and smaller islands. Chinese merchants continued to trade in the South China Sea, but the Chinese emperors had decisively abandoned their bid at constructing a maritime empire.

Regional maritime powers in the Baltic and North Seas also seem to have had the potential to develop global empires. The Hanseatic League had dominated commerce in the Baltic since the late medieval period and might have transitioned into a maritime empire, but the growing kingdom of Denmark controlled the Sound, the crucial passages between the Baltic and the North Sea. Danish kings constructed a navy around 1500, arming ships with artillery. Christian II of Denmark demonstrated the power of his fleet in 1520 by occupying Stockholm and suppressing rebellious Swedish nobles. Denmark seemed poised to dominate the Baltic Sea and construct an Atlantic, or even global, empire. The emergence of a powerful kingdom of Sweden in the mid-sixteenth century would prevent Denmark from competing with the global maritime empires.

In the Atlantic World, changing circumstances pointed to future possibilities for maritime development. Flemish mariners played a significant role within the broader Spanish Empire and Antwerp became one of the principal ports on the Atlantic coast of Europe early in the sixteenth century, but the Netherlands' position within Habsburg territories prevented independent imperial ambitions developing until civil war divided it in the late sixteenth century. England had a significant commercial and fishing presence in the Irish Sea, North Sea, and English Channel. The Venetian navigator Zuan Cabotto (John Cabot) led an English maritime expedition across the north Atlantic, charting the coast of Newfoundland. English fishing craft found abundant cod and expanded their fishing operations to Greenland and Newfoundland coasts, but the kingdom would only gradually launch Atlantic and global maritime expeditions. French mariners already traded in the Atlantic and the Mediterranean, but French monarchs were slow to instigate policies to develop a maritime empire. François I sponsored the navigator Jacques Cartier, who led three voyages to Canada between 1534 and 1543 in an attempt to found a colony of New France. Cartier mapped much of the Gulf of Saint Lawrence and the Saint Lawrence River valley, establishing several small settlements, which were ultimately abandoned. A French maritime empire and colonization would have to wait until the early seventeenth century.

Global slave trade

Prior to the rise of global navigation and colonization, several major supra-regional slave markets existed. The Mediterranean slave trade involved dual circuits of Muslim slaves within Christian lands and

70   War and Conflict in the Early Modern World

Christian slaves in Muslim North Africa and the Levant. A trans-Saharan slave trade transferred black Africans to North African slave markets. An Indian Ocean slave trade dealt in African and South Indian slaves. Enslavement in all these areas was normally directly linked to warfare. Prisoners of war were enslaved by their captors, and then employed as galley rowers, laborers, or domestic servants. Slaves could be resold at slave markets, mostly for domestic service. Laws in many areas restricted slave status to individuals beyond the boundaries of the locally dominant religion, since co-religionaries normally could not legally be enslaved.

Slavery gradually became linked to sugarcane cultivation in the late medieval Mediterranean. Muslims had long grown sugarcane in Cyprus and the Levant, but Europeans only encountered sugar cultivation during the Crusades. Mediterranean warfare between Christians and Muslims produced many new slaves, since both religions considered idolatrous war captives as subject to enslavement. Enslaved captives in the Mediterranean generally worked as domestic servants, but could also be employed in mining or agricultural labor. As Venetians expanded sugar production in Cyprus and other islands within their *stato da mar*, they increasingly employed Muslim and Orthodox Christian slaves as laborers. Growing, harvesting, and refining sugarcane required intensive labor, and produced a highly concentrated product that was transportable and very lucrative on export markets. Other Europeans experimented with sugarcane cultivation on Sicily and islands across the Mediterranean, also employing slave labor. As Portuguese and Spanish forces occupied Atlantic islands, new noble landholders enthusiastically embraced sugarcane cultivation. The Spanish brought sugar to the Canary Islands. The Portuguese first planted sugar in Madeira in 1455, and their plantations' output rapidly expanded. Sugar from the island very soon competed with Cypriot and Levantine sugar, and then came to dominate the northern European market by 1500. Fernão de Mello, the Portuguese governor in São Tomé, established some of the first sugar plantations to employ black African slaves, due to the island's proximity to the West African coast.

The plantation complex pioneered in the Mediterranean and Atlantic islands gradually spread to the new Portuguese and Spanish Empires in South America and the Caribbean. Christopher Columbus brought sugar to the Americas, initiating sugarcane cultivation on Hispaniola during his second voyage. Early Spanish plantations imposed forced labor on conquered Amerindians in Caribbean islands and coastal Mexico, but the demographic collapse of the Amerindian population prevented a rapid expansion of sugarcane and the severe lack of forced labor created a bottleneck in sugar production. Only in the 1540s did sugarcane cultivation take off in the Americas, when Portuguese settlers in Brazil developed the fully articulated plantation complex, which relied on a steady stream of black African slaves via a trans-Atlantic slave trade.

Portuguese and Spanish settlers in the Americas initially enslaved some Amerindian populations to perform labor in their early colonies. But diseases devastated the Taínos and other Amerindians in the Caribbean and South America, leading to labor shortages. In the early sixteenth century, Portuguese and Spanish expeditions gradually began to transport African slaves to the Americas. The perceived insufficiency of local slaves in the colonial territories presented legal and moral complications for European colonizers, who were familiar with Mediterranean slave systems. In the Mediterranean, slaves were normally taken in piracy and warfare across religious boundaries. Enslaved individuals could receive manumission, either by negotiating ransoms or through peace and prisoner exchanges. Established charity organizations grew up that were dedicated to negotiating the release of captives. The trans-Atlantic slave trade, in contrast, instituted a new condition of permanent slavery.

In the Atlantic World, slave acquisition operated in a very different way, gradually resulting in an entirely new form of slavery. Black Africans normally entered slavery as war captives who were taken in the fighting between West African kingdoms, and then were sold in regional slave markets. As the Portuguese established trading posts on the African coast in the late fifteenth century, they began to purchase African slaves for resale. Once sugar plantations, or *fazendas*, were established on São Tomé around 1510, Portuguese planters began to import African slaves from the nearby coast. By the 1530s and 1540s, Portuguese and Spanish slave traders were shipping Africans across the Atlantic. The Middle Passage was thus born.

Triangular trading systems gradually developed in the Atlantic Ocean, linking Europe, Africa, and the Americas through precise patterns of navigation and commerce. Armed ships departed European ports bearing cargoes of manufactured goods, and then navigated to the African coast, where captains traded goods and purchased slaves. With the chained African slaves confined below decks, slave ships then made the long trans-Atlantic voyage, or Middle Passage, to the Americas. Slaves were offloaded in Caribbean or Brazilian ports, sold in dedicated slave markets, and sent to sugar plantations.

The trans-Atlantic slave trade established new forms of brutality and Atlantic slavery became overwhelmingly associated with the institution of the plantation complex. It also racialized slavery, targeting black Africans as the only legitimate population group that could be converted into commercial property. The racialization of slavery prompted new ethical questions and debates about the morality of slavery. Many Europeans believed that slavery could be properly imposed on infidels, as they considered Muslims, but now they constructed new categories to describe black Africans as idolaters. The Portuguese used *asientos*, contracts issued to slave traders, to regulate the slave trade. Despite some Europeans' moral qualms about the trans-Atlantic slave trade, it grew rapidly.[26]

Brazil's proximity to slave supply sources together with steady trade winds made it the first trans-oceanic slave trade route destination to be lucrative. Major civil warfare within the kingdom of Kongo in the 1550s expanded the supply of slaves entering the markets on the West African coast, allowing Portuguese traders to purchase more slaves for transportation to the growing plantations in Brazil. This coincidence allowed for the rapid development of the Atlantic sugar industry: "Brazilian sugar had to travel farther to reach Europe, but Brazil had easier access to African labor."[27] Sugarcane production could rely on the purchase of an enslaved labor force because sugar was in such high demand.

Although the new system of slavery is often referred to as a trans-Atlantic system, it was truly global. The Atlantic World merely showcased regional dynamics of the emerging global patterns of slavery. The plantation complex that had been developed in the Mediterranean and Atlantic Worlds was being adapted to other lucrative cash crops worldwide. Many features of the trans-Atlantic slave economy were later exported to India and Southeast Asia.

Conclusion

Maritime conflict suddenly became global in scale in the wake of the voyages of the 1490s. Regional merchant activity became increasingly entangled with emerging global commercial patterns. Carracks brimming with artillery now ranged across the world's oceans and seas, preying on commerce. Merchant ships in the Indian Ocean were subject to Portuguese policies of systematic seizure. Spanish and Portuguese maritime forces exerted global claims of imperial possession, even as the Columbian Exchange began to alter Mediterranean slavery and stimulate the early Atlantic slave trade. The three-masted warship redefined naval warfare and maritime commerce globally, as shipwrights gradually developed galleons to meet the new demands of global navigation and commerce.

Ferdinand Magellan, a Portuguese mariner who had become a naturalized Spanish subject, organized an expedition aiming at finding a passage to the ocean on the western side of the Americas. Charles V supported Magellan's expedition, providing detailed instructions to the captain. Magellan's fleet of five ships departed from Spain in September 1519 on its epic journey. The fleet successfully crossed the Atlantic and descended the eastern coast of South America, before a mutiny erupted in Patagonia. Magellan navigated through the treacherous straits that have since borne his name, leading his small fleet into the Pacific Ocean after a terrifying 38-day passage. The fleet crossed the vast Pacific, nearly running out of supplies before reaching Guam. Magellan was killed in a combat in the Philippines, as his fleet worked its way westward. The surviving crewmembers managed to return in one ship across the Indian Ocean, rounding the Cape of Good Hope and sailing north to Spain, where they completed the first circumnavigation of the globe on September 1, 1522. Magellan's expedition confirmed the realization of global navigation and the possibilities of imperial overseas expansion. New circumnavigations followed, along with searches for a northwest passage around North America. Trans-oceanic routes increasingly wove a web of sustained connections and round-trip voyages that established vast global maritime empires.

3

Schism and Social Conflict, 1510s–1560s

Shah Ismail I (1501–14) led the Safavid Sufi order to power in Iran in the early sixteenth century, founding the Safavid dynasty and locating his capital at Tabriz. Political concerns over the new dynasty's legitimacy and rivalry with the Sunni Ottoman Empire emboldened Ismail to identify himself with Imam 'Ali (the Hidden Imam) and to claim divine inspiration. Shah Ismail designated Twelver Shiism as the official religion of his empire, attracting important Shia scholars to his court and patronizing religious art and poetry. The Safavids erected shrines, mosques, and madrasas to promote the Twelver Shia form of Islam throughout their rapidly expanding empire. The Safavid rulers of Iran and their armies articulated a particularly Shia notion of sacred conflict that would have a lasting impact on Central Asia.

The Shia revival in Iran was only one of the major religious reforms of the early sixteenth century that produced conflict. Apocalyptic belief seems to have represented a powerful force across different religious and social boundaries in this period.[1] New research on religious violence in the early modern world demonstrates strong correlations between spiritual crises and social conflicts in this period. Religious conflict did not represent a simple "clash of civilizations" between monolithic religious blocs, however.[2] Instead, complex spiritual movements within different religions fueled various forms of conflict, including schism, iconoclasm, sacred violence, and interreligious warfare. Spiritual crises and religious reform movements created powerful motivations for violence and social conflict in the early modern period.

Spiritual Crises

A wave of spiritual crises swept across much of the world around 1500. Every historical period witnesses new religious formations, but the early sixteenth century stands out as a particularly fertile time for religious revival movements and entirely new religions. Diverse religious movements arose, promoting devotional renewal and moral reform to cleanse pollution and re-establish purity.

Apocalyptic fears and millennial hopes

Dire prophesies spread millennial expectations of the imminent arrival of diabolical destroyers and divine saviors. New techniques of numerology and textual criticism were employed to interpret omens, horoscopes, and prophesies with seemingly striking precision. Mystical visions encouraged fresh spiritual renewals and devotional movements. Mechanical printing technologies now diffused apocalyptic beliefs across vast regions, affecting many religious communities.

Many Christians waited impatiently for the second coming of Jesus Christ, anticipating his arrival during the jubilee year of 1500. Orthodox Christians in Russia and Greece could regard invaders and occupiers as agents of God's punishment prior to a hoped-for redemption. Meanwhile, the Latin Christian Church seemed terribly split by clerical incompetence, rival claimants to spiritual leadership, and a conciliar movement that challenged papal authority. Latin Christian theologians advanced divergent interpretations of the Last Days, fomenting millennialism and apocalyptic fervor among Christian adherents.

Muslims held similar expectations for a Last Judgment in the early modern period. Both Sunni and Shia teachings prophesy the coming of the Mahdi, a righteous leader who would be sent by God to defeat the forces of evil in an apocalyptic battle before the Day of Judgment. Some Shia believed that the Twelfth Imam would be born just prior the Last Judgment, identifying this Hidden Imam with the figure of the Mahdi. Islamic eschatology enumerates signs heralding the appearance of the Mahdi, including a world filled with tyranny, immorality, and injustice.[3] Some Muslims believed that a *mujaddid* (renewer) would arise every century to revitalize Islam.

Early modern Jews hoped for the arrival of a long-awaited messiah. The expulsion of Jews from Spain in 1492 heightened apocalyptic belief among refugees and new converts to Christianity, or *conversos*. Kabalistic scholarship and Jewish mysticism flourished in the sixteenth and seventeenth centuries, as rabbis such as Judah ben Bezalel Loew explored relationships between mathematics and the natural world. Works such as Menasseh ben Israel's *The Hope of Israel* encouraged Jewish expectations for the imminent arrival of the messiah and imagined connections between the Ten Lost Tribes and Amerindians. A number of early modern Jews claimed to be the messiah, attracting devoted followings.[4]

Religious change strengthened apocalyptic strains in Asian religions in the early sixteenth century. Hindu epics provided models for apocalyptic violence, since Hindu millennialism envisions Kalki as an avatar of Vishnu who will destroy an immoral world and replace it with a golden age. The rise of Sikhism and the spread of Islam in India in the early sixteenth century shook some Hindu practitioners' beliefs and encouraged conversions.

Buddhist apocalypticism envisioned a period of immorality and evil that would destroy the age of the *dharma* before a new age of peace and truth. Divisions between the Mahayana, Theravada, and Vajrayana sects of Buddhism created competing monastic movements. Thai Theravada Buddhists allowed for the possibility that meritorious persons could perform miracles, presaging the arrival of Maitreya, a new Buddha. During political and social crises, Buddhist revival movements could coalesce around monastic leaders in Southeast Asia.

In the Americas, Mexican and Incan societies had their own apocalyptical beliefs that seemed to be confirmed by contact, disease, and conquest. Global exchanges produced radically changing understandings of geography, cartography, humanity, and nature that challenged accepted sacred knowledge within many religious traditions. Spiritual and religious reform movements often inspired deep apocalyptic fears, which could motivate wars or explain ongoing conflicts.

Prophets and religious fervor

Charismatic prophesy excited listeners and spurred religious reforms in many societies. Print media distributed prophetic writings, allowing spiritual leaders to attract broad audiences even at a distance. Radical prophecies destabilized social order and fueled conflicts in some places.

The Dominican monk Savonarola led a radical movement for repentance and moral renewal in Florence in the 1490s. Many of his followers participated in the infamous Bonfire of the Vanities, burning artwork and other worldly possessions that they considered immoral or extravagant. Savonarola's radical preaching provoked fear and suspicion among clerical and political authorities, who tried and executed him in 1498. But the prophet's brief theocratic leadership of Florence contributed to growing Christian revival movements.

Guru Nanak, a Punjabi ascetic, forged a new spiritual path in northwestern India in the 1520s–30s. The teachings of Guru Nanak critiqued Hindu and Muslim teachings and practices. This new religion, known as Sikhism, began to attract significant followings in northwestern India under the leadership of Sikh gurus (teachers). By the late sixteenth century, Sikh gurus had compiled a set of sacred texts and teachings, known as the *Adi Granth*. Sikhs began building a monumental religious complex, the Golden Temple, at Amritsar during the late sixteenth century, as Sikhism gained new converts among Hindus and Muslims. The growth of Sikhism seemed threatening to Hindu and Muslim leaders, creating social tensions in religiously diverse northwestern India.

New religious practices emerged as epidemic diseases decimated Amerindian political and religious leaders and devastated entire societies. Shamans and healers confronted horrifying new diseases that existing rituals and medicines did nothing to stop. Amerindians of northern Mexico may have developed their beliefs in "devil sickness" in response to the spread of disease in the early sixteenth century.[5] Early European imperialism and epidemic diseases devastated Native American societies and destabilized their religious systems.

Religious Reform in the Islamic World

Religious revival and schism produced extended social conflict and sectarian violence in the Islamic world in the sixteenth century.

Shia revival in Iran

As we saw in the chapter opening, Shah Ismail I's charismatic rule and his promotion of Shia revival rapidly transformed Iran. The Safavids embraced mystical Sufi versions of Twelver Shiism and sought to convert Iranians to their version of Shia devotion. Safavid collective religious practices aimed to purify Iran and prepare for the imminent arrival of the Mahdi. Safavid propaganda associated the shah with righteous rule and some Iranians seem to have greeted Ismail himself as the returned Hidden Imam.[6]

Safavid religious leaders sought to expand their leadership of Shia communities beyond Iran. Iraq held enormous significance for Shia believers as the vital center of Shia sacred geography. Ali ibn Abi Talib, one of the early caliphs, had been assassinated in the mosque of Kufa, and he is entombed in a shrine at Najaf. His son Hussain ibn Ali was killed at Karbala in 680, along with most of his followers, and the shrine constructed to commemorate his martyrdom is one of the most important Shia pilgrimage sites. Muhammad al-Mahdi, the Twelfth Imam, went into concealment in the Iraqi city of Samarra, according to Twelver Shia accounts. A religious scholar explains Samarra's significance: "Twelver Shias believe that the last imam did not die but has been in concealment since 260/872 and will return to usher in an age of justice at the end of time."[7] The density of Shia mosques and shrines in this region makes clear why the Safavids regarded Iraq as a sacred landscape.

The Shia religious reform in Iran and Iraq threatened the Safavids' Sunni neighbors. Shia imams – religious leaders – preached in rural areas of eastern Anatolia and Iraq, converting many Turkish peoples. The growing Shia revival alarmed the Ottoman Sultan Bayezid II (1481–1512), who was already struggling to maintain imperial control in eastern Anatolia.[8]

Ottoman expansion and the Islamic caliphate

Ottoman imperial expansion entered a new phase as Sultan Selim I (1512–20) launched a stunning series of conquests that greatly expanded the Ottoman Empire and inspired new religious dimensions to Ottoman rule. Selim I ascended the throne in 1512 and quickly solidified his control over Istanbul and Anatolia by suppressing rebellions and eliminating his fraternal rivals. The sultan was outraged by the Shia revival in Iran and called on the Mufti of Istanbul to issue a *fatwa*, or legal opinion, in 1514 declaring the Safavids heretics. Selim I organized a major military campaign against the Safavids, mobilizing his *kapukulu* (household) troops – including janissaries armed with arquebuses, imperial *sipahis*, a large artillery train, and a wagon laager – in addition to provincial *sipahis* and *timariot* light cavalry. An Ottoman army of perhaps 60,000 men engaged a heavily outnumbered Safavid force at the battle of Chaldiran in 1514. The Safavid army, which had no artillery or firearms-equipped infantry, was no match for the well-organized Ottomans. Selim I's forces captured Tabriz, forcing the Safavid Empire to reorganize.[9]

In 1516, Selim I then attacked the Mamluk Empire, a Sunni sultanate that comprised Egypt, Syria, and parts of Arabia. Selim I's main army engaged the Mamluk forces in Syria, defeating them at the battle of Marj Dabiq, where the Mamluk sultan was killed in the fighting. Ottoman forces capitalized on their victory to seize Aleppo and Damascus. The new Mamluk Sultan Tumanbay reorganized to resist the Ottoman advance at Raydaniyya the following year, but the Ottomans outflanked his position and destroyed the Mamluk army.[10] The armies of Selim I consolidated conquests in Syria, Egypt, and Arabia, establishing Ottoman control of the sacred sites of Mecca and Medina.

The Ottoman Empire now claimed the caliphate, protectorship of the holy sites of Islam, which included responsibilities for caring for the shrines and providing Muslim pilgrims with safe passage to Mecca. The *hajj*, or pilgrimage to Mecca, is one of the five pillars of Islam, and each Muslim believer is expected to undertake this holy voyage at least once during his or her lifetime, if at all possible. The protection of Muslim pilgrims during the annual *hajj* was thus a pious duty for any state that ruled in Arabia.[11] "By advancing a claim to supreme leadership of the Muslim world based on the twin titles of caliph...and protector of the holy cities," Giancarlo Casale argues, "the Ottoman sultan assumed a sacred responsibility to keep open and safe the pilgrimage route to Mecca and Medina – a responsibility that became an essential component of his good standing as a ruler in the eyes of the faithful."[12] The Ottoman Empire began to present itself as the chief promoter of Sunni orthodoxy and protector of Islamic faith worldwide.

Selim I's new claims to sacred authority advanced a global vision of Islam under Ottoman protection. "Armed with these new credentials," Casale points out, "Selim began to actively promote himself as a universal Islamic ruler whose sovereignty, especially with regard to the Indian Ocean, extended far beyond the borders of the areas under his physical control."[13] Selim I and his successors actively sponsored Sunni Islam, even as fierce currents of Sunni religious revival swept through the entire Ottoman Empire. Reforming Sunni preachers and messianic figures led reform movements and protests in the Ottoman Empire in the first half of the sixteenth century. The reinforced Ottoman identification with Sunni Islam encouraged sultans to oppose Shia revival as well as Safavid expansionism.

Sunni–Shia conflict

The rapid religious transformations in the Safavid and Ottoman Empires fueled Sunni–Shia conflicts in the Muslim world. The dynastic rivalry between the Ottomans and Safavids became a competition for religious and political leadership of Islam. Tijana Krstić argues that "it appears possible to speak of an 'age of confessionalization' in which Ottomans and Safavids faced challenges similar to those of their European counterparts."[14]

Iraq became a major battleground in the sectarian conflict between the Sunni Ottomans and the Shia Safavids. Ibrahim Pasha organized an Ottoman invasion of Iraq in 1532, seizing lands that the Safavids had conquered under Shah Ismail. Ottoman armies captured Tabriz and Baghdad in 1534, solidifying Ottoman control of Iraq. Sultan Süleyman repaired the tomb of Ahmad ibn Hanbali, founder of the Hanbali legal school, an important Sunni shrine in Baghdad. The Ottoman sultan also constructed or rebuilt a number of mosques in Iraq, essentially converting them from Shia to Sunni religious centers.[15]

The Safavids faced a series of religious conflicts and civil wars as they promoted Shia Islam in Iran and Central Asia. Shah Tahmasp (1524–76) displayed exemplary piety by performing pilgrimages to important Shia shrines and restoring numerous Shia mosques. Tahmasp elevated a favorite Shia theologian as Deputy of the Twelfth Imam, essentially granting him supreme religious authority in Safavid territories. Sunnis in Iran resisted conversion to the Shia faith promoted by their Safavid rulers, who ordered ritual cursing of early Sunni caliphs and enforcement of Shia orthodoxy by religious inspectors. Tahmasp's brother Alqas Mirza fled to Istanbul, claiming to embrace Sunni Islam, but he was eventually executed on the Shah's orders. Meanwhile, Uzbek armies composed of Sunni horse archers threatened the eastern frontier of the Safavid Empire. Continuing attacks along the Ottoman–Safavid border prompted Sultan Süleyman to lead a new Ottoman invasion of the Caucuses in 1554. The Ottomans and Safavids eventually negotiated the peace of Amasya in 1555, the first formal peace agreement between the two empires, which defined lasting sectarian boundaries between Shia and Sunni Islam in Western Asia.[16]

Reformations and the Fragmentation of Christianity

The Lutheran reform

One of the best-known religious reform movements of the sixteenth century began when Martin Luther, an Augustinian monk and professor, posted a series of theses for debate at the University of Wittenberg in 1517. Luther criticized the pope and Latin Christian clergy for abuses in the use of indulgences, which were then being issued in large numbers throughout Germany to support the rebuilding of St. Peter's Basilica in Rome. Luther claimed that only God could forgive sins and that "those indulgence preachers are in error who say that a man is absolved from every penalty and saved by papal indulgences." Luther's *Ninety-Five Theses* were quickly copied and published on printing presses, spreading his radical critique rapidly across Europe.[17]

Martin Luther's call for Christian reform elicited sharply divergent responses from clergy and lay people across the Holy Roman Empire, which comprised most of central Europe. Theologians criticized Luther's radical ideas and the pope excommunicated the disobedient monk over his heretical teachings. Luther published three potent treatises elaborating his conception of Christian reform in 1520, including *To the Christian Nobility of the German Nation*, which attacked the spiritual authority of the pope and clergy, saying that "we are all consecrated priests through baptism."[18] When summoned to debate papal officials before Emperor Charles V at the Diet of Worms in 1521, Luther adamantly refused to recant. Immediately after the imperial meeting, the emperor issued an arrest warrant for Luther, but the Elector of Saxony provided him with protection. Luther continued to write prolifically from Saxony, encouraging Christians to embrace reform and repentance, yet he could not lead an organized reform movement from a position of hiding. Many evangelical reform leaders emerged, preaching about clerical failures, monastic abuses, ecclesiastical errors, and spiritual renewal based on the pure Word of God. Some radical preachers stressed a social gospel of justice and compassion for ordinary believers, often promoting the notion of a community of goods for all Christians. These egalitarian ideas threatened ecclesiastical authorities and social elites alike.[19]

The fragmentation of Latin Christianity began to produce violence in the 1520s as radical Anabaptists in Switzerland and Germany engaged in iconoclasm, invading community churches and smashing art objects that they considered idolatrous in order to cleanse pollution in these sacred spaces. Municipal governments and nobles viewed such actions as illegitimate disorder, attempting to prosecute offenders for vandalism and heresy.

The German Peasants' War

Peasants across central Europe organized assemblies and armed bands to demand evangelical reform and social justice in 1524–25, sparking what became known as the German Peasants' War. As growing bands of peasants pillaged castles and monasteries, German princes scrambled to organize military forces in a chaotic religious conflict without clear sectarian lines. Peter Blickle has interpreted this peasant revolt as a class conflict, but other historians emphasize the social diversity of the movement and the strong spiritual motivations of all the participants.[20] The scale of the conflict, along with its radical spiritual and social dimensions, would distinguish this movement from ordinary peasant revolts.

The evangelical pastor Thomas Müntzer formed an Eternal League of God with peasant and urban support, promoting the Twelve Articles, a list of grievances that became a rallying cry during the Peasants' War. Müntzer exhorted his followers, saying "So go to it, go to it, go to it! The time has come, the evildoers are running like scared dogs!...Pay no attention to the cries of the godless...they will whimper and wheedle like children."[21] Religiously inspired peasant bands seized the town of Würzburg, seat of a bishop who was an avowed papal supporter, but they failed to take the bishop's Marienberg fortress.

Martin Luther denounced the peasant movement, accusing its leaders of scriptural error. Luther published *Against the Robbing and Murderous Hordes of Peasants*, a pamphlet castigating the peasants and exonerating German princes who engaged in holy warfare against the peasant rebels: "So dear lords, free here, save here, help here. Have mercy on the poor, stab, slay, strangle here whoever can; if you die doing it, good for you: a more blessed...death you can never receive." Luther explicitly justified violence in God's service, saying: "Such strange times are these that a prince can be more deserving of Heaven by shedding blood than others by praying."[22] Despite the initial victories of peasants, the Swabian League (a southern German military association) and a group of German princes formed separate armies and advanced against the peasants. The princely armies destroyed the main peasant bands in the battles of Frankenhausen and Königshofen in May and June 1525, then brutally suppressed the rebellious evangelical movements, executing many peasants.

The German Peasants' War revealed powerful religious motivations and agendas among the combatants. Religious reformers on all sides in the conflict had claimed to act as God's servants and promoters of the true Word of God. Radical evangelicals who survived the war portrayed their defeats as apocalyptic events and proclaimed Thomas Müntzer, who had been beheaded, a martyr. Martin Luther's bloody propaganda in favor of the princely armies discredited his leadership of evangelical reform. The mayor of one German town wrote that "Doctor Martin [Luther] has fallen into great disfavor with the common people."[23] Without clear leadership, disparate Christian reform movements continued to develop in central Europe, rapidly fragmenting Latin Christianity.

The Sack of Rome

Rome itself became the center of religious controversy and social turmoil in the 1520s, as the spiritual leadership of the pope was undermined. The political and territorial dimensions of papal power became enmeshed in the continuing Italian Wars. During a dispute between Emperor Charles V and Pope Clement VII in 1527, an Imperial army blockaded Rome to pressure the Papal States to reach an accommodation. Charles de Bourbon, the Imperial army commander and a former constable of France, impetuously launched a general assault on May 6, 1527. Bourbon was killed in one of the initial attacks, but his troops broke into Rome and began to sack the city.

The pope took shelter in his Castel Sant'Angelo, while the Imperial troops ransacked the city for 10 days and killed around 8,000 Roman residents. Some of the Imperial troops included German Lutherans, who pillaged churches and the Vatican palace – one even carved graffiti of "Martin Luther" into a religious fresco by Raphael.[24] A Spanish source recorded that, "in Rome, the capital of Christendom, no bells ring, no church is open, Mass is not said, neither Sundays nor feast days are celebrated. The rich shops of the merchants are turned to stables; the most splendid palaces are plundered; many houses are burnt to the ground."[25] News of the atrocities in Rome embarrassed Charles V and shocked Christians across Europe. The Sack of Rome, the symbolic capital of Latin Christiandom, seemed to confirm that notions of Christian unity had completely dissolved.

Some rulers and religious leaders continued to try to restore Latin Christian unity and rebuild the ideal of Christian brotherhood. Members of various reform movements within the Holy Roman Empire debated religious issues and confessional statements at the Diet of Augsburg of 1530, but their sharply divergent views led the Protestant delegation to walk out of the meeting. Following the failed negotiations at Augsburg, Lutheran princes in Germany formed a Schmalkaldic League in 1531 for mutual protection and advancement of Protestant causes. Meanwhile, papal loyalists increasingly sought to preserve Christian unity using judicial mechanisms to suppress illegal "heretical" activity in France, Germany, Spain, Italy, and elsewhere. Their efforts would later become known as the Counter-Reformation, one part of a much broader set of Catholic Reformation initiatives that aimed to strengthen papal authority and restore Roman leadership of Christianity.

Confessionalization and Christian militancy

Confessional divisions polarized Europe in the 1530s as episodes of religious violence proliferated. Anabaptists and other radicals in Switzerland sought to cleanse churches of polluting elements by smashing offensive statues, crosses, stained-glass windows, and liturgical vestments. Such iconoclastic attacks and the practice of adult baptism outraged other Christians, who saw these actions as attacks on divine law. As religious leaders proposed divergent "confessions," or statements of faith, individual Swiss cantons adopted competing versions of reform and confessional violence erupted in the Kappel Wars (1529–31). Huldrich Zwingli, one of the early reformers, joined the Zurich army and died in the rout at the battle of Kappel.

Radical prophets and Anabaptist preachers took control of the city of Münster in 1533 and prepared for the Second Coming of Jesus, attracting numerous followers and the leadership of the prophet Jan Matthijs of Haarlem. The inhabitants of Münster and their allies defended themselves from attacks by princely armies, but their confidence in the prophesies of Jan Matthijs may have been shaken when their leader was killed in combat in 1534. Matthijs's follower Jan van Leiden then declared himself King of Münster, and led the defense of the besieged city until its capitulation in 1535. Jan van Leiden and other leaders of the Anabaptist movement were executed in January 1536, ending the millennial movement in Münster, but prompting an Anabaptist diaspora.

Henry VIII of England, who had been regarded as a champion of papal causes, became frustrated with Pope Clement VII's refusal to grant an annulment of his childless marriage. The king broke with the pope around 1530 and began a gradual Reformation of England. He issued an Act of Supremacy in 1534, asserting his authority as head of the Church of England, effectively creating a national church. The king's reforms would soon lead to the execution of opponents, such as Thomas More, and uprisings such as the Pilgrimage of Grace in 1536. Other princely rulers began to form their own national churches, adopting the versions of reform that they found most appealing.

Christianity became even more fragmented as dynamic reformed ministers continued to preach, producing new evangelical movements that aggressively proselytized. Jean Calvin's version of reform developed into the most widespread of these Second Reformation movements. Calvin, a preacher who had fled from repression in Paris, eventually settled in Geneva as the leading minister to implement Reformed Christianity in Genevan society. He preached regularly in Geneva and developed systematic commentaries on key biblical texts, which were published in French and disseminated throughout Europe. Calvin forged a rigorous theology of predestination and developed a consistory (council of church elders) to enforce discipline in Genevan society. Genevan magistrates, acting on Calvin's suggestions, condemned the radical refugee Michael Servetus to death in 1553. Calvin became militant in the 1550s, writing works that seemed to argue for the right of Reformed Christians to resist tyrannical and heretical authorities.

Confessional divisions became more clearly pronounced as papal loyalists distinguished themselves from Lutheran, Calvinist, and other reform movements, effectively creating the Roman Catholic Church. Catholic reformers built on earlier spiritual and devotional movements of the late fifteenth and early sixteenth centuries to promote religious renewal. The pope convened the Council of Trent, which met in a series of gatherings between 1545 and 1567, in order to define Catholic doctrine and reassert papal authority. Catholics reformed old religious orders and organized entirely new ones. Ignatius Loyola, an ex-soldier, received papal support to found the Society of Jesus, whose members became known as Jesuits, to promote clerical education and missionary activity. Cardinal Carlo Borromeo led a reform of episcopal leadership in the late sixteenth century, while serving as archbishop of Milan. All these aspects of Catholic reform confirmed the notion of a Church Militant, eager to reunify Christianity through persuasion, or by force if necessary. In Germany, Emperor Charles V led Catholic and Imperial armies against the Protestant forces of the Schmalkaldic League, defeating them at the battle of Mühlberg in 1547.

Conversions and Religious Transformations

Religion played an important role in shaping intercultural communications from the earliest globalizing contacts, as religious innovations transformed beliefs and practices in the sixteenth century. A broad range of clergy and laypeople participated directly in diverse religious movements and conversion campaigns.

Buddhist monasticism and competition

Buddhist sects competed with each other in East and Southeast Asia during the early modern period. Many Buddhist rulers promoted specific monastic movements, founding monasteries and protecting their monks. For example, Sri Lankan kings took the title of *sangharaja*, or ruler of the *sangha* (monastic community).[26] Buddhist religious disputes thus became enmeshed with political and military conflicts.

Mahayana Buddhism defined religious life in much of East and Southeast Asia, greatly influencing politics and society in these regions. Large Mahayana monasteries and temples came to dominate Tibetan life, establishing political rule in the Himalayas. Chinese elites also embraced Mahayana Buddhism, which they saw as compatible with the well-established Confucian ideology. Meanwhile, Khmer kings built massive Mahayana monasteries and temples.

Other forms of Buddhism influenced war and society in early modern Japan. Many Japanese people engaged in *kami* (spirit) worship, performing rituals to local deities at non-Buddhist shrines. These practices diverged from Buddhism and, by the sixteenth century, had become known as Shinto. *Samurai* warriors in Japan enthusiastically engaged in Zen Buddhism through meditation, tea ceremonies, and martial arts. A form of apocalyptic belief contributed to sectarian violence and civil warfare in Japan. The *Ikkō* monastic movement of the True Pure Land Buddhism produced uprisings and religious violence in the 1530s. Meanwhile, adherents of the Lotus school of Buddhism criticized the *Ikkō* as "single-minded." In one of the *Ikkō-Ikki* movements, in the 1560s and 1570s, Buddhist monks of the Honganji sect fought against the forces of Oda Nobunaga and Tokugawa Ieyasu. The Honganji used explicitly religious motivations and fought under a banner that read: "Advance and be reborn in paradise. Retreat and fall immediately into hell."[27]

Islamization

Islam is rarely considered as a proselytizing religion, but a profound process of Islamization was radically reshaping many regions of the world during the sixteenth century. Commercial relations between Mamluk Egypt, Arabia, Iraq, and India had led Muslim merchants to settle in numerous port cities on the Red Sea, Persian Gulf, and Indian Ocean. Sufi mystics and Arab merchants, rather than dedicated missionaries, seem to have been the key agents of religious transformation in these areas. Islam had already spread into the northern Indian subcontinent, where the Delhi sultans ruled a Muslim state.

In Southeast Asia, Muslim merchants had already established communities in Sumatra, Java, Malaya, and Champa, but increasing commercial connections across the Indian Ocean and Ottoman imperial expansion stimulated further Islamization in Southeast Asia. By the mid-sixteenth century, the rulers of Aceh, Johor Brunei, Patani, and other Southeast Asian states had adopted Islam as their official religion. Many Indonesians converted to Islam in this period and Southeast Asia soon became one of the most populous regions of the Islamic world.[28]

Islamic merchants and scholars were simultaneously expanding Islam across the trans-Saharan caravan routes into West and Central Africa. Timbuktu and other major cities in sub-Saharan Africa had already become major Muslim centers, fostering further Islamization in West Africa. With the sweeping growth in Southeast Asia and Africa, Islam was rapidly becoming a global religion.

Christian missionaries and global conversion campaigns

Christian proselytization produced religious conflict in colonial contexts around the world. Crusading ideologies, religious prophesies, and the ideal of holy war against Islam motivated many of the early global navigators.[29] Christian missionaries joined maritime expeditions, eager to found new missions and convert non-Christians worldwide.

The so-called Indian Inquisition of the mid-sixteenth century shows that Spanish missionaries often seem to have been more concerned with establishing "correct" religion and disciplining recent converts rather than with winning new ones. During the sixteenth century, Franciscan, Dominican, and later Jesuit missionaries fanned out through Spanish and Portuguese territories in Central and South America, promoting an increasingly militant Catholicism. With the papacy embattled in Europe, the threat of idolatry, blasphemy, and polygamy in New Spain could seem frightening to these missionaries. The Indian Inquisition officials who attempted to deal with these issues faced a dilemma concerning whether Amerindians should be treated like Jews or like Muslims – two groups whose ethnic and religious identities had long been considered problematic in Spanish culture. Interestingly, Spanish Inquisition officials operating on the other side of the Atlantic seem to have been just as concerned about "the threat of religious enthusiasm," as shown by the case of Eugenia de la Torre, who was tried for feigning rapture in Madrid.[30]

Spanish missionary efforts demanded such discipline because of the paternalism that underlay most contemporary Christian attitudes toward Amerindians. Early modern Christian missionaries generally believed that they were acting to bring the "true faith" to child-like Amerindians who were paradoxically close to Eden. Conversion processes were hotly debated during the sixteenth century, and only a public profession of a conversion experience would be accepted as sincere.

Missionaries operating in colonial borderlands often saw themselves as caught up in a great religious struggle, and they assessed Native Americans' religiosity according to their experiences with other non-Europeans. The missionary activity in New Spain coincided with other Catholic campaigns to convert heretics in Europe and to bring the "true faith" to "savages" in the Americas, Africa, the Indian Ocean, and Japan.[31] "From the perspective of the French Franciscans," Megan C. Armstrong suggests, "the Wars of Religion was one of several fronts in their global war on sin, a war that embraced the rise of an aggressive form of Islamic rule in the East and encounters with New World peoples as well as the spread of Protestantism in Europe."[32] J.H. Elliott shows that Franciscans in New Spain inspired Cortés's belief that "there would arise in Mexico a 'new church, where God will be served and honoured more than in any other region of the earth.'...The Francisan vision was a world-wide vision."[33]

The Franciscan missionaries were not alone in conceiving of religion in terms of global struggle. Portuguese Capuchin missionaries ventured into Central Africa to evangelize in African kingdoms. According to John K. Thornton, "the Kingdom of Kongo, which became Portugal's and the Catholic Church's most successful and durable voluntary conversion of people who could not be conquered by force or made to convert, shows how important the role of continuous revelation was in validating co-revelations that created the African vision of Christianity."[34] King Afonso I adopted Christianity and led an energetic religious reform that swept through his entire kingdom, but also created tensions across Central Africa.

The Jesuits, members of the newly formed Society of Jesus, played an integral role in the expansion of Catholicism in Asia. They founded colleges to train priests in Goa, Kochi, and other cities in India and East Asia. Father Francis Xavier, a Jesuit priest, arrived in the Japanese port of Kagoshima in 1549 and quickly established a Catholic mission. Jesuits expanded their missionary activity in the city of

Nagasaki and throughout the island of Kyushu, winning numerous converts. The Jesuits received support from Portuguese and Spanish rulers, rapidly expanding their missionary activity in East and Southeast Asia. The Jesuits printed Christian texts in Asian languages at presses in Goa, Macau, Nagasaki, Beijing, and Manila during the late sixteenth and early seventeenth centuries.[35] By the 1580s, an estimated 150,000 Japanese had converted to Catholicism, while Jesuit missionaries were spreading into India, Indonesia, and the Philippines. Jesuits' public preaching and overt attempts to convert rulers created controversy almost everywhere they went. Together with their Christian *daimyō* converts, they engaged in iconoclastic attacks and forced conversions in Kyushu.[36] Matteo Ricci, a Jesuit who was trained in Goa, traveled to China in 1582 and managed to establish a mission in Beijing in the late sixteenth century.[37] The Jesuit missionaries did not always succeed in gaining converts, but their conversion campaigns produced religious upheaval and social conflict across much of Asia.

Syncretic religious revivals

Religious leaders in the Americas and Africa seem to have freely drawn from foreign and indigenous sources for their prophecies, mixing political resistance and religious creativity. Mayas, Tupis, and other Amerindians who encountered Christian missionaries often developed syncretic religious practices that fused aspects of their indigenous religions with Christianity. Religious nonconformists and heretics acted as members of "religions of the oppressed" that combined piety practices with the advancement of social interests.[38]

In Central Mexico, the swift collapse of the Mexica Empire did not bring a sudden end to Mesoamerican religious beliefs and practices. Instead, social and demographic crises prompted religious experimentation and syncretic fusions of Christian and Mesoamerican religions. Amerindian shamans and prophets led religious renewal in the Americas. Religious groupings in mid-sixteenth-century Mexico were fluid and decentralized, allowing shamans to promote various religious interpretations of the catastrophic violence that destroyed the Mexica Empire.[39] Contact with Spanish *conquistadores* and Catholic missionaries prompted resistance movements and religious revivals. Shamans joined a chief named Tenamaxtli in organizing a rebellion by the Caxcanes and other Amerindians in the mountains of western Mexico during the Mixtón War of the 1540s. Christianized Nahua chiefs, who had formerly been part of the Mexica Empire, joined with

Spanish colonial forces against the rebels, whom they described as *Chichimecas*, or barbarians.[40]

In South America, the Taki Onqoy (Dance of Disease) religious movement seems to have developed among the Incas in the 1560s as a response to epidemics and conversion campaigns in the Andes Mountains. According to a Spanish missionary, the Taki Onqoy "believed that all the *huacas* [divinities] of the kingdom, as many as the Christians had overthrown and burned, had come back to life, ... that now the world had turned, and God and the Spanish would be conquered this time and all the Spaniards would die, and their cities be flooded, and the sea would rise and drown them." Spanish missionaries apparently stamped out the Taki Onqoy's ecstatic dancing and apocalyptic teachings through their conversion efforts and coercion in the 1570s.[41]

African religions seem to have undergone significant transformation in the early sixteenth century, partly in response to increased contacts with Christianity and Islam. Indigenous African religions employed village rituals and ancestor veneration as central aspects of religious life. African priests used divination practices to interpret situations in everyday life and adjudicate disputes. For example, Yoruba priests performed Ifa, a form of divination using cowrie shells cast on a board, to communicate with the other world. West and Central African priests and possessed mediums could have powerful visionary experiences and revelatory dreams. Local cosmologies and ritual practices began to be recorded by European travelers, missionaries, and colonizers in the early sixteenth century, giving us some idea of transitions then under way. African societies expected their spiritual leaders to provide communication with the other world through continuous revelation, making priests vulnerable. In one instance, "in 1563, the king of Ndongo had eleven rainmakers put to death because they failed to deliver rain and were thus charged with chicanery." West African religious leaders had to adapt to the Islamic teachings that were spread by imams and merchants along the trans-Saharan trading routes, as well as to the encroaching Christian doctrines brought by missionaries and slave traders along the coast.[42]

Interreligious Conflicts

Interreligious warfare erupted frequently along several major religious frontiers in the early modern world. The religious borderlands between Christian and Muslim regions formed perhaps the most bellicose interreligious zones, with organized military frontiers in the Mediterranean, North Africa, and the Balkans.

Ottoman military expansion

In addition to Islamic proselytization (discussed above), Islam expanded through Ottoman military expansion against Christians in the Balkans and the Mediterranean. Ottoman *mujehedeen* and *gazi* waged *jihad* – a term encompassing various forms of holy warfare – against Christians, whom they regarded as infidels. Religious motivations figured in the successes of the Ottoman military system, as Ottoman armies overran most of Hungary and besieged the city of Vienna in 1529, although they failed to take it. Militant Christians organized their own latter-day crusades against Muslim enemies they called "Terrible Turks" or "Barbarous Moors." Muslim and Christian versions of expeditionary warfare promoted state religions and interreligious warfare, especially in the Mediterranean World.

Following their expulsion from Rhodes by the Ottomans in the 1520s, the Knights of Saint John of Jerusalem had settled on the island of Malta with the support of the Holy Roman Emperor. Malta held a strategic position in the central Mediterranean, controlling the key maritime passage between the eastern and western Mediterranean. The Knights of Malta, as the Knights of Saint John became known, adopted the Catholic version of reform and attracted militant noble adventurers from across Catholic Europe. Catholic galleys operating from Malta raided incessantly against Muslim shipping in the eastern Mediterranean and along the North African coast.

Sultan Süleyman the Magnificent launched a vast Ottoman amphibious force to conquer Malta in 1565, aiming to vanquish his old enemies and halt their naval raiding. Ottoman janissaries, artillery, and auxiliary troops debarked on the island and opened an epic siege of the fortified city of Valetta, which was fiercely defended by contingents of Knights from "nations" across Europe. The Ottomans came close to overwhelming Valetta's defenses, but finally had to abandon the siege. Prints and pamphlets across Europe celebrated the successful defense of Malta as a miraculous delivery by God.[43]

Christian crusading and expeditionary warfare

Christians periodically responded to the Ottoman expansion through expeditionary warfare based on the model of the earlier crusades. Spanish, Venetian, Maltese, and Italian galleys answered Pope Pius

V's call to form a Holy League and launch a grand crusade against the Ottoman fleet in 1571. The Holy League fleet met the main Ottoman fleet off of Lepanto in October 1571, destroying and capturing numerous Ottoman galleys. The great Christian victory of Lepanto was celebrated in publications and ceremonies across Europe, becoming a powerful symbol of ostensibly pan-Christian and pan-European unity. The Holy League rapidly disintegrated, however, allowing the Ottomans to rebuild their fleet and to continue their domination of the eastern Mediterranean. In the Ottoman Empire's long conflicts against the Habsburgs, Ottoman officers and soldiers seem to have maintained religious motivations, although one historian claims that Ottoman warfare "was much more a matter of controlling land, resources and trade routes than a desire to impose its spiritual views on subject peoples."[44]

Muslims resisted Christian crusading expeditions in the Balkans, the Mediterranean, and North Africa. Moroccan forces destroyed a crusading army led by King Sebastien of Portugal in 1578 at the battle of Al-Qasr al-Kabir (Alcázarquivir), killing Sebastien and provoking a succession crisis in Portugal. The victory confirmed the power of the Sa'dian dynasty even though the sultan died on the battlefield. The new sultan, Ahmad al-Mansur (1578–1603), shifted his capital from Fez to Marrakech and reformed his army in the 1570s and 1580s, combining elements of the Arab and Ottoman military systems.[45] He then launched his own campaign of conquest against the vast Songhay Empire in 1591–93. Ahmad al-Mansur referred to his conquest of Songhay as "this kingdom of the Blacks and the Touareg (*tarjiyya*) which has been added, by God's grace, to our realms, and threaded, by divine conquest and the shining sword, on our necklace."[46]

Persecution of religious minorities .

In the early modern world, religious minorities often suffered persecution by religious and legal institutions. Institutional religious persecution occurred especially in areas where new reforms encountered mixed religious populations. Christian, Jewish, and Muslim populations had long lived together in the mixed communities in Iberia, for example, despite occasional episodes of violence. But, as the *Reconquista* was completed and Christian reform intensified, Jews began to seem more threatening in the context of the growing Christian militancy in Iberia. The Spanish monarchs Ferdinand and Isabella issued a royal edict expelling Jews from Spain in 1492, and the Portuguese king followed their example, banishing Jews in 1496. Henry Kamen estimates that approximately 40,000 to 50,000 Jews emigrated from Spain – a figure much lower than previous estimates. Kamen argues that "the 'expulsion' decree of 1492 was a decree aimed not at expulsion but at conversion."[47] Indeed, most Jews seem to have responded to these laws by converting publicly to Christianity rather than going into exile.

The unsure religious status of the New Christians, as *conversos* were also known, prompted continuing worries by Spanish and Portuguese authorities. The Spanish Inquisition investigated persons suspected of continuing to practice Jewish faith or espousing heretical ideas. A Portuguese Inquisition was established in 1531 to investigate *conversos* for relapses and heterodox practices. The Inquisitions inspired fear across Iberia, but their most serious punishments seem to have been reserved for proselytizing Jews. The Inquisition's most serious legacy may have been "to institutionalize the prejudices and attitudes that had previously been commonplace in society."[48]

Although the Spanish Inquisition gained a lasting reputation for intolerance and persecution, Jews also experienced troubles beyond Iberia. Lithuania expelled its Jewish population in 1495, providing an example for other central and eastern European cities and states. Prague, for example, expelled its Jewish inhabitants in 1541. Such expulsions were often short-lived, however, as municipal governments frequently permitted Jews to return after a period of repression. Individual Jews and families were sometimes accused of ritual murder and subjected to special trials in Germany and Eastern Europe.

Cities and states in other areas of Europe rarely expelled Jewish populations from their boundaries, but instead applied other forms of discrimination. Frankfurt forced its Jewish residents to move into a separate neighborhood in 1462. The Venetian Republic created a ghetto in 1516, segregating Venetian Jews from the city's Christians. Other Italian cities, including Florence, created their own ghettos modeled after the Venetian one. Early modern Jewish ghettos were sometimes enclosed by walls and gates, which would be closed at night. The boundaries between Jewish and Christian communities remained permeable, however, and ghettos rarely prevented mobility within cities.[49] The expulsions and persecutions of Jews nonetheless prompted new migration patterns as some Jews fled from repressive city and state laws, seeking residence in the Ottoman Empire, Morocco, the Netherlands, Eastern Europe, and other regions.

Muslims who continued to live in Iberia following the *Reconquista* faced persecution from Portuguese and Spanish authorities, who referred to them as *mudéjares*. Municipal governments and Catholic clergy in cities like Granada imposed restrictions on the *mudéjares*. As Castilian Christian immigrants migrated southward, some Muslims converted to Christianity, becoming known as *moriscos*. Nonetheless, these New Christians continued to face discrimination.

Religious repression led rural *moriscos* in the Alpujarras mountains in the province of Granada to rebel in 1568–69. The rebels consisted primarily of peasants, but a few *moriscos* from the city of Granada, such as Fárax aben Fárex, played roles as leaders of the revolt. Fárex daringly led a rebel contingent into Granada on Christmas Eve in 1568, hoping to incite a broad urban revolt of the city's *morisco* population. However, he received little support. The peasant revolt continued to grow in the mountainous countryside, reaching perhaps 30,000 *morisco* rebels, who received supplies and reinforcements from Muslims in North Africa. Despite the Granadan *moriscos*' loyalty during the fighting, the urban minority suffered as a result of the revolt. In March 1569, Christian immigrants in Granada invaded the city jail and massacred about 150 *morisco* prisoners. In June 1569, Spanish authorities expelled the vast majority of Granada's *moriscos* from the kingdom as Don Juan of Austria took control of the royal response to the rebellion. Don Juan's forces led a coordinated military campaign against the *moriscos* in 1570, suppressing the revolt by the end of the summer. In the aftermath of the revolt, tens of thousands of *moriscos* from the province of Granada were forcibly resettled to other parts of Spain.

Conclusion

Religious reforms and schisms generated significant persecution and sacred conflict in the first half of the sixteenth century, but some religious and political leaders attempted to create new forms of accommodation to cope with the realities of religious pluralism. Religious unity remained an ideal for many polities, meaning that confessional reforms and conversions presented serious contradictions and created social confusion.

Emperor Charles V and the Protestant princes of Germany negotiated the Peace of Augsburg, one of the most ambitious attempts at religious accommodation, in 1555. This peace effectively allowed each territorial prince within the Holy Roman Empire to adopt the Lutheran or Catholic confession following the legal principle of *cuius regio, eius religio* (each prince, his religion). This religious arrangement was fragile, however, and its provisions denied princely rulers in Germany the choice of adopting the new Calvinist version of Reformed Christianity.

The Ottoman Empire seems to have been more successful at establishing relative toleration of multiple religious communities – Sunni Muslim, Sufi, Greek Orthodox, Syriac Christian, Latin Christian, Jewish – within its borders. The patriarchs of the Greek Orthodox Church negotiated with the Ottoman sultans to ensure the status of Orthodox religious practice and monasticism within Ottoman territories.[50] Some of the Jewish refugees who had fled from religious persecution in Portugal and Spain resettled in Ottoman cities. The Ottoman judicial and administrative systems seem to have implemented generally permissive laws and lenient enforcement policies for religious minorities, but acts of religious intolerance could still occur within the Ottoman Empire.

Indeed, prophetic movements and schisms would continue to create social conflict in the early modern world. But, by the mid-sixteenth century, confessional and sectarian identities seem to have been hardening in a number of areas, setting the stage for later religious warfare.

4

Dynastic War and State Development, 1520s–1580s

The Timurid prince Zahir al-Din Muhammed Babur dreamed of establishing a new empire based in the famed city of Samarkand, Temür's former capital and the vital center of Turco-Mongol culture. Babur managed to capture Samarkand three times, but he finally abandoned his attempts to re-establish Timurid rule after being forced to retreat once again from the city in 1511. Having failed to establish control of Samarkand, Babur began raiding the Indus valley and planning a conquest of India. In the 1520s, he launched a series of campaigns into the Punjab region and threatened the Delhi sultanate. Then, in December 1525, he organized an army of mounted archers, artillery, and infantry (including some armed with firearms) to march on Delhi itself. Babur's army crushed the forces of the Delhi sultanate at the battle of Panipat, outside the capital city, in April 1526.

This victory allowed Babur's forces to seize Delhi and overrun much of northern India. Babur established a new dynasty in Delhi and forged the Mughal Empire. Stephen F. Dale argues that "Babur's victory is the clearest case possible of dynastic imperialism, unleavened with any self-serving suggestions of religious sanctity." Babur wrote an autobiography, the *Baburnama*, which celebrated Turco-Mongol warrior values. "Babur conquered India simply because he had lost the hope of establishing an empire in [Central Asia] or anywhere else," according to Dale, "and so he turned his *mulkgirliq*, his 'kingdom-seizing' ambitions, to India, where the perpetual factional disputes of its Afghan rulers offered him an opportunity."[1]

The foundation of the Mughal Empire offers a stunning example of a new dynastic state, forged by conquest. New forms of dynastic monarchies and empires emerged in the sixteenth century, with expanded administrations, court cultures, patronage powers, and military organizations. Major empires ruled by the Mughal, Ottoman, Safavid, Ming, Habsburg, and Askiya dynasties threatened to overwhelm smaller states and regional neighbors. Dynastic monarchies in England, France, Russia, Sweden, and the Kongo asserted themselves and challenged their rivals. This chapter will examine how early modern dynasties ruled, administered their states, waged war, and managed crisis.

Dynastic Rule

Although kingship was common around the globe, monarchical principles and legal systems varied widely. Some societies embraced elective kingship, in which political and social elites selected a monarch from among their ranks. More often, monarchy was hereditary, allowing rulers to establish dynasties over multiple generations. As Niccolò Machiavelli famously pointed out, monarchs established dynastic rule through conquest or inheritance, but the complications of dynastic succession frequently resulted in conflict.

New monarchies

A series of new monarchies was carved out by conquering elites such as Babur in the early sixteenth century. Shah Ismail I seized power in Iran, founding the Safavid dynasty, as we saw in chapter 3. Several new Turco-Mongol states emerged in Central Asia, as Timurid successor princes, Afghan horsemen, and Uzbek warriors struggled over control of the major cities of Samarkand, Herat, and Kabul in the late fifteenth and early sixteenth centuries.

Albrecht von Hohenzollern, an important Prussian noble, managed to create a new principality in northeastern Europe. Hohenzollern was elected Grand Master of the Teutonic Order in Prussia in 1511, but this crusading military order had already been weakened by warfare against Poland. The Grand Master pursued negotiations with Poland to dissolve the Teutonic Order in return for granting ducal status for Prussia. In 1525 Albrecht paid homage to King Sigismund I of Poland as the first Duke of Prussia. The Prussian *Junkers*, or nobles, had considerable influence in the new principality through the *Landtag*, or diet, and the institutions of Polish monarchy.[2]

Civil warfare in Scandinavia allowed Gustav I Vasa (1523–60) to create a new dynasty in Sweden, which broke away from the Oldenburg kingdom of Denmark in 1523. The fledgling kingdom of Sweden was nearly surrounded by the Danes, since the Oldenburgs maintained control of the Sound, Norway, and territories of Skåne, Halland, and Blekinge along the southern tip of Scandinavia. The Swedes fought an amphibious war against Lübeck in 1534–36, greatly diminishing the Hanseatic League's control of Baltic commerce. Gustav I's heir took the name of Erik XIV (1560–68) in order to link himself with a mythical heritage of early Scandinavian warriors, revealing how anxiously new monarchies sought to establish their legitimacy.[3]

A number of small new principalities and monarchies emerged through fierce conflict and chaotic warfare in the early sixteenth century. Machiavelli famously commented on rulers of new principalities, using Cesare Borgia as one of his prime examples. Borgia, the illegitimate son of Pope Alexander VI, had commanded the armies of the Papal States, and had effectively fashioned his own principality in the region of Romagna in northern Italy. Other Italian city-states were struggling to maintain their independence, however, as were many city-states in other parts of the world. Swahili city-states on the coast of East Africa had to fend off Portuguese attacks, adapting new commercial and political organizations to survive.[4] City-states and kingdoms such as Aceh, Burma, Johor, Patani, and Pegu arose or strengthened in Southeast Asia in this period, as economic competition and maritime warfare disrupted established political systems and allowed princes opportunities for new conquests.[5]

Dynastic inheritance

Dynasties accumulated territories through progressive acquisitions of lands and titles that family members then inherited. Ruling families asserted collective territorial claims and rights, then sought to protect their patrimonies by transmitting possessions directly through a clearly determined lineage. Matthew Vester argues that "dynasticism provided a mechanism – inheritance – by which junior members of a house always had an interest in maintaining the integrity of the dynasty's sovereign claims, since devolution was always a possibility."[6] Inheritance practices varied significantly across different societies, but many principalities attempted to articulate rules of succession to ensure an orderly succession to a legitimate heir. Inheritance laws and customs thus provided the basis for dynastic rule and power through various succession strategies.

The principle of primogeniture was becoming common in many regions of the early modern world, privileging the ruler's eldest child as sole inheritor of dynastic authority and landholding titles. The Ming dynasty in China insisted on strict rules of primogeniture, establishing male preference to ensure transition from an emperor to his eldest son, but the imperial court sometimes intervened in the succession process. When the Jaijing Emperor died in 1566, his son inherited the throne, but "the high civil bureaucracy had the leading role at a critical moment in the dynastic succession," taking advantage of the succession to institute administrative reforms.[7] The Safavid rulers of Iran followed strict male primogeniture, buttressed by a notion of divinely inspired kingship. The kingdoms of France, England, and Scotland had long established primogeniture in their inheritance laws, although only France relied on exclusively male primogeniture. Some African kingdoms, notably Benin, used primogeniture rules, and other West African rulers seem to have gradually adopted similar inheritance customs in the early modern period. The Wittelsbach rulers of Bavaria began to assert primogeniture in the early sixteenth century, trying to ensure the integrity of the duchy of Bavaria.

Another dynastic inheritance strategy emphasized patrilineal descent, preferring brothers as the closest heirs. The Askiya dynasty ruled the Songhay Empire in West Africa using patrilineal rules of succession, allowing a series of brothers to rule in succession. Patrilineal succession provided opportunities for multiple males in the same generation to rule, perhaps easing tensions among a ruler's siblings. The Ottomans preferred sons as heirs throughout the fifteenth and sixteenth centuries, although siblings often competed for dominance during succession struggles, with the winner executing his rivals. Then, in 1618 Ottoman succession customs suddenly altered, when brothers became the preferred successors.[8]

Other kingdoms and principalities relied on partible inheritance laws, which required a roughly equal division of territories and wealth among princely sons. Partible inheritance was common in many societies across Eurasia and Africa. As Babur's case shows, the partible inheritance practices of Timurid princes could weaken dynastic unity in the Afghan, Uzbek, and Mughal Empires. But partible inheritance could also strengthen imperial rule through the corporate leadership of fraternal princes, as in the Mughal Empire.[9] Eldest sons were often favored in unequal arrangements of partible inheritance, giving them primacy over other sons. Partible inheritance did have the potential to fragment dynastic states, however. The partitions of inheritance among the princely heirs in Morocco led to the kingdom being divided up several times during the early modern period. In 1485, the Wettin dynasty divided its landholdings and titles in Saxony between two separate family branches, the Albertines (dukes of Saxony) and Ernestines (electors of Saxony). Over the next century, the Albertines attempted to use primogeniture to hold together its territories, while the Ernestines "divided and redivided their lands several times in the latter third of the sixteenth century."[10]

Elective kingship provided an alternate mechanism for succession in certain early modern polities. Some monarchies established electoral procedures in which assemblies of nobles selected one of their peers or a foreign prince to become their ruler. The vast kingdom of Poland-Lithuania is certainly the best-known elective monarchy in the early modern period. Polish nobles assembled in a *Sejm*, normally at the death of their king, to elect a new monarch. Although a system of elective kingship might seem to diminish the potential for dynastic control, the Jagiellon dynasty managed to secure successive elections and rule continuously in Poland-Lithuania from 1386 to 1572. The Habsburgs similarly succeeded in gaining control of the elective process of the Holy Roman Empire in the fifteenth century and a member of the dynasty would rule almost without interruption until the empire's dissolution in 1806.

Dynastic continuity

Genealogies presented dynasties as living trees with strong trunks and branches, but these were legal and propaganda documents that often presented an illusory image of dynastic continuity and strength. Indeed, dynastic households were rarely solid structures. Each member of a ruling family organized his or her own princely household – possessing significant landholdings, maintaining large entourages, and holding court. When rulers died without direct descendants, remote cousins could suddenly inherit entire new principalities. Competing family members enunciated their claims to rule and asserted their princely rights. Inheritance customs in some societies permitted rulers to simply designate a family member, even an adopted child, as heir.

The question of female rule posed a problem for dynastic continuity in many early modern polities. Realms with primogeniture often preferred male succession, even when their succession laws did allow direct female rule if no direct male heir existed. Mary Tudor (1553–58) and Elizabeth I (1558–1603) both ruled England in their own right during the sixteenth century, while Mary Stuart (1542–87) reigned in neighboring Scotland. John Knox famously decried the influence of women rulers in politics as a "monstrous regiment of women," but his attack was intended as anti-Stuart propaganda.[11] Jeanne d'Albret (1555–72) exercised full sovereignty as queen of Navarre, ruling her kingdom directly, although she did have a king consort. The well-known Salic Law established exclusively male primogeniture in France, denying women the right to inherit, but not to act as regents. Dynasties that used patrilineal and partible inheritance systems generally barred princesses completely from succession, but women could still rule indirectly as mothers and regents. The sixteenth century seems to have been a period of extraordinary female sovereignty and feminine power.[12]

Dynasties depended on managing the rights and titles of female family members to maintain their landholdings and authority. With each dynastic marriage, dowries placed lands and properties under the control of princely women, who might stand to transmit dynastic territories and rights to their husbands' families. Ottoman sultans often limited marriages and instead assumed multiple concubines, who could exercise custodianship but not inheritance rights. The Lorraine ruling dynasty and its cadet Guise branch creatively managed inheritance rights and succession through complex legal maneuvers and legal fictions, often with noblewomen playing key roles in judicial procedures. The princes and nobles from this dynasty operated in the duchy of Lorraine, the Holy Roman Empire, and the kingdom of France. Members of the Lorraine dynasty were able to rely on legal immunity in various countries and on privileged access to French law courts when they needed judicial support for their claims.[13]

Even in areas where the principle of primogeniture dominated inheritance laws, monarchs often created temporary cessations and permanent partitions in an attempt to defuse disputes over successions and ensure continuity. One dynastic mechanism was the creation of *apanages* as "parcels of the dynastic patrimony that were set aside to provide the household expenses of younger sons of the ruler, and were generally inherited by the eldest son of the apanagiste until the direct line ended. Then they reverted to the ruling branch of the family."[14] Jacques de Savoie, duc de Nemours (1531–85), a cadet of the ruling Savoie dynasty who served as a military leader and courtier in France, provides an interesting case of such partitions. Jacques deftly negotiated with his cousin, Emanuel Filibert de Savoie, duc de Savoie, to maintain his *apanage* privileges and succeeded in getting the Genevois erected as a duchy in 1564. The duc de Nemours-Genevois utilized the prestige and wealth of his *apanage* and other landholdings to construct châteaux in the Genevois and residential palaces in Paris. The *apanage* thus represented the key source of

Jacques de Savoie's prestige and honor, but also ensured the Savoie dynasty's solidity.

Dynastic succession in Renaissance Europe

The near contemporaneous successions of Henry VIII, François I, and Charles V in the early sixteenth century offer an excellent vantage point to observe the processes of succession in the Tudor, Valois, and Habsburg dynasties. These well-documented cases of succession demonstrate well the practices of early modern dynastic inheritance.

The Tudor dynasty reasserted royal authority in England in the wake of the Wars of the Roses (1455–85). Henry VII had subdued rebellions and increased royal finances, while preparing his eldest son, Arthur, for succession to the throne. Henry VII negotiated an alliance with Ferdinand of Spain, but Arthur died soon after marrying Catherine of Aragon in 1501. Henry, the second son of Henry VII, now become heir and was married to his brother's widow, with a papal dispensation. When his father died in 1509, the young prince inherited a revitalized kingdom of England as Henry VIII (1509–47). As a descendant of Yorkist and Lancastrians, Henry VIII represented a unified England and a strengthened Tudor dynasty, leading the poet John Skelton to write: "The Rose both white and red / In one Rose now doth grow."[15] Henry VIII soon began to assert his dynastic claims to French sovereignty, organizing military expeditions to Guyenne and Flanders in the 1510s.

Across the English Channel, the Valois dynasty managed a difficult succession in the 1510s because King Louis XII failed to produce a male heir, as required by France's Salic Law. When the king died in January 1515, his cousin François d'Angoulême inherited the throne as François I (1515–47). The royal family held a magnificent *sacre* (coronation) in the cathedral at Reims, where François I took oaths to protect ecclesiastical privileges and to defend Christianity, before being anointed and crowned to shouts of "*Vive le roi!*"[16] The new king made a ceremonial entry into Paris in February 1515, followed by a service at the cathedral of Notre-Dame and a festive banquet. In the summer, François I performed a triumphant entry to the city of Lyon, before leading his army to Italy. The ephemeral art and theatrical displays at this entry constructed representations of royal authority and military power, including a depiction of "the garden of France – guarded by two armed men, one holding a flaming sword, the other leaning on a halberd." This elaborate ceremony celebrated Valois dynastic sovereignty and continuity, linking François I with Clovis, founder of the kingdom of France.[17]

Perhaps the most spectacular case of early modern dynastic inheritance was Charles V von Habsburg, who inherited the largest territorial empire in Europe since Charlemagne – an inheritance that was entirely unexpected. Charles was born in February 1500 to Philip "the Fair" von Habsburg and Juana of Castile, who were then governing the Burgundian Netherlands for Philip's father, Emperor Maximilian I. Philip had married Juana in 1496, at a time when it looked as though she would only be able to provide children and a dowry, since she was the third child of Ferdinand of Aragon and Isabella of Castile. But by 1500, Juana's elder brother and sister had both died, leaving her as heir to the throne of the Spanish monarchy. Juana and her husband traveled to Spain to claim her part of her inheritance, but before she could so, Philip the Fair suddenly became ill, and died in September 1506.

Charles von Habsburg gradually inherited entire kingdoms and duchies from each of his four grandparents in the 1500s and 1510s. He received the Habsburg domains in Upper and Lower Austria, Tyrol, Styria, and Carniola from his paternal grandfather, Emperor Maximilian I. From his paternal grandmother, Mary of Burgundy, he took possession of the duchy of Burgundy and the Burgundian provinces in the Netherlands that had belonged to her father, Charles the Bold. He also inherited the newly united kingdom of Spain from his maternal grandparents, Ferdinand of Aragon and Isabella of Castille. After the death of Philip the Fair, Emperor Maximilian I carefully prepared Charles as his heir to the imperial throne.

Emperor Maximilian I died in 1519, prompting the seven German Electors to assemble to elect a new emperor. Maximilian I's grandson Charles "naturally saw himself as Maximilian's 'heir presumptive' and sought to preserve the imperial title in his family both for reasons of prestige – to lose it after three generations would imperil his reputation – and to safeguard more effectively the Habsburg lands in southeast Germany inherited from his grandfather."[18] King François I opposed Charles's election, however, and announced his own candidacy. Both candidates offered the electors massive gifts and gratifications, and Charles emerged as the leading contender with the backing of the banker Jacob Fugger. François I finally withdrew his candidacy and Charles was elected emperor.

Charles V (1519–56) was crowned as king of the Romans (acting Holy Roman Emperor) in the cathedral of Aachen in June 1520. He had to rule his vast empire by exercising sovereignty over a series of separate principalities and kingdoms. He held the distinct titles of king of Spain, king of Naples, archduke of Austria, duke of Burgundy, and duke of Luxembourg, in addition to ruling Franche-Comté and each of the provinces within the Burgundian Netherlands. We have already seen how the kingdom of Spain resulted from the fusion of crowns that merged the Iberian kingdoms of Castile and Aragon. Charles V could make additional claims to the duchy of Milan, the duchy of Burgundy, and various other territories in central and southern Europe. Soon after his coronation, he ceded his archduchy of Austria and other titles and territories to his brother Ferdinand, in order to ensure his loyalty. Charles secured his dynastic inheritance by marrying Isabel of Portugal in 1526 and by fathering a son and a daughter during the next two years. By then, he was already confronting the daunting challenges of administering his immense dynastic empire.

Dynastic Administration

Monarchs organized administrative institutions to deal with the complexities of ruling dynastic lands, subject territories, and new conquests, each with its own local laws and customs. Rulers attempted to promote their own personal interests, while managing competing family members' roles in composite dynastic states. Rulers employed delicate political and diplomatic negotiations to preserve their dynasties from internal and external threats.

Dynastic legitimacy

When a ruler assumed a throne, whether inherited or newly created, he or she had to establish the legitimacy of princely rule. Monarchs and emperors could never rule alone, however, instead relying on various strategies of legitimacy and complex systems of government administration. Consultative bodies and institutions – including councils, judicial bodies, and noble assemblies – were employed to provide advice and assistance in policy formulation and resource mobilization. Dynastic states often promoted the notion that the ruler embodied a *body politic* in service of the common good of the society. Historians following Ernst Kantorowicz's influential analysis of the political theology of medieval monarchies have discerned multiple "bodies" of a monarch in some early modern political theories.[19] Such theories could promote the personal rule of the monarch in the service of the common good of society.

Despite rulers' consultation with ostensibly representative bodies, most monarchs collaborated more intimately with appointed ministers and advisors. Monarchs relied on royal secretaries and ministers to handle their correspondence, gather information, and administer their dynastic states. Emperor Charles V utilized a mobile Imperial court, administered efficiently by Nicolas Perrenot de Granvelle, his secretary of state, and Mercurino Arborio di Gattinara, his chancellor. The Ming dynasty developed a much more elaborate ministerial bureaucracy to govern the immense population of China. Ministers played important roles in confirming the legitimacy of dynastic legislation and law enforcement.

Russia offers an example of reinforced dynastic legitimacy and noble consultation. Ivan IV (1533–84) revived the title of tsar in 1547 and created a new notion of Russian monarchy during his long reign. The *boyars* (nobles) played a prominent role in the expanding Russian state, through their military activities and their participation in the *Zemsky Sobor* (assembly), which was created in 1549. Ivan IV established a *strel'tsy* corps of arquebusiers in 1550, which was accompanied by light artillery. Russian field armies combined these infantry with significant contingents of *pomestie* cavalry. Russian forces conquered the Khanate of Kazan in 1552 and Astrakhan in 1556, beginning to colonize the steppe in these subjugated territories. Russian forces also fought against the Livonian Order and seized the Baltic port of Narva in 1559, giving the monarchy direct access to seaborne trading routes and enhanced prestige in northern Europe.[20] Growing Russian aggression in the Baltic produced a First Northern War (1562–70), which confirmed the kingdom's ascent and administrative growth.

Early modern ruling dynasties articulated various principles of authority through their courts and ceremonies. European rulers spent astonishing amounts of money on sumptuous clothes, luxurious palaces, extravagant festivities, and lavish gifts in stunning displays of magnificence. In West Africa, in contrast, kings' authority rested on human labor power rather than on land ownership. John K. Thornton argues that "because land was not viewed as a source of revenue, only rights over people counted, which made state institutions critically important and control over the state crucial on the one hand, and also gave special impetus to slavery as an institution for private, revenue-producing wealth." Capturing slaves in raids and battles could greatly enhance a king's power, since "ownership of slaves in Africa was virtually equivalent to owning land in western Europe or China."[21] Amerindian *caciques*, or chiefs, engaged in elaborate gift exchanges, which may have helped some chiefdoms solidify ruling dynasties.

Sixteenth-century monarchs rarely remained sedentary, as political and military demands often forced them to travel around their dispersed territories. The Valois kings of France were itinerant rulers, despite Paris's central role as a capital city for the realm. François I and his court moved between the palais du Louvre in Paris and a number of residences in the surrounding Île-de-France, including the château de Madrid in the nearby Bois de Boulogne, the château de Saint-Germain-en-Laye, the old château de Vincennes, and the sprawling château de Fontainebleau. The Valois also used several magnificent châteaux in the Loire valley, especially those at Blois, Chambord, Amboise, Chenonceau, and Chinon.

Dynasties increasingly espoused global claims to universal imperial authority (*imperium mundi*) in the sixteenth century. Emperor Charles V's motto, *Plus ultra* (further beyond), along with twin columns symbolizing the Pillars of Hercules, signified an ambition for imperial expansion and Christian proselytization worldwide. Charles V also claimed the superlative of *maximus* (the greatest) in order to assert his pre-eminence over Charlemagne, who had titled himself *magnus* (great). The Habsburgs and Valois both incorporated the Pillars of Hercules and the Twelve Labors of Hercules into their artistic and architectural patronage. Images of Hercules (or, alternatively, Atlas) holding the entire globe in his arms communicated a dynasty's global claims of imperial power. Some sixteenth-century Ottomans hailed Süleyman as the world conqueror associated with the Last Days. The Safavid Shah 'Abbas enunciated similar universal claims to be the Padishah of the World. Habsburg, Valois, and Ottoman rulers all commissioned works portraying themselves as Roman emperors, since ancient Rome was still regarded as the model for universal empire.

Regency governments and indirect rule

Individual monarchs were rarely able to rule all of their far-flung princely realms simultaneously, forcing dynastic states to rely on regency governments or viceroys to rule territories that were distant. Regents also acted in the name of rulers during temporary periods of absence, minority, or incapacity. Most dynasties chose family members to act as regents whenever possible, but sometimes powerful nobles played such roles.

The Habsburg dynasty's extensive use of regents in the sixteenth century reveals the advantages and disadvantages of regency government. Emperor Charles V acted as an itinerant ruler, almost constantly moving between his domains in Spain, the Netherlands, Austria, and Italy. Charles's mother, Juana of Castile, theoretically acted as joint ruler of Castile with her son, but her alleged madness created a tense relationship, especially after Juana was forced to sign embarrassing concessions during the *Comuneros* revolt in 1520.

Three women served as regents of the Habsburg Netherlands during the sixteenth century. Margaret of Austria acted as regent for Maximilian I in the Netherlands from 1507 to 1531. Margaret's entry with Charles into Bruges in 1515 was one of the most famous of the "Joyous Entries" staged by the Habsburgs in the Netherlands. Charles V designated Mary of Hungary as regent of the Netherlands in 1531, several years after her husband, Louis II Jagiellon, had been killed at Mohács. Mary was an astute political leader who administered the Netherlands well until 1555. Margaret of Parma later acted as regent in Brussels for Charles V's son, Philip II, from 1559 to 1567.

Many dynasties recognized male regents as indirect rulers of territories. Charles V's brother, Ferdinand von Habsburg, acted as his regent in the Habsburg domains in Austria. Charles V's son Philip, who would later succeed as King Philip II of Spain, also served as a regent for his father. In Tuscany, Francesco de' Medici served as regent for his father, Cosimo I de' Medici, until the aging Grand Duke finally retired. Rulers and their advisors sometimes selected prominent noblemen from beyond their ranks to act as regents during succession crises. Despite the problems of regency governments, Charles V advised his own son to use dynastic regents: "As you cannot be everywhere at the same time, the best way of keeping your kingdoms together is to make use of your children."[22]

When family members were unavailable or impractical, rulers could use viceroys and governors-general to act in their name. The Habsburgs, Portuguese, and Ottomans all used powerful representatives of royal or imperial power in their conquered territories and colonial possessions. The Spanish monarch used viceroys in his distant realms of Naples and New Spain, granting them power to act in the permanent absence of the king. The Ottoman *beglerbegi* (governors-general) in Egypt and other key provinces had sweeping political and military authority.

Temporary regencies were sometimes created for adult rulers who departed from their princely courts to lead military operations. Louise de Savoie acted as regent in France for her son, François I, when he directed a campaign in Italy in 1515. She again served as regent during a critical period from 1523 to 1526 – when the king fought in southern France and Italy and then was held prisoner following the disastrous battle of Pavia. King Henri II later named his wife, Caterina de' Medici, as regent when he went off to war in 1552.

Female regents exercised growing authority during the sixteenth century. Female concubines wielded considerable power at the Ottoman sultanate as advisors and regents. Female regents were largely accepted as part of the systems of dynastic government in much of the early modern world. William Monter argues that "the gradual acceptance of women rulers in Europe...was greatly assisted by various printed, painted, sculpted, and engraved endorsements of women's capacities for ruling," especially those commissioned by female regents.[23]

Diplomacy and alliances

Diplomatic practices were becoming increasingly regularized in the sixteenth century, as dynasties maintained more sustained relations with each other. Many dynasties established permanent embassies for their resident ambassadors at foreign courts, complete with secretaries, clerks, and support personnel. The Venetian *bailo* in Istanbul became an important model for resident ambassadors serving abroad and managing complex multilateral relationships.[24] Even fierce dynastic rivals, such as the Habsburgs and Ottomans, usually maintained permanent ambassadors at each other's courts. Dynastic rulers and their representatives often pursued diplomacy and warmaking simultaneously.

Diplomatic summit meetings between princely heads of state became important ceremonial affairs in the sixteenth century. One of the most famous examples of a summit was the meeting between Henry VIII of England and François I of France in 1520, which became known as the Field of Cloth of Gold. This summit, held near Calais, celebrated the recently concluded peace of London of October 1518. François I prepared a series of tents and pavilions, covered in extravagant gold and silver cloth, and a banquet hall in order to host Henry VIII's entourage. The two-week summit included tournaments, banquets, music performances, masses, and negotiations. Despite the amiable relations between members of the Tudor and Valois dynasties, they would be at war once again merely two years after the Field of Cloth of Gold celebrations.

As the kingdom of Kongo expanded in the early sixteenth century, competing with the kingdom of Ndongo, its forces encountered Portuguese expeditionary forces along the coast, opening up new possibilities for diplomatic activity. King Nzinga a Nkuwu of Kongo converted to Christianity, taking the name of João and inviting Portuguese troops to serve in Kongolese armies. João's son, Afonso I

(1506–43), promoted Christianity as the state religion of Kongo and actively worked to extend its influence in Central Africa. The kingdom increasingly organized its monarchical institutions around Christian principles. Kongo conducted diplomacy with Portugal on a peer-to-peer basis, with both monarchs referring to each other as "brother." This did not prevent a succession struggle when João I died, but may have ensured that his son Afonso Mvemba a Nzinga eventually succeeded in 1509.[25] The growing Portuguese diplomatic relations with Ndongo in the 1520s strained the Kongolese–Portuguese relationship, however. An invasion of Kongo by the Jagas in the 1560s forced the Kongolese King Alvaro I to flee for his life and seek Portuguese military assistance. The rulers of Kongo ably exploited the new possibilities of global diplomacy in order to preserve their kingdom and extend its influence in Central Africa.[26]

Humanist scholars and writers reformulated European political concepts and revised diplomatic practices during the sixteenth century. Although Niccolò Machiavelli had served as chancellor for the Florentine Republic, his writings championed princely rule. Machiavelli was perceived as advocating a ruthless realism, yet he also promoted the notion of a common good and envisioned a role for common people through militia service. Thomas More's *Utopia* (1516) satirizes European dynastic politics by contrasting European monarchs' duplicity and dissimulation with the Utopians' truthfulness and openness. Baldassare Castiglione's witty dialogue in *Il Libro del Cortegiano* (1528) provides useful advice for noble courtiers who wished to serve a princely court. Many humanists served as ambassadors, providing a new language for diplomatic relations, stressing sovereignty, reciprocity, decorum, and formality.

Dynastic states often formed alliances with other states, sometimes joining grand leagues or unions. Popes periodically initiated Holy Leagues to oppose Ottoman imperial expansion. France, Spain, the Papal States, and the Holy Roman Empire had all banded together to form the League of Cambrai against Venice in 1507–09. One of the most fascinating alliances of the sixteenth century was the League of Cognac, a Valois-led alliance that formed in 1526 to oppose Emperor Charles V's increasing influence in the Italian peninsula.

Dynastic Rivalries

A series of sustained rivalries flared up during the sixteenth century, fueling repeated wars between competing dynastic states. The

Ottoman dynasty simultaneously combatted the Safavids and the Habsburgs. The Valois kings of France faced Tudor challenges, even as they waged war against their main rivals, the Habsburgs. Despite the widespread use of monarchical political systems in the early modern world, however, dynastic warfare was not universal. Ruling families did not always have direct dynastic rivals, but instead faced other challenges. Ming emperors, for example, combatted repeated Manchu incursions from the steppes, resulting in sustained warfare in northern China. This section will focus especially on regions where dynastic rivalries fomented warfare and shaped military practices.

Renewal of the Habsburg–Valois Wars

The long struggle between the Habsburgs and Valois is often seen as the classic sixteenth-century dynastic rivalry. François I at first accepted the results of the election of Charles V as Holy Roman Emperor, but his resentment simmered. Martin du Bellay described the outbreak of hostilities between François I and Charles V: "It has many times been seen, in our times and in the past, that a *great fire is lit from a small spark*, insofar as there is nothing easier than to provoke princes one against another. Then, once they have started, it is amazingly difficult to stop them."[27] The Habsburg–Valois Wars broke out once again in 1521 as François I orchestrated an attack on Luxembourg.

Italy again became the center of Habsburg–Valois dynastic competition. Charles III de Bourbon, duc de Bourbon and *connétable* (constable) de France, planned a rebellion to support Charles V's cause in Italy and Henry VIII's claims to the French throne. When the plot was discovered, the duc de Bourbon fled, but was unable to link up with the English and Imperial troops that invaded northern France in 1523. François I stripped the rebellious Bourbon of his offices and titles, but Charles V offered him a command in the Imperial forces in Italy. The duc de Bourbon led an Imperial army into Provence, besieging the key port city of Marseille. François I's rapidly assembled field army marched to relieve Marseille and successfully forced the Imperial troops to abandon their siege.

François I pursued the retreating Imperial troops, leading his army into northern Italy in fall 1524 and besieging Pavia in October. The siege of Pavia wore on through the winter, and the Imperialists launched a surprise nighttime attack on the French encampments on February 23–24. François I personally led his *gendarmes* in repeated charges against Spanish infantry, but he was wounded and taken captive. The Imperialist garrison of Pavia sortied and routed the remaining French forces, completing a dramatic victory that threatened the stability of the Valois dynasty. François I was held prisoner for months and transferred to Madrid, as negotiations proceeded to secure his release. Charles V demanded that François I renounce his claims in Italy and the Netherlands, cede the province of Burgundy, and give two of his sons as hostages to implement the humiliating agreement, known as the treaty of Madrid (1526).

Although Habsburg and Valois armies waged major offensives in Italy, other forces were involved throughout the Italian Wars. Renaissance military entrepreneurs negotiated contracts, recruited troops, obtained weapons, provided food, and managed military forces during the Italian Wars. Giovanni de' Medici, known as Giovanni delle Bande Nere, was one of the most famous sixteenth-century *condottieri*, fighting in successive campaigns along the Italian peninsula.

French, Venetian, Florentine, Sforza, and Papal diplomats crafted the League of Cognac in 1526 in reaction to Emperor Charles V's stunning victory at the battle of Pavia the previous year. François I successfully convinced his allies that Charles V's dominant position in northern Italy posed a threat to the stability of the entire Italian peninsula. Pope Clement VII had vacillated between the French and Imperial camps during the War of the League of Cognac, but he finally joined the League against the emperor in 1527, leading Charles V to send an Imperial army against Rome.

The Sack of Rome, discussed above in chapter 3, produced chaos in the Papal States and across much of the Italian peninsula. With Pope Clement VII, a leading member of the Medici family, surrounded in the Castel Sant'Angelo, anti-Medici citizens restored the Florentine Republic in May 1527 and allied with the French. When Giovanni delle Bande Nere was killed in combat that year, the Florentine Republic took nominal control of his infantry companies, which were referred to as the *Bande Nere* (Black Bands) because of the black flags with devils embroidered on them. Florence sent the Black Bands to join the League of Cognac's army and invade the kingdom of Naples in 1528.

The Black Bands' contradictory roles in Florentine defense and in League offensive operations reveal the complexities of dynastic war in Renaissance Italy. While the captains of the Black Bands formed a semi-autonomous union to protect their interests, the units became caught in a political struggle between the fledgling Florentine Republic and Orazio Baglioni, their new military entrepreneur. Baglioni, a Perugian, eventually gained control of the Black Bands and led them to join the League of Cognac's main army in its campaign to take

Naples from Habsburg forces. Social, political, and medical factors combined to produce the disastrous failure of the League army's siege of Naples in 1528, and the dissolution of the Black Bands.[28]

Meanwhile, Clement VII had escaped from Rome and negotiated peace with the Emperor Charles V, who was embarrassed by the behavior of his Imperial troops during the Sack of Rome. Papal and Imperial forces now allied to attack the Florentine Republic, besieging Florence in October 1529. Michelangelo Buonarotti designed bastioned fortifications to enhance Florence's defenses, but family rivalries within the city and weakened loyalties in outlying towns undermined the Republican position. Florence capitulated to the besieging Papal-Imperial army in August 1530, and then pro-Medici forces "banished, imprisoned, or executed some 150 of the leading citizens and confiscated the estates of their families."[29] The occupying forces soon dismantled the last Florentine Republic and installed Alessandro de' Medici as duke of Florence. Conflicts and conspiracies continued between Italian princes and states following the consolidation of the Medicean duchy of Florence.

The Italian Wars showcased the intense personal rivalries between the Habsburg and Valois rulers. François I and Charles V each issued challenges to personal combat in defense of their honor during the Italian Wars. François I challenged his Imperial rival to an individual duel in 1528 to settle their differences. Later, Charles V publicly challenged François I to a duel without armor, but this staged event in 1536 at Saint Peter's Basilica in the Vatican was probably intended to sway public opinion in Rome rather than to result in an actual duel.

Despite this personal animosity, Margaret of Burgundy and Louise of Savoy and their ambassadors negotiated the peace of Cambrai in 1529, effectively establishing an extended truce between the two competing dynasties. Charles V orchestrated an elaborate second coronation ceremony and was crowned by Pope Clement VII in Bologna in February 1530, reinforcing his Italian prerogatives. The Valois and Habsburg dynasties still maintained their opposing claims in Italy, but François I was not the only dynastic rival with whom Charles V had to contend.

Süleyman I and Ottoman dynastic rivalries

As Ottoman armies expanded throughout the Balkans in the early sixteenth century, the Ottoman sultans came to see Christian rulers as dynastic rivals. Ottoman society was multicultural and the Ottomans maintained commercial, diplomatic, and cultural relations with

various European, Asian, and African societies. Selim I had conquered Syria, Arabia, and Egypt in the early sixteenth century, allowing the Ottomans to establish legitimacy as an Islamic empire. Sultan
Süleyman I (1520–66) reinforced Mehmed II's dynastic claims to a
Roman imperial legacy and reoriented the military policy of the
Ottomans toward Europe. He would become known as "the Magnificent" for his military conquests and his sumptuous extravagance
during his long reign.

Süleyman I acceded to the sultanate in 1520 and almost immediately launched campaigns against some of the previous Christian
enemies of the Ottomans. An Ottoman army seized Belgrade from
the Hungarians in 1521. A major amphibious expedition to the islands
of Rhodes in 1522 besieged the fortress city of Rhodes and forced
the Knights of Saint John of Jerusalem to capitulate and migrate to
the island of Malta. Ottoman armies then overran most of Hungary
following the rout at the battle of Mohács in 1526. With the death of
King Louis II Jagiellon, Emperor Charles V inherited the remaining
Jagiellon possessions in Hungary and Bohemia. Charles V now effectively became Süleyman I's direct rival for imperial hegemony in
southeastern Europe.

Süleyman I led an enormous army from Istanbul to besiege Buda
in 1529. The city fell after a brief five-day siege. The Ottoman army
invested Vienna in September and began digging approach trenches.
Ottoman batteries bombarded the fortifications of Vienna and gunpowder mines created a breach in October. The Ottomans launched
two major assaults into the breaches, but failed to break into the city.
The sultan's army abandoned the siege and withdrew, but left a
lasting impression in Austrian historical memory.

A contested, but relatively stable, imperial frontier zone gradually
developed in between the Habsburg and Ottoman fortification lines
in Hungary. Wallachia and Moldavia and Transylvania also represented borderlands, under indirect Ottoman rule. Ottoman sultans
allowed relative autonomy in these regions, but occasionally intervened to enforce their imperial tribute system. During Süleyman I's
reign, the Grand Vizier Sokullu Mehmed led an army to crush a
rebellion by Sigismund II, prince of Transylvania, in 1551.

Ottoman sultans did not merely have Christian rivals, however. In
the early sixteenth century, an intense rivalry developed between the
Ottomans and the Safavid rulers of Persia. The Ottomans and Safavids fought a series of wars over territories along their borders. These
dynastic wars were intensified by the religious dimensions of the
conflicts, since the Ottomans represented Sunni Islam and the Safavids promoted Shia Islam. Pro-Ottoman polemical works, such as

al-Baghadadi's *Hisnu al-Islam*, regarded Shia as unbelievers. The dynastic rivalry between the Ottomans and Safavids became a competition for leadership within the Islamic world.

Despite Christian depictions of the "Terrible Turk," some historians argue that the Ottomans were quickly becoming part of the European system of dynastic states in the sixteenth century. Süleyman I adopted aspects of European diplomatic ceremonial and began to receive ambassadors seated on a new jeweled throne in the 1530s. He also commissioned a "magnificent crown – designed and assembled by Venetian artisans – that markedly united motifs from the coronation crowns of the Holy Roman Emperor Charles V and the Pope Clement VII."[30] Süleyman I conducted a series of grandiose imperial entries to Belgrade and Nish in 1532, demonstrating his authority, perhaps in direct response to Charles V's recent imperial coronation ceremony in Bologna.

Under Süleyman I, the Ottomans articulated a pragmatic and flexible grand strategy. Ibrahim Pasha consolidated Ottoman rule in Egypt, then led an Ottoman army into Iraq and seized Baghdad in November 1534. Ottoman armies gradually established control of Yemen and fought a series of conflicts against the Portuguese under the leadership of Hadim Süleyman Pasha from 1536 to 1546. During Süleyman I's long reign, a new literary genre developed around the memoranda and treatises offering advice to sultans. Rustem Pasha, who served as grand vizier from 1546 to 1561, negotiated a truce with the Habsburgs in 1547 and managed palace conspiracies in Istanbul.[31]

Süleyman I was also known as "the Lawgiver" for his codification of Ottoman laws and systemization of *timar* land grants. Ibrahim Pasha issued a new law code in Egypt in 1525 and managed the newly conquered territories effectively. An increasingly pious Süleyman I constructed the Süleymaniye Mosque in Istanbul, renovated the Dome of the Rock Mosque in Jerusalem, and repaired the minarets of the Great Mosque in Mecca. Süleyman I at times exacted a harsh justice, removing threats to his rule. The victorious Ibrahim Pasha was executed in 1536, soon after his conquest of Baghdad, and Prince Mustafa, the sultan's eldest son, was executed in 1553. The failure of a major Ottoman military campaign in Hungary in 1566 and the death of Süleyman I seemed to confirm the limits of Ottoman dynastic expansion.

Marriage politics and peacemaking

Marriage alliances were central aspects of diplomacy and peacemaking among dynastic allies and rivals. Diplomats often negotiated marriage contracts between dynasties during peace talks. Princely marriage negotiations were always delicate, since they had the potential to produce new dynastic claims and to instigate new wars. Disappointed princely suitors could consider their rejection as a just cause for war. Rulers also might worry that the failure of prolonged marriage negotiations could lead their children to engage in clandestine marriages.

Dynastic rule required sophisticated marriage politics to produce carefully crafted princely unions. Marriage laws and customs varied widely around the early modern world, and marriage patterns also changed over time. Historians have identified several changing models of marriage in the early modern period. Frances E. Dolan explains that "marriage...moved from patriarchal to companionate, from obedience to intimacy, from sacrament to contract."[32] Marriages were integral to families' attempts to ensure succession and to preserve dynastic holdings, although Ottoman princesses who married did not bring territories or titles with them.[33] By avoiding succession crises and inheritance partitions, a dynasty could maintain its power through marriage politics and reproduction.

Rulers sought partners for their princely children and extended family members through elaborate marriage markets. Dynasties exchanged portraits and lyrical descriptions of their children with eligible princes and princesses, either within the realm or beyond its borders. Interested potential partners conducted complex negotiations relating to dowries, gifts, titles, landholdings, and dynastic rights. Successful negotiations concluded with detailed marriage contracts to solidify transactions and dowry terms among the families. The Ming emperors preferred to arrange marriages with military and administrative elites who held princely rank within their empire.[34] Many other dynasties exchanged partners with members of foreign ruling families, sometimes in elaborate double marriages. Parents could exert control over the choice of marriage partners, but they generally consulted closely with children and sometimes allowed them a role in negotiating their own marriages. Individual family members, and sometimes entire dynasties, were capable of pursuing coherent marriage strategies. Wives and mothers of rulers were able to assert considerable authority in brokering dynastic marriages. Dynasties were conscious of their princely rank and status in selecting marriage partners for their family members.

Caterina de' Medici's wedding to the Henri de Valois, the second son of François I, in 1533 demonstrates how unpredictable marriage alliances were. François I arranged this marriage as part of his alliance with Pope Clement VII, who was Caterina's uncle and a prominent member of the Medici family. Clement VII died just months after the wedding, however, and a Farnese cardinal was elected as Pope Paul III, diminishing the Medici family's influence in Rome. Caterina was at first a relatively minor figure at the Valois royal court, but the death of *dauphin* François, the eldest son of the king, in 1536 suddenly left Caterina's husband as heir to the French throne. Caterina's position remained vulnerable, however, since she and Henri did not produce their first child until 1544, creating concerns at the Valois court.

A ruler could seek an annulment if his or her marriage did not produce an heir within a few years of a princely wedding. Papal approval was normally necessary in order to obtain an annulment and then remarry. Henry VIII of England requested an annulment of his marriage to Catherine of Aragon, despite having already fathered a legitimate daughter. By this time, the Reformation movements had begun to challenge papal authority, leading the pope to deny Henry VIII's request. A furious Henry VIII broke from the Latin Christian church and declared himself head of a newly created Church of England so that he could divorce Catherine and marry Anne Boleyn. Dynastic marriage politics were thus more decisive than religious concerns in the initial stages of the Henrician Reformation in England.

Although Henry VIII's political situation was remarkable, he was not alone in remarrying. Widowed rulers often remarried in the sixteenth century, sometimes upsetting well-established relations with the dynasty of the deceased spouse. The politics of remarriages had the potential to create political tensions and conflicts, especially between rival dynasties.

Dynastic Crises

Dynasties periodically suffered serious political and financial crises that threatened to destabilize ruling families and their states, despite the adoption of a variety of defensive mechanisms. Prolonged disputes over inheritance claims and continual wars to uphold dynastic rights could prove costly for dynasties. When a ruler failed to produce a direct heir or to manage inheritance disputes, a succession crisis could ensue – challenging princely authority and endangering the dynastic state.

Dynastic preservation and defense

Early modern royal and imperial dynasties implemented measures to preserve their rule and provide security. Dynastic states pursued various approaches to dynastic preservation, developing military institutions and political strategies as survival mechanisms. One historian remarks that "the central fact of Ottoman history is surely the extraordinary survival of the ruling dynasty, unmatched in the Islamic world."[35] The emperors of Japan also achieved dynastic longevity, but by withdrawing from politics and playing no direct role in imperial administration or warfare. Despite internal and external challenges, some dynasties were able to construct familial political systems to rule large states over an extended period.

Dynastic stability could be threatened by various internal tensions, including cadet branches and other unincorporated family members. The Safavids reinforced the Shah's position within the dynasty by asserting divine kingship and closely associating his rule with Sufi religious leaders. Monarchs around the world had to manage incredibly complex relationships within their large ruling families. Illegitimate family members, routinely referred to as bastards, could sometimes claim inheritance and often demanded that rulers spend exorbitant sums to maintain their luxurious lifestyles. Political struggles and rebellions could result in members of ruling families being exiled or imprisoned indefinitely.

The Songhay Empire had developed into a strong dynastic state in West Africa by the early sixteenth century, constructing institutions to protect the royal family. Askiya Muhammad (1493–1529) created a permanent royal guard and led strong Songhay armies on campaigns of conquest against the kingdom of Fulbe along the Senegal River. Ironically, Askiya Muhammad's son Musa was able to depose him in 1529, however, eventually placing him under house arrest for the rest of his life. The Songhay Empire gradually descended into civil conflict, threatening the rule of Askiya's dynasty and weakening the empire in the late sixteenth century.

The kingdom of Kongo demonstrates some of the changing methods of dynastic defense. In the fifteenth century, the king of Kongo was already deploying powerful armies of shield-bearing heavy infantry, composed of noble elites, flanked by archers. But the Kongolese faced several hostile African states and searched for improved defenses. Kongolese soldiers gradually incorporated Portuguese crossbows, arquebuses, and bombards into their military system. An invasion of Kongo by the Jagas in the 1560s forced the Kongolese king Alvaro I to flee for his life and seek Portuguese military assistance.[36] Dynasties could seek assistance from increasingly far-flung allies in the sixteenth century.

Dynastic states invested in palace building and new fortifications to protect rulers and their courts. Many ruling families invested in constructing extensive fortifications systems in the sixteenth century, in order to defend their authority. In the early part of the century, the Ottomans engaged in extensive fortification-building campaigns around Istanbul and its military frontiers. Mughal emperors built strong new fortifications to guard the imperial palaces at Delhi and Agra. The grand princes of Muscovy strengthened the Kremlin as the main royal palace complex in Moscow. New fortified residences and palace complexes provided dynasties with secure refuges in times of crisis.

Military exhaustion in the Habsburg–Valois Wars

The intense dynastic rivalry between the Habsburg and the Valois ruling families demonstrates the dangers of military and financial exhaustion. The Habsburg–Valois Wars resumed in 1536 as Emperor Charles V personally led an army to invade Provence, but his siege of Marseille was unsuccessful. Valois armies attacked Artois and Pie-monte the next year, allowing the French to control part of northern Italy for the rest of the war. A truce was negotiated in 1538, but it crumbled once again in 1542. The final phases of the Habsburg–Valois Wars in the 1540s and 1550s were fought not only in Italy, but also in the Netherlands, Germany, France, and Spain. The demands of fight-ing across such expansive theaters of war strained the human and financial resources of both dynastic states.

Charles V created new infantry formations, the famed *tercios*, to fight the ongoing Habsburg–Valois Wars. The earliest *tercios*, composed of several infantry companies, were probably created in the early 1530s, even before the *tercios viejos* (those of Naples, Sicily, Milan, and Lombardy). By the 1540s, each *tercio* was composed of approximately 3,000 infantry, divided into about 10–12 compa-nies of roughly 250–300 soldiers. Individual *tercios* were raised in particular territories within the Habsburg Empire, but might fight anywhere that Charles V needed to deploy his armies. The Habsburg *tercios* would later influence infantry regimental organization.[37]

The Habsburgs and Valois raised increasingly large field armies to fight successive campaigns in the 1540s. The growing scale of warfare could be observed at the siege of Perpignan in 1542. Multiple Habsburg and Valois armies engaged in warfare in the Netherlands, Germany, and Italy in 1544, resulting in the battle of Ceresole in April 1544 and fighting in Luxembourg. Charles V launched an invasion of northern France in 1544, coupled with Henry VIII's parallel invasion from the English Channel.

King Henri II (1547–59) of France altered his father's strategy for intervention in Italy, sending small French expeditionary forces – rather than large contracted armies – to support Italians in Parma and Corsica who had adopted anti-Habsburg stances. The French war of diversion in Italy allowed Henri II to organize a large army to capture Metz in spring 1552 and to pursue campaigns against the Habsburg Netherlands. Charles V organized an army to retake Metz the next year, but his siege failed. In 1554, Henri II was able to field three separate armies for operations in Luxembourg, Artois, and Hainault.[38]

Cosimo I de' Medici, who had become duke of Florence in 1537 and allied with the Habsburgs, launched a surprise attack on the Republic of Siena in 1554, in a bid to annex the entire republic. The Medici troops tightened their siege of Siena as French forces, including Blaise de Monluc, assisted in the defense of the city. After an epic siege, Siena and its French garrison finally capitulated in April 1555, allowing Cosimo I to establish Medici dynastic rule over an expanded Tuscany. The Medici victory in Siena helped to force yet another short-lived Habsburg–Valois truce.

The Habsburg–Valois Wars had became costly wars of attrition by the 1550s, as both dynasties faced financial exhaustion. A physically drained Charles V gradually abdicated each of his sovereign titles during 1555 and 1556, dividing his vast empire between his son Philip and his brother Ferdinand. Charles then retired to a Spanish monastery for the final two years of his life. François de Lorraine, duc de Guise, led a French expedition to Naples in 1556–57, but the Habsburg victory at the battle of Saint-Quentin in August 1557 forced the French forces to withdraw from Naples. Attritional warfare had seemingly led to military stalemate and war weariness in Habsburg and Valois territories.

Succession crises

Despite the incredible power of some ruling families, early modern dynastic states could be incredibly fragile. Dynasties needed biological continuity and familial coherence to maintain control of their patrimonies and to exercise power. Inheritance disputes created serious political crises in a number of dynastic states, however. Elective monarchies, such as the kingdom of Poland-Lithuania, could experience succession crises when strong groups of nobles backed opposing candidates.

Lack of heirs, contested inheritance, illegitimate children, and the creation of collateral branches all had the potential to produce succession crises, which threatened to escalate into civil wars. Collateral branches of a dynasty could at times vie for a throne, producing princely revolts by cadets and cousins. Some succession crises resulted in sustained periods of civil conflict, as rejected successors refused to accept their status as cadets.

Even if outright succession crises were avoided, the minorities of rulers could present opportunities for opponents of regents and their ministers to challenge their authority. Regency governments frequently encountered serious difficulties of asserting princely authority, especially when acting in the name of a child ruler. Opposition by military and administrative elites could easily produce widespread political instability and civil conflict.

Monarchs often attempted to avoid succession crises by abdicating in favor of an heir. Emperor Charles V's abdication, discussed above, split his empire between his son Philip and his brother Ferdinand, a move that divided his dynasty into two separate branches: the Spanish Habsburgs and the Austrian Habsburgs. Cosimo I de' Medici effectively retired from ruling in the 1560s, allowing his son Francesco to formulate policy. Cosimo I later abdicated in 1574 and Francesco officially took up the title of Grand Duke of Tuscany.

The Ottoman succession procedures were uncodified, leading to numerous conspiracies and civil wars of succession in the early modern period. Prince Bayezid, one of the sons of Süleyman I, was accused of participating in a rebellion in the 1550s, leading him to seek exile at the Safavid court in 1559. Before he could negotiate a return to the Ottoman Empire, Bayezid was assassinated along with his sons in 1562. The threat of Safavid political intervention in Ottoman dynastic succession processes produced renewed warfare in the 1560s. Süleyman I once again led an Ottoman army into Hungary to besiege Szigetvár, but the sultan died in his army's camp in September 1566. The grand vizier kept his ruler's death a secret until the army could withdraw and Selim II could be installed as the new sultan.

The early Mughal Empire experienced severe succession struggles, in part because Babur had created a system of shared rule based on Timurid *apanage* practices of dividing regional control among male family members. Emperor Humayun (1530–66) thus faced competition from his male relatives when he ascended to the Mughal throne and spent much of his reign trying to consolidate his imperial authority.

Not all succession crises produced civil wars, however. Dynasties frequently were able to absorb the landholdings and titles of princely branches that failed to produce legitimate offspring. The Habsburgs progressively absorbed Burgundy, Hungary, and Portugal during the late fifteenth and early sixteenth centuries. The Stuart dynasty of Scotland inherited the entire kingdom of England in 1603, when the death of the childless Queen Elizabeth I effectively ended the Tudor dynasty.

Conclusion

Dynastic rivalries instigated many conflicts throughout the sixteenth century, as inheritance claims and practices shaped the dynamics of warfare. Imperial and monarchical rulers and their families managed succession processes and administered their dynastic states, even as they waged war and coped with crises. Rulers used elaborate ceremonies as demonstrations not only of their personal power, but also of their dynasties' prestige.

King Henri II of France assembled his forces in August 1558 near Laon, organizing a ceremonial review of his field army, which included 6,000 French infantry, 2,000 Swiss infantry, 19,000 Landsknechts, 1,750 *gendarmes*, 1,400 light cavalry, and 8,000 Reiters. Blaise de Monluc described this impressive force as "the finest and largest army a King of France had ever had."[39] The duc de Guise, now the pre-eminent French military commander, led this force to confront an Imperial army near Amiens, but the two armies cautiously maneuvered rather than engaging each other in battle. Guise's forces seized the towns of Calais and Thionville, but this operational advantage was offset by a Habsburg–English victory at Gravelines. Henri II's great military review may have worked as a dramatic display of dynastic power, but the Valois army proved unable to win an impressive victory to end the war.

The Habsburgs and Valois dynasties had now waged near-constant warfare for an entire generation. Soon after Charles V's death in September 1558, Valois and Habsburg ambassadors began intensive negotiations to hammer out the peace of Cateau-Cambrésis of 1559, which finally ended the long Habsburg–Valois conflict and the closely related Italian Wars. Paris hosted elaborate celebrations of the peace in June 1559, but a triumphant Henri II was mortally wounded in a jousting accident, plunging the kingdom of France into crisis. Dynastic interests would continue to shape politics and conflict throughout the early modern period, but by the mid-sixteenth century new issues were increasingly motivating warfare.

5

Noble Violence, 1520s–1620s

German knights frequently engaged in feuds with nearby nobles as local disputes were aggravated by the complex mixed sovereignty of the Holy Roman Empire, which was composed of hundreds of distinct principalities. Veit von Vestenberg, a noble from central Germany, entered into a protracted feud with his relatives over possession of landholdings and property rights in the 1470s and 1480s. Veit asserted his rights by building a new castle at Fürstenforst and then leading his forces to harass shepherds, damage pastures, destroy fences, cut down trees, and kill livestock of his enemies. The feuding Vestenbergs apparently all engaged in abducting their rivals' peasants, extorting money, and seizing taxes. Nonetheless, Veit von Vestenberg seems to have eventually won the feud, becoming an advisor to the Margrave of Brandenburg, and finally gaining confirmation of his right to fortify castle Fürstenforst from Emperor Maximilian I in 1495.[1]

The feuds between German knights have sometimes been interpreted as private wars fueled by personal animosities, but feuding could also be closely connected to princely politics. The practice of multiple vassalage ensured that most German nobles owed loyalty simultaneously to several different princes. In the Holy Roman Empire, territorial princes competed for the loyalties of German noblemen who could serve in their armies and state administrations. Friedrich IV Margrave of Brandenburg thus referred to nobles as the "greatest treasure" of princes.[2] German knights often received political and military support from princes when rivalries turned violent. Some historians have seen the noble conflicts of the early sixteenth century as representing the end of feuding, but in many ways familial conflict and noble violence was getting worse during the early modern period.

In many early modern societies, warrior elites dominated the political culture and everyday life through armed violence. To understand the pervasiveness of noble violence, Stuart Carroll proposes the concept of "vindicatory violence," a category encompassing "acts of violence, such as revenge killing and the duel, which repair an honour or injury and which are suggestive of a reciprocal relationship between the parties, such as one finds in the feud." This approach effectively considers disparate types of violence – including dueling, assassination, murder, feuding, and private war – as operating through a similar process of escalation and reprisal. Carroll details the techniques of vindicatory violence that nobles employed to insult, curse, intimidate, humiliate, challenge, maim, and kill their rivals, as well as members of their families and entourages.[3] This chapter probes the various ways in which warrior nobles and their clienteles engaged in armed violence and warfare.

Warrior Nobles

In many early modern societies, local and regional elites acted as warriors or military officers. The social origins of nobilities are obscure, but many Asian, European, and African elites seem to have acquired noble states through mounted military service, leading to extended historical debates over the concepts of "feudalism" and a medieval "horse revolution" across Eurasia.[4] The imagery of warriors continued to draw on medieval precedents, but warrior nobles exercised military and political power in early modern societies.

Military elites and lordship

The concept of "nobility" can be employed globally, even though the conditions for noble status varied widely across societies. Referring to "nobles" avoids the political associations of the term "aristocracy" – which is often associated with a highly restricted and ossified elite in governing positions. Noble status had become hereditary in most societies by the sixteenth century, as noble families reinforced their lineages through successive marriage alliances with other noble families. Yet, social mobility was still possible. Michel Nassiet's research on noble mortality and marriage patterns in fifteenth- and sixteenth-century France demonstrates that the nobility was continually renewed, as commoners entered the nobility through ennoblement and marriage. The high mortality rates among warrior nobles meant that perhaps 25 percent of the nobility was renewed each generation.[5]

Early modern nobles usually held some sort of lordship, or *seigneurie*. Lordship comprised a series of status distinctions, landholding privileges, legal rights, and judicial powers, collectively referred to as seigneurial rights. Noble families had accrued these rights over generations through military service and negotiations with local peasants. Lordship was often attached to a particular fief or landed estate, which became associated with a noble title. Lordship could alternatively be associated with wealth and authority over peasant farmers or enslaved peoples. Concepts of lordship varied widely even within dynastic states and provinces, since seigneurial rights were continuously contested and renegotiated. Notions of a "crisis of the aristocracy" or a "decline of lordship" proposed by some historians have grossly exaggerated the weakness of evolving systems of lordship.[6] Nobles in many societies continued to exercise their seigneurial rights effectively throughout the early modern period. Not all noble elites pursued military activities, but those who did acted as warriors and military officers – sharply distinguishing themselves from common soldiers, who were recruited from among socially inferior urban residents and peasants.

In the Caribbean and South America, the Caribs, Arawaks, and other Amerindian peoples had relied on warrior elites in the pre-Columbian period. The *caciques*, Amerindian chiefs, seem to have waged warfare over the possession of female bodies and ritual objects prior to contact with Europeans. As Spanish and Portuguese colonies were established in the sixteenth century, Amerindian warriors gradually shifted the focus of their warfare to competition over access to manufactured goods imported from Europe. Early Spanish sources depict the Caribs of the Caribbean islands as fierce savages and describe cannibals living on the mainland, yet such accounts clearly promoted imperialistic aims and demonized groups of Amerindians who resisted European colonial expansion. French, English, and Dutch traders and missionaries established posts along the South American coast, spurring a process of "tribalization" that divided indigenous peoples and produced warring "tribes" affiliated with different European colonial states. Amerindian warrior elites seem to have been constantly shifting and recombining as sustained contact and "tribalization" progressively disrupted indigenous societies.[7]

The Spanish conquest of Central and South America in the 1520s and 1530s greatly altered the situation for Amerindian nobles. Epidemic diseases such as measles, mumps, and smallpox devastated

Amerindian societies, wiping out many elite families and disrupting political relationships. Mesoamerican nobles from Texcoco and other cities joined with Hernán Cortés to overthrow Mexican imperial rule. The nobles of the Incan Empire divided over a contested imperial succession. As *conquistadores* established Spanish rule in the Americas, Amerindian elites gradually assimilated into colonial society and administration, converting to Christianity and taking Spanish names. The Amerindian warriors were transformed into a *mestizo* (mixed-ethnic) social elite, but some continued to lead resistance against Spanish rule. Don Carlos Ometochtli, a member of the Texcoco nobility, was tried by the Spanish Inquisition in Mexico and executed for heresy and sedition in an *auto de fé* in 1539.

Amerindian societies in North America also had warrior elites, although historical records are sparse for pre-Columbian periods. The Iroquois Confederacy established peace between the Mohawk, Oneida, Onondaga, Cayuga, and Seneca peoples – often referred to as the "five nations" – with a council of 50. Iroquois warriors waged "mourning war," in which a kinsman's death required retaliation through revenge killing or captive taking. Iroquois warfare would later change significantly as Europeans expanded into the interior of North America.

West African horse warriors attained noble status, while Central and East African nobles often fought in specialized infantry formations in the armies of large kingdoms. The shield-bearing heavy infantrymen of Kongo armies were considered military and social elites, while their counterparts in the neighboring Mbundu lands wielded battle axes. Many African elites enslaved enemy soldiers who were defeated in expansionist campaigns as well as individuals taken captive in raids.

Across the early modern Muslim world, warrior nobles dominated societies. North African warriors engaged in cavalry warfare and corsair raiding in the Mediterranean, taking captives as slaves. Turkish nobles served as *pashas* and *sipahis* in the Ottoman imperial armies, but non-Turks could gain status as officers in the janissary infantry. Persian nobles served as mounted warriors in Safavid armies in the sixteenth century.

South Asian nobilities were in flux in the early sixteenth century. The warriors of the Delhi sultanate were overwhelmed by Babur's Turco-Mongol army at the battle of Panipat in 1516, as we saw in chapter 4, leading to the rapid collapse of the sultanate. Rajput warriors in northern India had never been subordinated to the Delhi rulers, so the disintegration of power allowed the Hindu *raja* to assert themselves. Rana Sanga of Mewar forged a confederacy to oppose

Babur's invasions in the early sixteenth century, but Babur's army defeated the combined *raja* army at the battle of Khanua in 1527.[8] Afghan and Uzbek armies periodically raided in northern India, threatening local warrior elites' positions.

A multiethnic Mughal nobility gradually formed, incorporating Shia Iranian, Sunni Turco-Mongol, and Hindi warriors. Emperor Akbar (1556–1605) built enormous fortified cities at Agra, Allahabad, and Lahore to consolidate Mughal rule, but he also promoted religious curiosity and syncretism at his imperial court, apparently blending elements of Islam, Hinduism, Buddhism, and divine mysticism. Religious experimentation at court did not prevent Akbar from upholding Sunni Islam as the leading religion in the multicultural empire.[9] Early in his reign, Akbar established elaborate honorific ranks, known as the *mansabdari* system, for the diverse military elites in the Mughal Empire. Each *mansabdar* held a rank correlating to the number of soldiers he commanded, from 10 to 10,000, but nobles could be promoted for meritorious imperial service. Mughal emperors required the *mansabdars* to recruit and maintain their contingents, allowing the empire to mobilize large armies without assuming the enormous burden of paying for them. The empire compensated nobles holding *mansabdar* commands by granting them rights to collect taxes within *jagir* lands assigned to them, but they did not hold direct lordship of these lands. As a result, Mughal armies never coalesced into a permanent military force.[10]

Competing models of warrior elites structured societies in East Asia. Chinese military elites operated within an extensive imperial system that celebrated Confucian ideals. The Chinese imperial military commanders had to negotiate a complex imperial bureaucracy with entrenched officeholders established through civil service exams. Chinese cultural influence spread elements of this bureaucratic system into Korea and Southeast Asia in the fifteenth and sixteenth centuries. The authority of the *shoguns* (military generals) of Japan was eclipsed by the militant culture of *samurai* warriors and *daimyō* warlords during the sixteenth century.

Early modern European nobles are well documented, allowing us to consider the changing compositions of nobilities. The numbers of nobles and their relative status varied across early modern European societies, expanding and contracting over time. Most early modern European states had tiny nobilities that represented less than 1 percent of their populations. Nobles comprised a mere 0.3 percent of the population of the province of Holland around 1550. In Renaissance France, nobles represented approximately 1 percent of French society, but the nobility would gradually contract, composing only 0.5

percent of French subjects by the end of the seventeenth century. The Republic of Venice extended noble status to between 1.5 and 2.2 percent of its population. Hungary had an even broader nobility, perhaps constituting 5 percent of that society. The kingdom of Spain seems to have had a similarly large proportion of nobility, but the geographic distribution of the nobles was very uneven. Castilian nobles dominated the other Spanish elites, constituting a stunning 10 percent of the population of Castile. The kingdom of Poland-Lithuania seems to have had one of the widest elites in the early modern period, with almost 10 percent of society holding noble status.[11]

Not all of these nobles actually served as military officers or engaged in warfare, however, so it is very difficult to determine how many European nobles should really be considered as warrior elites. My own analysis of noble culture in southern France suggests that only a restricted group of provincial nobles embraced the profession of arms, but that they were the key organizers of warfare.[12] Many European nobles articulated their notions of nobility in terms of personal military service and leadership. The Danish Lord Admiral, Herluf Trolle, explained his notion of nobility and armed service in 1565:

> Know you not why we are called lords, and why we wear golden chains, and have estates, and would be superior and more greatly respected than others? We, rather than others, have this honour because when our king and lord, the country and kingdom have need of it then shall we ward off the realm's enemies, protect and shield our father's country with all our might and wealth, so that our subjects may live in peace and tranquility.[13]

Despite their small numbers, warrior elites wielded incredible power in early modern societies. Warrior nobles recruited and led military forces for the armies of growing states and empires. Warriors attended the princely courts of sovereign rulers, acting as courtiers and advisors to princely rulers. Some warrior elites, such as the *condottieri* of Renaissance Italy, inherited or carved out their own small principalities.

The nobles of Poland-Lithuania enjoyed sweeping institutional power through the *Sejm*, a bicameral Diet that elected monarchs and passed legislation, and judicial tribunals. Polish magnates limited the taxing authority of the elective monarchy and raised their own substantial armies in times of war. As a result, "by 1600 Poland-Lithuania seemed to be – and was seen to be – a state run by the nobles for the nobles."[14]

The kingdom of Hungary was largely occupied by Ottoman forces in the sixteenth century, but many Hungarian nobles continued to fight to recover their country. Competing groups of nobles backed either John Szapolyai or Ferdinand I von Habsburg to assume the title of king of Hungary, producing serious divisions among the Hungarian nobility. Ferdinand I eventually consolidated his control over the crown, and Hungarian nobles joined in the Habsburg defense of the military frontier against the Ottomans for the next century.[15]

Clientage and military entourages

Early modern nobles surrounded themselves with armed followers and political supporters, who were linked to their patrons through clientage relationships that included a broad range of interpersonal connections. The households and regular clienteles of some warrior elites are well documented, but other clientage relationships are more difficult to discern. Military governors and regional nobles paid stipends to certain household members and bodyguards, but also maintained more extensive clientele networks. Powerful nobles acted as patrons, cultivating informal alliances and clientage relationships with numerous provincial nobles and their own entourages.

Early modern rulers' bodyguards provided a model for nobles' armed entourages. Royal and imperial bodyguard units, generally composed entirely of high-ranking nobles, provided rulers with personal protection and palace security. Rulers who were itinerant also relied on bodyguards to escort them, to control highways, and to garrison fortifications. Mughal Emperors Akbar and Humayun both had numerous Persian nobles in their personal entourages. Bodyguards sometimes threatened imperial stability, however, as when palace *coups d'état* were periodically launched by the janissaries housed in the Ottoman sultan's Topkapı Palace in Istanbul. Princes and regional nobles imitated larger monarchies by creating their own elaborate household arsenals. Immediately after his accession, Elector Christian I of Saxony (1586–91) began building a *Neuer Stall* (or New Stable) to provide an extensive military complex complete with armory, stables, and jousting yard.[16]

Regional nobles formed clienteles of noble followers who provided political and military support, as well as social and cultural status. Warrior elites relied heavily on military entourages that included bodyguards, armed noble companions, and cavalry forces. During periods of warfare, nobles recruited infantry companies composed of peasants from their *seigneuries* and urban residents of nearby towns. Military officers personally distributed pay and rations to their personal entourages and troops. Some powerful regional nobles could raise entire field armies through their clientage networks.

The relationships between noble patrons and their clients were complex and constantly negotiated. Some historians propose distinguishing between the *grands* (magnates) and a *noblesse seconde* composed of provincial nobles who held considerable rank and titles.[17] Yet, such distinctions are misleading, since nobles arguably had strong self-identities defined by their specific noble ranks and their precise placements within precedence order in every social, political, and military activity.

The relationship of noble clienteles to dynastic states is also incredibly complicated. Most warrior nobles served as military and administrative officeholders, often holding multiple offices simultaneously. Nobles purchased venal offices that could be transferred to family members, associating clientage and lineage with military officeholding. Historians of absolutism have argued that hierarchical arrangements of *fidelités* (loyalties) structured nobles' engagement in royal service, but more recent research has seriously challenged statist attempts to order noble loyalties.[18] Noble intermediaries conducted politics and negotiated with state institutions through a "patron-broker-client relationship."[19] Kristen Neuschel demonstrates that nobles could express "episodic" loyalties, easily engaging and disengaging their honor at different times.[20] Some rulers did attempt to order their elites into hierarchical arrangements of noble ranks. King Erik XIV of Sweden, for example, introduced new titles in 1563, but could not restructure the entire Swedish nobility. New titles and offices that nobles acquired through inheritance, marriage, land sales, partitions, and rewards constantly altered the relative positions between noble individuals and families.

Familial and Clientage Violence

Nobles and their armed entourages often engaged in revenge killing through vendettas and feuds, linking individual and collective violence. Although the concept of feuding tends to be associated with medieval nobles, early modern military elites and their clients frequently utilized dueling, assassination, and multiple murder in pervasive noble violence that marked local communities.

Vendetta and feuding

Interfamilial violence between military elites has often been described as feuding or vendetta. Feuds can be considered as hostile relationships between groups involving relatively limited reciprocal exchanges of violence acts, which were governed by collective norms and by a principle of collective liability.[21] Similar approaches have revealed numerous cases of noble vengeance and feuding in Italy, France, Germany, Ireland, and England. Highland clans famously feuded over land disputes, marriage promises, and local politics, but other Scottish clans clashed in the Lowlands and the Border regions of Scotland.[22]

Clan feuding and vendetta violence seem to have been prevalent in many societies around the world in the sixteenth century. The Safavid prince Hamza Mīrzā was stabbed to death in his sleep in 1586 in an act of clan violence. One scholar analyzes the social response to the killing, arguing that "Iskandar Beg-i Munshī treated the assassination of Hamza Mīrzā less as a crime to be adjudicated in a court of law, and more as an act governed by a personal code of retribution for wrongs done."[23] In another case, Bir Singh Dev, a Rajput prince, orchestrated the assassination of Abul Fazl in northern India in 1595. Bir Singh became a powerful regional authority within the Mughal Empire, but his son rebelled against Shah Jahan and was killed when he fled into the neighboring kingdom of Chanda.[24]

The Savorgnan-Della Torre rivalry in the Friuli region of Venice's *terraferma* empire is one of the best documented cases of vendetta. Antonio Savorgnan, a minor noble, led a political group known as the Zambarlani and gained significant influence in Friuli through his military service and leadership of the regional peasant militia against the Holy Roman Empire. Savorgnan's increasing power produced tensions between his Zambarlani supporters and the Strumieri noble families, who were well established in the Friuli countryside. Alvise Della Torre, leader of the Strumieri, maintained connections with Habsburgs and seems to have been involved in pro-Imperial politics. Savorgnan and Delle Torre both attracted numerous *bravi*, young armed nobles, to serve in their entourages. Attempts to promote peace brought members of the two rival factions together for a banquet in Udine during Carnival celebrations in 1511.

Early in the morning of Fat Thursday, alarm bells rang and Savorgnan's militia rushed out of Udine, expecting an Imperial attack. When Savorgnan's militia found nothing, they returned to the city and were met by an excited crowd of supporters, who then marched to the

Della Torre *palazzo* (noble residence) and broke into the building. The angry crowd, perhaps directed by Savorgnan, attacked Della Torre family members and their Strumieri noble allies. Savorgnan's "dog pack" – a group of *bravi* and professional soldiers – seems to have been particularly vicious, murdering dozens of nobles and mutilating their corpses. Carnivalesque culture emphasized corpulent bodies, violent images, and transgressive practices. Butchery, dismemberment, gluttony, and drunkenness during Carnival all contributed to the forms of killing and mutilation that the Zambarlani used during what became known as the Cruel Carnival massacre.[25]

As news of the massacre in Udine circulated, violence spread to the Friuli countryside. Peasants and militiamen attacked Strumieri castles across the region. Savorgnan's control over Friuli did not last long, however, as renewed Habsburg invasions and warfare compromised his political position in the region and forced him to flee into Imperial territories.

Members of the Della Torre family and their Strumieri allies who survived this massive wave of violence regrouped, and then engaged in a series of revenge killings against their Zambarlani enemies. A band of Strumieri tracked down Antonio Savorgnan in an Austrian town and stabbed him to death in a church cemetery. With the death of Savorngan, the Zambarlani coalition quickly collapsed and the Della Torre family gradually resumed its place of prominence in Friuli society. Yet, descendants of the Savorgnan, Della Torre, and Colloredo noblemen who had been involved in the vendetta violence in 1511–12 continued to engage in revenge killings through a new series of assassinations and duels in the 1540s and 1550s.

Luigi da Porto, a nephew of Antonio Savorgnan, later transformed his experiences of the Savorgan–Della Torre vendetta and the Cruel Carnival massacre into a *novella* entitled *Giulietta e Romeo*, moving the setting for his tale of a love affair and vendetta to the city of Verona. This *novella* seems to have been a source for Shakespeare's beloved *Romeo and Juliet*, probably the most famous of all vendetta stories. Shakespeare sets the scene in the play's prologue:

> Two households, both alike in dignity,
>   In fair Verona, where we lay our scene,
> From ancient grudge break to new mutiny,
>   Where civil blood makes civil hands unclean.[26]

Shakespeare's treatment of vendetta focuses on two noble families embroiled in perpetual violence, as bands of young noblemen prowl the streets and squares of Verona, ready to draw their swords at the slightest provocation. The play includes a series of group fights and ambushes, which are often described as one-on-one informal duels.

Early modern societies attempted to manage vendetta violence by banishing nobles who committed murder or other serious personal crimes. Venetian nobles who were banished could often simply migrate temporarily to colonies in the Venetian *stato da mar* or to the Venetian community in Istanbul until they could obtain permission to return to Venice.[27] Other banished warrior nobles migrated from court to court in Europe offering their military services. Amerindians may have allowed banished warriors to join other tribes. Iroquois "mourning war" in the Great Lakes region allowed for the adoption of some warrior captives after a period of torture and assimilation. Banishment did not always alleviate violence, however, since nobles were commonly able to return after a period and carry out reprisals for old grudges.

Dueling and ritualized violence

Individual nobles often engaged in personal violence beyond the bounds of vendettas and familial conflicts. A new dueling culture gradually replaced vendetta practices in the sixteenth century. Judicial duels, formal trials by combat, had previously been sanctioned by medieval law courts, but were progressively outlawed in the late fifteenth and early sixteenth centuries. The last judicial duel in France occurred in 1547, when François de Vivonne, seigneur de La Châtaigneraye, fought against Guy Chabot, comte de Jarnac, in the presence of King Henri II. Even as trials by combat were banned, unsanctioned personal combats were proliferating among warrior nobles as dueling cultures developed in many areas.[28]

The *rapier*, a narrow sword developed in Italy in the sixteenth century, spawned a dueling craze across Europe in the mid-sixteenth and seventeenth centuries. The *rapier* emerged as a specific weapon with its own material culture that transformed dueling completely. Complex steel weapons technologies and artisanal industries permitted the production of this lightweight, sharp, but durable sword – which could be used for slashing, thrusting, and piercing. The *rapier* fulfilled warrior nobles' needs for self-protection and their desires to display wealth and distinction, but was not useful for battlefield or siege combat. *Rapiers* were not considered appropriate for military uses, but they represented perfect weapons for personal protection in urban environments, since they were lightweight and razor sharp.

European noblemen embraced this weapon in the mid-sixteenth century, wearing *rapiers* everywhere they traveled.

Sixteenth-century *maîtres d'armes*, or weapons masters, became "artisans of violence," diffusing fencing skills and the material culture of the new *rapiers* as key aspects of noblemen's physical and moral education. Young nobles attended colleges and academies for an education in mathematics, philosophy, and history, as well as training in dancing, horse-riding, and fencing. By the mid-sixteenth century, Italian *maîtres d'armes* were opening their own academies in cities across Europe, teaching fencing and encouraging the defense of honor through dueling.[29]

The organization of duels was sharply distinguished from the previous judicial combats. Individual nobles might challenge each other to duel over a perceived insult, but they often fought group combats accompanied by members of their noble entourages. François Billacois's classic study presents dueling as a "total social phenomenon" which represents a "touchstone" for a broader honor code throughout all of French society.[30] More recent histories of dueling stress the diverse political and social motivations for personal combats. For example, Spanish nobles' challenges seem to have involved evaluations of credit, not just an honor code. Disputes over debt repayment and fiscal reputation fused with concerns over honor, prompting duels among Spanish nobles.[31] Demobilized military officers, unemployed soldiers, and career duelists sought to join combats in urban areas. Such career duelists loitered in popular dueling locations, such as the Pont au Change in Paris, waiting to be recruited as seconds for group duels.

Dueling with *rapiers* spread across European societies and colonial settlements in the Americas, Africa, South Asia, and Southeast Asia, but ritualized dueling practices also emerged independently in several early modern societies. Anthropologists have examined challenges to honor and personal violence in clan and tribal societies. Bedouin heads of households apparently wielded power to kill any of their dependents who dishonored them. Personal violence between Arab elites in North African societies could resemble duels. West African elites also participated in ritualistic single combats, even if their practices differed.

The *samurai* warriors in early modern Japan engaged in dueling with elegant swords known as *katana*. *Samurai* fought armed encounters throughout the *Sengoku* (Warring States) period, but would also continue to duel well after the unification of Japan, perhaps using more ritualized forms of personal combat. Tokugawa-era *shoguns* outlawed firearms, reinforcing Japanese *samurais*' identification with the sword. Miyamoto Musashi, a consummate seventeenth-century duelist, provided advice on swordsmanship and martial behavior in his treatise *The Book of the Five Rings*. Musashi engaged in 66 duels, most famously fighting against a *samurai* named Ganryu: "Musashi killed him with a single blow of his wooden sword. It was faster than lightning, quicker than thunder."[32] On the basis of his own dueling experience, Musashi recommended aggressive attack in personal combat, saying: "Think only of your opponent's dying." Yagyu Munenori, son of a swordsmaster for Tokugawa Ieyasu, wrote another treatise on martial arts, applying Zen Buddhism to the practice of swordsmanship.

Some forms of cross-cultural dueling may have existed in the early modern world. Theories of a pan-Mediterranean honor have proposed that members of societies rimming the Mediterranean Sea shared common notions of honor and shame that governed interpersonal violence. Mediterranean masculinity supposedly involved hot-headed displays of violence at any insult in order to avoid feminizing shame. These theories have been criticized, however, for perpetuating stereotypes of Mediterranean peoples and for positing a Mediterranean cultural unity that never really existed.[33] Officers and soldiers in some early modern armies who fought each other regularly seem to have developed cross-cultural practices of dueling.

Dueling was not popular everywhere, however. Very few duels seem to have been fought in early modern England, with only 62 documented between 1580 and 1620.[34] Perhaps this anomaly resulted from the late arrival of the *rapier* and Italian fencing masters in England. Restraint also seems to have been particularly valued in English noble culture. When Gilbert Talbot, seventh earl of Shrewsbury, challenged his brother Edward to a duel in 1594, Edward refused to fight him.[35] Russian noblemen did not adopt European dueling practices until the late seventeenth century. Even then, Russian elites seem to have largely regarded dueling as an undesirable foreign import.[36] These societies appear to have been exceptions, however, as dueling became popular among nobles elsewhere, through association with honor and arms.

Noble Warfare

Warrior nobles, their clienteles, and military forces often engaged in noble revolts and civil conflicts during the early modern period. Historians have sometimes described localized noble conflicts as "private wars," but this term suggests individual feuding for purely private interests. The concept of "personal warfare" is useful in suggesting the conflation of public and private motivations in noble participation in civil warfare in the sixteenth and seventeenth centuries.

Noble revolts and personal warfare

Nobles' armed service in dynastic armies and political culture intersected with their personal agendas and aims during civil conflicts. Arlette Jouanna's groundbreaking study of noble violence, *Le Devoir de révolte*, contends that a "duty of revolt" motivated French nobles to take up arms in defense of constitutional principle of mixed monarchy.[37] My own research finds that southern French nobles instead pursued various religious and political causes within a "culture of revolt." I argue that "the king wielded a brand of revolt, designating disorderly opponents as guilty of *lèse-majesté*, but nobles could appropriate the king's authority to label their own rivals as 'quarrelsome,' 'seditious,' 'criminals,' and 'rebels.'"[38]

In many countries, noble titles and offices were expanding in the sixteenth century. An "inflation of titles" seems to have occurred, as monarchs granted new noble titles especially at the elevated ranks of dukes, marquises, and counts. In Spain, the number of noble titles quadrupled between 1506 and 1630, creating tensions among the Spanish nobility, or *hidalgos*.[39] Venal offices also created openings for provincial nobles to ascend in rank, as well as for non-nobles to enter the nobility. The expansion of nobilities may have averted widespread social conflicts as ambitious individuals took advantage of these new opportunities, but the processes also prompted some nobles to join rebellions in defense of their presumably eroding privileges.

The early modern Ottoman Empire has frequently been depicted as a stable multicultural society characterized by relative peace and religious tolerance, yet it also experienced periods of rebellion and civil warfare. Ottoman sultans attempted to provide social stability through an imperial system of rule that allowed for relative local autonomy and a *timar* system of landholding. Provincial governors, with titles of *pasha* or *bey*, held their positions for several years and then were rotated to new provinces. When sultans died or broader civil conflicts erupted, provincial governors could raise *timariot* forces and commit them to political struggles within the empire. Janissary commanders and soldiers based in garrisons could sometimes organize revolts along with local inhabitants who had grievances against the governors and *qadis* (judges) who were often seen as agents of a distant imperial power and as outsiders to communities.

Ottoman *sipahis* waged a more constant form of personal warfare on the military frontiers in the Balkans. Although some *sipahis* served in the six heavy cavalry units that were retained permanently and maintained in barracks in Istanbul, the vast majority of the *sipahis* were provincial holders of *timar* land grants in newly conquered territories. "In 1525 there were 10,688 *timar*-holding *sipahis* in the European side of the Empire, and 17,200 in Asia Minor, Aleppo, and Damascus." Protecting these *timar* holdings frequently led *sipahis* to engage in *gazi* warfare on borderlands with "infidel" Christians, sometimes against the desires of their sultans. Ottoman records from the 1590s show that "amid the inflation and shortages, the *sipahis* of Anatolia struggled to outfit their contingents for military service. Out of exasperation, many simply plundered or extorted from villagers." The *sancak beys*, regional military commanders, often struggled to keep order and prevent *sipahis* from rebelling.[40] Ottoman succession conflicts resulted in periods of broader civil warfare, as *sipahis* backed opposing claimants to authority.

Dissatisfied nobles could abandon their prince and pass between sovereign territories as members of a transnational nobility. Cadet branches of the Montmorency, Bourbon, Savoie, and Lorraine dynasties occupied privileged positions based on their princely potential to be sovereign. Jonathan Spangler argues that, "It was this potential for sovereignty that gave European princes their immunity, attracted clients hoping for favour from sovereigns, and necessitated a form of family foreign policy sometimes at variance with the monarchs they served."[41] Nobles who participated in failed revolts often had to seek refuge abroad, becoming exiles who then had to negotiate their amnesty or take up service with another ruler. Exiled nobles would sometimes attempt to foment noble revolts in their estranged countries, creating opportunities for them to return.

Noble elites could sometimes rise to princely power through revolt. The Afghan noble Sher Khan Sur rebelled against the Mughal Emperor Humayun in the 1530s, seizing Bengal. The rebellious Afghans routed the Mughal army at the battle of Chausa in June 1539, nearly capturing Humayun himself. This victory allowed Sher Khan Sur to assume the princely title of Sher Shah on the battlefield. Emperor Humayun fled into exile – eventually seeking refuge in Persia – while Sher Shah effectively ruled northern India from Agra until his death in 1545, when his son inherited the new dynastic title.[42] Such cases show the potential for powerful early modern nobles to raise large armies and to wage civil warfare.

Warring daimyō *in* Sengoku *Japan*

Warrior elites dominated Japan during the *Sengoku* period from 1467 to 1615, providing a fascinating case of early modern noble warfare. Japan became increasingly divided following the Ōnin War (1467–77), as the political instability in the *shoguns' bakufu* (military government) produced fragmentation. Street fighting occurred in Kyoto between supporters of two rival *shoguns* in the 1520s and 1530s. The eroding authority of the *shoguns* allowed regional *daimyō* to establish control over their *han* (provinces), administering their cities and villages as semi-autonomous states. Individual *daimyō* and their allies engaged in personal wars in the dozens of *han* across Japan during the most sustained fighting of the civil wars from the 1530s to the 1580s.

Through wars of conquest and alliances, certain *daimyō* succeeded in expanding their authority beyond their individual provinces. The Imagawa clan established control over the contiguous provinces of Suruga and Tōtōmi in part by linking tax authority and military service. The Takeda clan raised powerful cavalry forces and *samurai* in its province of Kai, allowing Takeda Shingen to launch successive invasions of the province of Shinano, which was defended by the Murakami clan and their allies the Uesugi of the neighboring Echigo province. The armies of Takeda Shingen and Uesugi Kenshin fought a series of battles at Kawanakajima between 1553 and 1564 that were celebrated in *samurai* culture for their brilliant tactics and courageous feats.

As Takeda Shingen could not eliminate his rival, he shifted his ambitions toward central Japan at a time when the practices of *Sengoku* warfare were changing. Takeda Shingen crafted alliances with other *daimyō*, notably Hōjō Ujiyasu and Imagawa Yoshimoto, in the 1550s. The so-called *samurai* armies had always employed a mixture of troop types and armaments, but many *daimyō* were now fielding larger armies that included numerous units of disciplined infantry units of *ashigaru*. Portuguese merchants had begun trading arquebuses and other firearms in Japan in the 1540s and they were becoming more common a decade later.[43]

Oda Nobunaga assumed leadership of a branch of the feuding Oda clan in 1551 and began consolidating control over the fractious province of Owari through ruthless raids and attacks. Nobunaga's forces ambushed a large Imagawa army in 1560 and killed its commander, Imagawa Yoshimoto. Nobunaga brokered temporary alliances with Takeda Shingen and Tokugawa Ieyasu in order to follow up his victory over Imagawa. Nobunaga seized Kyoto and installed a new *shogun* in 1568. Oda Nobunaga attracted numerous loyal followers among the *daimyō*, such as Toyotomi Hideyoshi.[44]

Powerful *daimyō* built impressive stone fortifications during the civil wars, creating the golden age of Japanese castle-building. Thousands of castles and fortified cities were constructed during the sixteenth century, many of them on isolated hills and mountains that allowed small garrisons to control roads and mountain passes. Oda Nobunaga and other ascendant *daimyō* constructed castles for their key *daimyō* supporters. Castles played a significant role in the fighting during the *Sengoku* period, but surprise attacks and assaults seem to have been more common than formal sieges.

The Oda and Takeda clans fought for control of central Japan between 1573 and 1582. Takeda Shingen was killed at a siege in 1573, but the Takeda clan remained strong under his son Katsuyori. Oda Nobunaga armed 3,000 his *ashigaru* troops with arquebuses – the largest firearms force yet seen in Japan – and defeated the Takeda clan at the battle of Nagashino in 1575 and slowly overwhelmed the Takeda in successive campaigns. Takeda Katsuyori committed ritual suicide following a final defeat in 1582. *Sengoku* politics remained volatile, however, with shifting alliances and all too common betrayals. Oda Nobunaga had conquered approximately a third of Japan when he was murdered by one of his own followers in 1582.

Noble Attitudes Toward Violence

Princes, courtiers, and noble writers promoted new ideals of noble behavior during the sixteenth century. Administrative and judicial authorities attempted to adjudicate noble disputes and to limit noble violence. Noble attitudes to violence gradually changed in response to these developments.

Warrior nobles and civilité

Courtly literature and treatises on honor by Baldassare Castiglione, Stefano Guazzo, Giovanni Della Casa, and others presented new ideals for noblemen at princely courts. Castiglione famously used the term *sprezzatura* to refer to the combination of manliness, virtue, merit, and grace required of a perfect courtier. Italian courtly literature influenced noble culture throughout Europe, since Italian continued to operate as the language of humanism and refined noble culture during the sixteenth century.

Norbert Elias theorizes that royal courts in Europe fostered a "civilizing process" to promote new manners within society and to subordinate nobles to state power. Elias envisions a "courtization of warriors" as a key mechanism in the "taming and preserving [of] the nobility" and the development of *civilité*, a social ideal that would gradually spread from the royal courts throughout European societies.[45] Historians such as Ellery Schalk have applied Elias's model, envisioning nobles as becoming progressively civilized by court culture and state institutions during this period.[46] Some historians have suggested that cultural and social changes may have curbed noble violence. Antonio Massa condemned the violence of dueling in his *Against the Use of the Duel* (1555), one of the first in a wave of publications criticizing dueling in the mid-sixteenth century. Although dueling culture remained pervasive, some nobles apparently refused to respond to insults and challenges. The popularity of neo-stoicism furthered such notions of self-control in the late sixteenth and early seventeenth centuries, perhaps buttressing notions of *civilité*.

This interpretation of a "civilizing process" has been sharply challenged by historians – including myself – who question whether *civilité* really pacified European nobles.[47] Early modern court culture actively promoted martial ideals and military displays that provided nobles with opportunities to enact militant roles even in peacetime. Dynastic states sponsored increasingly elaborate and theatrical expressions of violence, such as firearms displays, artillery salutes, horse ballets, cavalry carrousels, and military exercises.[48] Instead of disarming nobles, *civilité* seems to have encouraged expressions of noble honor and militant action.

Honor and the profession of arms

Although some historians, following Elias, have seen courtly literature as part of a "civilizing process," courtly literature and treatises often promoted arms training and fencing. Girolamo Muzio's treatise, *The Duel* (1550), drew directly on courtly literature in providing elaborate rules for the conduct of dueling. Such treatises formalized dueling practices, but also encouraged dueling culture among nobles. The arms training and practices popularized by the *maîtres d'armes* and their noble students transformed honor culture in complex ways.

Noble culture associated the notions of an *honnête homme*, or honorable man, directly with the profession of arms. Nicolas Faret wrote that "Since every man has to choose a profession…it seems to me that there is none more honorable or more essential to a gentleman than that of arms."[49] French treatises on honor and nobility became influential in the late sixteenth and early seventeenth centuries, diffusing bellicose ideals of the profession of arms. Many *maîtres d'armes* and military academies went well beyond fencing, offering weapons training and military education useful for budding military officers. Antoine de Pluvinel, a noted French academy master of the mid-seventeenth century, provided nobles with instruction on horseriding, later publishing his advice as *Instruction du roy en l'exercice de monter à cheval* (1666), which stressed order and control in managing horses and using violence.[50]

Noble honor distinguished some forms of violence, including dueling, as appropriate for noblemen, relegating other forms of violence to commoners. Personal violence was hardly confined to noblemen, of course, and many non-nobles engaged in ritual forms of personal violence using weapons other than *rapiers*. Greek and Italian peasants preferred knife-fighting, while workers in some other societies engaged in fistfights. Spanish non-noble settlers in New Spain seem to have routinely come to blows over disputes and debts. The lines between noble and non-noble personal violence could still be blurred, as with rank-and-file soldiers who readily participated in dueling.

State attempts to limit noble violence

Dynastic rulers and judicial authorities in many areas attempted to ban dueling and to limit noble violence. In Germany, feuding was already associated with lawlessness in the Carolina code of 1530, but by that time German nobles were engaging in religious violence that grew out of the Reformation movements. Magistrates in Italian city-states tried to control dueling by banning challenges and banishing duelists who killed their opponents. The Venetian Council of Ten issued new laws in the 1540s prohibiting duels and punishing those who issued written challenges with banishment. In Italy, nobles sometimes issued formal challenges by posting *cartelli di sfida*, written provocations to their adversaries, in public spaces. The *cartelli* were increasingly printed documents, which sometimes elicited responses from challenged nobles.

Litigation could provide opportunities for nobles to respond to challenges without a direct recourse to violence, but also had the potential to fuel further dueling. The use of printed *cartelli di sfida* resulted in exchanges of taunts in pamphlets rather than duels. A dispute between Francesco Varese and Count Carlo Thiene in Florence in 1568 resulted in a flurry of challenges and booklets between the two nobles, rather than any actual violence.[51] Military service may have declined among Italian nobles during the seventeenth century, perhaps weakening dueling culture.[52]

Henri IV and Louis XIII repeatedly issued edicts against dueling in France, but they seem to have only rarely been enforced. The most famous example of a trial for dueling in France involved the notorious duelist François de Montmorency, comte de Bouteville, who was found guilty of killing an opponent in the Place Royale (today known as Place des Vosges) in Paris and executed in 1627. Despite such efforts, French nobles and military officers continued to engage in duels, but often at night and in secluded sites rather than in prominent urban spaces.

The Court of Chivalry in England began to consider cases of insults and challenges in the early seventeenth century, which seems to have led to a reduction in dueling. When William Viscount Monson accused Robert Welch esquire of cheating at a game of cards in 1640, Welch reacted angrily and challenged Monson to a duel. Monson refused to take up the challenge, however, and instead filed a complaint against Welch at the Court of Chivalry.[53]

Some dynastic states attempted to limit noble involvement in revolts by including nobles in state militaries and administrations. Chinese elites served in a military system managed by a professionalized bureaucracy. In Europe, some states gradually expanded the notion of noble councilors and developed service nobilities to regularize noble administrative and military service. In mid-seventeenth-century Sweden, "half of all adult noblemen were in Crown service, two-thirds in the armed forces, the rest in the civil and judicial bureaucracies."[54] Peter the Great would later establish a table of ranks in an attempt to order noble royal service within the Russian Empire.

Conclusion

Despite dynastic states' attempts to halt noble revolts, many elites still articulated warrior identities and pursued militant activities. Violence remained popular among nobles and seems to have been associated with various revivals of chivalric culture in European societies. Nobles continued to engage in diverse forms of violence well into the seventeenth century, affecting their local communities and broader civil society.

Dueling and armed encounters remained part of everyday life during the Thirty Years War, when interpersonal violence among officers and soldiers often had political motivations and social implications. A drinking session in 1633 involving Lieutenant Colonel Johann Wachmeister, commander of the Swedish garrison at Nördlingen, and the occupied city's own captain of the guard turned into a violent brawl. The captain of the guard was evidently badly beaten after having made a toast that implied support of the Imperialist cause, enraging the Swedish Lieutenant Colonel. Meanwhile, Wachmeister claimed to have been stabbed, leading to an investigation of the officers' opposing charges. When the municipal leaders of Nördlingen refused to prosecute the captain, Wachmeister declared a feud against the entire city. The circumstances of war prevented the aggrieved Lieutenant Colonel from carrying out his threat, however.[55]

This episode is a reminder that everyday interactions involving nobles had the potential to erupt in violence. Noble participation in revolts would gradually decline as armies professionalized in the seventeenth century, leading nobles to adopt roles as commissioned military officers. Dueling practices would continue to change over time, but many nobles continued to engage in duels throughout the early modern period.[56]

6

Sectarian Violence and Religious Warfare, 1560s–1640s

Enthusiasm for the Calvinist Reform swept through France in the 1550s, prompting conversions of perhaps a third of the French nobles and mass conversions at many villages and towns in southern France. Perhaps 10 percent of France's population of 16 million people had embraced Calvinism by the end of the 1550s. The stunning growth of Calvinism in France produced serious social tensions, especially over clandestine Reformed worship services, which were illegal. Alarmed Catholics pressed for prosecutions of Calvinist ministers and investigations of the Huguenots, as adherents of the "so-called Reformed religion" quickly became known.

The tragic death of King Henri II following a jousting accident in 1559 produced extreme political instability within the religiously divided kingdom. Henri II's widow, Caterina de' Medici, became regent for a young and sickly François II, who would die later that year. A judge in the parlement de Paris, the pre-eminent judicial body in France, was found guilty of heresy and burned to death in front of the Hôtel de Ville, the Paris city hall. Many Calvinists seem to have believed that there was a real prospect of convincing the young king to convert and to instigate a complete Reformation of the kingdom. When an assembly of Huguenot nobles and their followers at Amboise was discovered in March 1560, they claimed that they merely wanted to present a confession of faith to the king. They were treated as conspirators, however, and their leaders were executed.

After François II died in December 1560 and an 11-year-old Charles IX ascended to the throne, the rivalries between Catholic and Reformed nobles created severe tensions at the Valois royal court.

François de Lorraine, duc de Guise, promoted policies to defend Catholicism within the kingdom, allying with Anne de Montmorency, duc de Montmorency, in a "triumvirate" along with the maréchal de Saint-André. Gaspard de Châtillon-Coligny, who was admiral de France and a fervent Calvinist, agitated for protections for his Reformed brethren. Caterina de' Medici and the Chancellor Michel de L'Hôpital sought to avoid conflict, but the kingdom soon descended into a series of chaotic religious wars that would devastate France for decades.

This chapter examines the dynamics of religious warfare and sectarian violence during the late sixteenth and early seventeenth centuries. The spiritual renewal movements and social conflicts, discussed above in chapter 3, gave way to more organized religious wars, in which noble elites and dynastic states articulated and advanced distinct religio-political agendas. Military commanders and their armies often supported confessional (or sectarian) causes and instituted religious reform programs in areas they controlled. Religion permeated diverse aspects of military activity throughout this period of pervasive religious warfare in France, the Netherlands, Germany, the Islamic world, and parts of Asia.

French Wars of Religion, 1562–1629

The outbreak of religious war in France signaled a new form of conflict, involving confessional causes and brutal violence in the name of God. The French Wars of Religion would become one of the most vicious and sustained religious wars in the early modern world.

Religious warfare in France, 1562–1571

Religious tensions grew throughout France as Calvinists occupied community churches and cleansed them of what they regarded as idolatrous images and objects. Catholics were horrified by this wave of iconoclasm, which they considered highly offensive to their faith and to God. In the vacuum of royal authority, emboldened Calvinists took control of some towns and held clandestine worship services across much of France. When the duc de Guise discovered one such service occurring in a barn on his lands in 1562, he led his bodyguard to suppress the service, resulting in the Massacre of Vassy. Calvinist nobles and towns responded by mobilizing military forces, instigating the first in a series of religious wars that would last from 1562 until 1629.

The early conflict in France revolved around control of urban centers and their religious sites in Paris and other major cities. The Huguenots established a stronghold at Orléans, and then advanced to threaten Paris. The main royal army soon blockaded the Huguenot base of Orléans and took Blois, before marching on to protect Paris and pursue the Huguenot army. The opposing armies met at Dreux and fought a bloody pitched battle that left thousands dead. The royal army won a crucial victory that buttressed the Catholic cause, but Anne de Montmorency, the royalist commander, was captured. The Huguenots were demoralized by their defeat and by the capture of their leader, Louis de Bourbon, prince de Condé. The duc de Guise, a dedicated Catholic, took control of the royal army and advanced to Orléans to transform the blockade into a full-scale siege of the Huguenot city. A Huguenot militant assassinated Guise in February 1563, throwing the royalist military leadership into chaos and prompting Caterina de' Medici to negotiate the peace of Amboise with the prince de Condé.

Charles IX and Caterina de' Medici conducted a royal tour of France in 1564–66 in an attempt to pacify the kingdom, but the limited protections granted to Calvinists were unpopular among Catholics. Localized conflicts between opposing confessional communities continued to erupt. Huguenot nobles launched a surprise cavalry attack on the royal entourage at Meaux in 1567, attempting to capture the king and convince him to convert to Calvinism. Charles IX escaped, however, and outraged Catholics mobilized to oppose the Huguenot militants as a second religious war engulfed France. The constable de Montmorency was killed at the indecisive battle of Saint-Denis in 1567, but conflict continued.

Foreign military forces increasingly intervened in the French Wars of Religion, with Swiss, Italian, Flemish, German, and English contingents serving to aid their co-religionists. Huguenots joined with German Protestant forces under Johan Casimir, Prince Palatine, in 1568. Royal forces attacked the Huguenot rear guard at Jarnac in March 1569, capturing the prince de Condé and executing him on the battlefield. The Huguenots nonetheless regrouped under the admiral de Coligny and besieged Poitiers. The main royal army fought a pitched battle at Moncontour in October 1569, breaking the Huguenot infantry. A royal siege of Saint-Jean d'Angély failed to overcome the Huguenot defenders, as Coligny, now the main Huguenot commander, waged extensive campaigns in southern France. The royal family negotiated the peace of Saint-Germain in August 1570, which granted concessions to the Calvinists.[1]

Saint Bartholomew's Day Massacre, 1572

A tenuous peace settled over the kingdom as the royal family attempted to broker compromises between Catholics and Calvinists. As part of the Valois policy of concord, Caterina de' Medici arranged a marriage between Henri de Navarre, one of the leading Calvinist princes, and her daughter, Margaret de Valois. Lavish wedding festivities were planned for this royal wedding in Paris in summer 1572, but unease gripped the capital city. Paris was the largest city in France and a bastion of French Catholicism. The vast majority of the city's residents were Catholic, and the practice of Calvinism was banned within its walls. A series of troubling clashes within Paris had occurred in 1571 after Calvinists had been discovered conducting clandestine services in the heart of the city. Parisian Catholics had burned down one of the secret worship houses and erected a great cross celebrating their victory. The king tried to calm tensions by having the cross moved to the cemetery of the Innocents, but it continued to attract crowds of devout Catholics who prayed for the elimination of heresy in their midst. Catholics throughout the staunchly Catholic capital felt offended by the arrival of hundreds of Huguenot nobles and their entourages in preparation for the August 1572 wedding.

Nonetheless, the marriage was celebrated without incident in the cathedral of Notre-Dame in a seeming victory for the royal efforts at compromise. Two days after the wedding, admiral de Coligny rode through the streets of Paris, heading to the Louvre to meet with the royal family. Shots rang out and Coligny was wounded in an attempted assassination. Huguenot nobles rushed Coligny to a residence nearby and tended to his wounds. Rumors spread throughout Paris that Coligny was dead, that the royal family was behind the attack, that the Huguenots would take vengeance on the Parisian Catholics, that a Huguenot army was approaching to seize the city, and that the Huguenot nobles lodged in the palace would take the royal family hostage. In this climate of fear, the Valois family and the royal council met in the Louvre late in the night of August 23–24, 1572, taking a fateful decision to launch a pre-emptive strike against the Huguenot leadership.[2]

Early in the morning of August 24, the king's bodyguards began to break down the doors of the apartments in the Louvre where the Huguenot nobles were staying, murdering them in their bedrooms. The bodyguards butchered hundreds of Calvinist nobles and their attendants. Henri de Lorraine, duc de Guise, the son of the slain Catholic leader, led the bodyguards out of the Louvre palace down the streets to the residence housing the wounded Coligny. The soldiers broke into the house, murdered Coligny in his bed, and dumped his body out of the window onto the street below. A crowd had already gathered, attracted by the noisy murder or by the ringing of the bell in the nearby church of Saint-Germain d'Auxerrois, the conventional signal for an emergency that would prompt city residents to assemble in the city squares. The duc de Guise stood over Coligny's corpse as the king's bodyguards beheaded it, ritually enacting royal justice. The pre-emptive strike against the Huguenot leadership was now complete, and the king's bodyguards returned to the Louvre.

The Catholic crowd clearly understood that the king had finally acted to suppress the Huguenots and extirpate heresy. Parisians now mutilated Coligny's corpse and began to search for their heretic neighbors, transforming the violence into a much broader Saint Bartholomew's Day Massacre. The Parisian civic guards joined in the killing, and may have been instrumental in the urban violence and cruelty of the so-called "popular" massacre. The guardsmen from urban quarters, who had become radicalized in the years leading up to the massacre, seem to have been especially vicious in attacking Calvinists in their neighborhoods. One young Huguenot girl was allegedly dipped "stark naked in the blood of her massacred mother and father, with horrible threats that, if ever she became a Huguenot, the same would happen to her."[3] Other accounts of the violence relate stories of forced conversions and murders of Calvinists who refused to abjure. The brutal massacre lasted more than four days and resulted in 2,000–4,000 slain Huguenots. News of the massacre spread throughout France, prompting additional violence in provincial cities. The stunned and disorganized Huguenots attempted to organize their defenses, even as shocked Protestants throughout Europe deplored the horrific massacre.

Renewed religious warfare in France, 1573–1598

In the aftermath of the massacre, the Valois royal family decided to launch a campaign to stamp out Calvinist heresy throughout the kingdom. A vast royal army assembled in 1573 and marched to besiege the major Huguenot center of La Rochelle, a well-fortified port city on the Atlantic coast. Catholic troops maintained an intense bombardment of La Rochelle's bastions and assaulted the fortifications at great cost, but failed to break into the well-defended city. The Catholic siege of Sancerre during the same year became infamous for its atrocities. The royal family had to abandon its attempt to extirpate heresy, however, as the Catholic armies were exhausted. "Easy to begin, the civil wars were too difficult and expensive to fight to any clear conclusion," according to James B. Wood. "The result was military stalemate."[4] Charles IX died in 1574, leaving France deeply divided and confused, awaiting the return of Charles's brother Henri from Poland for his coronation.

Henri III had extensive military experience, having led royal armies against Huguenots during several of the campaigns over the previous decade. Huguenot military forces were disorganized, but received assistance from German Protestants and from Henri III's younger brother, François de Valois, duc d'Anjou, who decided to support the Huguenot cause. Henri III had to make accommodations with the Huguenots and seek to repair the divisions within the Valois royal family. The resulting peace in 1576 granted Calvinists significant privileges and numerous *places de sûreté*, or security towns, to ensure that the peace was implemented. Meanwhile, Henri III had married Louise de Lorraine in 1575, but the couple failed to produce an heir, leading to speculation about the future of Valois dynastic rule. When the duc d'Anjou unexpectedly died in 1584, the Calvinist Henri de Bourbon, roi de Navarre, suddenly emerged as the heir apparent.[5]

The prospect of a Calvinist heir to the throne galvanized the Catholic Leagues, which had already begun to spring up in Catholic communities across the realm. Catholic League militant opposition to Huguenot influence produced a series of complex religious wars involving three major politico-religious groups: Catholic Leaguers, Huguenots, and *politiques*. This last group represented a diverse assemblage of Catholic moderates and Calvinists who were willing to accept a Calvinist presence in France and some Reformed participation in the royal government. These conflicts are sometimes described as the War of the Three Henries, referring to three of the principal political and military leaders. Henri de Lorraine, duc de Guise, emerged as the chief of the Catholic Leagues. Henri de Bourbon, roi de Navarre, became the principal Huguenot military commander, who represented Calvinist hopes to complete the reform of the realm should he accede to the throne. King Henri III can hardly be described as a *politique*, yet he pursued shifting religio-political positions in an attempt to maintain the Valois dynasty's tenuous control of the monarchical government.

Catholic Leaguers protested in Paris during the Day of the Barricades in 1588, forcing the king to flee and leaving the capital city in control of the duc de Guise and his Leaguer supporters. The Day of the Barricades showed the radical popular dimensions of the Leaguer movement. Henri III sought refuge in the Loire valley and then called for a meeting of the Estates General, which assembled at Blois in October. During the lengthy political negotiations, Henri III became desperate and ordered his bodyguards to murder the duc de Guise and his brother, the Cardinal de Guise, in December 1588. The assassinations, which occurred in the king's own bedchambers at the château de Blois, shocked the French people and outraged Catholic Leaguers across the kingdom. In the wake of the failed Estates General meeting, Henri III retreated to Tours and allied with Henri de Navarre, forming a joint *politique*-Huguenot army to retake Paris. As the siege of Paris advanced in 1589, Jacques Clément, a Catholic friar, came to the royal headquarters at Saint-Cloud and asked to meet urgently with the king. Clément then pulled out a hidden knife and plunged it into the king's chest, assassinating Henri III and ending the Valois line.[6]

In the aftermath of the assassination of Henri III, the *politique*-Huguenot forces threatened to fragment and the siege of Paris was abandoned. Henri de Navarre now became Henri IV, an uncrowned king without a capital, whose rule was sharply contested by the Catholic League. Indeed, the Leaguers not only challenged Navarre's right to rule as a "heretic," but instead recognized Cardinal Charles de Bourbon as king, calling him Charles X. Spain intervened in the conflict, sending troops and financial support to the Catholic Leaguers. Henri IV's army defeated a Leaguer army under the duc de Mayenne in a major cavalry battle at Ivry in March 1590, paving the way for a new *politique*-Huguenot attempt to take Paris. Henri IV's army invested the capital city in April 1590 and the siege lines advanced throughout the summer until a Spanish relief army under the duke of Parma raised the siege in August. The would-be king Charles X died during the siege, however, weakening the politico-religious position of the Catholic League. Henri IV negotiated a settlement with Parisian municipal leaders and converted to Catholicism at Saint-Denis in 1593, allowing him to enter Paris. He then pursued a series of military campaigns against the remaining Leaguer forces, gradually receiving the capitulations of Leaguer nobles and cities.[7]

Peacemaking and the military collapse of the Huguenots

Negotiations between Henri IV, the Catholic Leaguers, and the Huguenots produced the Edict of Nantes in 1598. This religious peace was a complex legal document and pacificatory program, which met with widespread popular disapproval and resistance from judicial courts. The king's ministers and royal commissioners found it difficult to implement the peace within the confessionally divided kingdom. The Edict of Nantes thus shifted the character of the religious wars, rather than really ending them.[8]

Catholic towns and cities forbade or limited Reformed services, denying Calvinists permission to build their own temples within city walls. Former members of the Catholic League blended into a more diffuse Catholic *dévot* (devout) movement, whose members founded new monasteries, participated in civic devotions, and agitated to restore Catholicism throughout the kingdom. Jesuits and Capuchins initiated missionary campaigns across southern France to convert Huguenots. These efforts found some converts among prominent Calvinist nobles and began to erode the Huguenot military system of protectors.[9]

Meanwhile, Huguenot communities throughout southern France vigorously disputed the re-establishment of the Catholic Mass and devotional practices, as called for in the peace agreement. Huguenots continued to maintain numerous *places de sûreté*, whose fortifications permitted these towns to maintain Calvinist majorities and to block Catholic religious orders from preaching within their town walls. Popular violence and armed clashes occurred in mixed-confessional towns, while low-intensity conflict continued in rural regions, often coinciding with peasant revolts and noble rebellions.

The uneasy religious settlement broke down after the assassination of Henri IV in May 1610 by François Ravaillac. The political instability of the regency government for young Louis XIII contributed to the widespread religious and civil conflict that erupted in the mixed-confessional areas of southern France throughout the 1610s. Repeated violations of the Edict of Nantes and the Catholic military occupation of Béarn, with its mostly Huguenot population, prompted Huguenot communities to unite in mutual defense in a full-scale religious war from 1620 to 1622. Louis XIII led a predominantly Catholic royal army on a campaign to conquer Huguenot towns in 1621, but met stiff resistance at the siege of Montauban, which had to be abandoned. A new campaign the next year saw atrocious sacks of several Huguenot towns, but a lengthy siege of Montpellier led to negotiations to end the war.

The Peace of Montpellier failed to halt violence, however, and violations of the peace produced renewed fighting between 1625 and 1628. Multiple armies waged intensive siege and raiding warfare across southern France, while royal efforts eventually focused on besieging La Rochelle in 1627–28. A few remaining Huguenot towns in Languedoc went to war yet again in 1629, but resistance quickly collapsed after Catholic troops assaulted Privas and sacked the town. The Huguenot military cause collapsed and the surviving Calvinist nobles fled to the Netherlands, England, or Germany. The French Wars of Religion were finally over and France's identity as a Catholic country was secure.[10]

Dutch Revolt, 1566–1609

Religious reforms and conversions undermined Habsburg rule in the Netherlands by the mid-sixteenth century, creating another site for religious conflict. Many of the same aspects of religious warfare that characterized the ferocious wars in France would recur in the Netherlands: iconoclasm, confessional activism, military intervention, forced conversion, assassination, execution, siege, and massacre. But, the outcome of the Dutch Revolt would be very different.

Confessional turmoil in the Netherlands, 1566–1572

Antwerp and Amsterdam were major commercial and financial centers in the Burgundian Netherlands, which Charles V had inherited in 1519. Martin Luther's protest against the papacy had attracted significant support in the Netherlands, but the Habsburg judicial system suppressed this reform movement through execution and exile. Charles V divided the vast Habsburg Empire in 1555, placing his eldest son on the Spanish throne as Philip II, with power over the Spanish Netherlands. Philip II departed for Madrid and subsequently governed the Netherlands as an absent ruler through his regent, Margaret of Parma.

Calvinist ministers, including many Dutch exiles in towns like Emden in Germany, began to spread evangelical reform in the Netherlands in the 1540s and 1550s.[11] By the 1560s, Dutch communities were organizing their own clandestine Reformed churches and pressing for a Calvinist reform. King Philip II initiated a plan to establish three archbishoprics and fourteen new bishoprics in the Netherlands to counter the growth of Calvinism and establish an effective Catholic reform in the Dutch provinces. A number of Dutch nobles opposed the new bishoprics and openly supported Calvinist calls for a relaxation of the anti-heresy laws in 1565. Eager Calvinist ministers launched an audacious campaign of evangelical hedge-preaching to large crowds in fields and public spaces. Many Calvinist ministers and their followers began to engage in widespread iconoclasm, cleansing churches across the Netherlands in what became known as the Icono-clastic Fury of 1566.

Philip II responded to news of this blasphemous activity with massive force, sending Fernando Álvarez de Toledo, duke of Alba, to the Netherlands along with an army composed of 10,000 veteran soldiers from Italy, who were organized in several *tercios* and desig-nated as the Army of Flanders. Alba's troops marched from Milan across the Alps and along the Spanish Road through Imperial terri-tories to reach the Netherlands. When the army arrived, the duke of Alba established himself as military governor of the Netherlands and cracked down on disorder. He instituted the Council of Troubles, a special judicial court to deal with disorder and heresy. This court prosecuted the counts of Hornes and Egmont, who had supported the Calvinists, sentencing them both to be beheaded in 1568. The Council of Troubles prosecuted Calvinists for heresy and iconoclasm, condemning 10,000 people to death, but very few people were actu-ally executed, since 90 percent of the accused were exiles tried *in absentia*. The duke of Alba implemented the stalled episcopal reforms, levied new taxes, and disrupted noble opposition through highly coer-cive means that were very unpopular. A contemporary propaganda woodcut depicted the duke as a bloody tyrant in league with the devil. A 1571 pamphlet accused him of atrocities, saying that "he filled the gallows and Gibbets full of the poor people...He destroyed many with the sword, he burnt many alive with a small fire, he beheaded many before their causes were pleaded."[12]

Religious warfare in the Netherlands, 1572–1590

Dutch Reformed nobles began to organize military opposition to the duke of Alba, and in the spring of 1572 a group of exiled Calvinists and privateers took control of several coastal cities in the northern Netherlands, igniting religious warfare. William I, Prince of Orange emerged as a key leader of the Calvinist cause. The duke of Alba's army waged a deliberate campaign of sieges against rebellious cities in the fall of 1572, massacring defenders who resisted at Zutphen and Naarden and terrifying other towns into submission. The Spanish besieged Haarlem in December, but the town's citizens and garrison resisted, constructing hasty defensive fortifications. As the siege dragged on, a Spanish captain described the suffering of the soldiers in the trench lines, saying that "it is amazing that there is no one to inform the king of the dreadful state in which things are...The way things are going I do not think that it will be possible to take this country."[13] When Haarlem finally capitulated in July 1573, Alba ordered the execution of the entire garrison and the town leaders. The heroic defense of Haarlem weakened the Spanish forces and inspired other Calvinist cities to resist Alba's armies. King Philip II grew frustrated with the duke's strategic approach and removed him from command in the Netherlands.

Despite these reverses, the Spanish armies had galvanized support for the war among the Dutch loyalists and still threatened to overwhelm the Calvinist rebels. In 1574, the Spanish army engaged in a lengthy siege of Leiden, aiming to cut Holland – the most solidly Calvinist province of the Netherlands – in two and isolate Amsterdam. But their failure to take the city allowed the Calvinists in Holland to remain united. The Spanish royal bankruptcy of 1575 produced massive mutinies by Spanish soldiers the following year. Spanish soldiers garrisoned in Antwerp rioted in 1576, sacking banking firms and burning the city hall in an orgy of violence that became known as the Spanish Fury. A contemporary ballad bitterly mocked the Spanish troops: "Adieu, plunderers, murderers, and wretches, killers, and tyrants. Your villainous deeds are shameful." The breakdown of order in the Army of Flanders forced the monarchy to accept a truce, the Pacification of Ghent. Cities across the Netherlands protested against Spanish military occupation and a chaotic situation emerged as Philip II was now discredited in the eyes of many Dutch subjects.[14]

Despite the truce, the Dutch Revolt increasingly took on the characteristics of a full-scale religious war. Calvinists seized churches in Holland and Zeeland, ending the Catholic mass in many communities in those provinces. In 1578, Calvinists also took control of the civic government in the major cities of Antwerp and Ghent. Co-religionists from France, England, and Germany intervened to support the Dutch Calvinists. The States of Holland became the key financial contributor to the States General and the Dutch cause by raising enormous sums through sales of *renten*, or bonds, to Dutch townspeople.[15] By 1579, a Calvinist Union of Utrecht formed, establishing the United Provinces in the northern Netherlands. Catholic loyalists to the Spanish king formed their own Union of Arras in the southern Netherlands. The Netherlands was now divided between a Calvinist north and a Catholic south, along with several key neutral provinces, including Flanders and Brabant.[16]

Sectional divisions gradually hardened between the northern and southern Netherlands along a military frontier. The fighting in the Netherlands involved intense siege warfare, with brutal sieges often followed by military occupations that could resemble sectarian cleansing operations. As Spanish armies consolidated their hold on the southern and central provinces, Calvinists from those regions had headed north as religious refugees or took flight as exiles. Catholic loyalists in Holland, Zeeland, and Utrecht fled south. Mixed-confessional cities such as Antwerp and Ghent experienced turmoil, since Calvinists controlled the municipal governments and refused to accept Spanish authority.

The new Spanish governor of the Netherlands, Alexander Farnese, launched major offensives to reconquer the Netherlands between 1579 and 1589. Farnese progressively seized the divided provinces of Brabant and Flanders, as well as parts of the rebellious northern Netherlands. Spanish troops took Brussels in 1583 and Ghent in 1584, pushing back Dutch Calvinist forces. William of Orange was assassinated in 1584, leaving the Dutch Calvinist leadership in chaos as the Spanish offensive continued. Farnese engineered a masterful blockade of Antwerp in 1584–85 using field fortifications, a pontoon bridge, and armed boats to force the city to surrender after the defenders had flooded the low-lying countryside. Philip II rewarded Farnese with the Order of the Golden Fleece and the successful general soon inherited the title of duke of Parma. By the end of 1585, Farnese's Spanish armies had isolated the province of Holland and seemed poised to crush the Dutch Calvinists.

At this point, Elizabeth I, queen of England and Ireland (1558–1603), intervened to save the desperate Dutch Calvinists, sending a large expeditionary force to counter the relentless Spanish advance in 1586. These English troops reflected a much larger pattern of intervention in the Netherlands. A broad Protestant international movement had been providing financial and military support to the northern Netherlands throughout the Dutch Revolt. Dutch exiles and privateers had been operating out of English ports to raid Spanish shipping in the English Channel and support Dutch rebels in coastal cities. Some German nobles and military adventurers had flocked to the Netherlands to fight for the Protestant cause. French Calvinists had sent military forces against Spanish troops in the southern Netherlands, and the duc d'Anjou, brother of the king of France, had become a leader of the Dutch Calvinists from 1581 to 1583. The famous Spanish Armada of 1588 aimed to transport the duke of Parma's veteran troops from the Netherlands for an invasion of England that would deny Dutch exiles a haven and halt English intervention in the Dutch Revolt. The disastrous failure of the Spanish Armada prevented Spanish military forces from crushing the rebellious northern provinces of the Netherlands.

Separatist politics and religious militancy

The States General declared itself sovereign in July 1590, establishing a Dutch Republic and officially separating the northern Netherlands from the southern provinces and from the Spanish crown. Maurits van Nassau, who had become *stadhouder* (literally place-keeper, but effectively governor-general) of Holland and Zeeland in 1585, reorganized the republican defenses and founded military academies to train its army officers. The province of Holland developed new financial techniques of raising credit in the 1580s and 1590s, providing a massive growth in war finance for the States General and its military forces. Dutch republican armies progressively rolled back the duke of Parma's conquests, regaining control of most of the northern Netherlands by 1602, while Spanish forces became embroiled in an epic siege of the coastal city of Ostend. Dutch Reformed leaders constructed an elaborate interlocking defensive system in 1605–06 by using lines of wooden redoubts to link bastioned fortifications to protect its southern border.

The Spanish monarchy, unable to defeat the Calvinist rebellion or occupy the northern provinces, ultimately accepted a Twelve Year Truce in 1609 that represented a *de facto* recognition of the Dutch Republic. Separatist politics and confessionalization during the Dutch Revolt had split the Netherlands, forging lasting divisions between a new Calvinist state in the north and a Catholic territory in the south.[17] While the Dutch Revolt shared many of the same forms of violence with the French Wars of Religion, a markedly different religio-political settlement emerged.

Religion and Violence in Asia

Sectarian violence and religious warfare characterized a number of conflicts in East and Southeast Asia during the late sixteenth and early seventeenth centuries.

Religious turmoil in Japan

In *Sengoku* Japan, civil wars had been raging for a generation, but they increasingly took on religious dimensions in the 1570s. Toyotomi Hideyoshi emerged as the most powerful *daimyō* following the assassination of Oda Nobunaga in 1582. Hideyoshi gradually gained the loyalty of Tokugawa Ieyasu and other former followers of Nobunaga. Hideyoshi was alarmed by the spread of Christianity in Japan, as some *daimyō* had begun to convert and the Society of Jesus had taken control of Nagasaki. Radical Buddhists, such as the armed *Ikkō ikki*, opposed Hideyoshi as they had Nobunaga before him. Hideyoshi defeated the Hōjō and other opposing *daimyō* in the Kantō region, finally taking Odawara castle in 1590. Hideyoshi had effectively subordinated the *daimyō* to his military authority, setting the stage for the unification of Japan.[18]

In the autumn of 1591, Hideyoshi ordered *daimyō* throughout Japan to mobilize their forces in preparation for an invasion of Korea. Hideyoshi seems to have believed that an invasion of Korea could forge religious and political unity among the *daimyō*, pacifying Japan and strengthening its emperor. In conjunction with his preparations for war, Hideyoshi expelled Jesuit missionaries from Japan, proclaiming:

> A few years ago the so-called Fathers came to my country seeking to bewitch our men and women, both of the laity and clergy. At that time punishment was administered to them, and it will be repeated if they should return to our domain to propagate their faith. It will not matter what sect or denomination they represent – they shall be destroyed.[19]

Hideyoshi may have also had dreams of conquering China and becoming a world emperor on the model of the Mongols, envisioning the conflict as a competition between two forms of Buddhism. An estimated 158,000 soldiers assembled in Kyushu for embarkation to Korea in 1592. Veteran Japanese *samurai* and arquebusiers at first swept the Korean forces before them. Ming imperial armies from China intervened in the conflict, leading to a truce and extended negotiations between 1592 and 1596. When the talks failed, Hideyoshi launched a second invasion of Korea in 1597–98, but he died suddenly and the invasion was abandoned. The linkage of religious conflict and unification in sixteenth-century Japan would have lasting consequences.[20]

Tokugawa Ieyasu completed the unification of Japan, creating the Tokugawa *bakufu* (shogunate government) and effectively establishing one of the first national states. A Tokugawa army defeated a major rebellion at the battle of Sekigahara in autumn 1600, allowing Tokugawa Ieyasu to consolidate power as *shogun*. Ieyasu punished the rebels harshly, confiscating the landholdings of 87 rebellious *daimyō* and creating new *daimyō* from his supporters.[21] The Tokugawa *bakufu* pursued centralizing policies that concentrated military power by monitoring *daimyō* warlords, demobilizing infzantry units, and confiscating weapons from peasants through a "politics of pacification."[22] By the early seventeenth century, imperial court ritual had been influenced by Kami worship, forging a compromise between Shinto and Buddhism that supported the Tokugawa order.

Tokugawa officials persecuted Japanese Christians and foreign missionaries in the mid-seventeenth century in an attempt to maintain order and impose religious uniformity. Japanese Christians revolted in the massive Shimabara rebellion in 1637–38, when perhaps 25,000 peasants and about 200 *rōnin* (masterless *samurai* warriors) seized Shimbara and the nearby Hara Castle. The movement took on messianic tones when a Japanese teenager declared that he was Christ reincarnated and galvanized peasant opposition with his preaching.[23] The brutal suppression of this rebellion led to even more strict enforcement of laws forbidding foreign missionaries from landing in Japan. Shinto practices and Buddhist mediation in village conflicts may have contributed to rural stability in Japan during the late seventeenth and eighteenth centuries. Under the Tokugawa *bakufu*, Japan was relatively peaceful, but isolated from global commercial and technological developments.

Religion and disorder in China and Vietnam

Ming China is often seen as an early modern society with a strong degree of religious coexistence, yet contradictions between the principles of Mahayana Buddhism and Confucianism could generate religious crises in the Chinese Empire. Buddhist monasteries and their teachings promoted law and order in Chinese society, while Confucianism provided the organizational principles and ruling rationales for the administrative institutions of the Chinese Empire. The Wanli emperor (1572–1620) displayed unconventional behavior at the Ming court, undermining the ideal of the sage emperor and eliciting religious and political condemnation. Timothy Brook indicates that "some objected to the free mingling of Buddhist and Confucian ideas, others to the donations that were going to Buddhist monasteries in preference to other needs."[24] Confucian academies, which often debated social and moral issues, began to criticize imperial tax policies openly. Imperial officials responded by arresting Confucian scholars and administrators who condemned the emperor's eccentric behavior and policies. Meanwhile, Chinese Buddhist masters promoted monastic revival and established branch temples within China and in tributary states. Internal dissent and Manchu invasions gradually weakened Ming rule, producing rural disorder and civil conflicts.[25]

Religion and kingship ideals also fueled conflict south of China, among the Vietnamese. The Tonkin rulers of northern Vietnam had adopted Confucianism, but many other Southeast Asian states had religiously mixed populations. A Vietnamese prince named Nguyen Hoang established a separate state of Cochin-China in southern Vietnam in the early seventeenth century, claiming lordship and opening trade relations with the Portuguese. Cochin-China organized an effective military that deployed regular forces including cannons, war galleys, and disciplined musketeers. Cochin-Chinese armies defeated successive Tonkin invasions between the 1620s and the 1670s, confirming the split between northern and southern Vietnam. Religious strife divided the neighboring kingdom of Champa, as Muslims, Hindus, Khmers, and Catholic Christians engaged in power struggles, allowing Cochin-Chinese troops to gradually absorb much of Champa.[26]

Buddhism and violence in Southeast Asia

Therevada Buddhism played a role in religious and political struggles in Southeast Asia during the sixteenth century. The Therevada form of Buddhism had spread earlier from Sri Lanka, but became linked to power struggles and empire-building. Chiengmai and Pegu became important centers of Therevada teaching in Burma, as a reinforced Buddhist monasticism spread into Cambodia, Laos, Siam, and adjacent regions.[27]

The restoration of the Thai kingdom of Siam demonstrates the power of Theravada Buddhism as a royal religion. Burmese armies had conquered much of mainland Southeast Asia in the 1540s–60s, devastating Siam and enslaving numerous Thai people. Prince Naresuen, a member of the Thai royal family, overthrew Burmese domination in a series of bold military campaigns that consolidated the kingdom of Siam around the city of Ayutthaya. King Naresuen (1590–1605) rode an elephant into battle and sometimes engaged in single combat – performing acts of bravery in a "demonstration of martial and spiritual skills."[28]

Therevadan Buddhist ideals and rituals shaped Thai martial arts and military practices in this period, becoming closely associated with Thai notions of kingship and royal authority. Ayutthayan kings constructed elaborate royal temples and Therevada monasteries, presenting yellow robes to monks in impressive ceremonies. Therevadan Buddhism seems to have provided strong motivations for Siamese soldiers in their campaigns against the Burmese and in subsequent expansionist wars in Laos and Cambodia. Muslim minorities in the kingdom of Siam were periodically subject to repression by Thai authorities.[29]

Military Reform and Religious Politics

Religious politics influenced military reforms and political organization in some areas during this period of religious warfare. Sectarian politics and conflict was especially pronounced within Islamic and Christian areas.

Sectarian conflict in the Islamic world

The coming of the end of the first Islamic millennium in 1000AH/1591CE seems to have unleashed renewed apocalyptical fervor in the Islamic world. Sayyid Muhammad Jawnpuri in India claimed to be the Mahdi, founding the acetic Mahdavi movement in Gujarat. The Mahdavi evolved into militant activists who were willing to suffer martyrdom, but the movement dissipated after the failure of the arrival of the Mahdi at the turn of the millennium. Several other Mahdi movements emerged in this period, including Ibn Abu Mahallah's campaign in Morocco. Many of these religious renewal movements promoted militant identities and adopted military reforms.

Muslim armies drew on this current of religious militancy to organize expeditionary religious warfare against infidel enemies. Ottoman military and naval forces continued to wage *gazi* war against their Christian rivals in the Balkans and the Mediterranean in the late sixteenth and early seventeenth centuries. The Ottomans could still organize major amphibious landings, as at the reconquest of Tunis in 1574. Ottoman armies conducted sustained warfare in Croatia and Hungary during the Habsburg–Ottoman war of 1593–1606. Later, Ottoman fleets ferried armies to invade the Venetian island of Crete in the 1640s.

Mystical Islamic reform movements in Morocco contributed to military reform and expeditionary warfare in North Africa. The Moroccan Sultan Ahmad al-Mansur (1578–1603) sent an army of 4,000 arquebusiers and lancers to invade the Songhay Empire in 1591. The Moroccan army defeated Songhay forces at Tondibi and rapidly occupied Gao and Timbuktu, but ongoing Songhay resistance resulted in a protracted war.[30] Meanwhile, the Fulani, among the first groups of sub-Saharan Africans to convert to Islam, waged campaigns for purity in West Africa.

Sectarian conflict between the Ottomans and Safavids reignited in the late sixteenth century. The Ottoman armies of Sultan Murad III battled against Shia Safavid armies in a major war in 1578–90. Ottoman troops seized the city of Tabriz, the former Safavid capital, as well as territories in Azerbaijan, Kurdistan, and Georgia. Shah 'Abbas (1588–1629) reorganized the Safavid military system, regularizing the *ghulams* (slave soldiers) as standing units. The Safavids waged new wars against the Ottomans in 1603–12 and 1623–39, defending their frontiers and retaking Tabriz. Some Sufis challenged the Safavids' claims to Shia leadership in Iran, but 'Abbas responded by having a number of them executed. By the mid-seventeenth century, the Safavids had succeeded in establishing Shia dominance throughout their empire.[31]

The complex religious landscape of India created tensions within the Mughal Empire, whose elites embraced Islam. Emperor Akbar had promoted religious pluralism, but the Mughal armies were still dominated by Muslim officers and soldiers, who sometimes clashed with religious groups that opposed imperial authority and Islamic law. Mughal armies gradually became more diverse, including contingents of Rajput warriors and Hindu *sadhu*, or armed ascetics.[32] Serious religious and ethnic conflicts developed in the Mughal Empire in the early seventeenth century. Akbar's son Jahangir (1605–27) feared plots by Sikh gurus and ordered his troops to suppress Sikhism. The Sikh guru Arjun blessed a rebel Mughal prince in 1605, bringing on a wave of persecutions of Sikhs, which solidified a Sikh culture of martyrdom. Shah Jahan (1628–58) built the Taj Mahal as a tomb for his wife and a powerful allegorical statement of a Mughal Islamic identity. Further religious conflicts erupted as Jain ascetics condemned Islam as a false religion.

Sectarian tensions produced social conflict among the diverse religious populations of the Ottoman Empire. Ottoman sultans promoted their own peculiar version of Sunni practice, which was sometimes criticized by non-Turkish Sunni Muslims and by the Sufi minority within the empire. Ottoman rulers allowed Sufi orders to practice mystical Islam within the empire, essentially promoting an "institutionalization of nonconformism."[33] Some imams and religious scholars condemned unbelief and immorality in Ottoman society. In the early seventeenth century, imam Kadizade Mehmed preached against tobacco and moral corruption, saying that "every innovation is heresy, every heresy is error, and every error leads to hell."[34] Ottoman religious flexibility allowed for a degree of social stability for its extremely diverse population. Tolerant laws sometimes appeared to devout Sunni as permissiveness, undermining Ottoman claims to the caliphate.

Military discipline and confessional identities

Meanwhile, religious politics and confessional identities became intertwined with military reforms in Europe. Maurits van Nassau had become captain general of the army of the fledgling Dutch Republic in 1588, and immediately began an army reform. Prince Maurits formed infantry battalions, composed of small infantry companies that closely coordinated the movements of their pikemen and musketeers. He also instituted a new system of infantry firearms drill, which coordinated and synchronized soldiers' motions in firing, countermarching, and reloading their muskets, which were now replacing the older arquebuses. The Dutch infantry performed well in the 1590s and 1600s, besieging cities such as Steenwijk in 1592 and winning victories at battles such as Nieuwport in 1600.[35]

Numerous Protestant noble adventurers and soldiers from England, Scotland, France, Germany, and Scandinavia served in the Netherlands during this period, allowing a diffusion of Dutch techniques abroad. Dutch military academies enrolled nobles from other Protestant armies, inculcating the new military discipline. Infantry drill manuals, such as De Gheyn's *The Exercise of Armes* (1607), provided an influential model for armies across Europe to emulate. Drill manuals became a distinct genre of military literature in the 1610s and 1620s, with hundreds of competing books claiming to offer new systems for drilling soldiers and coordinating infantry and cavalry units. The Swedish King Gustav II Adolf became excited about the possibility of new drill systems, issuing an *Ordinance for Military Personnel* to reform his military and institute a conscription system in the 1620s.[36] Michael Roberts sees the Swedish military reforms as a key stage in the development of a Military Revolution, but other scholars have challenged this notion.[37] Diverse Protestant contingents would later serve as allies and auxiliaries in the Swedish armies, ensuring that the Swedish way of war would be exported to England, Scotland, the Netherlands, and northern Germany.

Military training also became confessionalized in Catholic territories. The Spanish Army of Flanders became an informal military academy for Catholic military officers across Europe, attracting numerous noble volunteers and adventurers. The famed Spanish *tercios* became the model for contingents composed of Flemish, Walloon, Italian, German, English, and Irish Catholics who served in the polyglot armies of Philip II in the Spanish Netherlands.[38] The Wild Geese, as Irish soldiers fighting with the Spanish in the Dutch Revolt were known, seem to have forged a new political identity shaped "by

counter-reformation Catholicism, by a sense of 'national' consciousness and…by a militant separatism."[39]

New forms of military discipline also seem to have been linked to
confessional warfare in the late sixteenth and early seventeenth centuries. Soldiers attended public preaching and participated in collective prayer and devotions. Clergy served with armies throughout the
European Wars of Religion, often being attached to military units
and leading worship services prior to combat. Many soldiers carried
prayer books, psalm books, and catechisms to solidify their faith and
serve their devotional needs. Olivier Christin demonstrates that the
carrying and wearing of signs and symbols increasingly displayed
religious identities in the second half of the sixteenth century, height-
ening the confessional divide across Europe.[40]

Confessional politics in Germany

Confessional and sectarian animosities had been simmering in the
Holy Roman Empire during the second half of the sixteenth century.
The 1555 Peace of Augsburg had halted religious warfare in Germany
and instituted a pragmatic religious solution known as *cuius regio,
eius religio*: each prince had the right to choose his religion, and that
of his subjects. This settlement could work reasonably well as long as
confessional identities of populations remained stable and succeeding princely rulers respected their predecessors' religious choices.
Most of the princes of northern Germany territories had adopted
Lutheranism by the mid-sixteenth century, while most of southern
Germany was effectively controlled by Catholic princes and episcopal rulers. A series of Imperial Free Cities were scattered across
Germany, with Lutheran, Catholic, or mixed-confessional popula-
tions. Other versions of Reformed Christianity such as Calvinism and
Anabaptism, were forbidden in the empire.

The spread of Calvinism fundamentally upset the religious settlement in the Holy Roman Empire. The Calvinist Reform surged progressively through Germany, with the Lutheran rulers of the
Palatinate, Nassau, Hesse-Kassel, and Brandenburg converting to
Calvinism in the late sixteenth and early seventeenth centuries. Even
Martin Luther's homeland of Saxony briefly experimented with Calvinism. Meanwhile, the Catholic reform transformed those states that
had remained loyal to the pope and the old Latin Christian church,
as bishops implemented Tridentine reforms, educational initiatives, and
devotional practices. Despite continuing processes of confessionalization, some rulers and subjects continued to change their religious

affiliations, producing growing sectarian tensions into the seventeenth century.

Rival confessional groups also became increasingly politicized, as organizations formed to support their co-religionists. When Catholic clergy arranged processions in the mixed-confessional Imperial city of Donauwörth in 1606, angry Lutheran crowds protested. Emperor Rudolf II von Habsburg (1576–1612) authorized the Catholic Maximilian of Bavaria to occupy the city the following year and expel the Lutherans. The so-called Donauwörth Incident alarmed Lutherans and Calvinists throughout the Holy Roman Empire, leading to the formation of a Protestant Union in 1608 under the leadership of the Palatinate, providing an alliance and potential military support for Protestant causes in Germany. Prince Christian of Anhalt-Bernburg and other Calvinist activists vociferously opposed Catholic reform and conversion efforts in Germany.[41]

The crisis of Jülich-Clèves in 1609–10 showed the potential for a ruler's religious affiliation to upset the entire settlement within the Holy Roman Empire, as the Protestant Union mobilized to support a Lutheran claimant as successor. A Catholic League formed under the leadership of Bavaria in July 1609 in response to the Protestant Union's intervention at Jülich. The Protestant Union expanded, as Brandenburg, Hesse-Kassel, Pfalz-Zweibrücken, and a number of Protestant cities joined. Germans observed with trepidation a dramatic comet in 1618 – which seemed to represent a threatening omen of fervent confessional reforms, disputed Imperial rule, and growing conflict.

Thirty Years War, 1618–1648

Prague, the capital of the kingdom of Bohemia, turned out to be the crucial site of the next religious confrontation within the Holy Roman Empire. The outbreak of revolt in Bohemia would produce one of the most ferocious religious wars of the early modern period, the Thirty Years War.

Bohemian Revolt, 1618–1620

The Habsburg dynasty ruled Bohemia, with an emperor's son often taking the title of king of Bohemia, effectively signaling his position as successor. After the childless Matthias von Habsburg was elected emperor in 1612, his cousin archduke Ferdinand von Habsburg gradually maneuvered to become king of Bohemia by 1617. Ferdinand had been educated by Jesuits and had acted as an avid proponent of Catholic reform while administering the Habsburg territory of Styria. As king of Bohemia, he now ruled over a kingdom with an overwhelmingly Protestant population and sharply divided mixed-confessional nobility. Ferdinand decided to implement changes to promote Catholicism and found Jesuit colleges in Bohemia. In the spring of 1618, the Estates of Bohemia met at the castle of Prague to discuss the new religious policies, but when their absentee king ordered the meeting ended, angry delegates seized two of the king's regents and threw them out of a castle window, a bold act of defiance remembered as the Defenestration of Prague.

The Bohemian Revolt quickly spread, as the other territories ruled by Ferdinand fell into disorder. Emperor Matthias died in March 1619, worsening the political instability at the Imperial court. A serious civil war developed within Austria, as a rebel army besieged Vienna in May 1619. Charles Bonaventure de Longueval, count of Bucquoy, hastily raised an Imperial army of 30,000 men, relieving Vienna in June. Ferdinand reorganized and realized his election as Emperor Ferdinand II (1619–37) of the Holy Roman Empire in August 1619. The same month, the Estates of Bohemia formally deposed Ferdinand and elected the Calvinist Frederick V of the Palatinate as their new king. A contemporary critic mocked Frederick as "a prince who knew more about gardening than fighting," yet the Palatine prince was one of the key Calvinist militants in the Holy Roman Empire and was well connected with the Protestant Union.[42] As Bohemia prepared its defenses, a Transylvanian confederate army besieged Vienna for a second time in autumn 1619, but the Transylvanian prince later accepted a truce and demobilized. The Catholic League mobilized to support the emperor, organizing an army of 25,000 under the command of Maximilian of Bavaria. In the summer of 1620, Johann Tserclaes, count of Tilly, led another Catholic League army to join Bucquoy's forces and invade Bohemia. This Imperial army destroyed the Protestant Bohemian army at the battle of White Mountain in November 1620, crushing the revolt. Imperial troops executed captured rebels in the square in Prague, placing the heads of the beheaded Bohemian nobles on the tower of the Charles Bridge as a warning to the city's residents. An extended military occupation of Bohemia would result in a nearly complete re-Catholicization of the kingdom.[43]

Expanding warfare in Germany, 1620–1629

What had begun as a revolt in the Habsburg dynasty's own domains became a truly Imperial conflict as religious warfare expanded throughout Germany. Emperor Ferdinand was eager to punish Frederick V, now known as the Winter King, for his brazen intervention into Habsburg affairs. Imperial and Catholic League troops advanced beyond Bohemia, crossing neutral territories in central Germany as they headed for Frederick's own principality of the Palatinate. The Spanish Habsburgs allied with the emperor, sending Ambrosio Spínola's army from the Spanish Netherlands to invade the Palatinate. Alarmed members of the Protestant Union responded, mobilizing troops to oppose the advancing Catholic forces. Tilly's Bavarian army and an allied contingent of Spanish troops defeated Protestant armies at the battles of Wimpfen, Höchst, and Stadlohn in the summer of 1622, prompting surviving Protestant princes to flee or submit to Ferdinand II.[44] Tilly's Catholic League troops had successfully punished Ferdinand II's princely enemies, but the emperor now needed additional troops and decided to create his own army.

The dramatic rise of Albrecht von Wallenstein as commander of Imperial forces demonstrates the power of military entrepreneurs during the Thirty Years War. Wallenstein was a minor Bohemian nobleman who had gained a military reputation during the fighting in the 1620s. Emperor Ferdinand II selected Wallenstein to raise a new Imperial army in the summer of 1625 as the war continued to widen. Wallenstein developed close relationships with the colonels, who recruited cavalry companies and infantry regiments for his army. When Denmark intervened militarily in Germany, Wallenstein rapidly responded, sending his forces to overwhelm the Danish army at the battle of Lutter in August 1626. Wallenstein raised a stunning total of 103 regiments for the Imperial armies during the 1620s. He acquired the title of duke of Mecklenburg in January 1628, confirming his political ascent.

Emboldened by his armies' victories, Emperor Ferdinand II issued an Edict of Restitution in March 1629, decreeing the restitution of all Catholic churches and ecclesiastical properties seized by Protestant princes and communities in Germany since the beginning of the Reformation. This aggressive new religious policy antagonized Protestant opponents of the emperor and reinforced the confessional dimensions of the conflict.[45] Criticism of Imperial military and religious policies led the emperor to relieve Wallenstein of command in August 1630, but the war had already become a more international conflict.

Confessional violence and international conflict, 1630–1643

Gustav II Adolf (1611–32) invaded the Holy Roman Empire in July 1630, personally leading a Swedish army. The Swedish military system had recently been reorganized by employing Swedish conscription recruitment, Dutch infantry drill techniques, brigaded infantry formations, and infantry-support artillery. Some German Lutherans and Calvinists hailed the Swedish king as the Lion of the North and their new protector, supporting the rejuvenated Protestant cause. Protestant opposition to the Edict of Restitution and Swedish military intervention reinvigorated confessional violence in Germany.

French diplomats negotiated a treaty at Bärwalde in January 1631 to provide subsidies to the Swedish forces fighting against the Holy Roman Emperor. Historians have often pointed to Catholic France's financial support for Sweden as evidence that the internationalization of the Thirty Years War was by this point fostering the development of "reason of state" politics and a de-confessionalization of the conflict. French kings had previously supported Protestant and Ottoman military efforts against Imperial forces, however, since the Habsburgs represented their principal dynastic opponents and their rivals for leadership of the Catholic world.

In May 1631, an Imperial and Catholic League army under Tilly blockaded and then besieged the Protestant city of Magdeburg, which had supported Swedish intervention in Germany. The Imperialists assaulted Magdeburg on May 20, breaking through the city's defenses and massacring thousands of defenders and inhabitants. A fire broke out and engulfed the entire city, destroying almost all of the city's buildings. Although Tilly apparently attempted to restore discipline in his army, Imperial soldiers continued to pillage shops, plunder houses, and kill civilians. Surviving residents used valuables to bribe their way out of the occupied shell of a city. Around 20,000 of Magdeburg's inhabitants had been killed in the sack, and a 1632 census of Magdeburg reported only 449 remaining residents. Protestant pamphlets compared the sack of Magdeburg to the destruction of Jerusalem, describing in graphic detail the brutal slaying of children and other atrocities allegedly perpetrated by the Imperial troops.[46]

The utter devastation of Magdeburg represented an especially brutal application of the law of the siege that galvanized anti-Catholic sentiment in northern Germany and bolstered Gustav II Adolf's claim to deliver aid to Lutherans throughout the Holy Roman Empire. Swedish forces established themselves in Pomerania and gained support from the Elector of Brandenburg and other German princes, who sent armed contingents to join the Swedish army. When Imperialists crossed into neutral Saxony to forage, Saxon forces allied with the Swedes, sending a contingent to join Gustav II Adolf's growing army. The Swedish and Imperial armies met at the battle of Breitenfeld in September 1631. The Swedes deployed in a flexible checkerboard formation supported by artillery and cavalry, soundly defeating Tilly's army.

Following this victory, the Swedish army advanced into central and southern Germany, occupying Bavaria in early 1632. During the hard fighting in Bavaria, Tilly was killed at the battle of Rain, removing the best general active in the Catholic League. With the position of the Habsburgs and their allies collapsing, the emperor reinstated Wallenstein as commander of the main Imperial army. Wallenstein's forces met the Swedish army at the battle of Lützen in November 1632. Both armies suffered heavy casualties as the Swedes advanced into an Imperial position centered on a large battery. The Imperial general Pappenheim raced to lead reinforcements from the nearby town of Halle onto the battlefield to stabilize the Imperial line, but he was mortally wounded. Gustav II Adolf was killed during the battle, removing the great hope for the Protestant cause in Germany. After Lützen, the Swedish military system began to suffer from serious strategic overstretch and financial difficulties, leading to a series of army mutinies as a regency government led by Queen Christina and the minister Axel Oxenstierna managed the Swedish war effort.

Imperial forces were also in disarray. When Emperor Ferdinand II discovered that Albrecht von Wallenstein had been conducting secret negotiations, he removed him from command and ordered his arrest. Imperial officers and soldiers deserted Wallenstein's army, and he was assassinated in February 1634. Spanish forces intervened to support the Imperialists at this point, providing crucial support in the struggle for control of southern Germany. When a Spanish-Imperial army besieged Nördlingen, a Swedish army under Gustav Karlsson Horn attempted to relieve the town. Spanish and Imperial troops had time to dig entrenched artillery positions prior to the Swedish assault, inflicting horrific losses on the Swedish soldiers. The Swedish strategic position in southern Germany collapsed, leading to negotiations among German princes for the Peace of Prague of May 1635, but the exclusion of Calvinists from the talks ensured that the peace would never be implemented.

France now suddenly declared war on Spain, intervening directly in the Thirty Years War. Franco-Spanish rivalries had been brewing for over a decade and stemmed from longstanding dynastic ambitions and political disputes, as well as their religious rivalry for leadership of the Catholic cause. French military intervention initially stunned the Spanish Habsburgs, but Spanish forces took the town of Corbie in 1636 and plundered the countryside in Picardie, threatening Paris. The Imperialist cause was reinforced by a smooth succession, as

Emperor Ferdinand II accomplished his son's election as king of the Romans and heir to the Imperial title in 1636, and then died soon afterwards. The new emperor, Ferdinand III (1637–57), directed the reorganized Imperial forces against the Swedes and German Protestants, while the French and Spanish fought in Flanders. Louis II de Bourbon, duc d'Enghien, led a French army against the Spanish Army of Flanders at the battle of Rocroi in May 1643, when French cavalry swept Spanish cavalry from the field and surrounded five Spanish *tercios* – three of which were overwhelmed and another was forced to surrender. The French victory humiliated the Army of Flanders, but failed to produce a strategic breakthrough in the Spanish Netherlands.

Stalemate and armed negotiations, 1643–1648

By the 1640s, the Thirty Years War had become a brutal war of attrition, as each successive military intervention failed to break the relative stalemate and only further widened the conflict, as it became nearly pan-European in scope. The complex motivations and conflicting affiliations of the diverse warring parties have produced a debate over the religious nature of the conflict. Peter Wilson argues that the Thirty Years War "was not primarily a religious war....The war was religious only to the extent that faith guided all early modern public policy and private behaviour."[47] Other historians refute this interpretation of the conflict as essentially political, however, calling it a "religious war."[48] Tryntje Helfferich demonstrates that Amalia Elizabeth, Landgravine of Hesse, fought hard and negotiated vigorously to win religious concessions and legal protections for Calvinism in the Holy Roman Empire in the 1630s–40s, offering ample evidence of "the continued importance of religion in the second half of the Thirty Years War."[49]

The Thirty Years War is often characterized as the Golden Age of mercenaries, since almost every state employed military entrepreneurs to recruit and command some of their military forces. Albrecht von Wallenstein, Ernst von Mansfeld, and Bernard of Saxe-Weimar came to define the concept of "military entrepreneurship." Military officers such as colonels and captains tended to pursue lengthy careers in the service of different states, moving easily from one field army to another between campaigns. Scottish officers such as Sir Robert Monro gained their reputations in Swedish service, and then later returned to the British Isles. Common soldiers of diverse ethnic, national, and religious backgrounds frequently accepted a bounty to enter another field army when they were demobilized or captured. Nonetheless, many of these so-called "mercenaries" were motivated by strong confessional causes and religious politics, as well as by fame and fortune.

Soldiers in every army routinely pillaged villages and sacked cities, giving the Thirty Years War a lasting reputation for brutality. The historical memory of the conflict was forged through an astounding production of printed pamphlets and engravings that publicized outrages. When Magdeburg was sacked, "no less than 20 newspapers, 205 pamphlets and 41 illustrated broadsheets describing the horror were published." An English propaganda piece called *The Lamentations of Germany* depicted the horrors of the Thirty Years War graphically with prints of starving civilians eating snails, frogs, and human remains.[50]

As the military stalemate continued, conference negotiations began in 1643 to produce a compromise peace agreement. Two separate confessional congresses – one for Protestant and moderate Catholic negotiators at Osnabrück, and another for Catholic ambassadors at Münster – eventually assembled, with delegations meeting almost continuously from 1643 to 1648. The French victory against the Spanish at Rocroi encouraged Cardinal Jules Mazarin to attempt to pick up new military gains during the ongoing negotiations. Each successive military action brought new gains and losses at the negotiating table, drawing out the conflict.[51] Individual battles and sieges could still tantalizingly threaten to break the stalemate and force a state to submit. A Swedish army under Lennart Tortensson crushed an Imperial army at the battle of Jankov in March 1645, allowing the Swedes to advance to threaten Vienna, even if they lacked the forces to open a formal siege of the Habsburg capital. Meanwhile, a Franco-Hessian army commanded by Louis II de Bourbon, duc d'Enghien, defeated a Bavarian army under Jan van Werth at the battle of Allerheim in August 1645, forcing Emperor Ferdinand III to negotiate in earnest for a peace settlement.

The Thirty Years War finally ended in 1648 with the Peace of Westphalia, a complex religious peace within the Holy Roman Empire and a series of peace agreements between the warring states. Many political theorists and political scientists have designated the Peace of Westphalia as the first European peace agreement and portrayed the Westphalian congress as the foundational event of the modern international state system. The peace of Westphalia can alternatively be interpreted as a religious peace that legalized Calvinism in Germany, reinforced the Imperial constitution, and confirmed dynastic rule. The Peace of Westphalia ended the long religious war within the Holy Roman Empire, bringing peace between the Swedes, the French, the

German princes, and the Imperialists. The negotiations also brought Spanish recognition of Dutch independence and agreements between various states that had intervened in Germany. The Peace of Westphalia did not halt the Franco-Spanish war, which would continue until 1659, and failed to deal adequately with the difficulties of demobilization and rebuilding within the Holy Roman Empire.

Conclusion

The Thirty Years War left much of Germany desolated, as death, disease, and flight depopulated entire regions. An estimated 15–20 percent of the inhabitants of the Holy Roman Empire died during the conflict, with regions like Bavaria and Pomerania losing between 30 and 40 percent of their pre-war populations, and war-torn Württemberg and Lorraine losing nearly 60 percent of their populations. Areas particularly ravaged by war suffered serious economic contraction, visible through the abandonment of entire villages and significant reforestation. Although the myth of the "absolute destruction" of Germany during the Thirty Years War may be exaggerated, this religious war nonetheless destroyed many lives and left a lasting historical memory in German culture and European identities.[52]

New scientific methods, legal opinions, and skeptical philosophies began to limit religion's role in warfare in the mid-seventeenth century. Some communities forged tentative attempts at pragmatic coexistence across confessional lines. These local accommodations could occasionally provide for mixed-confessional communities, commercial exchanges, and common cultural activities.[53] The Dutch Republic gradually gained a reputation for religious tolerance, even if it was limited in practice. Yet, confessional animosities continued to disturb many societies and modern notions of religious toleration had not yet developed anywhere in the early modern world.

Attempts at coexistence repeatedly failed, reinforcing confessional identities, segregation, and conflict – as we saw in France in the aftermath of the Edict of Nantes. Indeed, Christians seem to have reinforced their confessional identities through confessional conflicts within Europe in this period, even as they confirmed their identities as Europeans through religious warfare against Muslims and animists around the world. Outright religious warfare declined in the late seventeenth century, but religious factors could still contribute to conflicts and motivate combatants.

7

Raiding Warfare, 1580s–1640s

Amerindian societies in North America valued individual courage and envisioned raids as opportunities for warriors to display their skills. Many Amerindian societies allowed warriors to wage war against individual enemies, and "young Indian men were encouraged to raid enemies to hone skills and achieve reputations."[1] Captive-taking and ritual violence were central to Amerindian raiding warfare, which developed distinct aims and dynamics. Iroquois warriors subjected captives taken in "mourning war" to ritualistic torture, testing their honor in complex ceremonies that resulted in the killing or adoption of captives. Amerindian raiding parties and nations also exchanged captives as gifts.

Raiding warfare may be the oldest form of warfare, utilized by diverse societies from prehistoric periods to today.[2] Yet, although it has long been practiced, few historians have seriously examined the history of its changing dynamics. Harry Holbert Turney-High's influential conception of raiding as a form of "primitive war" assumes that "a raid is hardly more of a war than is modern burglary." Turney-High presents a "military horizon" as sharply dividing "primitive war" from what he terms "true war."[3] This model of raiding warfare has long dominated military history, privileging conventional warfare between field armies of major states as the legitimate focus of historical investigation, while dismissing raiding activities as irrelevant to the history of warfare.

When irregular warfare has been considered, it is often treated as an aspect of guerrilla warfare, organized crime, or terrorist activity. Recent studies of raiding warfare and the "anthropology of war" have developed new approaches to investigate the motivations of raiders.[4] Early modern raiding warfare generally involved communication and collaboration between state and non-state actors. Regional and local military elites seem to have played important roles in organizing raiding warfare, but also in suppressing it.

This chapter traces the new forms of raiding warfare that emerged in response to global commerce and imperialism during the late sixteenth century. Certain regions experienced intensive raiding activity as a result of the development of "raiding clusters," areas in which particularly aggressive groups launched frequent offensive raids.[5] Where raiding became endemic, "raiding economies" seem to have developed, altering patterns of commercial exchange.[6] Localized pillaging, plundering, and captive-taking became increasingly associated with elaborate economic systems of distribution and resale that provided compensation for raiders. Although marauders actively sought financial compensation and profits, they often had broader political, social, cultural, and religious motivations for their attacks. Early modern raiders engaged in organized forms of maritime raiding, borderlands raiding, and economic devastation.

Maritime Raiding

Pirates and privateers engaged in incessant raiding warfare in the late sixteenth and seventeenth centuries, a period that some historians have characterized as a Golden Age of piracy. Sailing ships that mounted heavy artillery roamed the world's oceans, seeking opportunities to seize unprotected commercial vessels. The Caribbean Sea, Melaka Straits, and Java Sea all became dangerous waters where pirates and privateers plundered global commerce. These confined waters acted as key choke points along the global trade routes for the long-distance commerce in silver, gold, sugar, spices, medicines, and botanical specimens. Pirates and privateers targeted merchant ships, treasure fleets, and port towns in maritime raids that could obtain fabulous spoils.

Piracy and slavery in the Mediterranean

The expansion of the Ottoman Empire and the Ottoman–Venetian Wars in the eastern Mediterranean seem to have led to a sharp increase in Mediterranean piracy in the sixteenth century. The Knights of Saint John of Jerusalem conducted maritime raids from their base on the island of Rhodes until the Ottomans besieged the city of Rhodes in 1522. When the city capitulated, the Knights relocated to

Malta in the central Mediterranean, where they continued their piracy against Muslim merchants. The Catholic Knights of Malta continued to enslave Greek Orthodox sailors and merchants in the Mediterranean, refusing to consider them as fellow Christians.[7] The Dalmatian coast descended into chaos and Uskok pirates targeted merchant ships in the Adriatic. The Venetian Arsenale began to build larger and more heavily armed oared warships, known as *galeasses*, in the 1520s in order to counter the pirate threat. Each *galeass* was armed with eight or more heavy artillery pieces, as well as some lightweight anti-personnel guns.[8]

Christian and Muslim pirates terrorized Mediterranean islands and coastlines with their amphibious raiding parties throughout the sixteenth century. Mediterranean corsairs often captured fishing boats and merchant ships, holding the crew as hostages for ransom. Pirates sometimes landed along coasts or seized entire fishing villages to take captives. If hostages could not pay ransoms, captives were enslaved on galleys as oarsmen. When pirates returned to their home ports, local rulers would take some of their slaves while others were sold in slave markets.[9]

Mediterranean slavery was not a permanent condition, though, and many slaves were eventually freed through negotiated ransom payments provided by their families or communities. Many slaves had trouble winning their freedom, however. If corsair galleys were captured, the enslaved oarsmen were often forced to enlist as oarsmen in the victorious galleys. Some Christian captives converted to Islam to escape slavery, often then serving as "renegades" in North African armies. The system of Mediterranean piracy and slavery was highly complex, with some communities able to use protection money to avoid piracy and some merchants able to win compensation for their losses.

Mediterranean patterns of piracy continued through the seventeenth century and extended into the Black Sea. Various ports within the Ottoman Empire had commercial links with the overland trade routes that remained as legacies of the famous Silk Road caravans across Eurasia. Despite the Ottoman sultans' interest in profiting from this mixed overland and seaborne commerce, merchants were vulnerable to organized banditry and piracy. Cossack pirates operated in the Black and Caspian Seas throughout the early modern period.

Piracy and privateering in the Atlantic World

A very different pattern of piracy emerged in the Atlantic Ocean and the Caribbean Sea in the sixteenth century. The incredible wealth of the Spanish colonies in Central and South America attracted English, French, Dutch, and other pirates who were eager to plunder the growing trans-Atlantic commerce. In response to growing piracy and privateering in the Atlantic Ocean, Spanish naval officers began to organize an elaborate convoy system in the 1540s, using warships to protect fleets of merchant vessels crossing the Atlantic together. A system gradually evolved by the 1560s of sending two separate fleets each year to Veracruz, Mexico, and to Cartagena de Indias, in present-day Colombia. The fleets would then begin the return voyage to Spain, bearing fantastic amounts of silver and gold from the rich mines of Zacatecas and Potosí. The powerful Spanish warships and their convoy system provided vital protection to the Spanish Indies fleets, which represented attractive targets to independent pirates and privateers sponsored by Spain's enemies. After successfully making the Atlantic crossing, the fleets landed in the teeming port of Seville, the gateway to the Americas in the sixteenth and seventeenth centuries.

Sailors' motivations for joining maritime expeditions changed with the shifting conditions of maritime commerce. The initial voyages of "discovery" were incredibly risky, but offered great opportunities for mariners, as the terms of the payments for sailors demonstrate. But, the mid-sixteenth-century development of fixed trajectory annual voyages, which were increasingly regulated and controlled by Seville's House of Trade, altered the labor and payment conditions. Spanish mariners increasingly used capitalist mechanisms including joint investment, contracts, litigation, and customs inspection to conduct commerce, but they also resorted to cheating, bribery, fraud, and contraband.

Vague distinctions between naval and merchant vessels, coupled with the lure of fabulous wealth in the Americas and Asia increasingly made Spanish fleets targets for attack by opportunistic enemies. Some Calvinist Dutch exiles who fled from the Dutch Revolt became privateers operating out of English ports. A number of these privateers launched attacks on the coast of the Netherlands in 1572, and became known as the Sea Beggars. Dutch Calvinist and Catholic privateers raided their opponents' shipping in the English Channel and North Sea during the Dutch Revolt. Huguenot refugees from France also established themselves in England, sometimes organizing maritime operations to support their fellow Calvinists in France and the Netherlands. Spanish ships came under pressure from economic competition, naval rivalry, and religious conflict. Increasingly, the enormous costs of Spanish involvement in wars in the Netherlands, Italy, and North Africa eroded Spanish naval power, as Dutch and English privateers upset Spanish trade routes.

The rise of English privateering in the mid-sixteenth century produced heightened tensions between Protestant England and Catholic Spain. James McDermott's study of English privateering suggests that the English monarchy initially granted privateers *carte blanche* in the 1540s, encouraging naval raiding against Spain in the Atlantic Ocean.[10] Elizabethan privateers sailed with letters of marque justifying their seizures of Spanish ships. English courts paid rewards to privateers who brought prizes into ports. The privateers' seizure of neutral ships and their use of brutal violence blurred the distinctions between privateering and piracy.

A growing maritime rivalry widened into a "first cold war" between Spain and England in the 1560s and 1570s. English privateers were increasingly organized, using fast "race-built" galleons funded by bellicose English gentry. Francis Drake's famous circumnavigation of the globe in the *Golden Hind* in 1577–80 demonstrated the threat that such privateers posed to Atlantic commerce. Drake and his crew raided shipping in the Caribbean and along New Spain's Pacific coast, seizing numerous prizes and massive treasure before crossing the Pacific. The *Golden Hind* finally arrived in Plymouth, laden with a fabulous load of perhaps £264,000. Elizabeth I rewarded Drake with a banquet and a knighthood in 1581. Sir Francis Drake went on to lead privateering activity against Spain across the Atlantic.

Religious animosities and diplomatic misunderstandings complicated attempts to resolve incidents of ship seizures, leading to outright war between Spain and England in 1585. Aggressive Elizabethan naval policies and uncontrollable English privateering activity against Spanish shipping eventually brought retaliation in the form of a massive Spanish Armada bearing down on England. Many triumphalist accounts of this 1588 campaign credit English naval superiority with victory, celebrating the English national mythology surrounding the Spanish Armada. More recent historical works portray logistical difficulties, accidents, and storms as being primarily responsible for the ultimate failure of Philip II's attempt to invade England. English and Spanish diplomatic records reveal aspects of the famous clash between the two navies, presenting the conflict as a struggle "for the very soul of England" that played a role in forming "the English psyche."[11]

The failure of the 1588 Spanish Armada needs to be understood in broader European and global contexts. The naval warfare between Spain and England was closely linked to the contemporaneous Dutch Revolt, as Elizabethan military forces intervened in the conflict in the Netherlands. Recent scholarship demonstrates that Philip II's Spain was remarkably resilient, able to build a new Armada rapidly and

continue to maintain its overseas empire. Nonetheless, English privateers continued to raid Spanish commerce in the Atlantic, supporting
early English colonial ventures. English privateering sometimes
blended with organized naval activity, as when Robert Devereux,
second earl of Essex, led a naval raid on the Spanish port of Cadiz
in 1596, sailing into the harbor and briefly occupying the city while
Spanish sailors burned their ships to avoid their capture by the audacious English. Despite such dramatic raids, the Spanish naval recovery
and war exhaustion in the Netherlands eventually led to negotiations
for peace in 1605, ending one of the first trans-Atlantic wars.

The expansion of Atlantic commerce, the development of Spanish
colonies, and the vulnerability of the Spanish convoy system all point
to broader contexts of privateering and commercial rivalries. Privateering grew in the English Channel, North Sea, and the Baltic Sea
in an attempt to control herring fisheries and Scandinavian trade.
After defeating the old Hanseatic League in the 1530s, Danish and
Swedish fleets competed for Baltic naval dominance in the late sixteenth century. The Danes aggressively patrolled the Sound, enforcing tolls on merchant ships entering and exiting the Baltic Sea with
cargoes of timber, hemp, and other resources. King Christian IV (1596–
1648) later expanded the Danish fleet, but lost to the Swedish in a new
Baltic war in 1643–45. The Vasas arguably used Swedish naval and
military power to act as a "protection-selling dynasty" in the Baltic
region, eventually dominating the Baltic Sea with their navy.[12] Despite
the reputation of the Baltic Sea as a "Swedish lake" in the seventeenth
century, piracy and smuggling could still occur even in the Baltic.

By the early seventeenth century, English privateers were operating not only in the English Channel and the Atlantic, but also in the
Mediterranean. When warfare re-erupted between Spain and the
United Provinces after the Twelve Year Truce (1609–21), Dutch privateers and fleets resumed their attacks on Spanish shipping in the
Atlantic. Individual Spanish ships had long been vulnerable to attacks
if they became separated from convoys, but in September 1628, a
Dutch fleet of 32 ships under Piet Hein surprised a Spanish silver
fleet of four galleons and eleven merchant ships in Matanzas Bay on
the northern coast of Cuba. As the outnumbered Spanish fleet
attempted to reach the safety of the port of Matanzas, several of the
silver-laden ships ran aground. The Dutch warships captured the
entire Spanish fleet, seizing goods worth an estimated 11.5 million
guilders and burning the rest of the ships.[13] The close connections
between piracy and privateering that the English and Dutch developed to fight against the Spanish in the Atlantic influenced maritime
warfare around the world.

Piracy and naval conflict in the Indian Ocean

Imperial ventures and globalizing commerce altered piracy in the Indian Ocean in the late sixteenth century. The Ottoman Empire continued to compete with the Portuguese in the Red Sea and the Persian Gulf from its bases in Egypt and the Arabian peninsula. Urban elites in city-states such as Hormuz, Surat, and Bandar bought protection from pirates and military contractors to protect their merchant shipping. At times, city-states along the Indian Ocean coast organized "merchant resistance" and privateering against European commercial expansion. The Mappala of Malabar challenged Portuguese dominance along the southwest Indian coastline, while the Omanis and the Acehans contested Portuguese and Dutch trade.[14]

Piracy flourished alongside naval warfare in Southeast Asia in the early modern period. After seizing the strategic port of Melaka in 1511, Portuguese fleets operated throughout the Indonesian archipelago, but faced competition. The powerful sultanate of Aceh in Sumatra asserted control over commerce passing through the Sunda Straits. By the mid-sixteenth century, Aceh had built heavily armed ships, mounting artillery that could face off against Portuguese warships in the Indian Ocean and the Red Sea. Portugal's *cartaz* system, discussed above, had been developed precisely to protect Portuguese merchants from Acehan warships and pirates in the Indian Ocean.

The Dutch founded the *Verenigde Oost-Indische Compagnie* (VOC), or Dutch East India Company, in 1602 to assert Dutch commercial interests in Southeast Asia. Organized as a joint-stock company, the VOC operated as a military–merchant organization. The directors of the VOC developed a coordinated commercial and military strategy from their headquarters at the East Indies House in Amsterdam. The VOC outfitted its own armed trading ships, bristling with heavy naval artillery, in order to challenge the Portuguese trading monopoly in the Indian Ocean. VOC warships seized merchant ships carrying the *cartaz* passports and attacked Portuguese warships. VOC military and naval forces were capable of mounting joint amphibious operations against Portuguese *feitorías* on the coasts of Africa, India, and Indonesia. The VOC soon began to establish its own fortified trading posts, garrisoned by Dutch soldiers, at strategic points in the Indian Ocean. VOC officers operating from these bases were able to coordinate privateering, military conquest, and colonial development in Southeast Asia.

Portuguese, Spanish, Dutch, and English merchants simultaneously attempted to develop commercial relationships with China, which produced highly desirable luxury goods such as silk and porcelain. The Portuguese managed to establish a tenuous trading post in Macao in the 1550s and Jesuit missionaries initiated contacts with the Ming imperial court. Yet, Chinese emperors had long banned trade, except through special diplomatic tribute missions, using its Maritime Prohibition. Under the pressure of growing demands for expansive trade, Chinese imperial officials crafted a new policy in 1567 allowing Chinese merchants to trade abroad, except in Japan, which was accused of harboring pirates. Numerous Chinese smugglers nonetheless engaged in illegal trade with Japan, alongside the legitimate Chinese merchants who increasingly plied the China Sea.

Piracy rapidly expanded in the South China Sea, the East China Sea, the Sea of Japan, and the Inland Sea. Along the southern Chinese coast, many of the Dan people turned to piracy, taking advantage of the growing commerce through Macao and Hong Kong. Renegade Chinese pirates operated out of Japan and Taiwan, preying on merchant shipping in the China Sea and the Taiwan Straits. Japanese piracy often involved *daimyō* families, or sea lords, exercising dominion over important straits and sea lanes in the Sea of Japan and the Inland Sea. The Matsuya, for example, used the port of Hirado on the island of Kyushu as a pirate base, even as the city emerged as a hub of global trade with European merchants.[15]

European military leaders and merchants exploited Asian piracy and the destabilization of globalizing commerce. The Portuguese established a permanent trading post in Nagasaki in 1571, and the Dutch finally negotiated a base in 1638. But the Tokugawa *bakufu* greatly limited contact with European merchants, and clamped down on Japanese piracy. The VOC developed a coalition fleet along with renegade Chinese pirates in the 1630s to pressure the Chinese Empire to open its trading policies to Dutch commerce. Dutch privateers increasingly operated in the China Sea, aggressively attacking all Asian merchant shipping, sometimes in conjunction with local pirates. A Chinese pirate organization that the VOC had supported turned against the Dutch in the 1650s, ousting them from Taiwan.[16] Despite this reverse, the VOC emerged as "the world's largest and best-capitalized privateer enterprise."[17]

Navies and commerce raiding

By the mid-seventeenth century, maritime commerce raiding had become closely linked to states' naval policies. Defending and promoting maritime commerce became a major justification for declaring war on commercial and naval rivals. Naval warfare supported colonial ventures and aimed to control trade routes in mercantile wars. European states such as England, France, and the Netherlands waged intensive *guerre de corse* (naval raiding) using naval forces and privateers, often referred to as *corsaires*. Maritime raids in oceans around the world were fueled by economic globalization and international military and naval competition between the states that sponsored privateers.

Modern images of pirates seem to have grown out of seventeenth-century piracy in the Caribbean, when buccaneers and smugglers were able to operate autonomously from relatively lawless ports. The pirates of the Caribbean have often been romanticized in novels and films, in part because of the success of early eighteenth-century literary depictions of English pirates such as Edward Teach, who was known as Blackbeard.

However, much of this pirate lore harkens back to the raiding by seventeenth-century privateers such as Henry Morgan, an English privateer who operated out of Jamaica. Morgan and other privateers tested the limits of their commissions by plundering Spanish settlements, but continuing to submit captured ships and their goods to prize courts for adjudication. The notorious William Kidd exceeded his commission so spectacularly with his raids in the Caribbean and the Indian Ocean that he was tried for piracy and executed in England in 1701.

States commissioned naval and privateer captains to attack pirates, who were considered enemies of all humanity. Tales of pirate attacks and captivity narratives of slaves held in North Africa inspired fierce anti-piracy rhetoric in the seventeenth century. Prize courts attempted to control privateering by adjudicating seizures and prosecuting some captains for piracy.[18] Yet, actual anti-piracy campaigns were hesitant and largely unsuccessful in the early modern period. In response to English privateering, Spanish ports launched *guardacostas* (coastguards) to protect shipping, and by the early eighteenth century these vessels were engaging in their own privateering activities, sponsored by the Spanish crown.[19] Even in the Caribbean, then, state-sponsored privateering was always more prevalent than anarchic freebooting activity, despite states' failures to control the violence of privateers.

A much more significant historical development that emerged from anti-piracy attempts was the growth of international maritime law. Alberico Gentili, an important theorist of the laws of war, applied concepts of natural law and sovereignty to maritime spaces in the early seventeenth century. Hugo Grotius crafted a natural law theory of freedom of navigation, published as *Mare Liberum* (1609), which simultaneously envisioned states exerting authority at sea. Lauren

Benton argues that Grotius believed that "parts of the sea could be militarized and controlled," creating the basis for "sovereignty at sea."[20] Later political theorists and jurists worked to establish an international law at sea to justify naval action against pirates and legal measures to protect merchant ships from illegal seizures.

Borderlands Raiding

Raiding warfare on land intensified in regions where colonial empires and indigenous societies interacted. These regions have often been described in the past as "frontiers," but are now usually analyzed through "borderlands studies." Anthropologists R. Brian Ferguson and Neil L. Whitehead use a similar comparative concept of a "tribal zone," which can be defined as "that area continuously affected by the proximity of a state, but not under state administration."[21] Societies in such "tribal zones" were transformed and militarized, resulting in changing patterns of warfare beyond expanding empires. These related analytical concepts of cultural spaces beyond imperial control allow for a comparative examination of raiding violence in borderlands around the world in the early modern period.

Raiding war in the middle ground

The concept of "borderlands" is closely associated with Richard White's study of conflict in the "middle ground" of the Great Lakes region of North America. According to White, "the middle ground is the place in between: in between cultures, peoples, and in between empires and the nonstate world of villages."[22] Raids accompanied cultural exchanges and accommodations in this "middle ground," even as Amerindians and European colonists clashed.

Intense raiding war developed by the mid-seventeenth century in the woodlands near the English and French colonies along the Atlantic coast of North America. Amerindians would set ambushes in the dense woods, surprising enemies along trails. Raiding parties employed tactics developed in hunting game, relying on silence to approach targets for their ambush attacks with bows and arrows. Amerindian raiding tactics sometimes aimed to overwhelm isolated groups of enemies with war clubs and other weapons. In addition, raiding parties would conduct long-range forays, traveling far from their own villages to take captives. Some Amerindians conducted large-scale raids on enemy villages. English colonists, who had little understanding of Amerindian culture and habits, dismissively referred to Amerindian raiding warfare as "skulking," viewing concealment and hit-and-run attacks as improper conduct of war.

During the seventeenth century, European colonists developed their own practices of irregular warfare in North America. Jamestown and other English colonial settlements organized militias, which adopted brutal raiding tactics. Colonists fought against the Powhatan confederacy in Virginia in the 1610s, burning villages and crops. During the Pequot War in 1637, Connecticut soldiers and their allies massacred the inhabitants of a Pequot village. Narragansett warriors and their allies launched effective raids against English colonists in Massachusetts during King Philip's War in the 1670s.

English tactics in North America seem to have drawn on the experience of colonial warfare in Ireland. During the Elizabethan colonization of the northern counties of Ireland in the 1570s and 1580s, English planters appropriated lands and ousted Irish residents. Irish chieftains utilized raiding warfare to resist English colonization, but the English developed harsh tactics to suppress raiding and rebellion. Walter Devereux, first earl of Essex, invited Sir Brian Mac Phelim O'Neill and his entourage to a Christmas feast in 1574.

> They passed three nights and days together pleasantly and cheerfully....[Then], as they were agreeably drinking and making meery, Brian, his brother and his wife, were seized upon by the Earl, and all his people put unsparingly to the sword – men, women, youths, and maidens – in Brian's own presence. Brian was afterwards sent to Dublin with his wife and brother, where they were cut in quarters. Such was the end of their feast.[23]

Atrocities, such as assassinations and massacres, were part of the aggressive colonial warfare that the English brought to North America. They sometimes burned Amerindian villages in reprisal raids, appropriating land and settling in the borderlands regions of New England. Many colonial administrators actively promoted settlement and the expansion of cultivation in interior areas that their states claimed, but could not protect. English settlers often pushed westward ahead of their military forces.

Patterns of raiding warfare in North America were rapidly changing in the mid-seventeenth century. As French and English colonies expanded, the Amerindians in adjacent borderlands adapted and responded. The powerful Iroquois confederacy of the Cayuga, Mohawk, Oneida, Onondaga, and Seneca nations conducted joint diplomatic and military action to preserve their status and territories.

The Iroquois had long raided in order to control hunting grounds for beaver pelts, but growing global demand for beaver fur, which was used in manufacturing hats, fueled intensive resource warfare in the borderlands of North America. These "beaver wars" led to changes in Iroquois raiding practices as the adoption of captives became de-emphasized in favor of commercial priorities. By the mid-seventeenth century, the Iroquois were increasingly trading beaver pelts for muskets, acquiring substantial stocks of firearms.

In the woodlands of the Great Lakes region, the Hurons, Illinois, Miami, and other Algonquians faced different patterns of conflict in the borderlands created by the expansion of French colonies into what the French called the *pays d'en haut* (highlands). Algonquians sought refuge in this region from Iroquois expansion and raids, forming new communities and gradually developing alliances with French forces by the late seventeenth century. Many Algonquians intermarried with French traders and settlers, creating a *métis* (ethnically mixed) culture in settlements along Lake Michigan and Lake Superior. French colonists used marine detachments and *coureurs de bois* (fur traders) to conduct long-distance raids in New France when necessary, but otherwise relied on their Algonquian allies to conduct raiding warfare against their Iroquois and English enemies. The French soldiers seem to have instituted scalping bounties and slavery in the late seventeenth century in order to solidify their alliance with the Algonquians.

Raiding in badlands and steppes

In the arid plains and badlands north of New Spain (present-day American Southwest), Amerindians defined their territories using broad spaces as hunting grounds and settlement zones. Horses and cattle were first imported into the Americas by the Spanish, but they spread beyond the limits of New Spain as animals escaped and became wild. The Caddos raided mustang horses in the plains along the Gulf of Mexico. Apaches and Comanches raided across the Llano Escatado for human captives, horses, and livestock – fighting both the Spanish and each other. Spanish forces conducted raids in the badlands, enslaving their Amerindian captives.

As Spanish and Portuguese colonists and missionaries ventured into the interiors of Central and South America during the seventeenth century, some Amerindians resisted using raiding warfare. The majority of the colonists had settled along the coast in port cities and plantations, but cattle ranching spread across the Pampas of

Argentina and Brazilian grasslands, encroaching on Amerindian villages and forcing many to flee to mountainous and jungle areas
beyond the ranchers. *Bandeiras*, military companies of Portuguese
settlers, raided to capture and enslave non-Christianized Amerindians in the interior of Brazil. Jesuits organized converted Guaraní
militias to help defend their missions from both Amerindian and
bandeirantes raids in the mid-seventeenth century. Meanwhile,
"armed, mounted cowboys, or *vaqueiros*, were the shock troops of
the colonial advance," according to John F. Richards. "They defended
their herds from raiding Indians or bandit groups and, when necessary, could be mobilized to serve as militiamen in wars with the
Indians."[24] Raids sometime targeted sugar plantations, but coastal
settlements were more vulnerable to pirate attacks.

Another major borderlands region emerged in the steppes of
Eurasia in the seventeenth century as the Russian Empire expanded
eastward. Russian fur hunters and trappers ranged into Siberia in the
sixteenth and early seventeenth centuries, pursuing sable, ermine, fox,
and other pelts. The Russian hunting parties employed firearms and
competed with local Siberian hunters, killing massive numbers of
animals for their furs. "Throughout the seventeenth century," one
study finds, "a plausible Siberian harvest…would have ranged
between 200,000 and 300,000 sable pelts every year."[25] Russian fur
trapping and trading prompted raiding warfare with indigenous
populations in Siberia. The Russian Empire encouraged peasants to
settle frontier areas in the Caucuses and on the steppes of Central
Asia during the late sixteenth and seventeenth centuries. Russian
expansion southward threatened the Tatars, who retaliated by raiding
Russian peasants, taking more than 2,000 captives in 1637 alone.
The Russian military built several fortified lines to protect the southern frontier of the empire and prevent fugitive Russian serfs from
fleeing, but the fortifications could not effectively halt Tatar raiding
along the contested border until the 1650s. Cossacks raided in Ukraine
and Crimea in this period, but many of them were eventually co-
opted by the Russian military to serve as light cavalry in semi-
autonomous martial societies, each led by a *hetman*. Meanwhile,
various nomadic horsemen still raided across the sparsely populated
Eurasian steppes.

The Ottoman–Habsburg military frontier in the mountainous
region of the Balkans and Hungary generated perpetual raids. The
opposing fortress lines, garrisons, and militias along the frontier
between two major expanding territorial empires created a narrow
strip of contested territory. The Habsburg dynasty established a
defense-in-depth system along this military frontier. In Croatia, the

Habsburgs created *Militärgrenze* to protect villages from raiding Ottoman cavalry. Raiding in the borderlands in Hungary, Transylvania, and the Balkans was characterized by irregular warfare often conducted by mounted raiding parties. Armed refugees and military colonists who had fled from Ottoman occupied territories engaged in raiding.

Raiding warfare affected the mountainous and desert regions of Arabia and North Africa. Rebellions against the Ottoman Empire sometimes involved bandit raids and nomadic incursions in the late sixteenth and seventeenth centuries. Bedouin horsemen raided in the Arabian peninsula, along the edge of the Ottoman Empire, which controlled Mecca, Medina, and the Red Sea coast.[26] Berbers and other warriors raided in the Atlas Mountains of Morocco and at the heads of the trans-Saharan caravan routes. Complex credit mechanisms including loans, pawning, and enslavement supported the trans-Saharan camel caravans across the great desert, but also attracted raiders.

Raiding in grasslands and rainforests

On the West African coast and across the interior savannahs and rainforests, slave-taking became integral to warfare. Powerful cavalry armies enslaved men, women, and children in the regions formerly dominated by the Mali and Songhay Empires, and resold many individuals into the trans-Saharan slave trade. Localized slave-raiding operations seem to have been common aspects of African warfare in the seventeenth century. Raiding war in the rainforests of Gold Coast and Ivory Coast increasingly supplied slaves to Portuguese, Dutch, English, and French slave traders at ports along the Gulf of Guinea. Trading for firearms seems to have greatly stimulated slave-taking, a process analyzed by historians through the concept of "gun-slave cycles."[27]

The inhabitants of the grasslands of South Africa and East Africa faced colonial raids. Portuguese expeditionary forces began raiding the East African coast soon after rounding the Cape of Good Hope. Portuguese amphibious forces raided East African port towns that they could not conquer, sacking Mombasa successively in 1505, 1528, and again in 1589. Portuguese colonists built forts at Mozambique and other key ports, attempting to control commerce in gold and ivory from East Africa. The Portuguese settlers moved from Mozambique into the interior of Africa, inciting colonial warfare and rebellions by local Muslims.[28] The Dutch VOC established Cape

Town and other settlements in South Africa in the mid-seventeenth century to ensure passage of shipping between the Atlantic and Indian Oceans. Dutch settlers known as *trekboers* raised livestock, ranging over grazing lands and competing with indigenous herders.[29]

Despite the strength and relative stability of the Mughal Empire, raiding warfare developed in several regions of South Asia. The rugged mountains of Afghanistan sheltered Uzbek raiders on the northern borders of the Mughal Empire. Merchants from Gujarat's ports traded across the Indian Ocean with Swahili ports, becoming targets for raids. Indian cotton, pepper, and spice production generated highly lucrative commercial resources for the growing global market. Indian farmers could also act as small-scale military entrepreneurs, seeking employment in a huge military labor market in India in the early modern period, which could not be completely controlled by the Mughal administration. Local Indian elites were able to raise their own military forces, and by the late sixteenth century the Mughal Empire was facing growing rebellions and raiding warfare from the Rajputs and Marathas.

The rainforests of Southeast Asia hosted stateless peoples beyond the effective reach of sultanates and kingdoms. Arakanese slave raiders competed with the Portuguese along the Burmese coast in the early seventeenth century. Diverse hill peoples in present-day Myanmar, Thailand, Laos, southern China, and Vietnam ranged across the uplands of the Southeast Asian Massif. When organized states' military forces attempted to expand into the Massif, raiding warfare proliferated in these upland regions. These hill peoples have been referred to collectively as Zomians by some scholars, but whether or not they represented empowered anarchists or displaced refugees is hotly debated.[30]

Raiding parties in borderlands around the world often inflicted systematic rape, gendered violence, hostage-taking, and enslavement on men, women, and children abducted from rural and coastal villages. Captivity narratives tended to construct gendered discourses of confinement and liberation, simultaneously arguing for military action against pirates and "barbaric" indigenous peoples. Economic refugees, religious refugees, and borderlands inhabitants attempted to escape from the destruction of piracy and raiding warfare in the Atlantic and Indian Ocean Worlds. Maroon communities formed in the Caribbean and South America, as escaped slaves banded together to survive beyond colonial societies. Colonial raiding parties in the Caribbean and South America attempted to recapture maroons and return them to captivity.

Economic Devastation

All early modern military units conducted foraging activities, since states were unable to adequately supply field armies. Historians have often assumed that logistical services were virtually non-existent in the early modern period, in part because logistics tasks were typically handled by civilian merchants and administrators rather than official military organizations. The precise role that foraging played in early modern warfare has been debated, however. Martin Van Creveld's groundbreaking history of logistics depicts most European armies as essentially "living off the land" until 1914, when modern armies began to be able to organize their own supply systems.[31] John A. Lynn criticizes Van Creveld's thesis and develops a much more articulated history of logistics that distinguishes distinct periods associated with changing supply systems.[32] This approach allows us to consider logistical systems in diverse military systems around the world during the early modern period.

Pillaging and foraging

Certain early modern military systems had developed supply networks and procedures for moving troops within their societies. The *étapes* system in France, for example, established a series of posts along key royal highways for supplying troops that were traveling within the country. As the seventeenth century progressed, European states established regular winter quarters for their permanent military forces. Such supply systems rarely worked efficiently under the strains of massive mobilizations, heavy taxation, and food shortages during the Thirty Years War, however.

Field armies operating outside their own state's territories faced formidable challenges in feeding their hungry soldiers. Some were able to provide mobile ovens to bake bread for soldiers, but many relied on foraging. Foraging parties also had to find oats and fodder for cavalry and supply horses. Soldiers often received insufficient rations and suffered from pay that was months in arrears, so they resorted to pillaging farms to survive. This practice was so common that it was accepted as normal, and has been described as a "tax of violence."[33] Soldiers' wives and partners played crucial roles in pillage economies, carrying booty and protecting the couples' belongings on campaign. Looted goods were often resold to petty merchants and camp followers who accompanied field armies, or at markets in nearby towns.

The burdens of supplying armies were generally more than peasant villagers could bear. Incessant raiding warfare, contributions, and taxation in war zones during the seventeenth century prompted retaliation and resistance from peasants, as we will see in the next chapter. Peasants were often reduced to begging in their own communities, or forced to migrate as economic refugees. Civil wars created significant internal displacement as desperate peasants sheltered with field armies as camp followers. The plundering and destruction associated with raiding warfare created widespread poverty and revolts in many areas.[34]

Deserters and ex-soldiers ravaged the European countryside throughout the seventeenth century. Soldiers abandoned their military units because of consistent pay shortages, poor living conditions, and rampant disease. At the end of each campaigning season, numerous companies and entire regiments were disbanded, often leaving the now unemployed soldiers no way to survive other than by pillaging. Groups of deserters formed marauding bands of bandits, especially in the forests of Germany. Pillaging by deserters was certainly not unique to Germany during the seventeenth century, but some of the best documentation of early modern pillaging comes from the records of the Thirty Years War.[35] Soldiers could easily desert their units in the forests and marginally populated countryside of many regions of Eastern Europe. Mounted raiding parties crisscrossed the immense kingdom of Poland-Lithuania during the seventeenth-century civil wars known as the "Deluge."

Banditry and highway robbery tend to be seen as part of the history of crime, yet these forms of violence appear to have been closely associated with raiding warfare in dense forests and mountainous regions. We have already seen how exiled criminals and nobles often engaged in vendettas during the Italian Wars. Civil wars offered opportunities for town militias and cavalry units to engage in banditry. Groups of bandits could also align themselves with local militants, creating anarchic situations for civilian travelers and merchants in the countryside. Tales featuring vagabonds, rogues, and highway robbers became common during the late sixteenth and early seventeenth centuries, embedding a fear of forests into literary works written in this period. Picaresque novels such as *La vida de Lazarillo de Tormes y de sus fortunas y adversidades* (1554) and Miguel de Cervantes's *Don Quixote* (1605) present banditry as part of a disorderly world filled with begging, gambling, and misfortune.

Military historians have often dismissed non-European armies as marauding hordes, but recent studies suggest that many early modern armies used targeted pillage in their logistics. Nomadic horse archers ranged across the steppes of Eurasia, using milk and meat products to sustain themselves, while raiding for grain supplies and other goods. Some Amerindian war bands carried dried corn rations and necessary supplies on their raids. War parties in borderlands around the world could engage hunting and foraging while conducting raids.

Some military and administrative systems attempted to limit foraging. The Ottoman Empire developed an extensive bureaucratic administration to supply its armies, and especially the elite janissary corps. The sultan's kitchen provided meat for the imperial household troops on campaign. Merchants and camp followers accompanied Ottoman armies, exchanging goods in the *ordu bazaar*, or army market.[36] The supply of the large Safavid and Mughal armies similarly used a combination of bureaucratic and merchant logistics. In all these armies, auxiliary troops seem to have supplied their own equipment and had to forage for food. Military officers probably advanced food and supplies on their own credit to supply their troops. So, even the great imperial armies of the early modern period must have relied on extensive foraging operations. Smaller kingdoms and city-states around the world provisioned their troops by taxing staple crops and purchasing other food and supplies.

Fortifications and small war

In response to the disorderly conduct of mercenaries and mutinying troops who rampaged through rural and urban communities when pay or supplies ran short, some states began to fund sizeable permanent garrisons. Fortresses and citadels became elaborate fortification systems, which included barracks to house garrisons that might comprise several companies of cavalry and infantry. Bastioned fortifications became bases for defensive and offensive raiding warfare during the sixteenth century. The proliferation of bastioned fortifications and the creation of large permanent garrisons encouraged new forms of positional warfare.

Raids by garrison troops proliferated in the densely urbanized areas of Europe, which were contested by large field armies fielded by monarchical states. The numerous bastioned fortifications in northern Italy, the Netherlands, and Germany provided bases for small garrisons of soldiers who could launch localized raids. The divisions between the Spanish-controlled loyalist southern Netherlands and the rebellious northern provinces hardened during the Twelve Year Truce of 1609–21. Extensive bastioned fortress systems developed along this military frontier, lodging numerous Spanish and

Dutch garrisons, which engaged in raiding warfare once the fighting resumed in 1621. By the mid-seventeenth century, the Netherlands had become one of the main regions characterized by intensive and nearly perpetual raiding war. Municipal governments in the breakaway United Provinces struggled to maintain fortifications and lodge garrison soldiers.[37]

The fighting in the Netherlands during the seventeenth century helped to define a new type of raiding war, often referred to as *petite guerre*, or small war. Field armies largely conducted conventional warfare that focused on maneuvering to engage enemy armies in battle or to launch siege operations. At the same time, field armies occupied urban fortifications, attempting to control populations and strategic points. From these fortifications, garrisons launched extensive raiding parties to wage small war against enemy raiding parties and peasant communities. Small war thus supported the operations of field armies and was closely connected to operational and strategic aims, even if command and control tended to be highly localized. This type of small war was used across heavily fortified areas of Germany, Italy, and northern France during the Thirty Years War.

Bastioned artillery fortresses spread around the world during the sixteenth and seventeenth centuries, establishing bases for European garrisons to conduct raiding warfare. Geoffrey Parker provocatively argues that "the artillery fortress constituted the crucial link between the Europeans' naval mastery and their ability to attract and exploit local allies." This military advantage, Parker believes, allowed European colonial powers to establish footholds in far-flung territories around the world and eventually "to expand to global dominance."[38] The firepower of the artillery pieces positioned in bastioned fortifications offered relative security to even isolated garrisons. Such fortifications were certainly not impregnable, but they allowed garrisons to conduct localized raiding activities when necessary. Fortified port cities provided vital bases for European colonial, commercial, naval, and privateering expeditions.

Many territorial empires and states around the world acquired artillery pieces and constructed fortifications during the late sixteenth and seventeenth centuries. The Ottoman Empire employed artillery fortresses in its major cities and along its military frontiers. Mughal rulers built immense stone walls around major cities, later installing artillery platforms in some fortifications. Chinese cities relied on massive stone walls for protection. Many smaller principalities and city-states built impressive fortifications. The Mons of Pegu constructed major fortifications in their efforts to unify Burma in the sixteenth and seventeenth centuries. Societies that did not have artillery responded to the proliferation of bastioned fortifications by developing new techniques of raiding warfare beyond the firezones of emplaced guns.

Contributions systems

Early modern armies could be predators, engaging in systematic raiding warfare. Soldiers routinely pillaged villages in the path of war, stealing food and valuables from vulnerable peasants. Armies confiscated crops, oats, hay, and munitions from villages and towns, often compelling municipal leaders to requisition needed supplies from residents. But European armies began to employ more regulated forms of resource extraction in the early seventeenth century.

Field armies began to demand contributions, payments intended to supply troops, from villages and towns. Contributions could be paid with coins or with a mixture of crops and goods. Logistical officers often rode ahead of approaching field armies to arrange for contributions, which were normally assessed according to tax records. The contributions that peasants and townspeople paid to armies came to represent a form of protection money.

Albrecht von Wallenstein and other military enterprisers routinized contributions in Germany during the Thirty Years War, extracting installment payments from communities. Contributions became closely associated with taxation, which were often also raised by soldiers. The heavy burdens of taxes and contributions in France during the Thirty Years War led one pamphlet author to complain that the *taille* tax was "in part raised by the means of companies of fusiliers who are so many unchained devils."[39] The repeated extractions of contributions in France eventually led to protests and civil conflict.

Field armies punished villages and cities that failed to pay contributions or that supported enemy raiding parties. During the Thirty Years War, German villagers came to fear the figure of the *brandmeister*, a soldier bearing a lighted torch and prepared to set peasants' homes on fire if they failed to supply passing troops. Light cavalry companies and colonial militias sometimes adopted systematic burning of villages and crops to punish rural populations. Field armies could inflict massive agricultural and economic damage, resulting in food deprivation and depopulation across an entire region.

As armies became permanent in the seventeenth century, generals would choose untouched regions for winter quarters so that their troops could extract contributions and food supplies from communities. Henri de La Tour d'Auvergne, vicomte de Turenne, a renowned mid-seventeenth-century general and maréchal de France, believed that the selection of a region for autumn campaigning was crucial, "because then you can gain command of a tract of territory in which you have all winter to refresh and remake your army."[40]

The populations of many cities suffered directly from the pervasive siege warfare of the seventeenth century. Armies investing urban centers normally demanded that magistrates capitulate and provide contributions for their troops. When cities refused, besieging armies could blockade and bombard city walls for months before breaching key bastions and compelling garrisons to surrender or face assaults. When garrisons refused to capitulate, besiegers organized assaults and brutally applied the law of the siege. Following successful assaults, victorious soldiers would plunder homes and loot shops, resulting in some of the worst pillaging of the early modern period. Armies that seized cities subjected defeated communities to prolonged occupations, establishing garrisons and lodging troops in residents' homes in order to extract food and resources.

Conclusion

Raids on land and at sea afflicted communities and travelers throughout the early modern world. Attacks by marauding pirates, plundering brigands, and stealthy war bands could seem chaotic. Yet, raiding warfare became increasingly associated with armies and state power during this period. African kingdoms exercised indirect and direct state power through persistent raiding war and slave-taking. European states and empires employed privateering, military contracting, and contributions systems to wage lengthy wars, often at great distances.

The sultanate of Aceh in northwestern Sumatra offers an important case of raiding warfare and state power in the early seventeenth century. Aceh had become powerful during the late sixteenth century by constructing naval vessels and raiding Portuguese commerce in the Melaka Straits. The sultans maintained a close relationship with the Ottoman Empire, which provided arms and technologies, but also negotiated shifting alliances with Portuguese, Dutch, and English trading companies. The sultans of Aceh used contracted and slave recruitment to raise military forces composed of swordsmen, arquebusiers, and cavalry lancers, supported by artillery and an elephant corps. Acehnese armies secured the capital city and conquered adjacent territories, including ports that could be used for raiding warfare.[41]

Sultan Iskander Muda (1607–36) expanded Aceh's naval forces, constructing numerous large war galleys and arming them with cannons. He launched raids against trading outposts and merchant shipping in the Melaka Strait, as well as campaigns to conquer pepper-producing areas and important commercial ports on Sumatra and the Malay Peninsula, bringing back numerous slaves. His armies and fleets generated vast wealth by restricting the commercial independence of Acehnese merchants and operating a state monopoly on the pepper and slave trade. A major Acehnese army besieged Portuguese Melaka in 1629, but failed to take it. Nonetheless, Aceh demonstrated its ability to sustain state-sponsored raiding warfare against regional and European trading companies.[42] Raiding warfare in the early modern world was far from "primitive war."

8

Peasant Revolt and Rural Conflict, 1590s–1650s

A large group of bandits led by a former slave named Khlopko terrorized the countryside around Moscow in 1603, ambushing a contingent of *strel'tsy* musketeers who tried to disrupt their rapacious activities. An alarmed Tsar Boris Godunov sent a larger military force to destroy Khlopko's band, capturing and executing a number of the bandits.[1] Many peasants and slaves across Russia had taken up arms in the political chaos following the murder of the previous tsar's son in 1598. During the period known as the Time of Troubles (1598–1613), the Muscovite state experienced a series of succession crises, coupled with widespread famine, economic devastation, and civil warfare. Russian peasants believed that God would grant Russia their true tsar, allowing a string of pretenders to the throne to raise broad rural followings, composed of "Cossacks and other lower-grade servitors, non-Slavic tribesmen, fugitive peasants, and slaves." False Dimitri I, False Peter, Bolotnikov, False Dimitri II, and other pretenders led peasant armies during the Time of Troubles. According to John Keep, "these makeshift armies waged one campaign after another, under the banner of false pretenders to the throne or simple bandit chieftains, with the object of avenging themselves on their former masters and refashioning the social hierarchy to suit their sectional interests."[2] Rural conflict and banditry disrupted the agrarian lives of peasants across Russia until the Romanov dynasty finally began to restore order.

The rural conflicts in Russia during the Time of Troubles remind us that everyday life for most humans throughout the early modern world was dominated by agrarian societies and subsistence economies. Agriculture was frequently threatened by military extractions, environmental disruptions, and meteorological disasters. Severe monetary inflation and growing populations in many parts of the world produced a series of economic crises in the late sixteenth century. A period of global cooling, known as the Little Ice Age, then exacerbated the economic deprivation and ecological disaster, producing severe famines and social chaos throughout much of the seventeenth century.

Peasants in many regions responded to economic and social pressures by protesting and, at times, rebelling over crop failures, hoarding, and high prices. Many rural societies were disturbed by pervasive crime, banditry, and riots due to the ongoing crises. Studies of crowd actions in the early modern period demonstrate that peasant crowds should not be characterized as unruly "mobs," since they were hardly mindless or traditional.[3] Village inhabitants were capable of organizing armed bands, selecting their leaders, adopting specific rituals, and choosing specific forms of violence. This chapter explores everyday violence in agrarian societies, before considering peasant protest, resistance, and revolt.[4]

Everyday Life and Rural Violence

Peasant culture has often been presented as "traditional," based on supposedly unchanging agricultural patterns and social structures. It has frequently been assumed that agricultural societies can be defined in terms of "peasant conservatism," which is an inflexible attitude toward agricultural innovation and social change, but social historians have revealed complexities in peasant responses to economic changes. During the sixteenth and seventeenth centuries, peasants were adapting to new farming techniques, climate change, intensive agriculture, and global plant exchanges.

Agrarian societies and peasant culture

Classic Annales School studies of early modern peasants used a *longue durée* approach to social history, typically examining demographic and economic data in local peasant societies over several centuries. Emmanuel Le Roy Ladurie's landmark study, *The Peasants of Languedoc*, created a model for the social history of peasant societies, using rich economic and social data from market accounts, wage receipts, tax records, baptismal registers, marriage contracts, and burial registers to construct a complex demographic and economic history of the peasants of the southern French province of Languedoc in the early modern period.[5]

Recent research by social and cultural historians has revealed that early modern agrarian societies were more diversified than previously thought. Rural life was centered on the seigneurial estates and villages that organized farming and agricultural labor, which produced staple crops primarily for local consumption. Steven Kaplan has described "the tyranny of cereal-dependence in the pre- or proto-industrial world." Whether peasants consumed grains, rice, maize, or other staples, "cereal-dependence conditioned every phase of social life."[6] Farmers in Eurasia, Africa, and the Americas overwhelming depended on their own crops for food in economic systems that were still heavily reliant on subsistence agriculture. Yet, villages were also economically linked to nearby small towns, where excess staple crops could be sold, along with vegetables, fruit, and food specialties. Some early modern peasants engaged in market gardening and craftwork, which allowed them to generate income or barter for needed goods. Large towns and cities depended on the diversifying agricultural economies to import staples and other foods, usually using river and coastal transportation.

Since peasants constituted the vast majority of almost every early modern society, they could not represent a single monolithic group, much less a social class. Rural societies were made up of a broad spectrum of peasants, including landowning peasants, serfs, sharecroppers, migrant farmworkers, pastoral herders, foresters, and destitute vagabonds. In France, the term *coq du village* described a wealthy landowning peasant who occupied a position of relative dominance within a peasant community, perhaps owning half the properties in a village. Other peasants were small landowners, possessing a single family home and nearby fields. Many peasants owned a home, but not their fields, acting as sharecroppers. Bonded peasants and serfs across much of Eurasia worked on large seigneurial farms owned by elite landlords under onerous labor conditions and restrictions on their mobility. Peasants in many societies also had to perform *corvée* labor, doing maintenance work on local roads and collective projects.

Rural conflicts have often been characterized as "peasant revolts" or "popular revolts," but historians are increasingly discovering close political and social links between peasant farmers, rural elites, urban residents, and municipal governments. Rural poverty was pervasive and many peasants depended heavily on personal charity from social elites and religious organizations, creating close relationships between peasants and rural elites. Peasants actively defended their village liberties and privileges using negotiations, lawsuits, and protests.

Farmers were periodically able to air their grievances to judicial authorities or consultative bodies.

Despite high levels of illiteracy among rural populations, peasants were often well informed about political, military, and economic developments. Officials normally read royal edicts, court judgments, and administrative orders aloud in villages before posting them. Peddlers and colporteurs, who sold political pamphlets and prints, traveled through rural areas, spreading war news. Rumors of new tax policies and enforcement mechanisms could trigger protests and riots in villages and towns. Itinerant religious leaders preached in villages, spreading new religious ideas among peasants, who sometimes developed radical religious and political agendas. Peasant uprisings could be spectacular events with mass participation, as we have seen with the 1525 German Peasants' War, discussed above in chapter 3.

Seasonal cycles and carnivalesque violence

The rhythms of rural life revolved around plowing, planting, weeding, and harvesting crops, as well as tending and slaughtering livestock. The theme of the Labors of the Months illustrated rural life through representations of emblematic agricultural activities that drew on ancient and medieval precedents. Early modern almanacs, calendars, prayer books, and prints frequently depicted the Labors of the Months and the Four Seasons, diffusing images of seasonal cycles in popular culture. Christian, Islamic, and Confucian calendars all incorporated the signs of the zodiac and astrological information to assist in calculating the timing of agricultural activities. Although these scenes of everyday rural life could seem bucolic, peasant routines also included close relationships to violence. Harvest scenes show peasants wielding flails and scythes, farming tools that could easily become weapons. Depictions of November and December in European Labors of the Months often showed the slaughtering of pigs and sausage making.

Peasants routinely engaged in violence through hunting. In many regions, seigneurial rights prohibited peasants from hunting game – reserving deer, elk, wild boar, and other prestigious animals for the lord's use. Yet, at certain times, peasants could hunt in order to give gifts of big game to their lords. In addition, they served as beaters in the woods on noble estates during their landlords' hunts. Farmers were normally allowed to hunt rabbits, foxes, rodents, and other animals that were regarded as pests, permitting them to protect their crops and supplement their diets. Local peasant communities were sometimes able to challenge nobles' hunting privileges in law courts, allowing for broader peasant hunting practices. Some peasants were still hunting with bows-and-arrows or light crossbows, but across Eurasia they were increasingly developing skills with arquebuses, muskets, and other firearms through their hunting activities.

Rural life was punctuated by celebrations of religious and communal festivities, many of which had violent dimensions. Peasant marriage festivities often included the entire village's residents, who engaged in heavy drinking, dancing, and sometimes fighting. The Mahanavami festival in India involved martial display and military processions. Village youth in many societies engaged in charivaris, ritualistic shaming displays, to mock cuckolds or social transgressors. Charivaris always employed disruptive behavior such as banging on pots and pans, but could also direct physical violence at victims.

Many rural festivals involved ritual animal sacrifice or the slaughtering of animals for feasts. In Catholic territories, major saints' days were celebrated with feasting. Peasants across much of Europe slaughtered pigs and wild boars in the winter to make sausages and salamis, especially for Christmas festivities. European peasants utilized short swords and knives in slaughtering and butchering game and livestock during festivals at Easter and at intervals throughout the year.

Carnival is the best-studied festival of the early modern period, in part because of its reputation for carnivalesque violence, as riots erupted during the several weeks of boisterous Carnival festivities that prepared believers for the fasting and devotional activities of Lent. In the medieval period, the Latin Christian Church had celebrated Carnival across Europe, but during the sixteenth century Protestant rulers banned Lenten fasting and Carnival festivities as idolatrous excesses. By the seventeenth century, Carnival celebrations occurred only in Catholic territories, even though other forms of carnivalesque violence occurred elsewhere.

Peter Bruegel's famous painting, *The Combat between Carnival and Lent* (1559), evokes the violence and disorder of the festival through personifications of Carnival as a fat man jousting against an emaciated Lent. François Rabelais crafted literary expressions of carnivalesque humor and peasant misbehavior, which Mikhail Bakhtin interprets as being deeply subversive.[7] During Carnival, peasants could freely indulge in gluttonous feasting and excessive drinking. Authorities seem to have tolerated rowdy behavior, grotesque display, sexual humor, and foolishness. Carnival festivities utilized images of the world turned upside down to flaunt social order, representing women or animals in positions of power. The figure of the Wild Man, with a scraggly beard and woodsy attire, symbolized disorder and escape from society. A peasant could be King for a Day during one of the Carnival processions held on each of the major holidays, such as Fat Thursday and Fat Tuesday (Mardi Gras) throughout the Carnival season. These parades were often composed of costumed units, masked participants, and elaborate floats.[8]

Such temporary inversions of power relationships between rulers and ruled may have served as safety valves, releasing pressure and preventing social tensions from exploding in massive peasant uprisings. In other societies, municipal and state authorities organized controlled festivities to display their power theatrically. "The public festivals of Southeast Asia appear to have reinforced rather than challenged hierarchy," according to Anthony Reid. Festivals in Aceh, Siam, and Java often included cockfights, elephant battles, and noble jousts that showcased militant displays and sometimes brutal violence.[9]

Unauthorized violence would also take place during festivals. Brawls and riots often erupted during village festivities, induced by alcohol consumption and social inversion. At the same time festivities resulted in communication and sharing between peasant and urban cultures, especially in small towns that hosted major events. In some parts of Europe, teenage boys and unmarried young men formed organizations known as youth abbeys to participate in festive sporting matches. These youth abbeys also organized maypole dancing, charivaris, and other festivities in villages throughout the year. Sometimes, peasant youth groups became involved in clashes with urban youth.

Occasionally, festive celebrations resulted in serious rural violence. The Cruel Carnival of 1511, discussed in chapter 5, resulted in a massive wave of peasant violence against the Strumieri noble landlords across Friuli. Armed peasants and artisans seized the small southeastern French town of Romans during Carnival in 1579, maintaining control of it for an entire year. The following year's Carnival celebration there produced a violent massacre, as local elites retook control of Romans and pursued rebellious peasants in the surrounding countryside.[10] Such episodes of massacre far exceeded the normal routines of carnivalesque violence and were usually related to broader civil conflicts and peasant revolts.

Subsistence crises and food riots

Many episodes of rural violence corresponded to the rhythms of seasonal climatic patterns and disruptive weather events. Crop failures occurred with depressing regularity around the world in pre-modern periods, hitting a given local area an estimated once every four or five years, creating a famine cycle. Torrential rain, flooding, hail, excessive heat, drought, early frost, and other weather conditions could all destroy crops in the fields. Insects and disease could also ravage plants, resulting in meager harvests. Failures in staple crops resulted in higher prices on grains traded in market agriculture, but also severely stressed peasants who relied on subsistence farming for their daily sustenance. An estimated one half of a peasant family's income was spent on grain or bread in the early modern period.

Serious staple crop failures could easily lead to a subsistence crisis. Bad harvests of wheat, grains, rice, or maize meant poor diets and hunger for suffering peasants. Available grain reserves would be sold at inflated prices. Peasants unable to purchase food would be malnourished and weakened. Infants and the elderly were especially susceptible to disease and starvation during a subsistence crisis, which might last for months. Historians have traced the correlations between high bread prices, high mortality rates, and low birth rates. Recorded births fell during subsistence crises, presumably due both to malnourished women's lower fertility rates and to the undesirability of having additional children during a crisis. Although famines occurred during peacetime, many subsistence crises were either created or worsened by wartime shortages and depredations.

Peasants facing subsistence crises and the threat of starvation engaged in food riots to protest high food prices and the hoarding of staple reserves. Peasant women often led protests in towns, sometimes resulting in destructive attacks on granaries and municipal authorities' homes. Successful food riots frequently resulted in the distribution of granary reserves to rioting peasants, who paid a "fair price" for the grain to make bread. Food riots represented an important form of protest and, at times, violent action in early modern societies.

Even as intensive agriculture began to present the possibility of escaping from the famine cycle, peasant communities continued to use food riots to express their grievances. E.P. Thompson's history of bread riots in eighteenth-century England provides the most influential interpretation of the phenomenon, seeing it as evidence of a "moral economy" through which peasants enacted "collective bargaining" over food prices.[11] Earlier bread riots are not well documented, making analysis of changing patterns in food protests difficult.

Food riots also raise questions about issues of population growth and Malthusian interpretations of population limits. Political economist

Thomas Malthus constructed a famous theory of population growth in the late eighteenth century, asserting that nature regulated human populations by inflicting mortality through famine, disease, and war. Population growth, for Malthus, would always be checked when it outstripped agricultural production. Le Roy Ladurie and many other social historians have used Malthusian theory to describe the demographic situation of early modern peasant societies. Critics of Malthusian restraints argue that subsistence agricultural societies could limit populations in other ways, including infanticide and abortion. Other scholars point out that semi- and fully commercialized agricultural societies were not bound by Malthusian limits on their populations, and thus could instead experience rapid growth. New evidence that Malthusian limits did not always naturally limit early modern populations suggests that many famines may not have been natural, as Malthus had proposed.[12]

Warfare was all too common in the early modern period, often disrupting the routines of everyday rural life and causing additional subsistence crises. Peasants living in war zones suffered deprivations from field armies that maneuvered near their villages. Diverse groups of peasants probably experienced warfare very differently in the early modern period, although all of them could become victims of marauding soldiers. Relatively wealthy peasants were better able to sustain the burdens of war, but might be especially targeted for pillaging. Sharecroppers and the rural poor were especially vulnerable in wartime, often recruited as soldiers or forced to flee as refugees. For many desperate peasants, joining an army was a crucial survival mechanism, since soldiers were paid wages, issued bread and drink rations, and allowed to pillage.

Rural Transformations and Conflict

Even through staple crops remained central to agricultural economies around the world, new techniques were intensifying cultivation and new markets were altering the role of staples in war and society. The changing conditions of agricultural life in the late sixteenth and seventeenth centuries created new patterns of rural violence.

Agricultural change and peasant unrest

Wheat, barley, rice, maize, and other staple crops continued to provide the bulk of the calories that humans in most societies consumed.

Although historians have normally associated staple crops exclusively with subsistence agriculture, the food demands of increasingly large cities during the early modern period created regional markets for grain. Wheat and other cereal crops could be exported, as lucrative grain markets developed in the Mediterranean and some other regions. Small merchant ships transported grains from port to port along the Mediterranean coasts in *cabotage* trade, which relied on short-distance trade in bulk goods and agricultural produce, creating the dense connectivity that Peregrine Horden and Nicholas Purcell have described.[13] The populations of large port cities such as Istanbul, Naples, and Seville depended on a maritime trade in grains from Egypt, Macedonia, and Egypt.

The growth of army sizes in the sixteenth and seventeenth centuries created new markets for grain. Armies have historically depended on staple crops for sustenance. Early modern soldiers' rations often consisted substantially of staple foods. In early modern Asian societies, soldiers usually ate rice, whereas European soldiers received rations of wheat and grains. Seventeenth-century French soldiers consumed a standard daily ration of 24 ounces of bread, a pound of meat, and a pint of wine. Meat was difficult to provide, however, so soldiers often had to rely on bread. African soldiers relied on local staples of yams, rice, or grains, depending on the region in which they fought, since staples varied across the large continent. Amerindians used maize rations, but were also incorporating foods introduced by European colonists in the seventeenth century. Armies' horses also consumed massive amounts of cereals, especially oats, as well as hay. Field armies thus sent out forage parties to harvest their own fodder for cavalry and draft horses.

The expanded role of staple crops in feeding large armies created new strains on rural societies during wartime. Armies extracted grains through direct resource mobilization and coercion. Field armies could also divert grain shipments to prioritize supplying soldiers over townspeople and peasants. Grain merchants, bakers, butchers, and entrepreneurs accompanied field armies in order to supply their needs. Hungry soldiers also pillaged extensively to supply their daily dietary needs.

Other agricultural products figured in rural conflicts. Warfare always threatened both commercial and local alcohol markets. Early modern armies consumed massive amounts of alcohol in the form of wine, beer, and rice wine rations. Field armies often requisitioned entire stocks of alcohol from farmer-producers. Even when field armies paid for alcohol, they often diverted the beverages from their normal markets, disrupting the commercial networks of alcohol producers. The crops cultivated to produce alcoholic beverages thus usually had simultaneous uses as both food crops and cash crops.

Other dual food-cash crops held significance for peasant unrest. Cheeses manufactured from cow, sheep, and goat milk were important supplemental foods for many peasants, but they could also be sold or traded at markets for cash or goods. In a world where cane sugar was still a luxury, honey was an important sweetener for foods and drinks. Honey could be consumed directly by its producers or sold commercially. Disruptions in the trade of cheese, honey, dried fruit, and other food-cash crops could prompt protests in peasant communities. Around the Mediterranean, areas known for excellent olives produced olive oil as a food-cash crop for local consumption and for export. Peasants in these regions sometimes smashed olive presses during peasant revolts, halting olive production and exportation. Salt, an important mineral resource, played a similar role to dual food-cash crops. Diverse varieties of salt were harvested in shallow lagoons and estuaries, and then exported not only as a condiment but also as the key preservative for meat and fish. Disruptions in salt supplies or new salt taxes could lead to major conflicts in agrarian societies.

Global crop and food exchanges began to transform diets, cultures, and economies by the late sixteenth century. As global circulations of seeds and plant species increased, many agrarian economies incorporated new food crops and traded in staple commodities. Portuguese, Dutch, and English ships regularly transported plants and food products from South and Southeast Asia to Africa, Europe, and the Americas in the seventeenth century. The importation of new crops diversified some agricultural systems, benefiting peasants and alleviating famine conditions. Amerindian farmers played an important role in educating European peasant settlers about their indigenous crops. Many crops from the Americas seem to have spread once European colonial settlers accepted their taste and recognized their nutritional benefits. Potatoes, one of the most famous American crops, would only be adopted as a significant staple crop in areas around the world in the eighteenth century, but other American plants became global food crops much more rapidly.

Maize (corn) from the Americas spread throughout much of the world in the sixteenth century, but its adoption was extremely varied. Peasants in many parts of Africa seem to have incorporated maize into their agricultural systems in the mid-sixteenth century, but the crop did not become a major part of African diets until much later. In the Venetian *terraferma* territories of northern Italy, peasants began to plant maize as a garden vegetable crop by the 1550s. Cultivation of maize spread quickly throughout Italy as peasants experimented with the crop as a supplement to their staple wheat-based diet. Although historians have often depicted peasants as inherently conservative and resistant to agricultural and economic changes, Italian peasants seem to have been very innovative in adapting maize cultivation to their existing agricultural systems. By 1618, the Venetian Republic was accepting maize as payment for taxes – an indication of its rapid incorporation into the Italian agrarian economy and of its growing implication in tax protests.

Agricultural systems grappled with global monetary changes and inflation. Spanish colonial authorities shipped enormous amounts of silver and gold extracted from the mines of Zacatecas in Mexico and Potosí across the Atlantic. Spain's rulers minted much of the new metallic wealth, spending heavily on warfare and luxury goods, distributing the silver and gold throughout global economies. The massive influx of silver, used in the most circulated coinage, along with copper mining and new credit mechanisms, produced hyperinflation in Europe and seems to have increased the prices of goods and commodities worldwide. The rapid inflation between the 1520s and the 1650s transformed monetary economies in a process that has become known as the Price Revolution.[14] The severe economic disruptions caused by inflation can be seen especially in the records of steadily rising grain prices, which severely affected peasant livelihoods. European peasants' real wages seem to have fallen as the real cost of bread shot up with the increased wheat prices, fueling peasant unrest.

A major intellectual debate has emerged about how the inflation of prices and the depreciation of currencies affected global agricultural economies. Kenneth Pomeranz and other world historians argue that a "great divergence" between European and Asian economies occurred only after 1800, as a result of the Industrial Revolution.[15] Some economic historians have challenged this position, suggesting that agricultural intensification and rising labor wages in parts of Europe were already creating marked differences between western European agricultural systems and those of India and China in the sixteenth and seventeenth centuries.[16] Insufficient research makes it difficult to gauge the impact of global silver flows and regional agricultural changes on peasant societies worldwide. Global monetary fluctuations and price inflation may have contributed indirectly to peasant protests and rural conflicts in many regions.

Climate change and rural disasters

A period of global cooling, known as the Little Ice Age, exacerbated the rhythms of subsistence crises across much of the world in the seventeenth century. The Little Ice Age (c.1570s–1730s) was the most extreme phase of an extended period of global cooling from the late fourteenth century to the early nineteenth century. At the peak of the Little Ice Age, between the 1640s and the 1690s, average global temperatures were cooler than at any time during the Holocene Era. Historians such as Geoffrey Parker argue that the climate change of the Little Ice Age was closely connected to a series of social, economic, and political crises, collectively known as the Crisis of the Seventeenth Century.[17]

The evidence for this period of global cooling is massive and compelling, coming from diverse textual sources and numerous scientific studies. Anecdotal evidence in journals and chronicles certainly points to noticeably colder winters in this period, with numerous descriptions of ice-skating on rivers that had not usually frozen solid in previous centuries. Observers of disastrous famines described aberrant winter weather phenomena such as the deep freeze that allowed Parisians to ice-skate on the Seine. The painter Johannes Vermeer was one of many Europeans to purchase an iceboat to sail across frozen lakes in the early seventeenth century. English philosopher Francis Bacon stressed the effects of bad weather, arguing that "when any of the four pillars of government are mainly shaken or weakened (which are religion, justice, council and treasure), men had need to pray for fair weather."[18] Solar observations by astronomers using telescopes – beginning with Galileo in 1610 – left records of sunspot activity that reveal remarkably few sunspots during most of the seventeenth century. Based on these records, astronomers and historians have distinguished a period of low sunspot activity as the Maunder Minimum, 1643–1715. Scientists analyzing these sunspot patterns argue that the lack of solar storms, and their accompanying solar flares, may have caused a significant cooling of the earth's atmosphere. Polar ice core evidence shows significant deposits of volcanic ash from the 1630s and 1640s, reflecting the global dust veils produced by massive volcanic eruptions in Indonesia, the Philippines, Japan, New Guinea, and Chile. Tree ring evidence from North America shows stunted growth of trees from abnormally cool summers during precisely this period.[19] Ice core evidence also demonstrates that the Alpine glaciers in Switzerland advanced during the late sixteenth century, forming lakes of solid ice.

The combined evidence suggests that the Little Ice Age produced an average cooling of approximately 1 degree Celsius (or 2 degrees Fahrenheit) worldwide, when compared with the relative stable average temperatures of the preceding 6,000 years. The cooler temperatures of the seventeenth century translated into significantly shorter growing seasons for crops, which was especially severe in the northern parts of the northern hemisphere. The Little Ice Age seriously threatened agricultural economies and peasant life in many regions of the world. Global cooling also had a direct impact on military practices, since early frosts and long winters could shorten the duration of military campaigning seasons. Extreme cold and severe weather increased hardships for soldiers and peasants living in war zones.

Global climate change produced complex localized effects, with extreme weather conditions reported in diverse areas. The global cooling pattern had an uneven impact on local climates, creating exceptionally hot summers in certain regions and surprisingly mild years in others. The El Niño effect in the Pacific periodically produces temporary alterations in global weather patterns – resulting in mild winters in northern North America, droughts in South and Southeast Asia, and heavy rainfall in Central and South America. Recent scientific research identifies a number of El Niño events during the early modern period, and each occurrence created anomalous weather patterns. Despite variations in local climate change and weather, peasants across most of the world had to grapple with the implications of global cooling for their daily lives.

Climate change clearly contributed to numerous extreme famines across much of northern Eurasia, even if historians continue to debate the definitions of the Crisis of the Seventeenth Century. Cooler weather, heavy rains, and poor harvests prompted peasant revolts in Central Europe in the late sixteenth century. Peasant uprisings in Croatia in 1573 and in Lower Austria in 1596 have been blamed on climate change. Extreme cold gripped Germany in the 1640s, and Scandinavia experienced the coldest annual weather recorded in 1641. "Ice floes repeatedly clogged and even froze the Thames during the 1660s and 1670s, most spectacularly in 1683–4," according to Geoffrey Parker, who cites a contemporary source: "There was a whole streete called the broad streete framed quite over the Thames from the Temple to the Bear Garden, and booths built, and many thousands of people walking sometimes together at once."[20] Severe cold weather produced successive bad harvests in France in the early 1690s, leading to the disastrous famine of 1693–94. Grain prices skyrocketed and desperate peasants were reduced to begging for food. More than a million French people died from starvation and malnutrition during the famine.[21]

East Asia suffered severe droughts and famines in the 1590s and again in the 1630s–40s, perhaps compounded by dense volcanic dust veils in the atmosphere. Severe droughts in northern China in the early 1640s threatened the food supply for Beijing and created wide-spread famines, seriously weakening the Ming imperial government. The extremely cold winter of 1640–41 in Japan brought early snows and starvation in the streets of Edo. The Tokugawa *bakufu* developed famine relief policies and enforced strict social discipline, however, avoiding the extreme rural conflicts that occurred in much of the rest of the seventeenth-century world.[22]

Southeast Asia and the Indian subcontinent also suffered from the effects of the Little Ice Age. Mughal India experienced one of the most devastating famines in its history in 1630–31, when millions of people died of hunger. Climate change seems to have contributed to famine and rural disorder in Southeast Asia as well. Vietnamese chronicles recorded a series of severe famines during the civil wars of the late sixteenth century. Sustained droughts produced rice crop failures in Burma, Arakan, and Siam in the early 1630s. Spanish *tributos* records from the Philippines reveal serious population declines in the early seventeenth century. Parts of Indonesia seem to have avoided serious famines, however, perhaps due to variable local effects of global climatic patterns. The lush rainforests and abundant food plants of much of Southeast Asia may also have lessened the severity of staple crop failures when they occurred.

The temperate zones in Africa and South America were desolated by climate change. In the 1640s and 1660s, both cold winters and El Niño afflicted South America. After 1630, West Africa became more arid, leading to the expansion of the Sahara Desert and a shift southward of the semi-arid Sahel savannah, prompting migrations of nomads and conflicts in the region. East Africa suffered repeated droughts and famines in the seventeenth century. The records of floods in the Nile valley show extremely low levels of water in 1641–43, 1650, and again in 1694–95.[23]

Brutally cold winters gripped North America during the mid-seventeenth century. Amerindian populations were still suffering from the massive epidemics that had resulted from contact with new diseases. Epidemics continued to ravage Amerindians who came into contact with French and English settlers. The Little Ice Age seems to have threatened Amerindian agriculture and forced migrations in the interior of North America. Dire famine conditions in New England colonies in the 1630s exacerbated conflicts with Amerindians, such as the Pequots. Famine and epidemic disease weakened the Hurons in the 1630s and 1640s, as they waged desperate warfare against the Iroquois. The summer of 1675 was the coolest recorded over the previous 600 years, and resulting crop failures helped prompt King Philip's War in New England.[24]

Banditry and rural disorder

Transhumance patterns of livestock management contributed to rural violence in many regions of the early modern world. In the grasslands and savannas of Eurasia and Africa, pastoralists managed vast herds of cattle and sheep. The stark hills and steppes of Central Asia permitted goats, sheep, and camels to graze. More isolated mountainous regions and highlands served as summer grazing grounds for goats and other hardy livestock. Fernand Braudel described the complex patterns of short- and long-distance transhumance in early modern Spain and the Mediterranean, distinguishing this form of mobility from nomadism.[25] Seasonal patterns of transhumance often dictated pastoralists' movements, creating conflicts with farmers and other herders over grazing lands, as well as presenting opportunities for raids on livestock. Theft of livestock could easily lead to severe judicial punishments or retaliation in pastoralist societies. For example, the clan feuds in the Scottish Highlands seem to have been closely related to sheepherding and livestock theft.

Nomadic migrations across Central Asia continued to disrupt agricultural and pastoral societies on the steppes. The great Mongol states had fragmented by the sixteenth century, but entire clan groups of Turco-Mongols and other steppe peoples periodically moved *en masse*. Nomads often engaged in livestock banditry, which could expand into raiding warfare across the steppes. These nomadic groups rarely created elaborate military organizations, but a Manchurian leader named Nurhaci formed a banner military system and created a Manchu identity around the turn of the seventeenth century. Nurhachi led his cavalry armies against the imperial armies of China in the 1610s and 1620s, pressuring the Ming dynasty. Bandits became active throughout China during successive wars between the Manchu invaders and the imperial forces of the Ming.

Banditry proliferated throughout the great empires of West and South Asia in the sixteenth and seventeenth centuries. Although many historians have touted the centralized power of the so-called "gunpowder empires," R.J. Barendse argues that the "real strength" of the Ottoman, Safavid, Uzbek, and Mughal Empires lay in their organization of cavalry and of agricultural revenues, rather than their use of firearms. These great empires thus wielded great military and fiscal power, but generally did not dominate local populations. In the Mughal Empire, overland traffic moved over two systems of roads: royal roads and "smuggling routes," which were known for illicit traffic and banditry.[26] When banditry threatened an area in India, whole villages sometimes migrated in search of fertile land for resettlement. Bandits operated alongside roads in Anatolia and other regions of the Ottoman Empire, preying on livestock and robbing herders.

Banditry often overlapped with highway robbery, as marauding bands of brigands harassed pastoralists and travelers in rural areas. Highway robbery was common in the forests of Central Europe and in the remote foothills of the Pyrenees and Apennines. Even travelers on the Camino Real, or royal highway, across Spain could be robbed. Bandits held up the duke of Osuña's train in 1616, stealing belongings worth 14,000 *ducados*. European rivers also served as highways for bulk goods, such as grain, in the early modern period. Barges plying the major rivers of Europe had to pay tolls at successive towns and cities. The great Rhine River wound through numerous city-states and principalities, each demanding tolls. Organized outlaws exploited riverine commerce for their own illegal exactions and smuggling.

Banditry became rampant in contested war zones in the seventeenth century. Polish peasants suffered from bandit raids during successive civil wars in the seventeenth century. Mounted bandits roved over Scandinavian provinces, such as Skåne, that were disputed by Denmark and Sweden in the mid-seventeenth century. Political authorities sometimes launched anti-banditry campaigns using cavalry forces to patrol roads and to arrest bandits, who were typically hung as thieves.

Peasant Resistance

Peasants organized various forms of resistance to changes in agrarian economies and conditions in rural societies. In many societies, farmers opposed land management, protested military burdens, and resisted taxes.

Peasant responses to land management

New forms of intensive agriculture transformed some rural economies during the seventeenth century. In England and the Netherlands, improved techniques of crop rotation and fertilizers produced greater crop yields. Farmers in many regions of Europe and the Mediterranean expanded their use of market gardening, growing vegetables in their gardens and selling them in local and regional markets to earn monetary income. Intensive dairy production and cheese-making allowed some peasants to supplement their incomes.

Beer-brewing and winemaking increasingly served not only local clients, but also regional and long-distance consumers. In the Alps, Swiss farmers expanded the cultivation of hemp and flax as cash crops. Although most peasants continued to depend on subsistence agriculture, some sectors of agricultural economies were becoming commercialized, which began to affect the practice of warfare.[27]

Nobles and states in Central and Eastern Europe instituted a system of "second serfdom" in their territories, in part as a reaction to pervasive banditry and lawlessness. Many peasants in Poland, Brandenburg, and Bohemia were forced to accept legal conditions of servitude in order to receive protection from noble landlords. Although historians continue to debate the applicability of the term "second serfdom" to this new agricultural system, labor requirements clearly became more onerous. Eastern European peasants sometimes resisted these new legal systems of bound agricultural labor through protests and rebellions.

A new form of serfdom also developed in the Muscovite Empire during the early modern period. Until the mid-fifteenth century, Russian peasants lived under no mobility restrictions. Muscovite rulers and nobles gradually instituted decrees binding peasants to the land, however, first by narrowing their right to move to Saint George's Day and then by eliminating all freedom of mobility. Nonetheless, many Russian peasants fled from their noble landlords as fugitives, especially during the Time of Troubles from 1598 to 1613.

Changing agricultural economies provoked peasant resistance. The enclosure movement in England sparked peasant protests in the 1620s and 1630s. English gentry promoted enclosure as a remedy for rural disorder. A mid-seventeenth-century pamphlet complained that "the poor increase like fleas and lice, and these vermin will eat us up unless we enclose."[28] Many English lords and gentry engaged in usurping common lands, such as meadows and pastures that had previously been used as grazing areas for peasants' livestock.

Deforestation could be linked to rural disorder in the early modern world. The density of forests across much of Eurasia had grown following the decimation of populations by the Black Death in the mid-fourteenth century. Entire villages had been abandoned and forests allowed to grow. As European populations recovered during the late fifteenth and sixteenth centuries, more and more trees were felled to expand the arable land under cultivation. The Estates of Languedoc, a provincial assembly, complained in the mid-sixteenth century that "the country is being entirely cleared of wood."[29] Royal officials complained of encroachments on royal forests in France, as peasants harvested wood as fuel. In colonial Brazil and the Caribbean, extensive swaths of rainforest were cleared during the seventeenth century to create plantations along the coasts.

Despite such clearing, many forests were still very dense in many parts of the world in the seventeenth century, figuring in rural violence and warfare. In some communities, felling of trees and usurpation of forests created violent clashes between peasants and elite landlords. Religious refugees often sought protection in forests and mountains. In some regions, authorities maintained specialized forests for naval and commercial shipbuilding. The Venetian state managed its mainland forests in its *terraferma* empire using complex forestry laws and a sophisticated bureaucracy.[30] Such forests were reserved for state use by means of bans that prevented or limited peasant access – provoking opposition and protest.

Swamp draining and land reclamation projects allowed intensification of agriculture in some areas, but also produced social tensions in rural societies. In England, Parliament issued a General Draining Act in 1600 to encourage reclamation of land from marshes and fens, with the aim of "recovering many hundred thousand Acres of marshes."[31] Reclamation threatened the livelihoods of cottagers, refugees, and smugglers who dwelt within the marshlands. Before and during the English Civil Wars, fenland rioters attacked dikes and drainage projects, especially in Norfolk and Lincolnshire. In the Netherlands, elaborate systems of dikes not only protected the lowlands from sea incursions, but also allowed land reclamation. North Holland elites funded a series of major land reclamation projects from 1610 to 1640, using windmills to drain several lakes and to expand its agricultural land significantly. These land improvements came with significant costs for local residents, however, as the projects ended up "blocking access to the sea from many villages, and reducing inland fishing possibilities as they added a whole new class of large farmers and enlarged the marketing functions of the towns."[32] Less extensive land reclamation projects were initiated in other countries throughout the seventeenth century, often prompting local protests.

Rural protest against military burdens

Military recruitment practices produced disorder and tension in rural societies in the seventeenth century. Military labor markets varied across early modern societies, but usually drew heavily from the young males who lived in peasant villages and small towns.

Enlistment in many early modern armies was theoretically voluntary, but recruiting parties often employed coercion to compel men to join the ranks of ever-larger field armies in the seventeenth century. In many regions, sergeants and other junior officers led groups of soldiers to "beat the drum" in village squares, enticing bored young farmers to seek adventure in the military. Recruiting parties preyed on drunken peasants and travelers in taverns, inviting them to accept a free drink and a bounty. Noble landlords used their seigneurial authority to pressure peasants who lived within their own seigneurial jurisdictions, as well as in nearby small towns, to enlist. In war zones, recruiting parties competed with each other to win over peasants to one cause or another. Press gangs operating in port cities often forced men into naval service, sometimes abducting peasants who had no experience at sea.

Many peasants must have fled from recruiting parties, and the desertion rates could be shockingly high, especially for soldiers who had been forcibly recruited. Evidence for coordinated peasant demonstrations against recruitment and billeting is slim, but protests that turned violent offer some idea of the dynamics of rural resistance to military organizations. Peasants clearly feared field armies, and peasant culture depicted soldiers as marauding beasts that pillaged, raped, and spread diseases.

Acts of peasant resistance against compulsory recruitment systems are better documented. Eastern European societies that had implemented second serfdom often employed a more strict form of compulsory recruitment through levies on villages. European colonial authorities raised auxiliary forces through compulsory recruitment, sometimes leading to resentment and protest in the Americas and Southeast Asia. The Mughal Empire occasionally faced resistance as it recruited peasants in the Rajput, Maratha, and Nayaka regions of South Asia. The Ottoman Empire recruited Christian children as janissary soldiers through the *devshirme*. Despite the seemingly onerous conditions of the *devshirme*, even this form of compulsory recruitment could be negotiated through quotas on peasant villages that were then adjudicated by community leaders. But, if these negotiations broke down, peasants could organize resistance and outright revolt against military recruitment systems.

Tax resistance

Heavy taxation caused or fueled peasant resistance around the world in the seventeenth century. The burden of taxation fell overwhelmingly on the peasants in most countries, since social elites and urban citizens normally held exemptions from various taxes. In many societies, tax officials organized armed parties to conduct tax collection in mobile columns that could resemble raiding parties. Tax farmers profited from the tax system, managing the taxation process in return for keeping a percentage of the revenues that they raised from peasants. There is little surprise, then, that taxation often resembled extortion.

Most peasants paid direct taxes, which might be collected as monetary payments or contributions in staple crops. In the kingdom of France, royal taxation relied on the *taille* (direct tax) as its main revenue source, which was overwhelmingly levied on the peasants, since nobles, clergy, and many townspeople were exempted from this tax. Royal officials set the *taille* contribution levels for each community within a *généralité* (regional tax district), but "the peasants themselves assessed and collected their parish *tailles*."[33] In practice, tax rates and collection methods varied considerably even within individual provinces.

Peasants also normally paid indirect taxes on agricultural products and commercial goods that they purchased. Salt taxes were considered especially onerous because salt was the crucial meat preservative agent that all peasants needed. In France, a royal monopoly on salt ensured peasants a steady supply of salt, but also provided tax revenues for the king. Increases in the notorious *gabelle* (salt tax) often led to tax protests and peasant revolts in France in the late sixteenth and seventeenth centuries. Other indirect taxes such as the *aides* (sales tax) and *traites* (transit fees) primarily affected commercial goods, but peasants felt the effects of these taxes, too, especially on retail goods such as wine. Tax farmers purchased the right to collect many of these indirect taxes for the royal administration, allowing them to extract tax revenues from peasants and keep a portion of the sums they collected as profits.

Villages often protested augmentations in tax levies and changes in tax policies, which were generally related to the financial pressures of war. Peasants periodically gathered in village assemblies to discuss their grievances and organize protests against tax increases. Mughal peasants were well armed and tried to resist imperial tax collection.[34] Early modern taxes were always considerable, but peasants complained vociferously about the burdens of wartime resource mobilization and extraction during the wars of the seventeenth century. When a royal tax official visited the French village of Saint-Just-la-Pendue in 1649 to collect back taxes, he and his assistants "were gradually surrounded by a growing crowd of angry residents led by the local priest and by Claude Rey, a prominent farmer, who growled, 'By the death of the Lord you are all thieves, the *taille* has been paid.'"[35] Tax collectors and administrators often had to beat a hasty retreat in such situations and then engage in protracted negotiations to calm tensions.

Some governments seem to have managed tax policies and protest more effectively, preventing widespread tax resistance. The unification of Japan promoted stability and enforced order through new political and legal institutions, creating markedly different conditions in rural Japan. Tokugawa *shoguns* disarmed peasants and instituted regularized tax policies, halting the widespread peasant revolts and rural violence that had plagued Japan during the *Sengoku* period – when many farmers had resisted taxation and had joined the *Ikkō ikki* bands. A cadastral survey by Tokugawa Ieyasu in the early seventeenth century standardized legal definitions of village boundaries and of assessed yields of rice. The *daimyō* elites gained sweeping administrative and judicial authority in their districts, even as they lost political power. Tokugawa judicial institutions reacted against peasant unrest with severe punishments.[36]

Peasant Revolts

Tax protests could quickly escalate into broad peasant revolts, as villages across entire regions refused to pay taxes, while their residents took up arms. Many historians have attempted to quantify peasant violence by compiling lists to enumerate revolts and gauge their frequency. Provence experienced an estimated 374 peasant uprisings between 1590 and 1715, while Guyenne suffered an astonishing 459 peasant revolts in the same period.[37] Peasants frequently rebelled against taxes in Germany and Switzerland during the seventeenth century. Local gazetteers provide ample evidence of peasant revolts and rural violence in sixteenth- and seventeenth-century China.[38] Numerous incidents of peasant revolt in other regions of Eurasia, Africa, and the Americas during the seventeenth century have also been documented. Attempts at quantifying peasant violence have ultimately foundered on definitional problems and the diverse motivations that fueled incidents of peasant violence.[39]

Peasant revolts in France

The *croquants* of southern France who organized protests against the introduction or augmentation of the *gabelle*, or salt tax, in the late sixteenth century provide a classic case of early modern peasant rebels. French peasants came to hate the *gabeleurs* (salt tax officials), but also used their official title as a derogatory label against all royal tax officials. The depredations of the French Wars of Religion exacerbated such economic grievances, producing widespread tax rebellions. Nobles referred to peasant rebels as *croquants*, a pejorative term meaning "bumpkins" or "hayseeds."[40] The *croquant* uprising of 1594 in Guyenne coincided with the intense fighting and heavy contributions of the Catholic League wars. Another major *croquant* uprising occurred during the renewed religious warfare in the 1620s in Guyenne and Languedoc.

Other peasant revolts were linked to the tax burdens and economic disruption of the Thirty Years War. Peasants in southwestern France began attacking *gabeleurs* after royal officials augmented taxes in 1636. A massive *croquant* force of some 30,000 peasants assembled in May 1637 and marched on Bergerac, occupying the town. The *croquants* threatened Bordeaux, the provincial capital of Guyenne, only to be defeated by a royal army at La Sauvetat. Negotiations led to a truce and a demobilization of the *croquant* army.[41]

The revolt of the *nu-pieds* that erupted in Normandy in July 1639 also targeted hated *gabeleurs* during the Thirty Years War, but this time over the privileges of salt workers, who were referred to as *nu-pieds* because they were barefooted as they refined sea salt in proto-industrial works along the Norman coast. Peasants who brought wood to fuel the salt cauldrons joined the rebellion, as did local carpenters, bakers, and other workers. "It would seem that at this basic level," according to Le Roy Ladurie, "the contingent of combatants provided by the rebel parishes represented a broad cross-section of peasant society." The movement became associated with the figure of Jean Nu-pieds (John the Barefooted), their supposed leader, who was portrayed as a new St. John the Baptist. The rebellion continued to expand, as salt smugglers, village clergy, artisanal workers, and some urban elites joined the movement and participated in attacks on tax officials and their offices. The *nu-pieds* organized an army that they called the *armée de la souffrance* (Army of Suffering), but they were ultimately defeated by a royal army in November 1639.[42]

Peasant uprisings in Central Europe

Many of the large peasant revolts of the early modern period were indeed motivated by peasant reactions against state tax policies, but religious persecution, political conflict, and other rural issues also prompted widespread peasant mobilization. Peasant revolts have too frequently been described simply as tax rebellions. Often, localized peasant protest over specific grievances – whether related directly to taxes or not – gradually widened into complex, multilayered regional peasant revolts. Other economic motives relating to the intensification and commercialization of agriculture played a role in peasant movements in the seventeenth century. Land use policies and real estate markets increasingly pressured farmers in many regions. Cultural and religious changes in rural society could be perceived as threatening peasant communities. Peasant revolts thus were not motivated solely by economic motives, but also by religious and political motives.

Many peasants formed self-defense leagues to protect themselves from pillaging soldiers and marauding bandits. German peasants assembled to protest high taxes and excessive contributions that field armies levied on their villages during the Thirty Years War. Peasant organization produced revolts in Habsburg territories in Upper Austria in 1626 and 1632–36, as well as in Swabia. Bavaria experienced peasant uprisings that were responses to military predation and pillaging in 1633–34. Surviving documents from a 1630–31 revolt in Hohenloe reveal that "the leaders of this movement came from those who had the most to lose as the old order began to give way: the village elite."[43]

Peasant unrest could overlap significantly with religious conflict. Rural shrines and highway crosses attracted local devotion and regional pilgrimage in Catholic territories. Catholic clergy and parishioners organized rural processions to shrines and nearby churches for important religious festivals. Protestant peasants often protested Catholic religious activities near their villages. Calvinist peasants sometimes launched iconoclastic attacks on rural shrines, angering local Catholic believers. Such religious clashes could escalate into rural peasant conflicts.

Peasant unrest in the Ottoman Empire

The Ottoman Empire also faced considerable peasant unrest in the late sixteenth and seventeenth centuries. Severe droughts and famines struck southern Anatolia and parts of the Eastern Mediterranean in the 1590s, producing a breakdown in Ottoman provisioning systems and a rise in banditry. Then, a series of rural conflicts disrupted the empire in what historian Sam White has called "the worst crisis in Ottoman history." During the Celali Rebellion (1596–1610), many peasants abandoned farming and joined bands of marauders who terrorized the countryside. White explains, "mercenary leaders gathered rebel armies that plundered the provinces and defied the imperial government for more than a decade, laying waste to wide stretches of the empire."[44]

Another wave of peasant revolts followed in the 1620s, as the climatic effects of the Little Ice Age continued to disrupt the Ottoman agricultural system. Anatolia, the heartland of the Ottoman agrarian society, seems to have suffered severe depopulation, due to droughts and peasant flight from agricultural service. Movements of nomadic Turkic and Kurdish peoples further destabilized Anatolian, Syrian, and Iraqi peasant villages under Ottoman rule, creating widespread rural disorder and economic crisis.[45]

Widespread rural disorder continued through the mid-seventeenth century, as political disruptions, military burdens, and civil war prevented Ottoman authorities from re-establishing order in rural society. *Sipahis* encountered fierce tax resistance in the 1640s and many Ottoman administrative officials found it difficult to even enter peasant villages.[46] In the empire's frontier regions, the Ottoman tributary system periodically broke down. Wallachian peasants revolted in 1655, attacking the local officials who collected taxes on behalf of the empire. A disastrous drought across the Balkans in 1659–60 produced misery for peasants, some of whom rebelled against taxation and Ottoman rule.[47]

Conclusion

Seventeenth-century peasants clearly used violence to protest economic circumstances, oppose tax policies, and resist state power. The various forms of peasant violence did not necessarily represent class struggle, however. Peasant communities were remarkably diverse and it is difficult to discern evidence of any broad peasant solidarity even within a particular province or society. Peasants around the world organized rural violence in localized contexts, where tax protest was often linked with banditry, raiding warfare, urban rebellions, and even noble revolts. Large peasant revolts thus only occasionally coalesced and were seldom motivated by a single cause.

Chinese rural unrest in the late Ming period demonstrates the importance of considering the connections between peasant revolts and other forms of rural violence. Population growth, land consolidation, and excessive taxes prompted tenant farmers across China to rebel against their landlords and imperial tax policies. As the Ming dynasty struggled to suppress the revolts and defend the imperial borders, unpaid mercenary soldiers joined rural revolts in the 1620s and 1630s. Chinese writers described bitter winters and reported that the Yellow River froze solid in 1634. The exceptionally cold weather caused crop failures and made famines even more devastating for millions of farmers. Many peasants became roving bandits and "both country and people were trampled like mud and ashes."[48] Near continuous warfare against the Manchus on the northern frontier of China strained the Ming imperial state. Manchu banner armies invaded China several times, reaching Beijing in 1629 and 1636. The rural rebellions coincided with urban protests and grew into broad rebellions. Li Zicheng's peasant army captured Beijing in April 1644 and entered the Forbidden City, as the emperor committed suicide. The Ming dynasty dissolved, as Manchu armies, swollen by many Chinese allies, seized control of northern China in summer 1644 and declared the Qing dynasty.

Supporters of the Ming dynasty continued to struggle against the new Manchu regime for several years, as peasant unrest persisted across the empire. A Chinese observer described peasant motivations for violence: "Among the bondservants, some are cunning and they are stirring up a movement for the annulment of their bonds of servitude, saying that the dynasty is changing so how can the regulations for bondservants be as they used to be."[49] Widespread peasant revolts continued to erupt in remote areas of China. The genealogy of a family in southern China recorded in 1646 that "the bond servants...turned upon their masters and caused much disturbance. Fierce young men in seven villages followed them, set up camps and walled compounds, robbed, and could not be controlled...such that not even chickens and dogs were left in peace. Every family departed from the village to escape from their wrath."[50] Rural disorder and civil warfare lingered in southern China into the 1670s. The massive peasant revolts may have been the decisive factor in the collapse of the Ming dynasty in China and the transition to Qing rule.

9

Ethnic Conflict, 1620s–1660s

Soon after English settlers founded the colony of Jamestown in 1609, deep contradictions emerged in English paternalistic attitudes that portrayed Amerindians as "noble savages" who lived in an Eden-like paradise. English colonial voyager Thomas Harriot thought that Amerindians would eventually come to "honor, obey, fear, and love us," but English attitudes and colonial development soon antagonized the settlers' Amerindian neighbors.[1] The Powhatan confederacy attacked English colonial settlements in Virginia in 1622, killing hundreds of colonists and creating terror throughout the English colonies in the Atlantic World. Outraged English colonists referred to the attacks as the Virginia Massacre and called for revenge against the Powhatans.[2]

The Virginia Massacre produced a serious rupture in English–Amerindian relations and fundamentally altered English colonial policies. Captain John Smith wrote that "now we have just cause to destroy them by all meanes possible," and English colonists mobilized a brutal campaign of reprisal massacres and economic devastation against the Powhatans.[3] English political culture sanctioned extreme forms of violence against Amerindians as a justifiable means of upholding the colonial community and maintaining social order.

Ethnic and racial conceptions seem to have played a significant role in the explosion of intercultural violence in Virginia. The massacres committed by Amerindians and English colonists in Virginia suggest that warfare was instrumental in the construction of ethnic identities in many societies in the early modern world. This chapter will consider ethnic conflicts, slavery, and racial categories in seventeenth-century warfare. In the Americas, Africa, and Southeast Asia, European racism and imperialism were key components in atrocities carried out against indigenous peoples. The chapter will examine how ethnicity shaped intercultural violence and colonial conflicts, which in turn reinforced ethnic identities and racial conceptions.

Intercultural Violence

Historians have long portrayed early modern frontiers as violent, seeing New Spain, for example, as an area in which "war and the frontier advanced together."[4] We have already seen how conquest and early colonization created chaotic borderlands, discussed above in chapter 7. Recent borderlands studies offer new ways of considering intercultural violence that avoid casting violence as a mere by-product of disciplining colonial discourse. As settler colonies solidified in the seventeenth century, they produced more defined colonial frontiers that shaped intercultural violence.

Frontiers and ethnic conflicts

From the earliest contacts between Amerindians and Europeans, ethnic identities shaped violence in the Atlantic World. Christopher Columbus's own reports of his expeditions began to mold Europeans' attitudes toward the inhabitants of Caribbean islands and to construct ethnic identifications. Reports of Hernán Cortés's expedition to Mexico constructed elaborate conquest narratives and fixed representations of Amerindians that would have a long legacy in Spanish culture and beyond.

The colonial frontiers of the Spanish Empire forged ethnic categories of enemies. The latter stages of the *Reconquista* against Muslims in Iberia arguably represented a new type of conflict, "something like the more modern notion of 'ethnic cleansing.'"[5] Granada can be seen as a "frontier city" within Iberia, highlighting the importance of trans-Atlantic dimensions of Spanish violence against Muslims and Amerindians.[6] Spanish mission communities in northwestern Mexico created shifting social groupings, cultural endurance, and resistance tactics among Amerindians.[7] In South America, colonial expansion into the interior and changing conditions of warfare created ethnic realignments among Amerindians there.[8] Throughout the Spanish Empire, frontiers shaped ethnicity, religion, and violence.

Captives and ritualized violence

Organized intercultural violence in the early modern world often involved captive-taking and prolonged confinement or forced reidentification. Captured soldiers and civilians alike might experience resettlement, cultural assimilation, forced labor, and violence. In order to understand ethnic violence, we must consider the treatment of captives and the meanings of pain inflicted on human bodies through mutilation, torture, and other ritualized violence.[9] Early modern accounts of torture tended to sensationalize brutality and depict practitioners of ritual violence as cruel and inhuman. While captivity is often presented as a solitary episode, early modern captivity narratives can be read to suggest that "suffering is a social experience" and an important aspect of warfare.[10]

Ritual human sacrifice and cannibalism have generally been seen as the ultimate atrocities, perpetuated by monstrous beings. The most infamous alleged case of cannibalism in the early modern Atlantic World is certainly that of the Tupinambas of Brazil. Descriptions of Tupinamba cannibalism were related in sixteenth-century travel narratives written by Europeans, and then diffused through later texts on marvels and monstrosities.[11] While some scholars have questioned whether the Tupinamba actually practiced cannibalism, the ritualistic violence reported by several sixteenth-century European observers has continued to fascinate historians, anthropologists, and social theorists. The influential anthropologist Claude Lévi-Strauss read many of these early modern accounts before conducting fieldwork with Amerindians in twentieth-century Brazil. He carried with him a copy of Jean de Léry's *Histoire d'un voyage faict en la terre du Brésil* (1580) and thought of early modern travel narratives "as [he] set foot on Brazilian soil for the first time." Interestingly, Lévi-Strauss mentions cannibalism, but avoids directly discussing Tupinamba cannibalism.[12]

The supposedly cannibalistic Tupinambas served as a model for the contemporary Catholic cartographer André Thevet's cosmography.[13] As Stephen Greenblatt notes, "the very incoherence of [Thevet's] cosmography allows a jumbled confusion of remarkable observations, much like the unsystematized, wildly various contents of the 'wonder cabinets' beloved of Renaissance collectors. Thevet's Tupinamba are like living wonder cabinets."[14] Calvinist Jean de Léry's account, one of the other key sixteenth-century sources on Tupinamba cannibalism, is central to Michel de Certeau's analysis of ethnographic writing and voice. Certeau finds links between Léry's descriptions of Tupinamba women's eating of human flesh and contemporary European depictions of witches' nighttime Sabbath revelry.[15] Cannibalism represented devilish gorging to European travel writers who were attuned to issues of feast and famine, and who believed that "God's greatest punishment with famine was to induce cannibalism, and especially to thereby induce starving mothers to eat their own babies."[16] Europeans describing cannibals in this period of frequent famines and religious conflicts often wanted to emphasize their pious fasting and their "correct" interpretation of the Eucharist. Literary critic and philosopher René Girard, instead of focusing on European descriptions, treats Tupinamba cannibalism as a "real" practice. Rather than seeing ritualistic cannibalism as an aberration, however, Girard suggests that it is merely another form of ritualistic sacrifice – a fundamental purifying act common to all religious systems and necessary to remove the pollution of violence, or "mimetic desire," from the community. "All religious rituals spring from the surrogate victim," he argues, "and all the great institutions of mankind, both secular and religious, spring from ritual."[17] The very concepts of religion, violence, and ethnicity intersect in all these readings of the Tupinambas.

Whether or not the Tupinambas or any other Amerindians actually ate human flesh, images of cannibalism and human sacrifice shaped early modern conceptions of ethnicity. Hans Staden's captivity narrative suggests that the Tupinambas probably were not cannibals, but that they actively cultivated a cannibalistic image and successfully used the "subversive power of rumors in resisting imperialism."[18] Staden's religion-infused captivity narrative, intended for a Lutheran audience, provides the key source in this interpretation of the Tupinambas' supposed cannibalism. Staden's narrative can be seen as a Christian religious text that locates cannibalistic violence as an ethnic defensive smokescreen. These findings parallel Gananath Obeyesekere's interpretation of Spanish descriptions of human sacrifice and cannibalism in Central America, which concludes that the Mexica were "manipulating a human sacrifice for political purposes, utilizing a conventional sign system to frighten the Spaniards, and no doubt succeeding."[19]

Ritual torture and bodily mutilation also shaped intercultural violence. The treatment of captives in North Africa and the Americas proved shocking to Europeans. Captivity narratives written by Europeans seem to have misunderstood Amerindian ritualistic bodily mutilation practices and exaggerated their dimensions in their outraged descriptions of Amerindian "barbarities." The Iroquois and other Amerindian societies placed great religious significance on captives, ritualistic torture, and mourning.[20]

Ritualistic scalping and mutilation of cadavers provoked outrage. Some Amerindian warriors scalped wounded or already dead enemies, although the origins of scalping practices have also been hotly debated. Archaeological, linguistic, and textual evidence strongly suggest that scalping was practiced by pre-Columbian Amerindians, despite some previous claims that Europeans introduced scalping to Amerindian societies. However, European colonists clearly did encourage scalping in early modern colonial warfare through the use of bounties for scalps brought in by Amerindian warriors.[21] European religious leaders in North American colonies sometimes provided religious justifications for scalping and atrocious treatment of the dead bodies of enemies.

Europeans' captivity narratives can be compared with trial records of Amerindians who faced European judicial processes. The Indian Inquisition in Mexico meted out harsh punishments and executions to Mesoamerican captives in an effort to halt what the inquisitors considered idolatry.[22] Religious rationales sustained torture throughout European judicial systems and their colonial counterparts, not merely in Inquisition courts. A recent study of judicial torture in France finds that "much as chosen suffering sought to crush the rebellious will and thereby to make spiritual space for the indwelling truth of God, so too did judicial torture, by inflicting pain on an accused, seek to destroy the willfulness that diminished the truth of testimony."[23] European colonists subjected Amerindians to forms of judicial torture and execution that incorporated deliberate, ritualistic infliction of pain.

The most massive and systematic captive-taking operations in the early modern world arose in West Africa, as European merchants purchased growing numbers of African slaves. European planters' rising demand for slaves in the seventeenth century seem to have fueled warfare among West African states and societies, encouraging slave-taking operations and supporting an "ideology of militarism [that] was founded in the political economy of the slave trade."[24] While the European desire for slaves provided strong economic incentives for the slave market, the actual enslavement of Africans stemmed largely from wars conducted between kingdoms in West Africa, leading John K. Thornton to conclude that "African participation in the slave trade was voluntary and under the control of African decision makers."[25] If European slave traders had to compete with internal African economic use of slaves, they nonetheless controlled the transportation and reselling of slaves. The Middle Passage in the seventeenth century was a cruel, deadly voyage that killed over 20 percent of captive Africans shipped across the Atlantic.[26] Slaves challenged the plantation complex by means of subtle collective action, revolt, and flight. Africans who escaped from plantations often formed maroon communities in the Caribbean and South America, but they always risked capture and re-enslavement. The enormous scale of the early modern slave trade and the intense organization of the violence suffered by its captives should be contextualized by an examination of contemporaries' understanding of atrocities.

Mass violence and atrocity

Perhaps no single source had done more to shape our images of atrocity in the early modern world than Bartolomé de Las Casas's famous account of the brutal treatment of Amerindians in New Spain.[27] Travel narratives and polemical works written by Protestants built on critical Spanish accounts such as Las Casas's to fashion a Black Legend of Spanish cruelty in the mines and *encomiendas* of New Spain. Hans Staden's narrative probably criticized Portuguese slavery in order to please a Lutheran audience, and many of the facets of the Black Legend were undoubtedly a product of the religious propaganda of European wars of religion.[28] Yet, many of the horrific episodes recounted in propaganda pieces did relate horribly real excessive violence practiced by Spanish colonial soldiers and settlers against noncombatants, as well as by other Europeans and Amerindians embroiled in conflicts in the colonial borderlands. Analyzing early modern atrocities is complicated not only by the outrage that accompanied most of these descriptions of cruelties, but also by ambiguous legal distinctions and gender conceptions that often made defining "non-combatants" very difficult.[29] Tracing the connections between religion and ethnicity can help in understanding the massive scale and disturbing character of the atrocities committed in the early modern Atlantic World.

The increasingly brutal character of violence between English colonists and Amerindians highlights the failure of restraints in colonial warfare in the Atlantic World. All wars involve the forging of conventions between groups of combatants regarding the appropriate means and forms of violence, but these conventional practices of warfare and restraints on violence are periodically violated, and can at times break down.[30] Differing cultural expectations about violence and communication difficulties seem to have exacerbated problems in maintaining restraints on levels of intercultural violence in areas like Virginia and New England. Colonial military and militia units seem to have accepted the routine use of excessive violence, as settler colonists incorporated notions of a militarized frontier and a "militia myth" into their images of self-defense.[31]

Strong religious motivations often underlay the atrocities committed by the European combatants who fought in colonial wars. Sociologist Mark Juergensmeyer argues that "warriors" in religious conflicts experience symbolic empowerment through their performance of violence in what they perceive as a "cosmic war."[32] These approaches to religious conflict provide a way to interpret early modern European soldiers' commitment to a cause and their willingness to inflict violence. For combatants in the European Wars of Religion, heretics and infidels both represented agents of the Devil, with shared abominable characteristics. Colonial encounters with indigenous peoples became sites of religious and theological dispute in confessional propaganda of the religious wars. If the Tupinamba could be compared to witches by the Protestant French writer Léry, so too could Huguenot "heretics" be portrayed as witches and sorcerers by Catholic polemicists in France. For Christians anticipating the Apocalypse, waging warfare against the Ottomans in the Mediterranean or against the Powhatans in Virginia signified participating in the great struggle against the Antichrist. Many European soldiers and colonists who were directly involved in the production of violence in Europe's global expansion exported religious warfare into colonial contexts. Incidents of religious violence erupted among Europeans in colonial territories, such as the conflict between French Calvinists and Catholics at Fort Coligny. The English colonial leader John Smith explained that "the Warres in *Europe, Asia,* and *Affrica*...taught me how to subdue the wilde Salvages in *Virginia.*"[33]

A trans-Atlantic comparative perspective can make Smith's comment even more significant and the atrocities surrounding the Virginia Massacre more comprehensible. English colonization in Ireland and the Americas developed as serious religious divisions emerged in the British Isles in the sixteenth century between Catholic Ireland, Calvinist Scotland, and an Anglican-dominated but religiously mixed England. Elizabethan England seems to have become increasingly militarized, just as it began its imperial policies in the Atlantic as a result of the pressures of fighting in religious conflicts in the divided Netherlands and in Catholic Ireland during the late sixteenth century.[34] English colonists in the Americas in the early seventeenth century used "the same pretexts for the extermination of the Indians as their counterparts had used in the 1560s and 1570s for the slaughter of numbers of the Irish."[35] Aggressive English colonization in Ireland continued during the religious conflicts of the mid-seventeenth-century wars, which involved so much atrocity that it has been likened to late twentieth-century "ethnic cleansing."[36] English, Irish, and Scottish soldiers who experienced the atrocities of the British Civil Wars in the 1640s and 1650s may have been even more prepared to practice warfare beyond restraint. They had witnessed the erosion of conventional limits on warfare among Christians and the infusion of bitter religious hatred into European conflicts.[37] The atrocious nature of this sort of conflict arguably shaped later English attitudes toward both Irish and Amerindians.[38] The combination of ethnic stereotypes, imperial ideologies, and religious justifications not only sanctioned atrocities, but gave them expansive meaning.

Colonial Power and Coercion

Early modern colonization operated through armed coercion and brutal violence. Colonial power relationships involved elaborate conceptualizations of race, settlement, and slavery.

Trading companies and imperial race relations

Trading companies operating in the Indian and Atlantic Oceans employed ethnic stereotypes and racialized categories in their aggressive maritime operations and in the slave trade. Portuguese slave traders seem to have created racialized descriptions of Africans whom they purchased along the West African coast and transported into perpetual bondage in Brazilian plantations. Portuguese merchants and soldiers in India and Southeast Asia instituted racial types for subordinated peoples in their colonies in Mozambique, Goa, and Colombo. By the early seventeenth century, the Portuguese Empire was facing serious competition from Dutch and English forces. The English East India Company (EIC) was chartered in 1600 as a joint-stock company to develop English commerce and trading factories in the Indian Ocean. But, it was the Dutch who would refine the organization of trading companies and transform race relations in Southeast Asia.

The *Verenigde Oostindische Compagnie* (VOC), or Dutch East India Company, was established in 1602 as a joint-stock company with investment by the government of the United Provinces, as we noted in chapter 7. A VOC expedition under Jan Pietersz Coen attacked the kingdom of Sunda on the island of Java, seizing the port of Jakarta and burning the palace in 1619. The VOC founded Batavia on the ruins of the destroyed capital, constructing a fortified port city that soon became the VOC's principal administrative center in Asia. The fortress at Batavia had a massive arsenal, gun foundry, and powder mills. Maritime voyages from the Netherlands to Batavia could take eight months or more, so VOC administrators in Asia often coordinated trade and colonial policies themselves.

VOC officials in Batavia acted ruthlessly to monopolize the global trade in nutmeg and mace by invading the Banda islands in 1621, practically the only area where the prized nutmeg tree grew. Previous Dutch voyagers to Southeast Asia had marveled at nutmeg's medicinal power, claiming that it could cure headaches, improve memory, and prevent diarrhea. English traders had already established a fort in the Bandas in the 1600s, but VOC forces – now operating from their developing base in Batavia – were able to capture the fort in 1620.

The VOC used brutal methods in dealing with indigenous peoples in the Banda islands. When the VOC encountered resistance from the Bandanese people, Jan Pietersz Coen directed a cruel military campaign to depopulate the island. Dutch soldiers burned Bandanese villages and slaughtered the islanders, annihilating almost the entire indigenous population and enslaving a few hundred survivors. The VOC then imported African slaves to work newly established Dutch plantations on the islands, allowing the company to monopolize the global trade in nutmeg.

New ethnic and racial portrayals of Asians fueled the ruthless VOC policies in the Banda islands and other regions of Southeast Asia. Cloves attracted the attention of Dutch and English traders due to their supposed medicinal properties, leading the VOC to compete with the EIC for control of the Moluccas, where cloves grew. The island of Ambon became the critical site of Anglo-Dutch rivalry in Southeast Asia. In 1623, suspicious Dutch soldiers arrested Japanese and English personnel of the EIC in Ambon, accusing them of plotting to seize the VOC factory there. After using water torture to extract confessions from the prisoners, the local Dutch judicial body condemned the men to death for treason. This Ambona Massacre angered the English public and almost sparked a full-scale war between England and the Netherlands, but it did allow the VOC to consolidate its control of Ambon and the clove trade. The VOC justified its torture and execution of the English agents by associating their covert actions with those of Japanese pirates.

By the mid-seventeenth century, the VOC dominated three overlapping slave trade circuits in East Africa, South Asia, and Southeast Asia. Dutch ships raided and traded for slaves for resale in VOC port cities such as Batavia, Melaka, and Cochin. African, Indian, and Asian slaves were worked to raise pepper, nutmeg, mace, sugar, tobacco, and cotton on Dutch plantations scattered around the Indian Ocean World. By the late seventeenth century, the forced labor practices of Dutch planters, which included chain gangs and brutal violence, had become notorious. Markus Vink concludes that "the myth of a relatively 'benign' form of Indian Ocean slavery should therefore be quickly put to rest in the face of the continuous urge of slaves to escape their chattel status."[39]

Settler colonies and immigration

Large numbers of European males migrated to colonial settlements during the early modern period. An estimated 100,000–150,000 Portuguese merchants, soldiers, sailors, and settlers populated the far-flung colonies and trading factories of the maritime empire at any given time during the sixteenth century. About 3,900 Spanish migrants sailed for New Spain every year in the first half of the seventeenth century. Some *moriscos* and *conversos* who had faced persecution in Iberia migrated to Spanish and Portuguese colonies, successfully integrating themselves into the settler communities. Hundreds of thousands of Dutch males migrated to colonies in Indonesia and the Americas during the seventeenth century as sailors, soldiers, and laborers.[40]

Many European immigrants to the Americas and Southeast Asia became planters and slave masters. European plantation owners acquired near-absolute authority on their lands as masters of their slaves and administrators of their estates. Other European immigrants became urban residents, populating growing colonial cities such as Mexico City, Lima, Charleston, New York, and Boston.

Refugee migration fed colonial settlement in many areas. Religious refugees and ethnic minorities probably figured significantly in colonial settler migration. Many of the Huguenots who fled from France during and after the religious wars ended up in English colonies in North America. English Catholics and Puritans migrated to the Americas seeking religious separation. Poor Irish and English farmers migrated to the Americas as indentured workers, often working off their transport contracts as farm laborers. Others settled as independent farmers and pioneers, clearing land on the fringes of colonial territories and expanding the imperial frontiers.

The European immigration to colonial territories in the seventeenth century was dwarfed by the rapidly growing importation of

African slaves, however. Huge gender imbalances existed in the immigration to colonial societies in the Atlantic and Indian Ocean World. Studies of the seventeenth-century trans-Atlantic trade show the sharp gender disparity of African slaves transported to the Americas: 60 percent were adult males, 27 percent adult females, and 12 percent children.[41] The European immigration patterns were also heavily skewed toward male populations, although the precise numbers are not as well documented.

Plantation agriculture, slave labor, and violence

Ethnic violence needs to be understood in conjunction with the gradual development of the plantation complex, an organization using slave labor and brutal violence to produce an agricultural cash crop for export.[42] Early European settler colonies used a mixture of indentured and slave labor. Then, as sugar and tobacco plantations spread through the Caribbean, African slaves became the key workers in the plantation complex. The growing use of African slaves and the emergence of racism in the early plantations seems to have been linked to the unwillingness of Europeans to consider the possibility of using white slaves.[43] Some Irish immigrants who initially came to the island of Montserrat as indentured servants to work on tobacco plantations gradually became "hard and efficient slave masters," overseeing African slaves.[44] The plantations seem to have produced their own forms of violence, involving racist attitudes and the physical domination of Africans. Slave masters employed rape as a sexual weapon and established "breeder women" to perpetuate the slave population. European planters' racial fears prompted them to use brutal discipline, harsh punishments, and bodily mutilation implemented by dedicated overseers, who played a significant role in a plantation complex that was also sustained by religious values and beliefs.

New cash crops and plantation systems created new forms of institutionalized violence in the early seventeenth century. For centuries, Asian plants had been making their way into the Mediterranean via the Eurasian caravan and Red Sea trading routes, and the Portuguese and Spanish voyages into the Indian Ocean and across the Atlantic Ocean greatly accelerated the global exchange of plants and crops. Sugarcane, a Southeast Asian grass, became the first plant to radically transform global economies. Muslims in South Asia, the Levant, and North Africa had cultivated sugarcane in the Mediterranean for centuries. Europeans had adopted sugar by the fifteenth century, planting it in the Canary Islands, Madeira, and São Tomé to serve the growing European market for cane sugar. The demand for sugar prompted agricultural and commercial experimentation to improve the ways in which this cash crop was cultivated, refined, and transported.

The plantation complex developed first in the Portuguese colony of Brazil as an economic and labor system for the production of cane sugar. The Portuguese granted strips of land along the coast of Brazil to planters who would establish plantations using intensive agriculture by slave laborers. Amerindian slaves initially worked the sugarcane fields, but they were gradually replaced by African slaves bought from the West African coast. The number of sugarcane mills in Brazil grew from an initial 5 in the 1550s to 350 by 1629. "By the end of the sixteenth century," therefore, "Brazil emerged as the world leader in sugar production, replacing São Tomé, Madeira, and the Canaries as the chief source of European sugar."[45]

Sugarcane grew well in the Caribbean climate, and sugar plantations began to proliferate beyond Brazil. Spanish colonists established sugar plantations in Hispaniola and Puerto Rico in the sixteenth century, but a shortage of slave labor and the discovery of silver and gold mines on mainland Central and South America slowed the development of sugar colonies in the Spanish Caribbean. The plantation complex quickly spread throughout the English and French Caribbean islands in the seventeenth century, however. The population of Barbados grew from 1,400 in 1629 to at least 60,000 by 1713, as English colonists imported slaves to work their sugar plantations. French settlers in Saint-Domingue created a lucrative sugar colony on the island of Hispaniola, with a population of 92,000 by 1730. On these and other Caribbean islands, planters ordered their slaves to cut down woods and forests, clearing land for plantations and producing fuel wood for refining sugar. Thus, "the sugar revolutions created their own ecology as well as demography."[46]

The spread of sugarcane and the associated plantation complex spurred the development of a global sugar economy. Planters increasingly relied on the importation of African slaves from West Africa and Angola to work their sugarcane fields. Atlantic slavery became commercialized as the demand for African slaves rapidly expanded. Slave labor in Brazil and the Caribbean became specialized in order to serve the need for agricultural labor for sugarcane plantations.

The plantation complex gradually spread as a system of agricultural production of cash crops. In the late seventeenth century, colonial planters began to cultivate coffee, tea, cotton, and indigo on plantations in the Atlantic and Indian Ocean. In 1683, the French colony of Guadeloupe had 89 sugar mills and 12 indigo works.[47] Some individual plantations were diversifying in order to produce multiple cash crops. Spice production in Indonesia and along the Malabar Coast of India was gradually converted into a plantation system. Cocoa production in Central and South America also adopted the plantation complex.

The huge demand for plantation slave labor fueled the slave trade in the Atlantic and Indian Oceans. The slave trade also encouraged violence in rural Africa, as African kings and elites could now sell their war captives into lucrative global slave markets. The Middle Passage across the Atlantic Ocean must have terrorized African slaves bound for the Americas. Europeans operated specialized slave ships, with purpose-built slave decks and disciplinary equipment, along triangular trading routes in the Atlantic. The slave trade encouraged violence at sea, since privateers and pirates could seize slave ships and then sell their entire cargo of slaves. Cases of shipboard slave resistance and mutinies have been documented for the early modern period, but most of them stem from the eighteenth century.

The plantation complex produced new forms of systemic violence in the seventeenth-century world. Indeed, "violence was the chief characteristic of slave societies," according to James Pritchard. "Slaves constantly threatened European society, which employed enormous resources to suppress them."[48] Trading companies with their own naval and military forces established and protected plantation economies. Plantation systems employed brutal discipline and torture to maintain slave labor and punish resistance. Planters who held a land grant often possessed extensive legal authority on their plantations. The brutality of plantation discipline may have contributed to rural violence in slave colonies in the Americas and Southeast Asia. Planters and their plantation overseers exercised brutal discipline over slaves, using rape and torture to control them. Colonial authorities developed slave law codes and disciplinary systems, such as France's infamous *Code Noir* of 1685, which legitimized and institutionalized slavery.

Colonial Identities and Race

The seventeenth century represented an important period of "ethnogenesis" and acculturation – processes through which ethnic identities were forged or reformulated. Colonial societies both disrupted and created ethnic identities through complex processes of acculturation, assimilation, and ethnogenesis.

Ethnogenesis

Along colonial frontiers, individuals' identities seem to have been incredibly flexible and changeable. Studies of ethnicity and violence in the Atlantic World often oppose "colonizers" to "indigenous peoples," envisioning a statist imperial program suppressing resistance by the colonized. Yet, the importance of non-state actors in early modern ethnic violence makes such a focus on states extremely problematic. *Conquistadores*, military adventurers, and privateers may have acted vaguely in the name of European states, but they also had their own personal motivations and agendas. Many European travelers, traders, fur trappers, merchants, and castaways were able to construct supple "chameleon" identities, as Hans Staden's identity performances demonstrate. Runaway slaves, castaways, and maroons could integrate into new communities. Colonial frontiers and borderlands also allowed people to discard unwanted identities, whether robber, cheat, rapist, or murderer.

Ethnic identification was often structured through language, but imperfectly. Communication between Amerindians and Europeans required linguistic translation and cultural explanation, as literary theorist Tzvetan Todorov's provocative and fiercely debated work on interpretation and linguistic conquest suggests.[49] Interpreters such as Malinche, who served as Hernán Cortés's personal translator, had peculiar positions and could wield substantial power in the borderlands, where intercultural miscommunications and misunderstandings were routine. Amerindian groups seem to have used cultural interpretive strategies to address the threat posed by the arrival of European colonists.[50] Rumors, insinuations, and legends could be weapons used to defend against European incursions, at least for a time. Interpreters occupied ambiguous positions, despite the vital importance of intercultural communication. English explorers at times violently abducted Amerindians to serve as their informants. If Europeans were dissatisfied with the information supplied by such informants, they could apply brutal violence, as when English colonial leader John Smith whipped an Amerindian guide for supposedly misleading him. Such evidence fits well with research on the origins of the Pequot War, which shows that miscommunications and ethnic responses could also result in escalating violence and disastrous warfare.[51]

Amerindian societies' loose affiliations and permeability allowed flexible identifications, even when the proximity of European colonies prompted a more structured "tribalization." Amerindian war bands freely formed and reformed around leaders. The identifications presented by individuals could be challenged and transformed through contact and conflict, and perhaps the most important factor in limiting or fixing ethnic identifications was violence.

Where Amerindian and European colonial communities lived in close proximity in borderlands, blurred cross-cultural identities and mixed-ethnic populations emerged. English colonial writings reflected their authors' conflicting impressions of Amerindian relations with early English colonies and the possibilities of assimilating "noble savages" into a "civilized" transplanted English society. Widespread evidence reveals communication, trading relations, cultural exchanges, and intermarriage between Amerindians and Europeans throughout the Americas. Negotiations, political alliances, and military coopera-tion between groups of Europeans and Amerindians provide more examples of constructive intercultural relations that broke down bar-riers, or at least allowed passages across them. In many colonial areas, different European ethnic groups mixed, further destabilizing identi-ties. European settlement colonies promoted a "civilizing mission" that often challenged these cross-cultural identities, expecting conformity instead. English travel narratives and settlement histories reveal an ironic vision of harmony promoted by early English colonists in Vir-ginia and New England, as they envisioned a patriarchal dominion over subordinated, domesticated "noble savage" dependents.[52]

The possibilities of harmony and assimilation often ran afoul of Europeans' ethnic identifications, which defined their "civilized" soci-eties in opposition to "barbarous" ones precisely by depicting "savages" as engaging in brutal, as opposed to legitimate, violence. Ethnic identities, then, were also conceptualized and distinguished through the violent practices of warfare. Studies of the "skulking" way of war and Amerindian fortifications have shown the flexibility and adaptability of Amerindian warfare, suggesting that notions and practices of violence could change as ethnic identification shifted.[53]

New ethnicities also emerged elsewhere, outside colonial contexts. Although previous Persian empires had existed, the Safavid Empire crafted an Iranian identity that transcended regional attachments and clan networks. Shi'a rituals and imperial ceremonies celebrated a nascent Iranian identity. Shah 'Abbas confirmed Iranianness by reforming his army around 1600 by "bringing in peasants, Iranian tribesmen, and convert soldiers and equipping them with modern fire-arms on a large scale."[54] Iranian identity emerged through a century of near-constant warfare against the Sunni Ottoman Empire and may have been consolidated through the peace of Zuhab, which finally ended the Safavid–Ottoman conflict in 1629.[55]

Warfare in the multicultural Indian subcontinent contributed to the formation of strong ethnic identities. Mughal military campaigns of conquest in India sometimes prompted ethnic resistance. Emperor Aurangzeb's armies defeated the Hindu kingdom of Assam and occupied the realm in 1661, but the Ahom dynasty refused to submit and instead organized guerrilla warfare in the jungles of Assam for several years.[56] Mughals depicted the Marathas as members of a martial ethnicity based on characterizations of their diet and environment.[57]

Christianization and imperialism

Christianization reshaped ethnic and religious identities in colonial contexts. European soldiers, clergy, and settlers all saw God's agency at work in their colonies.[58] Millenarian beliefs implied that colonists represented instruments in a divine plan and participants in a "cosmic war" that involved "martyrs" in the struggle against "demons."[59] English colonists in Virginia could genuinely believe that they were fighting "the Lord's battles," and many of their European contemporaries reported visions of cosmic battles in the heavens.[60] Colonial adventurers considered their suffering through a religious iconography of martyrdom and sacrifice.

Contemporary Christian laypeople who experienced the broad religious transformations in the early modern world often espoused eschatological visions, perceiving their world as a "world turned upside-down." Imagery portraying the symbolic inversion of worldly order was integral to Reformation-era propaganda and to widespread belief in the Antichrist and the impending Apocalypse. Many sixteenth- and early seventeenth-century Christians believed that the unsettling "discoveries" of the Americas, the religious discord within Europe, and other portents signaled the arrival of the Last Days. While Protestants and Catholics had different ways of understanding God's power and human free will, almost all Europeans interpreted portents as evidence of Providence actively shaping the world around them.

Early modern European imperial ideologies incorporated religious commitment, fusing colonial expansionism with engagement in a "cosmic war." An early seventeenth-century pamphlet celebrating the appointment of Henri II de Montmorency, duc de Montmorency, as admiral of France linked his readiness to fight the "galleys of Mohammed" with his preparedness "to search for new kingdoms for his master, to found new Frances, and to plant *fleurs de lys* all around

the world."[61] Similar religious discourses underpinned Spanish conquest and expansion in Central and South America. European clergy
considered some indigenous peoples capable of assimilation through
global missionary campaigns. European colonists' personal religiosity
and faith became entangled in an all-encompassing struggle that
provided powerful religious justifications for violence, and even holy
war, in colonial warfare throughout the early modern world.

Islamization and imperialism

Islam continued to grow rapidly during the seventeenth century,
especially in Southeast Asia. The process of Islamization, introduced
in chapter 3, intensified in competition with an expanding Christianity in the same region, as "more than half the population of Southeast
Asia adopted Islam or Christianity in some sense during the age of
commerce."[62] Islamization advanced rapidly in Indonesia during the
seventeenth century. Islamic states throughout Southeast Asia
expanded their authority into rural areas, linking ethnic identities
with sanctioned religious practice.

Ottoman sultans actively promoted proselytization, seeking converts to Islam among conquered Orthodox and Latin Christian communities in the Balkans and the Adriatic. Ottoman military and naval
commanders sought conversions during their imperial campaigns in
the Indian Ocean, contributing to the spread of Muslim practice.
Mehmed IV used military ceremonies and armed tours as opportunities for mass proselytization in the Balkans in the seventeenth
century.[63]

Although Jewish–Muslim relations within the Ottoman Empire
seem to have been generally smooth, localized disputes could erupt.
Sabbatai Sevi, a Jewish mystic, claimed to be the Jewish Messiah and
attracted a large following of Jews in the Ottoman Empire in the
1650s–60s. The Sabbatarian movement became increasingly radical
as European and Mediterranean Jews traveled to Jerusalem in expec-
tation of the re-establishment of Israel. Worried Ottoman officials
imprisoned Sabbatai Sevi and pressured him into converting to Islam,
causing the Sabbatarian movement to disintegrate. Religious and
ethnic politics thus sometimes produced social conflicts that threatened to destabilize imperial rule.

Emperor Aurangzeb (1658–1707) led renewed Mughal expansion
and Islamic revival during the late seventeenth century, repressing
Sikhs and destroying Hindu temples.[64] Aurangzeb attempted to incorporate the Maratha confederation in southern India into his empire,

recruiting dozens of Maratha nobility into the Mughal armies and administrative services. But, the emperor humiliated and imprisoned the Maratha leader Shivaji, prompting outrage and resistance from the Marathas. Aurangzeb extolled an exclusive Islamic vision of martial service that excluded the Marathas, whom he regarded as infidels. The Mughal Empire waged successive campaigns of conquest in the 1680s–90s, but only reinforced Maratha perceptions of ethnic distinctiveness, bolstering their resistance.[65]

Indigeneity and soldiering

More subtle forms of acculturation developed in colonial military systems. Early modern dynastic states and trading companies often employed indigenous soldiers in auxiliary military units. The Ottoman Empire had long utilized various auxiliary units within their multi-ethnic empire. Ottomans recruited Christian children in the Balkans through its *devshirme* system, which involved converting recruits and training them in Istanbul to serve as elite janissary soldiers.

Extended contact between Amerindians and European settlers in the Americas during the seventeenth century allowed technology transfers and acculturation to gradually reshape colonial practices of warfare. Europeans and Amerindians certainly had differing cultural expectations about the practice of warfare, yet accommodation and cultural adaptation were at times possible.[66] In certain aspects of warfare, blurred ethnic identities could emerge. For example, many Amerindians acted as "ethnic soldiers," providing auxiliary, mercenary, logistical, and reconnaissance services for European colonial military forces.[67] Neil Whitehead argues that "ethnic soldiers" were linked to the processes of tribalization in South America and the Caribbean.[68]

The diffusion of European diseases, firearms, and animals forced Amerindians to adapt to increasingly deadly warfare. At the same time, European territorial encroachments and colonial economic priorities – especially fur trading and silver mining – intensified warfare among Amerindian societies.[69] Amerindians progressively adopted firearms and certain European military techniques, but maintained their "skulking" way of war, as English described the stealth and ambush tactics employed by indigenous warriors. During King Philip's War, "the Indian mode of warfare, actually a blend of aboriginal and European elements, proved so successful in numerous engagements that perceptive officers and government officials began to urge changes in colonial military doctrine," according to Patrick M.

Malone.[70] European coastal fortifications, trading factories, and military incursions forced social reorganizations and militarized Amerindian culture in the "tribal zone."

The VOC enslaved Southeast Asians and used some of them in its militia forces. VOC slaving policies constructed ethnic preferences and defined Dutch race relations in the Indian Ocean and around the world. "VOC authorities resorted to a wide variety of countermeasures in a desperate attempt to stem the continuous flood of slave escapees. A preferential slave import system promoted the introduction of certain 'ethnicities'...while prohibiting the trade in certain groups deemed troublesome."[71]

Other European trading companies and colonial settlements utilized indigenous peoples as auxiliaries. European colonists in the Americas allied with Amerindians during times of war and encouraged raids on enemy settlements. Iroquois and other Amerindians obtained firearms from Dutch West Indian Company (WIC) traders and subsequently fought with and against the English and French colonists in the Great Lakes region. European colonial forces thus included indigenous soldiers and support personnel long before the English EIC created sepoy units in Bengal and Madras during the eighteenth century.

Racial categories and ethnic identities

By the mid-seventeenth century, ethnic identifications were increasingly defined by racial categories and stereotypes that justified violence. Slave labor provided logistical support for European colonial and military operations in the Atlantic World. Amerindians were enslaved in the growing Spanish *encomienda* system (discussed above in chapter 2) and forced to work in agricultural operations and silver mines in Central and South America. A recent reassessment of Amerindian population collapse in Hispaniola attributes blame in part to the violence of the *encomienda* system.[72] From the beginning of European imperialism in the Atlantic, enslaved Africans played a role in colonial expansion and mining operations. When European colonies' demands for labor exceeded what the available Amerindian slaves could provide, Europeans turned increasingly to African slave labor, defined through a legal concept of blackness. European planters continued to use Amerindian slaves, however, and the transition from Amerindian to African slave labor was complex.[73]

European colonial governments attempted to prevent miscegenation (mixed-ethnic sexual relations), but many colonists engaged in sexual activity with African, Asian, and Amerindian men and women. Some of these mixed-ethnic couples intermarried, producing mixed ethnicity or interracial populations in most colonies. The terms *mestizo*, *métis*, and *creole* were employed to describe the offspring of biracial couples, who often unsettled the legal categories in colonial societies. Many *mestizo* people were automatically treated as slaves, but in some colonies *mestizos* could establish free status and even themselves become slave-owners.

Some ethnic identities seem to have had significant racial components. Spanish colonists expressed concerns over *limpieza de sangre* (purity of blood), which was also linked with purity of religion.[74] Early modern French notions of noble *race* seem to have paralleled Spanish discourses on *limpieza de sangre*. Claims for the existence of a *noblesse de race* implied that certain nobles were naturally superior and transmitted their noble qualities to their children through their blood.[75] French colonies and global missionary work developed simultaneously in Canada, the Mediterranean, and the Indian Ocean, perhaps shaping emerging French racial distinctions during the seventeenth century.[76]

A broader collective consciousness of Europeanness gradually formed, as the concept of Europe as a geographical space partially replaced older designations of Christendom.[77] Maps, artwork, and printed images reinforced European identities and sharpened notions of cultural difference between Europeans and other peoples.[78] A racialized notion of whiteness seems to have been simultaneously forming within Europe.

Conclusion

Conceptions of ethnicities were challenged and confronted in various ways during the seventeenth century. The shock of initial contacts between diverse peoples during earlier periods was replaced with uncomfortable closeness and sustained relationships. The practices of warfare and enslavement fueled ethnic and racial categories of enemies and conquered peoples by legal and military institutions.

New and more direct contacts over great distances reinforced notions of alterity, or otherness, in cultures. Cross-cultural diplomatic and military exchanges often exposed differences in cultural practices and reinforced stereotypes. In 1689, Chinese and Russian envoys met and negotiated the treaty of Nerchinsk, demarcating common boundaries and defining political relationships between the two empires, despite the vast distances between their capitals. Their meetings highlighted the distinct differences between their cultures, however, and did not lead to regular diplomatic interactions. Similarly, the Thai ambassadors' voyage to France to meet personally with Louis XIV in 1686 allowed the French king to demonstrate his worldliness even while simultaneously asserting his authority and superiority. European observers of the Thai embassy perceived strong ethnic differences, identifying certain character traits as Thai and reinforcing racial categories of whiteness. Louis XIV's reception of the Thai ambassadors did not, however, prevent French forces from launching an attack on Bangkok in 1688 to reinforce his prerogatives.[79]

10

Rebellion and Civil Warfare, 1630s–1660s

Peasants in rural Catalonia organized armed demonstrations in May 1640 to protest the billeting of Spanish soldiers in their villages during the Thirty Years War. In retaliation, Spanish troops sacked the small town of Santa Coloma de Farners, prompting widespread outrage and peasant mobilization across the province. Peasant rebels entered Barcelona and attacked administrative officials they considered traitors. A group of Catalan elites then attempted to gain control of the rebellion, using a council known as the Disputas to direct the movement. The Disputas raised taxes, mobilized a Catalan army, and began to articulate separatist politics. The Catalan leaders declared a Republic in January 1641 and allied with France, the bitter enemy of the Spanish monarchy. The Catalan Revolt became a separatist struggle and one of the most sustained rebellions of the seventeenth century. The conflict finally came to an end through a negotiated settlement in 1652, when the province of Catalonia was reincorporated into Spain with a full amnesty.[1]

The drama of the Catalan Revolt suggests the complexity of early modern rebellion and civil warfare. A wave of civil wars and rebellions occurred around the world in the mid-seventeenth century, sparked in part by transformations in political organization and state development. The elaboration of maritime empires, fiscal-military systems, and expanded imperial claims produced radical political activism and social change. Scholars have long debated whether or not conflicts such as the Dutch Revolt, the Fronde civil war in France, or the British Civil Wars can be considered genuine political or social revolutions. This chapter examines the political dimensions of civil warfare in the mid-seventeenth century through court politics, urban culture, parliamentary representation, and colonial contexts.

Court Politics and Civil Conflict

Early modern monarchies and empires situated power around the person of the ruler and the dynastic residence. Royal and imperial households were normally composed of dynastic family members, illegitimate children, great nobles, and semi-sovereign princes who resided at palaces or in nearby cities. Ministers, secretaries, officials, noble courtiers, and other officials also played important roles in policy formulation and courtly culture. Sociologist Norbert Elias famously linked the development of court societies and royal states, but critics have challenged his theory that a "civilizing process" sub-jugated and tamed court nobles.[2] Indeed, princely courts, as centers of dynastic power, remained sites of political intrigue and conflict in the seventeenth century.

Palace rebellions

Court politics and palace intrigues periodically produced conspira-cies and political *coups d'état* against royal ministers. One of the most famous seventeenth-century *coups d'état* occurred at the Bourbon court of France, when Maria de' Medici attempted to oust Cardinal Richelieu as her son Louis XIII's first minister during the so-called Day of the Dupes, on November 10, 1630. Louis XIII initially seemed prepared to accede to the queen mother's request, but later in the day he reversed his decision and instead exiled Maria de' Medici to the countryside. The following year, she fled to the Spanish Nether-lands and entered what proved to be permanent exile.

Assassinations and palace *coups d'état* became notoriously common in the Ottoman Empire. Early Ottoman rulers had limited male offspring and institutionalized dynastic fratricide among the imperial princes during successions. A sultan's grand vizier, military officers, wives, concubines, and eunuchs all vied for influence within the Ottoman imperial household. Sultan Süleyman set a new prece-dent by moving his imperial harem into the Topkapı Palace and mar-rying Hürrem, one of his concubines, blurring the lines between procreative and pleasurable sexuality.[3] Later, Mehmed II ordered the strangling of his 19 brothers in an attempt to enforce his authority.

Palace rebellions by the janissaries, elite infantrymen, occurred with increasing regularity in the Ottoman Empire. The janissary corps grew significantly in size during the late sixteenth and early seven-teenth centuries, gaining significant political power in Istanbul. "While they were still called up for war," Sam White indicates, "their military role increasingly came second to their position as a hereditary privileged class and a political pressure group."[4] Janissaries led a *coup d'état* in the Topkapı Palace in 1622–23, executing the young Sultan Osman II and selecting a new sultan. Janissary soldiers ousted Sultan Ibrahim in 1648, with the backing of the imperial dynasty. In addition to these outright *coups d'état*, janissaries periodically demanded that sultans remove their grand viziers, as when the grand vizier was executed in 1655. Köprülü Mehmed Pasha, who served as grand vizier from 1656 to 1661, instituted purges in the Ottoman military system to assure loyalty. In the second half of the seventeenth century, partly in response to the frequent palace rebellions, Mehmed IV began to reside in the city of Edirne, effectively displacing Istanbul as the imperial capital.

Muscovite residents and soldiers organized palace rebellions in Russia at several points during the seventeenth century. Urban protesters in Moscow burned numerous noble residences and merchant shops in June 1648, before invading the Kremlin Palace and forcing Tsar Alexei to dismiss his unpopular first minister. In 1682, a group of *strel'tsy* musketeers occupied the Kremlin and then seized control of the capital city with the support of Old Believers. These palace rebellions represented short-term disorders, however, and failed to topple the Romanov dynasty.[5]

Princely rebellions

Court politics and conspiracies could sometimes result in broader princely rebellions, aimed at removing royal ministers from their positions as key advisors. Rebellious princes and their noble allies could use their provincial and municipal governorships as bases for their military operations and political negotiations. Merely mobilizing military forces could force royal governments to negotiate with discontented nobles, leading to the removal of unpopular ministers. Princes claimed to have a right to counsel monarchs, enunciating claims to represent broader groups of subjects.[6]

Gaston de Bourbon, duc d'Orléans, who was the brother of Louis XIII and heir apparent to the still childless king, fled from France in 1631 in order to protest Cardinal Richelieu's influence at the royal court. The following year, Gaston led a small army of his supporters into France, hoping to spark a broad political rebellion. Henri II de Montmorency, duc de Montmorency and the provincial governor of Languedoc, raised an army to support Gaston, but few other great nobles joined the cause. A royal army under the duc de Schomberg marched into Languedoc, encountering Gaston's army at Castel-naudary. As the duc de Montmorency reconnoitered the positions, he stumbled into the *gardes françaises*, who wounded and captured him. The parlement de Toulouse tried Montmorency for *lèse-majesté*, the crime of treason, and sentenced him to death by beheading. The rebel forces disintegrated and a chastened Gaston negotiated a settlement with the king.

Monarchs and their ministers used a "brand of revolt" to label princely and noble opponents as seditious rebels during civil conflicts. Military authorities and judicial institutions could wield extraordinary powers against any protesters or militants who were designated as seditious in order to suppress disorder and rebellion. Noble officers and military commanders often usurped this state power to define sedition and revolt, effectively "branding" their rivals and enemies as rebels.[7]

Restraints on military practices often broke down during the civil wars that engulfed vast areas of the world in the mid-seventeenth century. Cities that were situated in major conflict zones could suffer catastrophic violence as the most extreme applications of the "law of the siege" became normal. Soldiers, who were often ill-supplied and underpaid, became habituated to pillaging and burning towns that attempted to resist them. Massacres of inhabitants and executions of civic leaders followed the end of many sieges as a result of the brutal conditions of early modern warfare and the excessive zeal of many soldiers participating in religious and civil warfare.[8]

Elaborate notions of the right to resist tyranny developed during the European Wars of Religion, as religious minorities formulated political theories to justify their rebellions against rulers they considered ungodly or heretical. Calvinist works such as François Hotman's *Francogallia* (1573) and Philippe du Plessis-Mornay's *Vindiciae, contra tyrannos* (1579) articulated arguments against Catholic rulers and condemned them as idolatrous tyrants. Such works effectively associated the concept of tyranny with impiety and heresy. Arguments for a right to resist came to be used against ministers as well as monarchs during the seventeenth century. Royal family members and nobles could mobilize extreme rhetoric of opposition to tyranny even in the context of dynastic disputes.[9]

Wars of succession

Numerous wars of succession occurred during the seventeenth century, as princes who were potential heirs battled to control dynastic states. These political struggles usually involved brothers and cousins disputing inheritance claims during dynastic transitions when direct male succession was contested or impossible.

Wars of succession could lead to state breakdown or division, as the case of Morocco shows. When Sultan Ahmad al-Mansur of Morocco died in 1603, a sustained war of succession erupted between Mulay Zaydan and several princely rivals. Morocco effectively became divided between competing spheres of power in the north and the south during a series of civil wars over the royal succession.

One of the most significant wars of succession in the mid-seventeenth century was the Mughal civil war of 1657–59 in northern India. As Emperor Shah Jahan aged, his princely sons jockeyed for positions within the imperial court and Mughal military administration. When the emperor fell ill in 1657, the princely rivalries produced a multi-sided war of succession. Dara Shukoh, the Shah's eldest son, quickly seized control of the palace and imperial court in Delhi. His brother Aurangzeb had just defeated the kingdom of Bijapur and commanded Mughal forces in the Deccan. The ailing Shah Jahan favored his eldest son's succession and sent an imperial army against Aurangzeb, but it was defeated. Aurangzeb accused Dara Shukoh of apostasy and idolatry, championing his own Islamic piety. The younger brother's army advanced toward the imperial capital, meeting Dara's forces near Agra in May 1658. Aurangzeb's disciplined troops defeated his brother's Rajput cavalry allies at the battle of Samugarh, and Dara fled the field as his army dissolved. Aurangzeb seized the city of Agra and forced his elderly father to surrender.

Aurangzeb's forces pursued the defeated Dara Shukoh and his supporters. Dara was nonetheless able to raise a new army and to gain the allegiance of many Mughal nobles. Aurangzeb's army defeated his elder brother's forces once again in another major battle at Ajmer in March 1659, allowing him to consolidate his control and organize an elaborate coronation ceremony in June. When the vanquished Dara sought the support of an Afghan noble, he was arrested and sent to Delhi, where Aurangzeb ordered his execution in August 1659.[10]

Emperor Aurangzeb reinforced his control of the Mughal Empire in the aftermath of the civil war. John F. Richards argues that "the succession crisis reaffirmed the unity of the empire and the authority of the victorious Timurid monarch. Partition of the empire into two or more appanages did not take place."[11] Aurangzeb ensured his rule by eliminating his other princely brothers in 1660 and 1661, then imposing a strict Islamic political culture across the Mughal Empire.

Urban Revolts

Population growth and urbanization drove substantial growth in city sizes throughout the seventeenth century, creating new tensions in urban societies. William Beik has shown that violent encounters in everyday urban life could intersect with organized forms of civic violence.[12] Urban revolts were common in cities around the world during the early modern period.

Municipal leaders and urban revolts

The political positions of civic magistrates were often tenuous, since mayors and city councilors were normally elected by elite male citizens for one- or two-year terms. City councils handled budgets, with individual city councilors paying for extraordinary expenses out of their own personal wealth. City magistrates often went deeply into debt when cities had to raise exceptional wartime taxes or pay contributions to passing armies.

Municipal leaders acted as crisis managers, grappling with urban protests by artisans and other urban inhabitants. Protests against taxes, grain hording, or electoral results could turn violent, producing civic disorder and threatening municipal leaders' positions and even their lives. Popular protest merged with political violence during episodes of urban conflict, producing what William Beik calls a "culture of retribution." Massive rioting broke out in Bordeaux in 1635, forcing the city magistrates to take shelter in the château du Hâ while crowds took control of the city for several days. Angry crowds of women and artisans protested against taxes in Montpellier in 1645, rioting in the streets and threatening the city magistrates and royal garrison.[13] Popular protests could result in extended periods of urban disorder, as with the serious urban riots that erupted in Istanbul in 1651 and 1656.

Civic magistrates also had to face external threats to their communities. Mayors, city councilors, merchant elites, and judicial officials often opposed tax policies and defended their civic privileges. Burdensome taxes during the extended wars of the mid-seventeenth century upset municipal leaders, who were responsible for raising taxes in their communities. Many of the tax rebellions in this period have been interpreted as resistance to state centralization, yet tax issues often intersected with local politics during civil conflicts. Wartime taxes, contributions, billeting, and pillaging strained already depleted urban economies, prompting artisans and urban poor to organize armed resistance or enlist in armies themselves. Economic exchanges between towns and countryside ensured that there were strong urban dimensions to religious wars and peasant revolts, as noted above in chapters 6 and 8. Municipal leaders thus had to cope with the growing power of dynastic states and their armies.

When municipal leaders' grievances overlapped with popular protests by artisans and poor residents, major urban revolts could develop. Certain urban revolts expanded into broader provincial rebellions, as magistrates called on other provincial cities to support their grievances. Some of these urban revolts widened into separatist provincial rebellions, as with Barcelona's role in the Catalan Revolt, discussed above. Similarly, civic magistrates and judges in Bordeaux, Aix-en-Provence, Rouen, and Paris took leadership of urban protests to mount rebellions during the Fronde.[14]

Civic guards and urban violence

Weapons seem to have proliferated throughout broad segments of early modern societies. Contemporary concepts of citizenship and service in the civic guards fostered an elaborate culture of arms in urban contexts. Municipal governments promoted local shooting societies and sponsored festive shooting matches. Sword-fighting schools, crossbow shoots, and sword dances forged a martial ethic among male citizens of towns and villages. Urban male householders could be arrested for failing to keep arms, skipping the annual oath-day, or missing musters.

Weapons were central to the practices of civic duty, since paying taxes and standing watch were often the two principal responsibilities of urban citizenship. All "free" German men had the freedom to bear arms and most of them exercised this privilege. German cities' weapons counts and militia musters demonstrate that urban residents were indeed well-armed. A 1610 weapons count of 6,160 householders in Augsburg shows that the city's homes bristled with arms: 11 percent of householders possessed firearms, 46 percent owned pole arms, and a stunning 91.6 percent had swords. A surprising 53 percent of households in Rothenburg had firearms in 1620 and the city of Hamburg called on all of its citizens to keep and maintain guns.[15]

Urban elites increasingly associated themselves with civic guards units, championing their role in armed service. Group portraits of civic guard officers, such as Rembrandt van Rijn's *The Night Watch*, highlight the civic pride of urban elites who commanded guard companies. Civic guards had their own armories and meeting halls, often located within the city hall or in an adjacent building. The prestige of civic guards arguably enhanced the militarized dimensions of urban identities.

Urban revolts in the Spanish Empire

Spain faced a series of urban revolts in its Iberian territories during the 1640s, even as the monarchy intervened in the Thirty Years War and attempted to prevent Dutch independence. The Catalan Revolt, discussed above, began as a peasant revolt in May 1640, but quickly became dominated by municipal elites in Barcelona. The outbreak of the Catalan Revolt destabilized the entire Spanish monarchy and threatened its ongoing war effort in the Netherlands and Germany.

The political crisis allowed cities in various parts of the vast Spanish Empire to revolt. Portuguese nobles seized control of Lisbon in December 1640. News of the revolt in Lisbon triggered a "panic in the Indies."[16] Goa, Mombasa, Mozambique, and other colonial cities supported Lisbon, creating a rebellion that would succeed in restoring the independence of the Portuguese monarchy. The Spanish Habsburgs continued to raise taxes throughout much of the Spanish Empire in the 1640s to cope with the financial burdens of waging the Thirty Years War and simultaneously combating Dutch, Catalan, and Portuguese rebels. Political plots in Mexico City threatened the government of New Spain in 1641–42, but inquisitorial investigations and arrests narrowly averted urban revolts.[17]

The costs of supporting Spanish military forces prompted riots and further rebellions in Spanish Italy. Crowds of Sicilian artisans rioted in Messina in 1646 and in Palermo the next year, attacking tax collectors and magistrates. News of these urban riots prompted widespread rural violence and peasant revolt across Sicily. Urban conspiracies and rural tax protests challenged Spanish authorities in the duchy of Milan in the 1640s, but the strength of the Milanese military and banking institutions ensured Habsburg control over this key territory in the Spanish Empire.

In Naples, market venders protested against the *gabella della frutta* (fruit tax) on July 7, 1647, sparking a broad peasant revolt that quickly became politicized. Tommaso Aniello, a fishseller better known as Masaniello, emerged as the leader of the market vendors and artisans who surrounded the palace of Spanish Viceroy of Naples. Riotous crowds attacked tax collectors' offices and magistrates' residences in the city. Although Masaniello was murdered on July 16, his rebellion continued without him, as peasants and some nobles joined the urban protesters and took control of the city of Naples. Villages and small towns across the Kingdom of Naples joined the rebellion in the summer and fall of 1647. Rebel leaders declared a Republic of Naples in October 1647 and sought French protection, but the movement never took on a fully revolutionary character. A negotiated settlement led to a collapse of the revolt, as Naples submitted to Spanish authority and opened its gates to a new garrison in April 1648.[18]

Revolts in the Swiss cantons

Residents of Swiss city-states developed their own complex forms of protest and collective action in the early modern period. Many male residents of Swiss cantons enrolled in stipendiary companies to serve in foreign conflicts in the late sixteenth and seventeenth centuries. Some of these young men may have been seeking adventure, but most probably enlisted to escape poverty and meager work prospects. During the Thirty Years War, agricultural changes, price fluctuations, and war refugees disrupted urban economies of the Alpine regions. Many Swiss farmers flocked to the cities searching for jobs, creating further challenges for Swiss magistrates.

A major revolt in the canton of Lucerne in 1652–53 involved democratic political organization by peasants and townspeople, leading some historians to characterize this as a revolutionary movement. Hans Emmenegger, a wealthy peasant who was literate, compiled the peasants' grievances and acted as their spokesperson. An army of about 16,000 farmers and townspeople from the Bern countryside surrounded the capital city in May 1653, pressuring the magistrates to negotiate with them. Some of the rebel bands were able to win significant political concessions from local authorities. Swiss cantonal authorities assembled an army, however, and routed the remaining rebellious peasants and townspeople in June, ending the revolt.

British Civil Wars, 1638–1649

A series of civil wars swept over the British Isles during the 1630s and 1640s, as unpopular royal policies and religious tensions combined to produce serious parliamentary opposition and military crisis. The British Civil Wars provide an opportunity to examine how princely, urban, and representative politics combined in seventeenth-century civil warfare.

Political crisis in the British Isles

King Charles I (1625–49) of England, Scotland, and Ireland disregarded principles of consultative monarchy throughout his reign. He organized military expeditions against Spain and France, but refused to call the English Parliament into session and used a series of financial expedients to raise new taxes, creating deep political opposition among the English gentry (minor nobility). He gradually transformed the English royal navy, replacing the Elizabethan race-built galleons with larger warships in an ambitious shipbuilding campaign that was financed with his controversial Ship Money program in the 1630s. The most remarkable of these new ships was *Sovereign of the Seas*, built in 1637 to project English claims of maritime domination, but the exorbitant costs angered many English subjects.

Tensions between the religiously mixed populations in England, Scotland, and Ireland aggravated the growing political crisis. Charles I used London as a base from which to rule over an England that was Anglican, but with a significant minority of Catholics, nonconformists, and a growing number of Calvinists and Puritans, who argued that the Church of England had not gone far enough in reforming itself. Scotland had remained staunchly Calvinist and Ireland was strongly Catholic, so the king generally promoted moderate religious positions that would allow him to govern the entire British Isles. Dissatisfied religious radicals nonetheless accused Charles I of popery for his lack of support of Reformed religion. When William Laud, the Archbishop of Canterbury, produced a new *Book of Common Prayer* that seemed conservative, many English Puritans protested. The publication of a version of the new prayer book in Scotland in 1637 sparked more serious outrage, leading to the Bishop's War.

When Scottish forces invaded England in 1639, Charles I's military forces failed to halt them, creating a panic. The king decided to call Parliament to seek financial support to fight the war, but the members of Parliament (MPs) instead focused on redressing their longstanding grievances over the king's unpopular taxation policies and governmental style. Political gridlock led to the dismissal of this Short Parliament in May 1640 and new elections for another assembly, which met in November 1640 and would become known as the Long Parliament.

Parliament imprisoned the unpopular Archbishop Laud and removed Charles I's advisor, Thomas Wentworth, earl of Strafford. The king failed to intervene, allowing Parliament to condemn Strafford to death and execute him in May 1641. A rebellion broke out in

Ireland in October 1641, as Catholic nobles and their followers attacked Ulster Protestants. The Irish Catholics claimed that that fought "only for the preservation of his majesty, and his rightful government over them...the defense of their religion, laws, and liberties."[19] News of the rebellion deepened the political crisis in England, and Parliament essentially took control of London while Charles I attempted to negotiate with the Scots.

Civil wars in England, 1642–1649

Charles I raised his royal standard at Nottingham in August 1642 and announced his intention to retake London, instigating the First Civil War (1642–46). The royalist army advanced southward in October, but was met at Edgehill by a parliamentary army under Robert Devereux, third earl of Essex. The armies fought to a bloody draw at the battle of Edgehill, which shocked the English public and prompted negotiations to resolve the conflict. The royalist forces, unable to subdue London, took up winter quarters in Reading.

Civil warfare expanded across the country in 1643, producing a series of localized and regional conflicts. Parliamentary forces seized towns and cities along the River Thames, while royalist troops under Prince Rupert captured castles and towns across northern and southwestern England. In August, the royalists began a siege of Gloucester, key to the communications on the River Severn. The earl of Essex led a parliamentary army to relieve the siege, fighting an intense battle at Newbury in September that resulted in a draw. The royalists seem to have been poised to destroy Essex's poorly supplied army, but they allowed the bloodied parliamentary troops to retreat back to London.[20]

A major parliamentary army marched north in 1644 to join the Scots and engage the royalists near York. Parliamentary and Scottish troops defeated the royalist army at the battle of Marston Moor, allowing the parliamentarians to take York and most of northern England. Parliament organized a New Model Army, which soon defeated the main royalist army at the battle of Naseby in June 1645, seizing the king's secret correspondence. Charles I surrendered in May 1646 and was later placed under house arrest.[21]

The parliamentary and royalist troops seem largely to have respected the laws of war in the initial phases of the fighting in England, but such restraint evaporated during the Second Civil War (1648–49) in England. The parliamentary siege of the royalist town of Colchester from June to August 1648 became infamous for its brutality and suffering. When the royalist garrison finally surrendered, parliamentary forces executed two of the royalist officers and pillaged the rank-and-file prisoners in punishment for their alleged treason.[22]

Religious militancy and atrocities in the British Civil Wars

The Irish Civil War (1641–52), which is also known as the Irish Confederate War or the Eleven Years War, was already filled with atrocities. Irish Catholics massacred numerous Protestants in the early months of the rebellion in 1641, killing around 4,000 of them. English depositions and print propaganda exaggerated the scale of the massacre, claiming that hundreds of thousands of Protestants had been killed. Religious motivations and agendas drove much of the conflict between Protestant and Catholic nobles, clergy, and soldiers. James Butler, duke of Ormond, and later Michael Jones directed the parliamentary war effort against the Irish Catholic and Confederate forces. Oliver Cromwell led a brutal war of reconquest in 1649–50. His parliamentary soldiers slaughtered the Catholic garrison at Drogheda in September 1649 and sacked Wexford a month later. Parliamentary forces gradually suppressed the remaining Irish Catholic rebels and ended the civil war.[23]

Religious radicals organized various movements during the British Civil Wars, although historians still debate the significance of the religious aspects of the conflicts. The Levellers attacked religious symbols and sites during the conflicts, at times committing acts of iconoclasm. Calvinists and other radical Reformed Christians attacked the Cheapside Cross and other public symbols that they found offensive. Parliamentary and Scottish soldiers removed the rood screens and liturgical implements from many English churches in an attempt to cleanse vestiges of Laudism. Quakers and other groups of Christian seekers formulated radical concepts of pacifism, encouraging their members to avoid participation in any form of violence.[24] When religious radicals threatened parliamentary order, Cromwell purged MPs, creating the Rump Parliament.

Military government

The Rump Parliament organized a trial of Charles I in January 1649, finding him guilty of treason and executing him. In the wake of the king's execution, Parliament essentially represented the executive power of England, instituting a republican Commonwealth government under the leadership of the parliamentary generals and particularly Cromwell. Meanwhile, surviving members of the Stuart dynasty and the cavalier nobles fled into exile in France and other countries. The Commonwealth government adopted oaths of loyalty and army purges to maintain political control during 1650, when radical protests and Stuart plots created a crisis of legitimacy. The Commonwealth and its military forces proved capable of waging war both within the British Isles and against foreign enemies.

Parliamentary forces instituted military governorships to direct the occupation of Scotland. A brief third civil war (1650–51) erupted in Scotland and northern England, as Stuart exiles and their supporters attempted to reverse English domination and parliamentary rule. By 1653, Cromwell had established personal military rule in the British Isles, implementing what some historians have controversially described as a military dictatorship. Although full-scale civil warfare died down, further plotting and civil unrest prevented demobilization. Cromwell exercised power with the title of Lord Protector and the backing of the armed forces until his death in 1658, when the Stuart dynasty began to prepare for a Restoration in 1660. The British Civil Wars had produced political experimentation and radicalization, but also bitter civil warfare and an intense backlash against republicanism.

Representative Politics and Civil Wars

The English Parliament was not the only representative assembly to become embroiled in civil warfare in the seventeenth century. Many nobles embraced ancient notions of consultative government, sometimes expressed through the Latin ideal of the *res publica* (common good), which could be fulfilled through noble assemblies that deliberated on state policies and offered advice to their princely rulers. During the mid-seventeenth century, consultative institutions often opposed ministerial politics and sometimes led political movements that turned violent.

The Fronde in France

In France, onerous taxation during the Thirty Years War and political instability during the minority of Louis XIV resulted in the Fronde civil wars (1648–53). Orest Ranum emphasizes that "the Fronde began as a tax revolt provoked by the monarchy's desperate need for funds to continue the war against Spain."[25] Anne of Austria, the young king's mother and acting regent, and her minister Cardinal Jules Mazarin struggled to manage tax protests and provincial disorder in the 1640s, especially after the Peace of Westphalia ended war across much of Europe in 1648. Then, the regency government's new fiscal policies, which aimed at raising funds by cutting payments to royal officers, resulted in stiff opposition by judicial officials and provincial officers.

When the regency government arrested leading judges of the parlement de Paris in August, Parisian crowds attacked the ministerial residence and erected barricades to control the streets of Paris. The rebellious Parisians became known as *frondeurs*, from the term used for the crude slings used by Paris youth. The judges of the parlement de Paris (an appelate court), known as *parlementaires*, became prominent leaders of the Fronde by claiming to represent the grievances of Parisians and by gaining the support of other *parlementaire* judges in Rouen, Bordeaux, and Aix-en-Provence. The royal family fled from Paris in the middle of the night, joining an army that Louis II de Bourbon, prince de Condé, had mobilized to besiege Paris. A peace that was negotiated in March 1649 allowed the royal family to re-enter Paris, but could not restore order in the provinces.[26]

Confusing politics and shifting alliances among powerful nobles soon led to the arrest of the prince de Condé, the prince de Conti, and the duc de Longueville. Outraged Condé allies and clients protested his unjust arrest and mobilized troops, resulting in a second Fronde led by princes and nobles. Louis XIV's uncle, Gaston d'Orléans, maneuvered for influence in Paris, declaring that he could protect the royal family. Nobles and jurists likewise claimed to act in the king's name and in the interests of the French people.

The royal family managed to hold a *lit de justice* ceremony in the parlement de Paris to pronounce Louis XIV's majority in December 1651, but still could not halt the civil war. Meanwhile, cities and towns across France chose sides as civil warfare spread across the provinces. A popular movement of merchants, artisans, and laborers known as the Ormée took control of Bordeaux in 1652–53, mounting massive marches and expelling city leaders. Thousands of printed pamphlets, known as *Mazarinades*, produced anti-government propaganda and Cardinal Mazarin was forced into exile twice during the chaotic civil war. In July 1652, a royal army cornered the prince de Condé's army outside the walls of Paris, but Condé's allies in Paris convinced the garrison to open the gates and allow the prince to enter the capital. Condé's troops took over the Hôtel de Ville (city hall), ransacking the building and killing dozens of judges and political opponents. The prince de Condé quickly lost support of Parisians and fled, joining Spanish forces.

Anne of Austria and her trusted minister Mazarin were gradually able to restore royal authority. Louis XIV and the royal family entered Paris in October 1652 and reoccupied the Louvre palace. A royal army finally forced Bordeaux to submit in August 1653, effectively ending the Fronde. *Parlementaire* opposition, noble division, and popular protest during the Fronde nonetheless left a lasting fear of radicalism in French political culture.

The deluge in Poland-Lithuania

The representative political system of Poland-Lithuania faced a serious political crisis in the mid-seventeenth century. The Sejm assembly had elected John II Casimir Vasa (1648–68) as king of Poland-Lithuania in 1648. The new king attempted to reorganize his military forces, but immediately confronted noble opposition and a Cossack uprising. The tsar of Russia backed the Cossacks, producing the Thirteen Years War (1654–67) between Poland-Lithuania and Russia. A Russian army invaded at the beginning of the war, over-running much of Lithuania and capturing Vilnius. The Russian forces included *strel'tsy* musketeers, new formation infantry, artillery, and foreign military advisors, in addition to noble cavalry, light cavalry, and conscripted infantry contingents.[27] Swedish and Brandenburger forces intervened, defeating the Polish army soundly at the battle of Warsaw in July 1656 and seizing the capital city.

John Casimir fled into exile as the conflict widened into what became known as the Second Northern War (1655–70). Sweden was now fighting against Russia within the borders of Poland-Lithuania, but also in the eastern Baltic. Denmark entered the war against its old rival Sweden, but was rapidly defeated. King Charles X of Sweden seemed poised to confirm Swedish imperial control of the entire Baltic coastline. The Sejm assembly was deeply divided and Poland-Lithuania seemed in danger of collapse. Brandenburg suddenly turned against Sweden in 1657, providing support for John Casimir's restoration in Poland-Lithuania.

Meanwhile, Poland-Lithuania descended into a civil war that Polish people remember as *Potop*, or the Deluge. Most of the Polish nobles backed Swedish forces, while many Lithuanian nobles joined with the Russians, accepting Tsar Alexei's claim as Grand Duke of Lithuania. The shock power that the nobles, who served as winged hussar heavy cavalrymen, normally provided for Polish armies was thus diluted.

The Ukrainian Cossacks were also divided in the confusing civil war. Poland-Lithuania received military assistance from the Habsburgs and gradually repelled Russian forces, but suffered terribly from warfare, military occupation, disease, and population collapse. John Casimir eventually managed to reach a diplomatic agreement with Russia to regain his throne in 1667, but at the cost of huge territorial concessions in eastern Poland and Ukraine.[28] The king abdicated in 1668, permitting a new election to be held and finally ending the Deluge. The elective monarchy of Poland-Lithuania was greatly weakened by the prolonged civil warfare, however, as consultative politics fell victim to foreign lobbying and military intervention.[29]

Civil conflict in Russia

Russian *boyars* (nobles) sought a different form of collaboration with the Romanov monarchs. In the mid-seventeenth century, Russian *boyars* and rulers acted to tighten legal restrictions on peasants, establishing a system sometimes called "second serfdom." The Law Code of 1649 merged the status of various types of peasants in Russia, contributing to the blurring of the conditions of peasants, serfs, and slaves within the empire. The law bound most peasants legally to the land, denying them mobility other than enlistment in the Russian army. Almost all Russian peasants were essentially serfs as a result of this legal reform, and "after 1649 serfdom had become increasingly more degrading and severe."[30]

The *boyars* exercised immense authority on their landed estates, periodically prompting civil conflict. The conditions of Russian serfdom sometimes led peasants to join rebellions, usually organized in the name of the tsar around the figure of a peasant pretender. Peasants apparently hoped that a "true" tsar would assist them against the *boyars*. Cossacks and peasants rose in revolt during succession crises in the Russian Empire in 1579 and 1614, asserting their role in upholding just rule.

Religious schism contributed to the disorder and civil conflict in Russia in the mid-seventeenth century. Patriarch Nikon, the leader of the Russian Orthodox Church, led liturgical reforms in the 1650s that met serious resistance among the peasants. Opponents of Nikon's reforms, who became known as Old Believers, actively resisted attempts at establishing religious uniformity and joined a series of peasant revolts later in the seventeenth century. Stenka Razin led an extensive peasant revolt along the Volga River in 1667–70, gaining significant support from Old Believers. Razin exploited the legend of the good tsar, whom he claimed to be assisting in implementing imperial justice.

Colonial Conflicts

Rebellions occurred in European colonies and maritime empires around the world in the early modern period. Colonial systems developed their own political cultures that generated conflicts within colonial societies during the seventeenth century.

Resistance in Africa

The establishment of European trading factories and colonial outposts in West Africa fueled conflicts on the continent. Some coastal Africans resisted the growing influence of the Atlantic slave trade, but others actively participated in the slave markets, which often involved reselling war captives from the interior of West and Central Africa. African kingdoms maintained wary relationships with the Portuguese *feitorías* at Angola and Sao Tomé that managed booming slave exports.

Agricultural changes and new agricultural products seem to have produced social conflict in Africa. West Africans grew yams, millet, rice, plantain, bananas, and other crops prior to contact with European trade, employing slaves as cultivators. Many African societies adopted maize, cassava, and other crops from the Americas in the sixteenth and seventeenth centuries as global trade reshaped local contexts. Droughts associated with the Little Ice Age may have aggravated rural crises.

Rural rebellions and civil wars occurred in Africa, but the political fragmentation of early modern Africa into thousands of small kingdoms and city-states and the lack of written sources in many areas makes documenting rural violence across the continent difficult. One of the best-known conflicts was a succession crisis in the kingdom of Kongo in the mid-seventeenth century. Portuguese troops and their African auxiliaries intervened in the civil war, defeating a Kongolese army and destroying the kingdom.[31] Many pastoral societies seem to have experienced repeated displacements and migrations as a result of continual political and ethnic regroupings in the rainforests and savannahs of Africa. The ability of West and Central African kingdoms to resist European encroachments and acceptance of the trans-Atlantic slave trade was progressively eroding.

Slave revolts

In colonial territories, plantation slavery created new forms of resistance. African slaves in the Caribbean and South America could resist by running away and forming their own isolated maroon communities to collectively resist recapture. Planters aggressively pursued runaway slaves, sending armed parties out to hunt them down. Maroon settlements in Brazil, known as *quilombos*, may have utilized Central African military organization, since their name derives from the Bantu term for war camp, or *kilombo*. Some of the maroon societies carried out raids on plantations and colonial settlements. Ex-slaves managed to create their own maroon kingdom of Palmares in Brazil during the late sixteenth century.[32] Other slaves organized resistance on the plantations themselves, attempting to disrupt the agricultural system through sabotage of equipment or work slow-downs. Some slaves chose to challenge their masters and escape slavery through suicide.

Occasionally, an entire plantation's slaves would rise in a violent revolt aimed at killing their masters and disrupting the local plantation complex. Reports of slaves poisoning their masters circulated in Caribbean colonies. Slaves in the English colony of Barbados rebelled in 1649, and alleged slave conspiracies were uncovered several times in Barbados and Jamaica during the late seventeenth century. Dutch planters in Southeast Asia confronted conspiracies and attempted revolts in Batavia during the same period. Unfortunately, limited evidence has so far been discovered on slave revolts during the seventeenth century, but colonial administrative records and correspondence demonstrates that a deep-seated fear of slave revolts already existed in dominant slaveholding cultures.

Colonial rebellions

Discontented settlers and colonized peoples resisted colonial authorities in highly diverse contexts. The colonial cities of Goa and Colombo revolted against Portugal in 1652–53. When Chinese workers in the Philippines rebelled in 1639, Spanish authorities retaliated with atrocious violence: "The Spanish governor had all Chinese held in captivity shot in cold blood, murdered all Chinese servants in Christian households, and set fire to Manila's Chinese suburb, incinerating all within it."[33]

Indentured laborers worked on many Caribbean plantations in the late sixteenth and early seventeenth centuries. Irish indentured workers in the English colonies on the islands of Montserrat, Barbados, and Jamaica. Some of these Irish laborers were former peasant rebels who had opposed English rule in Ireland during the British Civil Wars and who had subsequently been sent to the Caribbean as indentured servants to work on plantations. Irish indentured servants periodically protested their conditions, and English colonial officials worried that they might join slave revolts.[34]

The enormous wealth generated by sugar and tobacco plantations attracted raids and stimulated colonial rebellions. Dutch forces aggressively raided Spanish and Portuguese colonies in the Caribbean and South America in the 1630s and 1640s. The Dutch West India Company managed to carve out a Dutch colony in Brazil, seizing Portuguese plantations. But, a colonial rebellion by Portuguese settlers forced the Dutch to withdraw in 1654. Colonial wars and rebellions sometimes led to the temporary breakdown of plantation economies as imperial military and naval forces battled over colonial possessions.

The Pueblo Revolt in northern New Spain shows how powerful rural revolts could be in colonial territories. Franciscan friars had long conducted missionary activity among the Pueblos who lived along the upper Rio Grande River in present-day New Mexico. Franciscan friars gradually became frustrated with aspects of syncretism in the Pueblo practice of Christianity and sought to instill a more purified form of Catholicism. A series of droughts and famines in the 1660s and 1670s exacerbated the situation in Pueblo villages, apparently prompting attempts at reviving indigenous religion. Juan Francisco Treviño, a provincial governor, organized a campaign against idolatry in 1675, instituting new policies to stamp out indigenous religious practices by disrupting Pueblo ceremonies, confiscating liturgical implements, and imprisoning medicine men. Treviño's colonial forces tried to intimate the Pueblo, arresting 47 medicine men, executing three of them and whipping the others. When crowds of Pueblo people protested in Santa Fe, Treviño released the religious leaders.

One of the medicine men who had been whipped, named Popé, soon began to organize resistance from Taos Pueblo. In August 1680, Pueblo warriors seized Spanish horses and attacked the Spanish villages in northern Pueblo lands, desecrating Catholic churches and killing about 400 colonial settlers and 21 friars. Popé's Pueblo warriors then surrounded Santa Fe, prompting the Spanish colonists there to break out of the blockade and flee southward away from Pueblo territory. The Pueblo warriors succeeded in throwing off Spanish colonial domination and reinstituting indigenous religious and cultural practices for more than a decade. Colonial officials in

New Spain slowly reorganized, however, reconquering Pueblo settlements in the 1690s and founding new Franciscan missions. The Pueblo Revolt nonetheless demonstrated that colonial rebellions could seriously destabilize colonial regimes.

Exiles and refugees

Colonial territories sheltered exiles and refugees, many of whom had profound ethnic, national, and religious identities forged in searing defeats and exile experiences. Civil warfare encouraged the persecution and expulsion of religious minorities during the seventeenth century. Members of religious groups from England, the Netherlands, and Germany that were considered dangerous or ungovernable – such as the Calvinists, Anabaptists, Puritans, and Quakers – migrated to distant colonies. European settlers in Atlantic and Indian Ocean colonies often already had intimate personal experience with religious violence and civil warfare.

Other migrants were refugees from the chaos, political disruption, epidemic disease, and famine that accompanied civil wars. Civil wars and economic difficulties in Europe prompted migrations of refugees to colonies in the Atlantic and Indian Oceans during the seventeenth century. An estimated 248,000 English, 158,000 Spanish, 50,000 Portuguese, 45,000 French, and 13,000 Dutch migrants left their home countries between 1640 and 1700 for Atlantic colonies.[35] If there were seemingly few Dutch colonists in the Atlantic World, this was because the Dutch model of colonization relied on soldiers and sailors serving with the VOC in the Indian Ocean. Some 317,800 Dutch men departed on VOC ships for Asia between 1602 and 1700.[36]

Some refugees formed "national" contingents of soldiers based on their strong ethnic identities and exile experiences. Early modern concepts of "nations" often referred to common linguistic identities and a nascent consciousness of a "national" *patrie*, or homeland. Some historians suggest that patriotic expressions during wartime can be considered an early form of nationalism.[37] Stipendiary contingents and auxiliaries were normally composed of soldiers from a shared ethnic background who supported a common cause, often deepened though their extended service for "national" causes. Such military units represent some of the best cases for such "national" sentiment in the early modern world.

Many of the Huguenot refugees who fled France after the Revocation of the Edict of Nantes in 1685 remained bitter opponents of Louis XIV. Thousands of Huguenots migrated to the Netherlands,

Brandenburg, England, and its colonies in the late seventeenth century. Other French Calvinists formed five Huguenot regiments to serve along with the Grand Alliance against Louis XIV during the Nine Years War, responding to William III, Prince of Orange's call for a Protestant crusade against Catholic France.[38]

Civil conflicts in the British Isles during the late seventeenth century affected the entire empire and its colonies. William of Orange invaded England in 1688 with a veteran Dutch army, but faced little armed opposition and quickly ousted James II during the so-called Glorious Revolution. As William and Mary established a new royal dynasty in England, the exiled James II and his Jacobite supporters continued to organize rebellions in Scotland and Ireland until they were defeated at the battle of the Boyne in July 1690. The defeat of the Jacobite cause nonetheless spurred Scottish military adventurers to fight elsewhere. Scottish soldiers went off to diverse wars in search of opportunities to serve Protestant causes in Europe and the Atlantic World.[39] As the English domination of Ireland tightened, many Irish men took up their "national" cause by serving as Wild Geese in Louis XIV's army and fighting against the English.

Conclusion

Civil warfare seemed pervasive around much of the world during the middle of the seventeenth century. The Little Ice Age contributed significantly to the wave of political rebellions and civil wars that crashed over many states between the 1630s and the 1660s. Geoffrey Parker argues that "the fatal synergy that developed between natural and human factors created a demographic, social, economic and political catastrophe that lasted for two generations and convinced contemporaries that they faced unprecedented hardships."[40]

One of the last major civil wars of the seventeenth century occurred in China, where the Kangxi emperor (1662–1722) faced challenges in restoring order following the Manchu conquest and establishing Qing dynastic rule throughout China. Several former Ming generals had joined the Qing armies and led the conquest of southern and southwestern China. These generals were rewarded with lands and governing power in the regions that they had conquered. One of these generals, Wu Sangui, rebelled in 1673 and was soon joined by other disaffected military elites in what became known as the Three Feudatories Revolt. Wu Sangui's forces defeated several imperial armies, but the vast majority of the population remained loyal to the Qing dynasty. The Kangxi emperor and his loyal generals gradually suppressed the rebellion in southwestern China by 1681 and "the Qing state emerged from the Rebellion of the Three Feudatories firmly in control of China and ready to expand even further."[41] The Qing would go on to consolidate their control of the Chinese imperial administration and military forces, allowing the dynasty to rule into the twentieth century.

11

Mercantile War, 1630s–1690s

Dutch warships sailed into the Melaka Straits in June 1640 and began a naval blockade of the Portuguese port of Melaka. Antonio Van Diemen, Governor-General of the VOC (Dutch East India Company) in Batavia, had organized this expeditionary force in a bid to seize this vital harbor and fortified city, which the Portuguese had held since 1511. Melaka controlled commerce through the straits and served as one of the key entrepôts in the Portuguese Empire's global trade in spices, silk, and porcelain. The VOC had previously attempted sieges of Melaka in 1606 and again in the 1620s, but had failed to capture the port. The sultanate of Aceh, committed enemies of the Portuguese, provided military forces and logistical support for the new Dutch attempt, allowing the VOC to conduct a concentrated siege against the strong Portuguese defenses, which included bastioned fortifications and at least 70 heavy cannons. After a five-month defense and several attempts to relieve the siege, the Portuguese garrison finally capitulated in 1641 and VOC troops took control of Melaka.[1]

The fall of Melaka represented a major loss for the Portuguese maritime empire in Southeast Asia and a significant transition in commercial patterns in the Indian Ocean. A VOC officer celebrated the conquest of Melaka in a letter to the king of Burma:

> Your Majesty writes that we are continually at war with the Portuguese, which is indeed true. In fact, about four months ago, with God's help, our people took the famous old fortified city of Malacca [Melaka] from the Portuguese by great force of arms. During the siege, around seven thousand Portuguese either died of starvation or were killed in

combat so that this wicked and deceitful breed is increasingly being smitten and tormented by the Lord's castigating hand.[2]

The VOC now dominated the Melaka Straits and used its strategic position to threaten its European and Southeast Asia rivals and assert control over commerce in Southeast Asia.

This chapter examines the connections between warfare and global commerce in the seventeenth century. Maturing global commercial networks diffused commodities, stimulated new markets, and generated consumer demand. Trading companies engaged in intense economic competition and maritime conflict to control commercial routes, natural resources, and commodities. States sponsored these trading companies and increasingly directed their economic policies as they waged mercantile war.

Desired Commodities and Economic Competition

Consumer demand for rare and expensive commodities drove armed competition between maritime empires and their trading companies in global markets. Merchants and trading companies expanded commercial networks, attempting to profit from the lucrative and growing trade in spices, medicines, foods, beverages, and manufactured goods.

Commodities and global commerce

The spice trade had already become globalized during the sixteenth century as Chinese, Japanese, Arab, Indian, Portuguese, and Spanish merchants traded cloves, mace, cinnamon, pepper, and other spices. The prices for spices could be fantastic, as the rare plant products such as Malabar pepper were priced per ounce. A global monetary market in silver grew up to support the spice trade, and economic historians have traced the global silver flows from the Americas and Europe to East Asia in the sixteenth and seventeenth centuries. Spices were not merely used as condiments and flavor enhancers, but also as food preservatives, medicines, and health supplements.

Medical commerce became one of the most lucrative sectors of the early modern global economy. "While Spanish conquistadors had entered the Americas looking for gold and silver, by the seventeenth century Europeans increasingly turned their attention to 'green gold,'" according to Londa Schiebinger. Botanical samples from the Americas, Africa, and Southeast Asia could command astonishing prices. The botanical gardens of hospitals and universities expanded rapidly as they attempted to categorize plant specimens and understand appropriate medicinal uses for them. Schiebinger stresses that "botanical exploration – bioprospecting, plant identification, transport, and acclimatization – worked hand in hand with European colonial expansion."[3]

Portuguese warships had aggressively attempted to monopolize commerce in the Indian Ocean throughout the sixteenth century, but they faced escalating competition from Ottoman, Arab, Indian, and Southeast Asian opponents. Portuguese control of the spice trade eroded further toward the end of the sixteenth century, as Dutch and English privateers preyed on Portuguese merchant shipping in the Indian Ocean. English and Dutch began sending armed merchant ships to acquire spices directly. An early Dutch trading company called the Company of Far Lands sent eight ships to Southeast Asia in 1598, which "brought back 600,000 pounds of pepper and 250,000 pounds of cloves, along with nutmeg and mace. The ultimate return on the combined initial investment was a staggering 400 percent."[4] By the early seventeenth century, the incredible profits of the spice trade were stimulating armed competition and mercantile warfare.

Global foods, medicines, and beverages

Mercantile companies competed to dominate commerce in foods, medicines, and beverages. Salted cod became the first global seafood in the sixteenth century, as exploitation of the North Atlantic cod fisheries became heavily commercialized. The growth of global commerce brought various new fish into broader circulation, but salted cod was imported in high quantities into Europe, allowing it to become a supplemental staple food. Cod that was caught off New England, Newfoundland, and Greenland was preserved with salt before transportation across the Atlantic. Scottish, English, Dutch, French, and Basque fishing boats developed massive cod fishing operations. Cod consumption expanded rapidly in predominantly Catholic areas, where fish was already normally consumed as the main protein on fasting days. *Bacalao* and *baccalà* (terms for salted cod) became important dishes in Spanish and Italian cuisines by the late sixteenth century and salted cod quickly became a staple food in the diets of some European peasants.[5] Competition over cod fisheries provoked maritime conflict and privateering in the North Atlantic.

Sugarcane cultivation on plantations in the Americas rapidly transformed imperial economies in the Atlantic World, as we saw in chapter 9. The refined sugar that was shipped from Brazil and the Caribbean islands had become a global food commodity by the early seventeenth century. Fine-grained sugar began to replace other sweeteners in pastries, dishes, and beverages in societies around the world. Sold in small measures, sugar became a consumer commodity that was accessible to broad segments of society. European states with colonies in the sugar-producing Caribbean reaped the spectacular profits of the global trade in sugar and the expanding consumer societies. Colonial powers now attempted to control sugar islands and raid enemy commercial vessels transporting "white gold," as sugar became known.

Tobacco use spread rapidly throughout the world in the seventeenth century, provoking economic and social conflict. Amerindians had long employed tobacco spiritually in rituals and ceremonies, as well as medicinally. Smoking became extremely popular among soldiers, as shown by contemporary Dutch paintings of soldiers' revelries and smoking societies. As tobacco spread globally, moral concerns about the practice prompted many societies to ban consumption of tobacco. There were anti-tobacco urban riots in Istanbul, but the sultan's bans on tobacco failed, in part because smoking was so popular among the janissaries. Emperor Jahangir prohibited tobacco use in the Mughal Empire in 1617, although the edict seems to have had little effect. The Chinese were adopting tobacco smoking by the 1630s, prompting an imperial prohibition in 1640, which was abolished two years later by a military governor because it was so popular among his troops. "As the global community of smokers grew," according to one historian, "they were uninhibited in expressing their delight at discovering the pleasures of tobacco."[6] Plantations in the Americas struggled to keep pace with the growing global demand for tobacco, and cultivation spread rapidly to other areas of the globe. India, for example, became a major producer and exporter of tobacco by the mid-seventeenth century. The tobacco trade spurred further economic competition and mercantile conflict on a global scale.

Coffee and tea became major global beverages, supported by the spread of sugar, which could be added to these drinks. Coffee was made from the bean that originated in the Arabian peninsula and East Africa and had been cultivated since the fifteenth century in the Islamic world. Venetians had adopted coffee drinking from the Ottomans, but its use beyond Islamic territories initially seems to have remained limited. Then, coffee consumption expanded rapidly as the first coffee houses opened in London in 1652 and, soon afterwards, in Paris. Soldiers helped popularize coffee drinking and spread its consumption worldwide. Coffee bean cultivation spread to India and

Java as English and Dutch companies struggled to respond to the growing demand for coffee. English consumers began drinking tea imported from China and Japan soon after, and by the 1690s tea consumption took off. The English East India Company played an important role in the burgeoning tea trade, fighting to preserve its market share.

Chocolate consumption spread through its association with coffee and tea drinking. Cacao beans, originally used by Mayan and Mexican societies, were grown in the tropical rainforests of Central America and then exported to Europe and other colonies around the world. Chocolate was consumed as a warm drink that was thought to have medicinal value. Chocolatiers and merchants began adding sugar to the bitter raw product, making its taste more acceptable to global consumers. The popularity of chocolate led to smuggling and seizures of cacao shipments.

Alcoholic beverages produced from plants were mostly consumed locally, but certain varieties increasingly had broad markets. Some fine wines had long been shipped across the Mediterranean Sea as luxury goods. Venetians enjoyed sweet Cretan wines produced on the largest island of their *stato da mar*, until the Ottoman conquest of Crete halted the flow of sweet wines to Venice and ensured Ottoman naval and commercial dominance of the eastern Mediterranean.[7]

Brandies and Bordeaux wines were becoming famed as prestige wines that were sought in French, Dutch, and English markets. "Starting as early as the 1660s," according to one study, "premium producers began to focus on developing wines that were full bodied, with concentrated mellow flavors; luscious, rich textures; and deep, jewel-like colors."[8] Fortified wines such as *porto* and *madiera* began to be marketed throughout the Atlantic World by the end of the seventeenth century. London and Amsterdam merchant associations competed over the fine wines exported from Bordeaux.

Table wines, beers, ales, and rice wines had been used for centuries by laborers and soldiers around the world to fortify themselves for their work, but these beverages had mostly been locally manufactured and consumed. Global navies now transported soldiers, supplied colonial settlements, and ensured global commerce. The increasing numbers of sailors and soldiers serving in navies and colonial territories required alcoholic rations, generating a growing demand for alcoholic beverages. The English East India Company shipped India Pale Ale for sailors and soldiers in the Indian Ocean.

Intoxicants also became increasingly globalized. Dutch distillers began making gin from juniper plants in the mid-seventeenth century, and VOC sailors and soldiers serving around the world soon received gin as part of their daily rations. Sugar plantations in the Caribbean produced rum, which became popular with sailors and colonists across the Atlantic World. European merchants began to use alcohol as a trade good with indigenous peoples in the Americas, Africa, and Asia, sometimes disrupting social values. Alcohol both motivated soldiers and fueled colonial warfare worldwide.

Manufactured goods and consumer demand

Certain manufactured trade goods became available in abundance on global markets during the seventeenth century. Finished products from Asia were popular trading goods, but merchants also sought animals, minerals, and raw materials to use in manufacturing goods. Global commercial networks were now dense enough to circulate prized domestic goods in sufficient quantity to meet broad market demand, bringing down prices. Food products and manufactured goods that had previously been exclusively luxury goods now fed a consumer culture that was not merely for the noble elites, but was accessible to wider segments of society. Commercialism and marketing techniques increasingly aimed at broad communities of urban residents who could act as consumers. Consumer demand in turn drove mercantile competition and maritime warfare between the well-armed fleets of trading companies.

Chinese blue-and-white porcelain pieces became global luxury goods. Porcelain was already highly prized in the Islamic world before it entered Europe as early as the fifteenth century. Porcelain production was a carefully guarded secret, and the best porcelain was reserved for the Chinese emperor and his court. Yet Chinese potters also fired porcelain for various collectors within China, as well as export porcelain intended for markets in Southeast Asia, South Asia, West Asia, and Europe. By the seventeenth century, Korean and Japanese potters had learned how to create their own porcelain, but the majority of export porcelain was still produced in Jingdezhen. Ceramics makers imitated the look of Chinese porcelain, even if they were unable to reproduce the secret of true porcelain firing. Potters at Iznik in the Ottoman Empire, Delft in the Netherlands, and Puebla in Mexico all emulated Chinese blue-and-white styles. Dutch merchants commissioned *kraakporselein* (carrack porcelain) with designs sent from the Netherlands to potters in Japan. One of the popular styles of this export porcelain prominently displayed the VOC monogram. VOC ships brought back enormous cargoes of porcelain to the Netherlands, as Dutch merchants rushed to fill the growing demand. A single VOC ship, the *Wapan van Delft*, brought a total of 15,000 pieces of porcelain in two voyages during the 1620s.[9]

Clothing became increasingly globalized in the late seventeenth century. Wool produced in areas of significant shepherding – especially Scotland, England, and Spain – was increasingly traded globally. Indigo was cultivated in several regions of India, Asia, and the Mediterranean for use in dying textiles. Silk was produced in China and Japan, but shipped worldwide as a luxury textile by mercantile companies. Cotton grown along the western coast of India was woven into calicos, chintzes, and other textiles for export from the ports of Surat, Bombay, and Madras by the late seventeenth century. Proto-industrial production of clothing fed not merely the European demand, but also diverse markets of settler colonies and indigenous peoples worldwide.

Animal pelts from Russia and North America were transported to Western Europe for manufacturing coats and hats. Bear and fox furs were exploited for making coats. Ermine, mink, otter, sable, and other rare animal furs from Siberia were used for the linings of coats and mantles. Beaver furs from Canada became especially popular in manufacturing broad-brimmed hats in Europe during the seventeenth century.[10] English and Dutch companies competed over the animal pelts, which could be processed by artisans in their cities. Some articles of clothing were sold exclusively within Europe, but others were exported worldwide.

Manufacturing allowed for the growth of a global arms trade. A widespread trade in luxury arms had long existed, since weapons and armor often served as diplomatic gifts between princely rulers. Around 1600, "the international trade in arms began to concentrate in the northern Netherlands, especially in Amsterdam."[11] Dutch foundries produced artillery pieces for the VOC and for presentation to rulers worldwide as diplomatic gifts.

The growth of proto-industrial manufacturing in the late sixteenth and early seventeenth centuries greatly broadened the arms trade. Major arms manufacturing centers developed in Amsterdam, Utrecht, Rotterdam, and Maastricht. A putting-out system developed in the Netherlands to manufacture gunpowder, as merchants distributed their raw materials to peasant workers who would then refine and corn the powder. Massive amounts of Dutch gunpowder were used by the VOC or sold on the burgeoning global arms market. Dutch armorers produced large quantities of firearms, armor, artillery, and gunpowder for an ever-expanding global market in arms. As a result, "Dutch arms could be found in the farthest corner of the then-known world: with North American Indians, in the Spanish and Portuguese colonies in Central and South America, in Africa with rulers along the Guinea shore, and in Asia."[12]

Speculative bubbles and economic crises

Early stock markets grew up in Antwerp and Amsterdam during the sixteenth century, but remained limited in scope. New financial techniques developed in the Netherlands, as Dutch nobles and urban elites invested heavily in state bonds and annuities to finance warfare against the Spanish Empire during the Dutch Revolt.[13] By the early seventeenth century, stock markets had developed significantly as a wider set of elites and urban professionals became shareholders in the VOC, the EIC, and other companies in the Netherlands and England. The VOC attracted numerous investors: "With its capital of nearly 6.5 million florins divided into 22.5% annually on the original share capital for the next 120 years, the VOC provided continuing opportunities for investment and profit taking for shareholders."[14] Intensive investment and speculation could drive rapid inflation and reselling, however, leading to the creation of "bubbles." The most famous early modern example of a speculative bubble was the tulip bubble of the 1630s, which became knows as "tulipmania."

Exotic flowers became prized domestic consumer products in European and Mediterranean urban culture in the late sixteenth century, especially in the Ottoman Empire and the Netherlands. Armed merchant ships brought botanical specimens from colonies in the Americas and Southeast Asia in increasing numbers and varieties. Tulips soon became the most popular of all the flowers newly available on global markets. By the 1630s, Istanbul reportedly boasted 80 flower shops selling tulip bulbs that were cultivated by 300 different growers. Because tulip bulbs could be transported and then planted in plots, they quickly became commodified. A virus on some bulbs would sometimes create spectacular multicolored tulip varieties that were incredibly rare, highly prized, and thus extremely expensive. Dutch growers gave these rare varietals names – such as *Semper Augustus*, *Admirael van der Eyck*, and *Gouda* – that could be used in marketing bulbs. Tulip companies in the Netherlands began to offer futures in tulip bulb plots, allowing investors to cash in on the profits that would be generated from a particular group of tulips that bloomed in the summer. Futures were already used in the Baltic grain trade, but tulip futures became extremely speculative in the 1630s, leading one Dutch observer to comment that "no one speaks asks about or talks of anything but Flora, so that they have their heads so full of it, that they can neither think nor dream of anything else." A single *Admirael van Enkhuizen* bulb sold at an auction in Alkmaar in February 1637 for a stunning price of 5,200 guilders.[15]

A few weeks later, the tulip bubble collapsed when prices fell dramatically, as growers could not deliver sufficient numbers of bulbs and investors refused to pay their debts. Satirical prints and songs ridiculed the tulip traders and investors as "Flower-fools." Some shareholders indeed lost considerably, but few seem to have experienced immediate bankruptcies. Despite this dramatic collapse of the tulip market, Dutch tulip cultivation continued and the flower market gradually recovered. The Netherlands successfully captured the global trade in flowers in the seventeenth century, a dominance they have maintained ever since: "The Dutch flower industry today is world-renowned, with a market share of 70 percent of the international production of flowers and 90 percent of the trade; and of these flowers tulips are by far the most important."[16]

The bursting of the tulip bubble did not shatter the Dutch economy, as some legends have claimed, but it did question commercial practices based on credit and reputation, creating "a crisis over a culture of value."[17] Debates over commerce and credit became common in the seventeenth century. The spectacular profits of the spice trade seemed ephemeral, since "following the effective monopolization of nutmeg, mace, and cloves by the VOC in the 1650s, 'there followed a prolonged slump in export values.'"[18] EIC shares and other stocks were traded regularly in English coffee houses in the late seventeenth century, even though a formal London stock exchange did not yet exist. Moralists in London and elsewhere worried about the informality of stock markets, the transferability of shares, and the potential volatility of stock prices. These concerns greatly troubled war planners, too, since stocks had become crucial to financing the war efforts of joint-stock companies and the mercantilist states that backed them.

Resource Wars

Dutch trading companies waged aggressive maritime and amphibious warfare in the Caribbean Sea, the Atlantic Ocean, and the Indian Ocean. By the mid-seventeenth century, trading companies were engaging in direct economic competition and mercantile warfare to control natural resources and human labor supplies on a global scale.

Trading companies and monopolies

The VOC represented the prototype of a new wave of mercantilist companies that arose in the early and mid-seventeenth century. The company offered Dutch urban elites a new form of capital investment with a high rate of return, and it reaped fantastic profits on its spice trade, occasionally as high as 1000 percent. VOC officers became the key agents of the trade between Japan, Indonesia, and India, establishing commercial dominance in Southeast Asia – effectively monopolizing trade on key commodities and resources by the 1630s. The VOC developed a convoy system that used trade winds to speed armed merchant ships between the Netherlands and its colonies in the Indian Ocean. It maintained a complex military and naval system of warships, sailors, soldiers, and fortifications across Southeast Asia. The trading company organized blockades of Goa and other Portuguese-controlled ports during the 1630s, preying on Portuguese and Spanish galleons. The VOC grew rapidly, deploying 85 warships in the Indian Ocean by 1639 and invading Ceylon.

The VOC received direct support from the Dutch Republican government, which organized massive shipbuilding campaigns and began to maintain a permanent navy. A Dutch fleet under Maarten Tromp had engaged a Spanish armada in the English Channel, fighting a series of engagements known as the battle of the Downs in September and October 1639. This naval victory confirmed the ability of the Dutch Republic to wage mercantile war on a global scale.[19]

The spectacular profits of the spice trade were unpredictable, however. Even with monopolization, spices were subject to changing supplies and fluctuating prices in an unstable global market. In addition, "the financial costs imposed by policing the monopoly – building fortifications, garrisoning them, launching punitive raids, and patrolling the waters – were substantial."[20] Monopolies were always imperfect, since unauthorized production and smuggling continued. Prices periodically slumped and bouts of colonial warfare sometimes disrupted commerce. The VOC fleet nonetheless defeated the English East India Company (EIC) fleet in successive engagements during the Anglo-Dutch Wars of the mid-seventeenth century and maintained its commercial dominance throughout most of the seventeenth century.

The States General of the United Provinces recognized the effectiveness of the new VOC model and copied its organization in its global mercantile empire. The Dutch West India Company (WIC) was formed in 1621 in order to wage privateering campaigns and economic warfare against Spanish shipping in the Caribbean. The WIC soon administered Dutch colonies in North America, Brazil, Guiana, and the Caribbean, developing its own military and naval forces, based in Dutch Brazil under the command of a governor-general. The WIC actively waged trade warfare in the Caribbean, aiming to threaten the Spanish control of silver and gold flows and to break the Portuguese dominance in the global slave trade. In 1628, a WIC fleet commanded by Piet Hein caught a Spanish treasure fleet in Matanzas Bay, along the coast of Cuba, as we saw in chapter 7. Dutch warships seized an estimated 11.5 million guilders of captured silver, filling the coffers of the WIC and funding its war effort. The WIC had seized the island of Curaçao in 1634 and expanded Dutch colonial control in northern Brazil. As the Spanish threat to the Netherlands receded, Dutch fleets extended their mercantile warfare to English colonial targets in the Caribbean and North America during the Anglo-Dutch Wars. Admiral Michiel de Ruyter's squadron conducted destructive raids on commercial shipping throughout the West Indies in 1664–65.[21]

Global mercantile wars

The military victories and enormous profits of the VOC and WIC inspired other European states to emulate them by forming their own mercantilist companies to stimulate colonization and economic development. The English EIC was restructured to incorporate investments in 1659. Companies negotiated for commercial privileges and monopolies on lucrative spices and crops. French ministers launched several mercantile companies in the early seventeenth century, including the Levant Company.

During the middle of the seventeenth century, competition between colonial companies gradually became orchestrated by ministerial officials and military officers, operating from royal courts and capital cities. The EIC asserted the power to mint coins and impose martial law in 1685, challenging Mughal authority as well as the French presence in South Asia.[22] Companies could still occasionally wage wars of conquest independently of government ministers in the metropoles, as when the EIC essentially fought its own war against the Mughal Empire in 1686–90.

Ottoman mercantilism provides an excellent example of the combination of naval competition, colonial development, and war finance. The *bazaars* of Istanbul retained their importance in global commerce throughout the early modern period, incorporating new features such as coffee houses, tea rooms, and *hookah* smoking lounges. Anatolian, Syrian, and Egyptian artisans produced Turkish rugs, silk fabrics, cotton textiles, Iznik ceramics, firearms, and other goods for consumption within the vast Ottoman Empire, as well as for export to markets across the Mediterranean, Eastern Europe, Central Asia, and the Indian Ocean. Artisans accompanied Ottoman armies on campaign to supply soldiers, sell them merchandise, and purchase any pillaged goods.[23] Ottoman fleets and armies pursued aggressive amphibious warfare to defend Ottoman trading routes and open new markets in the eastern Mediterranean, the Black Sea, the Red Sea, and the Indian Ocean. Daniel Goffman argues that because of the exchanges in diplomacy, commerce, and migration, "what emerged by 1700…was an almost universal perception of the Ottoman Empire as a European state."[24] Whether or not the Ottoman Empire was fully accepted as a European state, it certainly waged mercantile warfare.

Although the Portuguese global empire gradually shrank due to losses against the Dutch and English in Southeast Asia, Portugal still maintained a number of colonies in the Atlantic World. Angola and Brazil continued to generate considerable wealth through the slave trade and sugar cultivation. Portuguese gold mining seems to have actually expanded in Brazil during the 1690s and 1700s.

Fiscal controversies and scandals associated with the costs of waging mercantile warfare led to the reorganization of a number of joint-stock companies. Company losses and wartime expenditures strained government finances in the United Provinces and England in the second half of the seventeenth century. The foundation of the Bank of England in 1694 provided the English royal government and its trading companies with greatly expanded credit through perpetual loans, stockholding investments, and customer deposits.

The plantation complex and slave mercantilism

The plantation complex, discussed in chapter 9, was initially developed for sugarcane cultivation, but could easily be adapted for the production of other lucrative cash crops, such as tobacco, coffee beans, and tea leaves. During the seventeenth century, slave mercantilism emerged as colonial agricultural economies increasingly depended on the importation of new slave laborers.

Plantation slavery grew dramatically during the seventeenth century, fed by the rapidly expanding global slave trade. A trans-Atlantic slave trade increasingly competed with the older trans-Saharan, Mediterranean, and Indian Ocean slave trades. Portuguese merchants had established a near-monopoly on the overseas transport of African slaves during the sixteenth century, but this broke down as Dutch, English, and French trading companies developed their own slave commerce along the coasts of West Africa. European slave ships purchased slaves at the ports of African rulers who had enslaved captives in wars between African states. Some African militaries and European contingents may have engaged in dedicated slave-taking operations at times along the African coast, but most of the trade seems to have been handled by merchants operating in the trading factories.[25]

In the Atlantic World, multiple triangular trading routes developed in the seventeenth century. Settler colonies in the Americas, South Africa, and Southeast Asia generated a growing demand for finished products from Europe. Colonial governors and elites purchased porcelain, silk cloth, fine fabric prints, silver, wines, and other luxury goods from around the world. Colonists and *mestizos* in the Americas and the Indian Ocean desired English cloth, German linens, tin, and Moroccan leather. A journal of the voyage of the slave ship *Diligent* shows that the slave trade in Africans had become normalized by the early eighteenth century, even as it reveals the complexities of the triangular trade in the Atlantic.[26]

Colonies with profitable plantation agricultural systems prompted intense economic competition over the trade in cash crops produced by slaves. Pirates and privateers routinely raided colonial ports and shipping during the seventeenth century. During major wars, mercantile companies and states fought to occupy fertile agricultural lands and developed colonial ports. Mercantile warfare involved conquests to control colonial resources, urban settler populations, and port facilities. Colonies came to be thought of as mercantile investments in and of themselves, but historians disagree about whether or not they were profitable for the states that sponsored them.[27]

Mercantile conflict prompted European colonial settlers to organize protests and revolts in colonies in the Atlantic and Indian Ocean Worlds during the seventeenth century. French colonists in Martinique rebelled in 1666, and settlers in Saint-Domingue led a sustained revolt in 1670–72. James Pritchard emphasizes that "troubles broke out again in 1680 at Cap Français following the collapse of the French market for colonial tobacco and the enforcement of the Senegal Company's slave trade monopoly."[28] Colonial settlers were deeply invested in plantation economies and slave mercantilism, sometimes opposing broader interests of metropolitan governments that dealt with other forms of commerce and broader conceptions of mercantile warfare.

State Economic Direction

As trading companies and global commercial networks expanded, philosophers and economic analysts developed theories of mercantilism beginning in the early seventeenth century. Maritime empires increasingly attempted to direct commercial competition and economic development through mercantile theory, resource management, and naval force.

Mercantile theory and state development

Mercantilists equated wealth with natural resources, especially precious metals. Antoine de Montchrestien's *Traité de l'économie politique* (1615) advocated that the kingdom of France enrich itself through global commerce, colonial expansion, and mercantile warfare. Francis Bacon offered a similar mercantilist theory of aggressive expansion for the king of England in his *Essays* (1625). The theorists of mercantilism assumed that natural resources must be finite, and they thus considered the world's wealth to be static. States would capture and exploit resources in a zero-sum game of winners and losers in direct economic competition.

Mercantilist theories adapted expansive conceptions of wealth in the mid-seventeenth century as plantation economies and colonial production took off. In England, Parliament's passage of the Navigation Acts of 1651 and 1660 produced a heated debate concerning the appropriate relationship between commerce and state authority. Benjamin Worsley justified the Navigation Act of 1651, arguing that: "It is by trade, and the due ordering and governing of it [by the state] and by no other means that wealth and shipping can…be increased and upheld."[29] European mercantilist governments passed numerous laws to ban trade with competing states, protect monopolies, and enforce tariffs.

Jean-Baptiste Colbert, minister of finance for Louis XIV, refined mercantilist theories while supervising French royal finances, commerce, buildings, and naval affairs in the 1660s and 1670s. Colbert reorganized the French navy and oversaw the formation of the *Compagnie des Indes Orientales* (French East India Company) beginning in 1664. He refined earlier mercantilist theories and implemented state-sponsored economic projects. With his *intendants* (royal provincial administrators), he improved ports, shipyards, and maritime stores to outfit and provision commercial and naval ships. An industrial infrastructure developed to handle the enormous demands of shipbuilding, cannon founding, and provisioning for Colbert's naval administration.[30]

Mercantile theorists devised new taxes on popular commodities and consumer goods. The lengthening Franco-Dutch War (1672–78) pushed the French monarchy to seek additional taxes and to enforce collection of previously existing taxes. Colbert issued new taxes on commodities entering France, requiring a *papier timbré* (stamp) on certain commercial goods such as tobacco, tinware, and pewterware. The new taxes on commodities prompted protests and tax rebellions in Brittany and Guyenne in 1674–75. News of initial protests in and around Bordeaux led to a massive tax rebellion in Brittany, which involved peasant and urban participants who refused to pay the taxes. Urban crowds sacked tax collection offices in Rennes and Nantes, while peasants donning a *bonnet rouge* (red cap) attacked tax collectors in the countryside. Royal military forces quickly suppressed the rebellion and occupied Brittany, enforcing the new tax regime.

Resource management and economic development

Mercantilism involved various methods of direct state intervention in economies. Cities and royal states invested in botanical gardens to further medical research and economic development. Merchants and trading companies imported seeds from around the world. Botanists worked to classify diverse plant specimens from distant environments, producing treatises on a rapidly expanding botanical universe. They also experimented with plant varietals and cultivation techniques that would allow for the exportation and plantation of desired plants in colonial settings.

Royal states launched major economic and urban development projects during the seventeenth century. The Bourbons instigated various urban projects in Paris, building new bridges and squares in their capital city. The ducs de Savoie rebuilt their capital of Turin as an ideal fortified city. The disastrous Great Fire of London in 1666 destroyed more than 13,000 houses and left at least 100,000 inhabitants homeless, prompting the Stuarts and the municipal government to engage in urban planning on a massive scale.

Major land reclamation and water management projects promoted economic development in many societies. The draining of the marshes in eastern Paris in the late sixteenth century allowed the Marais district to become one of the preferred neighborhoods for noble residences in the city. French engineers constructed the Île-Saint-Louis in the middle of the Seine in the early seventeenth century. Provincial *daimyō* and Tokugawa *shoguns* promoted rural economic growth through land reclamation and tax regulation. Marsh draining and land reclamation were vital for intensive agriculture and economic development in many parts of the Netherlands. In the mid-seventeenth century, Dutch provinces and cities invested in building complex *trekvaart* canal networks for passenger barges, which were pulled by horses. By 1665, the canal systems linked 30 cities in the Netherlands, and "the barges were a wonder of comfort and punctuality."[31]

France launched a massive commercial enterprise to construct a canal across southwestern France to link Atlantic and Mediterranean commerce and circumvent the naval forces of its chief rival Spain. Pierre-Paul Riquet, a tax administrator in Languedoc, proposed the Canal du Midi project to Jean-Baptiste Colbert and eventually received his approval. The project involved engineering a complex water reservoir system and constructing a lengthy canal from the Mediterranean, near Béziers, to the Garonne River at Toulouse. Engineers built a new port at Sète on the Mediterranean coast to control the entrance to the canal, as well as a canal bridge near Béziers, so that boats could cross over the Orb River. The Canal du Midi allowed ships to bypass Iberian coastlines, but never fulfilled its ambition to surpass the commerce that passed between the Atlantic and the Mediterranean at the Straits of Gibraltar, but it was nonetheless considered a major engineering marvel.[32]

Permanent navies

Mercantile warfare transformed maritime conflict, as certain states began to build and maintain large and expensive navies. Prior to the mid-seventeenth century, most governments relied on armed merchant ships or converted civilian vessels to act as warships during major maritime conflicts. Few states maintained fleets in peacetime, except in the Mediterranean, where persistent galley warfare had encouraged the construction of specialized war galleys that were dedicated naval vessels. The Ottoman, Venetian, Spanish, and French governments all maintained fleets of rowed galleys and galleases throughout the early modern period. These fleets had limited uses for mercantile competition, however, since they normally only operated in the relatively calm seas of the Mediterranean. The logistical demands of global mercantile trade began to alter maritime warfare during the seventeenth century, encouraging mercantile companies to construct specialized heavily armed merchant sailing vessels. Global economic competition fueled naval rivalries between the Portuguese, Spanish, English, Dutch, and French governments, which sought to protect their merchant vessels and commercial interests worldwide.

Mercantilist governments began to invest in the construction of purpose-built sail-powered warships that would be incorporated into established permanent navies. The Swedish royal navy established its presence on the Baltic Sea to support Swedish military operations against Denmark, Poland, and Russia. Although the flagship *Vasa* famously foundered on its maiden voyage, the Swedish fleet grew to 28 warships by 1650, outpacing the Danish fleet. Jan Glete argues that "the Vasa Kings originally created the navy as a defense against blockade and invasion...but they could also use it as an instrument of imperial expansion."[33] Denmark struggled to keep pace with Swedish and Dutch naval building, but the Danish navy still effectively controlled traffic between the North Sea and the Baltic Sea, enforcing the Sound tolls.

In the Atlantic World, the once mighty Portuguese fleets had been eclipsed by their Spanish and Dutch rivals by the seventeenth century. Meanwhile, cardinal de Richelieu directed a major reorganization of French naval forces, allocating significant funds for building new ships. The States General of the United Provinces organized its navy through a federal system of five admiralties, constructing a powerful fleet to protect its global mercantile empire. In chapter 10, we already encountered Charles I's attempts to build an English royal navy to rival the Dutch fleets. When the British Civil Wars broke out, the Long Parliament appointed Robert Rich, earl of Warwick, as commander of the fleet in 1642, and Charles I lost control of his navy. A royalist fleet was formed in 1643 to support Charles I's military operations in England and Ireland. The republican navy reorganized in 1649, eventually destroying the royalist fleet during the British Civil Wars.

Naval rivalry and economic competition

The republican governments of England and the Netherlands emerged as the principal naval rivals in the mid-seventeenth century. The naval and economic warfare between these two republican governments challenges some theories of representative governments and their willingness to wage war on each other.

The English and Dutch navies began to build increasingly large warships, referred to as great ships or first-rate warships that mounted huge arsenals of heavy shipboard artillery. By the 1650s, a single first-rater might carry 50 guns, as many artillery pieces as an entire army. Navies began to use classification systems to categorize their vessels based on their ratings, from the first-raters to small frigates and support vessels. Admirals and naval theorists developed linear naval tactics to employ the concentrated firepower of fleets' artillery. The first-rate and second-rate ships were considered ships-of-the-line, capable of participating in these linear tactics because of their awesome firepower and staunch hulls. Smaller naval vessels performed escort, raiding, and logistical duties for their fleets.

The English and Dutch navies fought three successive mercantile wars. In the First Anglo-Dutch War (1652–54), the new English fleet inflicted heavy losses on the Dutch navy, which had fewer ships-of-the-line. Under the leadership of Johan de Witt, the Dutch States General responded by completely transforming the Dutch Republican navy. Alfred Thayer Mahan's classic analysis of the Second Anglo-Dutch War (1665–67) stressed the Dutch navy's dramatic victories and downplayed the intense economic impact of Dutch privateers.[34] The Dutch fleet under Michiel de Ruyter won a significant engagement against the English fleet of George Monck and Prince Rupert at the Four Days' Battle in 1666, but then lost the Two Days' Battle. The next year, de Ruyter led a bold attack up the River Thames, capturing the *Royal Charles* and several other ships, and effectively ending the war. The English Restoration government of Charles II invested heavily in shipbuilding, expanding the navy to 95 warships by 1675 and allying with France to fight an indecisive Third Anglo-Dutch War (1672–74). These conflicts damaged both English and Dutch commerce, as both sides' merchant shipping suffered heavy losses to privateering. Wartime economic losses were often followed by peacetime recoveries, and it is not clear whether the successive wars led to a decline of the Dutch mercantile empire.[35]

France suddenly presented a challenge to Dutch maritime dominance, entering into Atlantic naval rivalry through Colbert's mercantilist policies. Colbert began to administer the French royal navy as controller-general of finance in 1661, becoming secretary of state for the navy in 1669. He established a French East India Company in 1664, and in the same year claimed that "an almost unlimited multiplication of the number of ships would…multiply the glory and power of the state."[36] Over the next decade, Colbert oversaw a major shipbuilding campaign that by 1672 had produced at least 120 major warships. French shipbuilders incorporated new principles of naval design, engineering, and hydrodynamics to build sleek, powerful ships. Increasing standardization and rationalization governed all phases of shipbuilding and naval procurement, from timber production to artillery founding. Colbert's naval ordinances instituted a new classification system to organize the expanded navy, led by 33 first- and second-rate warships, each of which mounted 80 guns or more. Arsenals and artillery foundries were established and a series of new fortified ports were constructed or expanded at Dunkirk, Toulon, and Brest, offering French vessels improved harbor facilities. The *Soleil Royal*, a massive 120-gun warship built in 1669–71, became the pride of the French navy. The French navy effectively competed with both the English and Dutch navies in the 1670s and 1680s, winning a victory at the battle of Beachy Head against a combined Anglo-Dutch fleet in 1690.

The draining expenditures in the Nine Years War later forced Louis XIV to chose between financing either his armies or his fleets. The king did not hesitate to prioritize his armies, which were needed to face a broad coalition of enemy armies. He abandoned Colbert's fiscal and economic policies when the financial pressures of supplying his royal armies during the Franco-Dutch War (1672–78) forced a shift in priorities.[37]

Conclusion

Mercantilism has too often been considered an exclusively European phenomenon, an aspect of narratives of the expansion of capitalism and the rise of the West. But, throughout the seventeenth century, indigenous peoples in North America and Africa participated in the dynamics of mercantile warfare as they traded with foreign merchants, interacted with colonists, and fought both for and against armed forces. Empires and states in India, East Asia, and West Asia forged their own new systems of warfare and commerce that had mercantile aspects, since they too were closely involved in the processes of globalization.

The Ottoman conquest of the Venetian island of Crete can be considered a mercantile war. Sultan Ibrahim declared war on Venice in 1645 because the Venetians had provided protection for Maltese pirates who had been preying on Ottoman merchant shipping in the Eastern Mediterranean. The sultan directed an Ottoman fleet of 78 galleys and numerous smaller vessels to transport an invasion force from Istanbul to the island of Crete. An Ottoman army that included large contingents of janissaries disembarked in northeastern Crete in June 1645, rapidly seizing the cities of Chania and Rethymnon and overrunning the Cretan countryside. The Ottomans invested the heavily fortified Cretan capital of Candia in 1647 and began a sustained naval blockade of its port. The blockade became an epic struggle, with extended bombardments of Candia's fortifications, vast mining operations, and three formal sieges. Ottoman janissaries and auxiliaries reportedly assaulted the Venetian bastions of Candia 69 times during the final siege in 1667–69.[38] When Candia finally surrendered in September 1669, one of the Venetian negotiators exclaimed: "We have come to surrender a fortress whose equal does not exist in the entire world. It is a priceless pearl the likes of which no sultan possesses."[39]

Even before the fall of Candia, Crete was being incorporated into the Ottoman mercantilist system. Local Cretans enhanced their existing trading relations with Istanbul and other Ottoman ports. The janissaries who played a leading role in the conquest of Candia became merchants, entrepreneurs, and landholders in the city and throughout the island. The Ottoman conquest of Crete thus created a "janissaries' island" that thrived in the mercantile economy that the empire had created across the Eastern Mediterranean.[40]

Territorial War, 1660s–1700s

Louis XIV and his military advisors decided to make the capture of Maastricht, a key Dutch city, the main goal for the entire campaign of 1673. French armies had invaded the Netherlands the previous year at the beginning of the Franco-Dutch War (1672–78), but had avoided attacking the well-fortified city of Maastricht, which straddled the Meuse River and held a strong garrison of 5,000 infantry and 1,000 cavalry. The maréchal de Turenne led one French army to feint against Imperial forces in the upper Rhine valley, disguising the main theatre of war. Meanwhile, another army under the prince de Condé screened Dutch forces, allowing the main French army of 40,000 soldiers to invest Maastricht in June 1673. Sébastien Le Prestre de Vauban, the leading French military engineer, took charge of the siege attack, ordering thousands of pioneers and conscripted peasants to dig zigzagging approach trenches on the northern side of Maastricht, facing the city's Brussels gate. The king himself joined the besieging army to observe the progress of the siege, but he allowed his engineer to direct the siegeworks. Vauban employed three parallels, linked by approach trenches, to position batteries closer and closer to the defensive fortifications. French troops methodically assaulted the fortified outworks and their siege guns opened a massive bombardment, firing at least 5,000 shots into one section of the city walls. The desperate garrison capitulated after only 25 days of siege.[1]

The siege of Maastricht displayed a highly systematic form of positional warfare. Vauban predicted that an army utilizing his system of siege warfare could take any fortress in a mere 45 days.[2] The dashing comte d'Artagnan, captain of a company in the *gardes*

françaises, was killed during one of the attacks on Maastricht's outworks – providing a symbol of royal service for French propaganda
and model for Alexandre Dumas's later novel *The Three Musketeers*.
Paintings, prints, and triumphal artworks celebrated the victory with
images of Louis XIV in front of the siegeworks at Maastricht.

At the time of the siege of Maastricht, many European military
officers and ministers already considered Louis XIV's army and military administration as organizational models to emulate. New associations of territoriality and sovereignty underpinned warfare and
state development processes in the second half of the seventeenth
century. Lauren Benton observes that "although empires did lay
claim to vast stretches of territory, the nature of such claims was
tempered by control that was exercised mainly over narrow bands,
or corridors, and over enclaves and irregular zones around them."[3]
Legal theories and cartographical developments enunciated coherent
claims of sovereignty over peoples and geographic spaces. Dynastic
states and empires had long battled over inheritance rights and possession of titled landholdings, but new territorial imperatives increasingly drove warfare between states that each claimed an abstract
sovereignty over defined frontiers.

State-Commission Armies

New techniques of recruitment and army formation changed the relationship between states and war during the mid-seventeenth century.
Dynastic governments increasingly used a formal commissioning
process to recruit and maintain military units on a permanent basis,
gradually replacing the features of the older aggregate-contract processes of army formation. The emerging "state-commission armies"
provided the basis for new operational and strategic approaches to
territorial warfare.

Recruitment

The rapacious behavior of aggregate-contract armies led some states
to reform their military systems in the mid-seventeenth century.
Several dynastic states established state-commission armies that relied
on commissioned military colonels and captains to recruit soldiers for
their proprietary infantry and cavalry units. State-commission armies
maintained permanent armed forces and provided regular salaries
and quarters for soldiers. John A. Lynn argues: "A state-commission

army took longer to raise than did its predecessor, but had advantages to compensate: it was better disciplined, more loyal to the ruler, and cheaper man for man, as well as being more uniform, with a standardized, permanent regiment as its basic building block."[4]

The new recruitment patterns associated with state-commission armies gradually coalesced, in conjunction with military reforms in firearms drill and discipline. The Dutch techniques of firearms drill developed by Maurits van Nassau required regular practice and military discipline. In the mid-seventeenth century, the Swedish, Brandenburg, and Austrian armies incorporated firearms drill, instituted regimental organization, and enforced strict discipline. France, Spain, and other kingdoms gradually adopted state-commission recruitment and developed permanent military forces. Some Mughal and Ottoman military forces began to be recruited through commissioning processes, too, suggesting that elements of the state-commission army were not exclusively European.

Recruitment techniques changed as military forces sought soldiers who would engage in long-term service, rather than serving merely for a campaigning season. States commissioned officers to recruit soldiers through a system of "voluntary" enlistment often ritualized through an oath of loyalty and the acceptance of a bounty. Recruiting parties of soldiers nonetheless resorted to coercive methods to entice men to enlist. Taverns proved to be perfect recruiting grounds for officers seeking to prey on unemployed and drunk men who could be tricked or abducted into military service.

New recruits entering permanent military units faced a lifetime of strict discipline. Regiments commanded by proprietary colonels became the key organizations in most states' military systems. Infantry companies had previously been the basic organizational units, assembled into ad hoc brigades and temporary regiments for an individual military campaign or for the duration of a war. Colonels now purchased their offices and retained command of permanent regiments even in peacetime, providing their soldiers with uniforms, arms, equipment, munitions, wages, and rations – based on established standards. Permanent infantry regiments, often composed of 10–20 companies, became the backbone of state-commission armies.

Permanent armed forces

State-commission military systems began to maintain permanent armed forces in the mid-seventeenth century. The term "standing armies" has frequently been used to describe permanent military forces, but this is somewhat confusing since regiments were often dispersed into garrisons during winter and peacetime. Garrison troops had previously been billeted in the homes of urban residents, who were in theory compensated for providing soldiers with room and board. Soldiers now enlisted for longer terms of service, receiving pay and rations even when campaigns and wars were over.

The growing size and permanence of garrisons required new systems to lodge and feed troops, leading state military administrations to invest in constructing barracks for their soldiers. Military engineers began to build dedicated barracks – complete with dormitories, kitchens, mess halls, and armories – within bastioned artillery fortifications to house and feed permanent garrisons for extended periods. The construction of barracks never fully satisfied the demand for housing troops in wartime, but they helped establish permanent military units and averted massive demobilizations at the end of each campaigning season.[5] Louis XIV built the Hôtel des Invalides in Paris as a residence for his retired veterans in the 1670s, in effect creating the first permanent veterans' home.

A number of states instituted comprehensive army reorganizations in order to establish state-commission armies. Permanent military units effectively created an officer corps, since nobles who were commissioned to recruit units could now rely on regular salaries and permanent employment. Colonels controlled subordinate appointments and discipline within their proprietary regiments, transmitting offices to their kin and clients. Officers cultivated a sense of professionalization in the nascent officer corps and among their units through rituals, regular inspections, and military reviews. Expanded cavalry units were increasingly filled with non-noble recruits, except in guard cavalry and other elite mounted units. States invested in cannon foundries, producing large numbers of heavy artillery pieces. State-commission armies employed large trains of siege artillery, which was used extensively in positional warfare throughout the second half of the seventeenth century.

Military professionalization

State-commission armies fostered military professionalization during the second half of the seventeenth century. Elector Frederick William of Brandenburg-Prussia reformed his military in the 1650s and 1660s, creating a state-commission army. By the 1680s, regularized recruitment and taxation had resulted in permanent armed forces composed of 31,000 soldiers and hundreds of siege artillery pieces.[6] Despite frequently changing alliances, the Great Elector often provided political support to the Holy Roman Emperor and upheld Imperial law, now that Calvinism had been legally recognized by the Peace of Westphalia. The army of Brandenburg-Prussia defeated a Swedish army at the battle of Fehrbellin in 1675, allowing his troops to briefly occupy Pomerania.[7] The Mughal Empire attempted to institute its own versions of military professionalization through the *mansabdari* system. Qing generals likewise instituted professional military officers and administrative systems in the Chinese Empire.

The army of Louis XIV became the principal model for military professionalization under the war ministers Michel Le Tellier and his son, François-Michel Le Tellier, marquis de Louvois. When Louis XIV began his personal rule in 1660, the young king expressed a strong desire for *gloire* (martial glory), aggressively pressing his legal and territorial claims. Louis XIV expanded his permanent military forces in preparation for war. Jean Martinet, named inspector-general for infantry in 1667, instituted rigorous infantry drill and instilled strict military discipline in the French army. Louis XIV pressed his territorial claims in the War of Devolution, 1667–68, but the Dutch joined England and Sweden in a Triple Alliance to check the king's advances, forcing the French to conclude peace with Spain in 1668.

Louis XIV felt personally betrayed by the Dutch and sought vengeance against them. For four years, French ambassadors worked to diplomatically isolate the United Provinces, while Louvois expanded the royal military forces and prepared war material. In the spring of 1672, Louis XIV suddenly declared war on the United Provinces and launched a massive invasion by three separate armies. The war would showcase the reorganized French royal military system and its techniques of professionalization.[8]

Positional Warfare

Positional warfare aimed to capture city sites and control urban populations. Cities served as key bargaining chips in peace negotiations, since urban centers held enormous economic and tax value for rulers and their states. John A. Lynn uses the expression "war-as-process" to describe the strategy of late seventeenth-century positional warfare, which was defined by "the indecisive character of battle and siege, the slow tempo of operations, the strong resolve to make war feed war, the powerful influence of attrition, and the considerable emphasis given to ongoing diplomatic negotiations."[9]

Franco-Dutch War, 1672–1678

At the beginning of hostilities, the outnumbered and ill-prepared Dutch troops were overwhelmed as the French armies rapidly advanced, seizing Deventer, Utrecht, and Nijmegen. Desperate Dutch negotiators sued for peace, but Louis XIV refused, seeking even more humiliating terms. As French troops began to encircle Amsterdam in June 1672, the Dutch opened the sluices at Muiden, allowing the North Sea to inundate the countryside around Amsterdam. French forces were unable to capture Amsterdam, and had to turn to face the threat of an approaching army from Brandenburg, which had allied with the Dutch. Imperial troops also mobilized, as the emperor considered entering the war. The flooded countryside of the United Provinces prevented the French armies from advancing further. Louis XIV's chance to win a quick war evaporated, as the conflict grew into a major European conflict, which would become known as the Franco-Dutch War.

Unable to knock the Dutch out of the expanding war, French forces withdrew from the United Provinces and invaded the Spanish Netherlands and Franche-Comté. During 1673, Vauban conducted a masterful two-week siege of the Dutch fortified city of Maastricht, discussed above. Meanwhile, fighting erupted in the Rhineland, Roussillon, Sicily, and the West Indies. The French maréchal de Turenne orchestrated a series of offensives in the Palatinate and Lorraine in 1674, outmaneuvering Imperial forces near Philippsburg and personally leading cavalry charges at the battle of Sinzheim on June 16, 1674. After defeating the Imperial army there, Turenne claimed: "I have never seen such a dogged battle."[10] Turenne's forces extracted contributions from the Palatinate, and then cleared Imperial forces out of Alsace in a brilliantly conceived winter campaign in 1674–75. Louis XIV shifted his armies into a largely defensive posture in 1676, but still sought gains in the Spanish Netherlands, which became the main theater of war. A Dutch army attempted to retake the heavily fortified city of Maastricht in 1676, but was finally forced to abandon its siege. Military operations in the Spanish Netherlands continued to revolve around sieges of well-defended cities in 1677 and 1678, while fighting continued in Germany, Roussillon, and other theaters of war.

Negotiations proceeded at Nijmegan throughout 1678, producing a series of separate peace agreements between August 1678 and February 1679, ending the hostilities. The conduct of the Franco-Dutch War had demonstrated Louis XIV's concern with territorial gains and defensible frontiers. Following the war, Louis XIV pursued a policy of *réunions*, annexing cities and districts along the French borders that had at least theoretically been subject to kings of France in the past. French law courts and military forces implemented these *réunions*, seizing Metz, Toul, Verdun, Luxembourg, and Strasbourg between 1679 and 1684. The Dutch War and the ensuing *réunions* displayed a territorial imperative for positional warfare on a grand scale.

Artillery fortifications and siege warfare

Positional warfare became more systematic in the second half of the seventeenth century, as bastioned artillery fortification designs continued to develop, utilizing well-emplaced cannon to lay down a concentrated crossfire. The density of defensive artillery increased as permanent bastioned fortifications became more common and states invested in additional gun foundries. Military operations had become closely linked to the rhythms of siege warfare, as field armies targeted major fortresses and fortified cities for attack using methodical approach trenches and intensive bombardments by well-positioned batteries of siege artillery. Meanwhile, battles often developed as opposing field armies attempted to relieve beleaguered fortresses. New treatises on fortifications and siege warfare, such as Blaise François, comte de Pagan's *Les Fortifications* (1645), popularized techniques for attacking and defending artillery fortifications.

Bastioned fortresses proliferated at port cities, colonial towns, and strategic sites around the world during the seventeenth century. English, French, and Spanish colonial troops improved fortifications in the Caribbean Sea and the Americas. Portuguese, Spanish, and Dutch engineers built elaborate bastioned fortresses in Indian and Southeast Asian colonies, especially at fortified cities like Goa, Manila, Melaka, and Batavia. Similarly, fortresses ensured Swedish control over that kingdom's widespread Baltic possessions in Pomerania, Livonia, Estonia, Finland, and along the Sound.

In certain densely populated regions and war zones, bastioned fortresses became linked with broader fortified systems that relied on interdependent fortresses and defense-in-depth. Ottoman and Habsburg rulers enhanced fortresses along the military frontier in Hungary and along the Danube River. Fortification lines came to define the boundaries between the Dutch Republic and the Spanish Netherlands during the Dutch Revolt and the Thirty Years War. Linked fortresses also guarded key mountain passes through the Alps and in northern Italy.

Beginning in the 1670s, Vauban developed a complex fortification system known as the *pré carré* to defend the entire kingdom of France with mutually supporting artillery fortifications. Vauban constructed a *frontière de fer* (iron frontier) along France's northern border with the Spanish Netherlands, with fortified cities at Dunkirk, Lille, Valenciennes, and other sites, forming two dense interlinking lines of bastioned fortresses. To complete the *pré carré*, Vauban built dozens of entirely new fortresses and improved the fortifications at hundreds of other sites. Vauban became the most influential military engineer of the early modern period through his numerous fortresses, his siege attacks, and his treatises on fortifications.[11]

In response to Vauban's fortifications and the experience of the Franco-Dutch War, the Dutch Republic intensified its defenses in the 1680s and 1690s. Military engineer Menno van Coehoorn became known for his fortifications treatise, *Nieuwe Vestingbouw*, published in 1685, and William III appointed him to improve the citadel at Namur. Coehoorn then directed new fortification construction at Bergen-op-Zoom, Coevorden, and other fortresses along the Dutch frontier in the 1690s.[12]

Various designs of artillery fortresses emerged during the late seventeenth century. Bastions and geometric designs did not completely dictate fortification construction, since military engineers adapted to local topography, political needs, and social factors. As a result, artillery fortresses often employed irregular designs, improvised additions, and peculiar outworks. Rounded towers with artillery platforms could be used effectively in place of angled bastions, for example, and earthwork outworks could sometimes disrupt besiegers' approaches. Ottoman engineers utilized a variety of designs for artillery fortifications, mixing bastions with other approaches. Mughal emperors built enormous fortifications at Agra, Delhi, and Lahore with thick mud brick or stone walls that could potentially absorb cannonballs and gunpowder mines, but that did not depend principally on artillery for defense. Russian engineers built bastions and earthworks around the pre-existing Kremlin fortress at Moscow in 1707–08.

By the late seventeenth century, bastioned citadels watched over urban populations worldwide. Bastioned fortifications had been used to ensure state control over conquered territories and rebellious cities as early as the mid-sixteenth century, but the use of dedicated citadels increased during the seventeenth century. Citadels were often built on hilltops outside city walls, where military garrisons could enforce loyalties and suppress urban disorder. Following protests in Marseille in 1660, for example, Louis XIV ordered the construction of Fort Saint-Nicolas to observe the city's inhabitants from across the old harbor.

War and State Development

The rapid growth of state-commission armies required new techniques of war administration, and royal states struggled to meet their needs. "The study of state-formation is inherently historical, because it focuses on the creation of durable states and the transformations of basic structural features of those states," George Steinmetz points out, "... but states are never 'formed' once and for all. It is more fruitful to view state-formation as an ongoing process of structural change and not as a one-time event."[13] Rather than constructing a strict typology of early modern states, this section will examine the patterns of state development that affected the practices of warfare.

Fiscal-military administration

The growth in army sizes in the second half of the seventeenth century spurred the development of new financial institutions and techniques of managing war finances. Some historians use the term "fiscal-military states" to describe the expanding military and financial organizations that emerged in the early modern period.[14] Perhaps it is more useful to see war administration as adopting "fiscal-military" systems, whether or not individual polities can be effectively described as "fiscal-military states."[15]

The demands of engaging in colonial and European warfare drove the English monarchy to create the Bank of England and a financial community of creditors in order to continue waging warfare while running up enormous debts. John Brewer argues that "between 1688 and 1714 the English state underwent a radical transformation, acquiring the main features of a powerful fiscal-military state: high taxes, a growing and well-organized civil administration, a standing army and the determination to act as a major European power."[16]

The growth of "fiscal-military states" is often associated with "absolutism" and government centralization, yet many of the key roles in war finance and logistics continued to be played by non-governmental organizations and individuals. Civilian merchants, bakers, and butchers provisioned field armies on the march. Samuel Oppenheimer of Heidelberg became the principal contractor for Emperor Leopold I's armies, supplying the Imperial war effort in

Hungary and in Germany during the late seventeenth century. The firm of Antonio Alvarez Machado and Jacob Pereira in the Hague provisioned William III, Prince of Orange's Dutch, and later Anglo-Dutch, forces in the 1670s and 1680s.[17] Civilian teams maneuvered artillery and carted supplies for the field armies of most early modern states.

Fiscal-military institutions attempted to transform regional and local administrative practices in order to extract taxes and resources to sustain their military activities. The province of Franche-Comté, which Louis XIV had annexed during the Dutch War, provides an excellent case for examining regional government and war finance. The marquis de Louvois, secretary of state for war, became the key royal administrator of Franche-Comté and all other conquered provinces, striving to make war pay for war. The integration of Franche-Comté "largely unfolded without a preconceived plan," following an approach that has been described as "pragmatic opportunism." When Louvois lost patience with provincial elites' attempts to renegotiate the terms of their relationship with their new ruler, royal officials completely restructured Besançon's municipal government. The newly crafted relationships between royal financial officials and the local elites were tested during the Nine Years War and the War of the Spanish Succession. During these lengthy conflicts, "an increasingly desperate royal government first exploited every existing source of revenue, then invented entirely new ones."[18]

Resource mobilization by armies provoked widespread tax resistance in France during the personal rule of Louis XIV, despite the absolutist rhetoric of his ministers and bureaucratic officials. The Lustucru rebellion erupted in the Boulonnais in 1662, as peasant bands attacked tax officials and the soldiers who accompanied them. The duc d'Elbeuf led an army to engage the peasants, who barricaded themselves in a village. The royal troops quickly overwhelmed the peasant forces, executing four of the captured ringleaders and condemning 365 peasants to galley service.[19] Peasants in the Pyrenees foothills waged a sustained campaign of attacks against tax collectors during the Audijos revolt of the 1660s. Perhaps 4,000 peasants mobilized in the Vivarais during the Roure rebellion of 1670. Most of these rural tax rebellions were led by provincial noblemen and drew support from artisans in small towns, although the majority of the supporters were peasants.

Fiscal-military administrators developed new techniques of information management in order to direct and supply multiple field armies in different theaters of war. Louis XIV and his ministers centralized war planning through elaborate information-gathering and communications services. The circulation of official correspondence, military intelligence, and logistical information prompted the creation of new officials who could act as information managers and produce their own reports to synthesize the information flows.

Cartographic and military engineering services improved mapping techniques, producing numerous maps and surveys to meet the global and local demands of military and naval forces. Louis XIV's enormous palace and gardens at Versailles became the center of the king's vision of an orderly and peaceful kingdom defended at a distance by heavily fortified frontiers.[20] At the same time, cartographers in France, Spain, England, and the Netherlands worked to produce detailed world maps and globes that could aid military planners in formulating global strategies.

The Ottoman Empire also constructed fiscal-military administrative institutions. The Ottoman imperial administration developed effective information-gathering services for policy formulation, military planning, and espionage by the late century. These institutions allowed Ottoman sultans and their grand viziers to articulate a pragmatic grand strategy encompassing imperial territories in the Mediterranean, the Balkans, and West Asia.[21] The janissary corps of musketeers remained large throughout the seventeenth century, but lost its elite status as janissary soldiers posted to provincial garrisons took on administrative and civilian roles. Meanwhile, changes in the *timar* system weakened the ability of the sultan to raise provincial *timariot* cavalry, even as provincial governors' own forces were increasing in size. "As a result of these transformations," according to Gábor Ágoston, "the formerly cavalry-heavy Ottoman army also changed significantly: In the late 1690s infantrymen made up 50–60 percent of deployed troops, mirroring the infantry-to-cavalry ratio of their Habsburg rivals."[22] The Ottoman military and administrative systems remained capable of sustained warfare on multiple fronts, despite some historians' claims that the empire had entered into a period of "decline."

National identities and patriotic war

Territorial warfare and ethnic conflict in the late seventeenth century seem to have contributed to the stronger national identities. The concept of "nations" had previously referred to language groups or ethnicities, especially when describing ambassadors, merchants, sailors, and soldiers who were traveling or fighting abroad. Historical sociologist Charles Tilly argues that "through most of history, national states – states governing multiple contiguous regions and their cities

by means of centralized, differentiated, and autonomous structures
– have appeared only rarely."[23] Now, printed propaganda increasingly
stressed patriotic rationales for war, defining officers and soldiers as
protectors of nations.

Prolonged peace and the governing policies of the Tokugawa *bakufu*
fueled a growing national identity and a steady economic recovery in
Japan during the seventeenth century. The Tokugawa capital of Edo
developed from a small city of 30,000 around 1600 into one of the world's
largest metropolises, with a population nearing a million by 1700. The
commercial center of Osaka, with a population of some 200,000 residents in 1610, grew to approximately 360,000 by 1700. Despite the
sweeping authority of the Tokugawa *bakufu*, its military system was
untested by warfare, except against periodic peasant revolts.[24] The Tokugawa *shoguns* pursued diplomatic isolation and enforced strict separation of Japanese society from global connectivity.

The Dutch Republican state also took on national aspects in the
seventeenth century. The long Dutch struggle against the Spanish monarchy produced a republican militancy and heroic national identity. The
States General and its armies crafted a sense of militancy and Dutchness,
even before the Republic finally won official recognition of its independence in 1648. The VOC and its maritime empire in the Indian Ocean
provided the Dutch public with news of ongoing commercial enterprises,
colonial expansion, and naval operations against the Spanish, Portuguese, and English fleets, as well as Southeast Asian militaries. All of this
imperial and war news excited popular interest in the VOC's activities
and forged a strong Dutch identification with its empire.

The United Kingdom, as it gradually became known, was also
asserting its own sense of national identity. The establishment of the
Church of England and participation in religious wars of the sixteenth century had already forged nascent conceptions of English
national identity. This notion widened into a distinct British identity,
or Britishness, which was forged by military expeditions in North
America, the Caribbean, and Ireland. Linda Colley's research demonstrates that English-led military operations by English, Scottish,
and Irish forces against Louis XIV's France stimulated anti-French
sentiment and reinforced ideas of Britishness.[25] At the same time, the
union of the kingdoms of Scotland and England, made official in 1707,
threatened to undermine nascent British national identity. Scottish
soldiers displayed competing loyalties to their clans, their military
units, the kingdom of Scotland, the still abstract ideal of the United
Kingdom, and to the person of their monarch.[26] The British maritime
empire was directed from London, and its dispersed settler colonies
in the Atlantic World only further complicated British national

identity. British empire-building and state development reinforced each other as British trading companies, chartered colonies, military governors, and naval forces forged close relationships.[27]

Small kingdoms and city-states around the world developed fledgling national identities, often in response to military pressures. The Venetian Republic expanded older patrician identities with a broader sense of Venetian distinctiveness following the loss of much of its *stato da mar* to the Ottomans by the late seventeenth century. The kingdom of Denmark-Norway seems to have forged a common identity through its repeated confrontations with Sweden in the seventeenth century. The kingdom of Portugal regained its independence from Spain and reinforced its particular nature through its crusading history and empire. In the aftermath of a Manchu invasion in 1637, Korea became increasingly isolated, constructing "national memories" through accounts of its previous resistance to Japanese invasion.[28] In Southeast Asia, Aceh maintained its independence through its military strength, while the Ayutthayan state expanded significantly, developing a strong Thai identity that was closely linked to the monarchy. Many of these small states used artillery fortresses and alliances to preserve their independence.

Some large royal states began to articulate national identities and notions of patriotic service. Royal ministers and geographers asserted concepts of "natural frontiers" to designate idealized forms of kingdoms. Political pamphlets and military treatises justified war and motivated soldiers through national identities that fused religious and political identities. Louis XIV's annexations of German- and Flemish-speaking regions and his fiscal-military policies may have inhibited the full development of a national identity within his kingdom. Yet, the expression of patriotic ideals of royal service and military duty during Louis XIV's wars arguably allowed for a powerful sense of Frenchness. Although David Bell argues that the "cult of the nation" only emerged in the eighteenth century, the strong association between *patrie* (fatherland) and *nation* seems to have emerged even earlier.[29]

National identities and patriotism laid the groundwork for the later development of nation-states with exclusive loyalties and citizenship laws in the late eighteenth century and beyond.

Imperial rule and territorial expansion

Multiethnic and multilingual empires could not deploy national propaganda, but instead relied on other forms of identity. The Ottoman,

Russian, Mughal, and Chinese Empires all incorporated mixed populations (with diverse ethnicities, languages, and religions) that often cohabited in regions and communities. The very concept of national identification threatened these empires' multicultural compositions, paving the way for later national separatist movements that would challenge their capacity to wage territorial war.

The Russian Empire promoted sweeping territorial expansion, encouraging peasant migration and settlement of the Eurasian steppes. Russian military forces fought against Tatar cavalry in Crimea and indigenous peoples in Siberia. The Russian imperial state built fortifications to enhance its defenses on the steppes while fighting a Russo-Turkish War (1676–81). Tsar Peter the Great (1689–1725) launched campaigns against the Ottomans in Crimea, resulting in two sieges of the fortress of Azov in 1695 and 1696 respectively. The Ottoman garrison of Azov capitulated in June 1696, giving the Russian Empire a fortified base on the Sea of Azov. Peter the Great reorganized the Russian artillery services and recruitment practices in the late 1690s and 1700s, gradually transforming Russian military administration during the Great Northern War (1700–21) against Sweden. These organizational adjustments certainly assisted the Russian army in retaking Narva in 1704 and winning the battle of Poltava in 1709, but recent historical research questions how "modernizing" Peter the Great's reforms really were. Carol B. Stevens argues that "'Europeanization' was only one element in the transformation of Russian military forces, and Peter's efforts were only a part of the broad military changes that took place in the late seventeenth and early eighteenth centuries."[30]

Qing armies began to operate in the Central Asian steppes, fighting Mongol khanates and the growing Russian Empire. The Kangxi emperor personally led four military campaigns against the Zunghar Mongols under Galdan in the 1690s, culminating in the battle of Jao Modo and the death of Galdan in 1696. Kangxi commissioned a history of his campaigns, called *Outline History of the Personal Expeditions to Pacify the Northwestern Frontier*, which "began the Qing project to establish a definitive demarcation of the dynasty's position in imperial space and time."[31] The Qing Empire expanded rice cultivation and strengthened its administrative and logistical services to support its territorial expansion into Central Asia and Tibet.

The Mughal Empire established a powerful imperial state in South Asia in the seventeenth century based on a multiethnic army and administration. Emperor Aurangzeb built on the governing innovations of his predecessors and consolidated Mughal administration in northern India. Aurangzeb pursued a policy of territorial expansion, waging successive wars of conquest in the Deccan plateau of central and southern India. Aurangzeb finally conquered the kingdoms of Bijapur and Golconda in the 1680s, extending the Mughal Empire's borders to their maximum extent.

The Marathas, a Hindu group in southern India, actively resisted Mughal domination, however. Shivaji, king of the Marathas, organized effectual raiding warfare and skirmish defense against the Mughal invasions from the 1674 until his death in 1680. Aurangzeb led numerous military campaigns against the Marathas in the late seventeenth century, succeeding in capturing Shambaji, the new Maratha king, and executing him in 1689. Aurangzeb ultimately failed to subdue the Marathas, and when he died in 1707, the Mughal Empire seemed dangerously weakened by the rise of an effective Maratha confederacy.[32]

The Safavids never seem to have developed a strong imperial state apparatus in Iran. Safavid Iran continued to operate as a dynastic state, but could not assert control over the lucrative silk trade. Beginning in the early seventeenth century, Safavid princes were raised in the *haram*, where courtly women and eunuchs contributed to imperial policy formulation. Shia *imams* opposed women's influence in politics and gained enormous religious power in Iran. Some of these *imams* criticized Shah Sulaiman (1666–94) for being an alcoholic and an ineffectual ruler, further weakening the image of the Shah. The Iranian military system suffered from these dynastic struggles, leaving the Safavid Empire extremely vulnerable at the turn of the eighteenth century.[33]

Other multiethnic empires remained significant in the late seventeenth century. The Austrian Habsburg Empire retained its Germanic, Czech, and Slovak core, but added new territories with Italian, Transylvanian, Hungarian, and Slavic populations. The Spanish Empire continued to rule vast multiethnic territories in Latin America as well as scattered colonies in North Africa and the Philippines. The Portuguese Empire was equally multiethnic in character, with diverse colonies in Brazil, Africa, India, and Southeast Asia. All these multicultural empires relied on imperial law and administration to maintain order in their diverse societies.

Armies and State Authority

Permanent armies could act as direct agents of state authority by the late seventeenth century. New military administrative techniques permitted territorial rulers to project organized violence on a grand scale, attempting to control military operations from their capitals.

Even if rulers' mechanisms of command and control were incomplete, they directed their armies' movements, logistics, and combats in detail.

Targeted devastation

Territorial states' armies sometimes went beyond routine pillaging and foraging, deliberately inflicting massive economic devastation on entire regions in war zones. Field armies often occupied enemy villages and towns, allowing soldiers to harass terrified civilians. Burning crops was a popular method of devastating a region's agrarian economy and denying food and fodder to opposing armies. Targeted devastation purposefully inflicted suffering on civilian populations and sometimes involved mass atrocities. Light cavalry forces, such as the Cossacks, acquired reputations for rapacity in their campaigns in the Balkans and the Caucuses.

During the second half of the seventeenth century, state-commission armies organized raiding warfare throughout war zones. Louis XIV and his generals integrated *petite guerre* with the siege warfare conducted by large field armies during the Franco-Dutch War (1672–78), allowing France to wage effective positional warfare in the Netherlands. The persistent raids organized by French garrisons acted both defensively to protect French supply lines and offensively to sever enemy communications and to blockade enemy fortifications.[34] Although these techniques of raiding warfare were not entirely new, they seem to have been organized more meticulously by central military planners than ever before.

The Habsburg–Ottoman war of 1683–99 brought extensive deliberate destruction to southeastern Europe and the Balkans. The Ottoman Empire still held portions of Hungary and periodically attacked the Habsburg domains in Austria. General Raimondo Montecuccoli had destroyed an advancing Ottoman army at the battle of Saint Gothard in 1664, but the Ottoman military system remained capable of threatening central Europe. At the outbreak of renewed warfare in 1683, Grand Vizier Kara Mustafa led a large Ottoman army to invade Austria. Ottoman forces devastated Lower Austria and besieged Vienna itself in July 1683. The Austrian defenders of Vienna destroyed suburbs surrounding the city walls to improve artillery fire zones. Emperor Leopold I appealed for aid and Pope Innocent XI called on Christian princes to join in a crusade to assist Vienna. A combined army of Imperial, Bavarian, Saxon, and Polish troops marched to the aid of the beleaguered city, defeating the

Ottoman army at the battle of Kahlenberg outside the walls of Vienna in September and relieving the city. Jan III Sobieski (1674–96), king of Poland-Lithuania, was hailed across Europe as a great hero for his military leadership against the Ottomans. This dramatic victory dramatically altered the military situation in southeastern Europe. Resurgent Austrian armies forced the Ottomans onto the defensive and began a steady expansion into Hungary and the Balkans.

Imperial forces of the Habsburgs and their allies pursued the defeated Turks and launched a new Holy League in 1684 to invade Hungary, which had been occupied by the Ottoman Empire for several centuries. Imperial armies carried out numerous sieges, capturing Buda, Kanizsa, Belgrade, and several other Hungarian cities by 1688. The fighting then bogged down into a war of attrition from 1689 to 1696, as Imperial and Ottoman forces raided the Hungarian, Transylvanian, Bosnian, and Wallachian countrysides. The military frontier between Habsburg and Ottoman territories shifted further and further southeast, resulting in brutal destruction by opposing troops. Large numbers of janissaries were posted in defensive fortifications along the military frontier. Prince Eugène de Savoie, the leading Imperial general, orchestrated a brilliant campaign in 1697, maneuvering his army to catch a major Ottoman army as it attempted to cross the Tisza River. During the ensuing battle of Zenta, the Ottoman army was annihilated: an estimated 25,000 Turkish soldiers were killed, along with the grand vizier.[35]

Negotiations soon began, eventually leading to the peace of Karlowitz in 1699, confirming the Imperial conquest of nearly all of Hungary. Yet many Hungarians hardly saw this as a liberation. "From the 1680s, Hungary had suffered heavily from the military operations on its soil, but also from the billeting of troops and immense fiscal pressure," according to one historian. "The situation was aggravated by forcible re-catholicization as well as the brutality with which Imperial generals dealt with resistance, whether real or imaginary."[36] The misery of many Hungarians would lead them to support an anti-Imperial rebellion just a few years later.

Targeted devastation could also accompany more subtle forms of coercion, as armies punished populations on a regional or even national scale. Louis XIV developed a military policy of *dragonnades* against Huguenots still living in France in the 1680s. French army officials billeted dragoons and other troops in southern French Protestants' homes, pressuring them to convert to Catholicism in order to obtain relief from the burdens of lodging the soldiers. The *dragonnades* were expanded in 1685 as a prelude to the official Revocation of the Edict of Nantes later that year. Economic pressure and military coercion here served as tools of forced conversion and cultural homogenization. Tens of thousands of Huguenots refused to convert and instead migrated to the Netherlands, England, and Brandenburg-Prussia. The artisanal and technical expertise of many of the approximately 40,000 French Calvinists who settled in and around Berlin provided a stimulus to economic development in Brandenburg-Prussia.

Racism often fueled campaigns of brutal devastation in colonial wars. English colonial troops and Amerindian warriors both targeted civilians during King Philip's War (1675–76). An Algonquian chief known as King Philip led Wampanoag warriors to attack English settlements in New England in June 1675, apparently in retaliation for the execution of two Wampanoag men at Plymouth. Algonquian raiding parties burned isolated farmhouses and villages, destroying agricultural implements and economic infrastructure. One English colonist wrote: "Many of our miserable inhabitants lye naked, wallowing in their blood, and crying, and whilst the Barbarous enraged Natives, from one part of the Country to another are on Fire, flaming forth their fury, Spoiling Cattle and Corn and burning Houses, and torturing Men, Women, and Children; and burning them alive." In March 1676, a Narragansett war party attacked Providence, Rhode Island and burned the entire town. English colonial troops and their Amerindian allies responded with ruthless force, destroying numerous Algonquian communities and imprisoning captives on islands. English soldiers sold captive Algonquians into slavery. Jill Lepore argues that "in every measurable way King Philip's War was a harsher conflict than any Indian-English conflict that preceded it." Lepore finds evidence of a growing "sense of racial identity" among English colonists.[37]

Such campaigns of targeted devastation suggest the extremes of violence against civilians that were practiced during the early modern period. Willful and orchestrated campaigns on this scale were certainly rare, yet they highlight the ability of state-commission armies influenced by territorial imperatives to carry out atrocities against civilians.

Nine Years War, 1688–1697

A brutal episode of targeted devastation occurred soon after the outbreak of the Nine Years War (1688–97). Louis XIV's desire to rationalize the French frontier and improve its defenses had led to the creation of the League of Augsburg in Germany in 1686. Following a succession dispute in Cologne, French armies invaded Germany in the autumn of 1688, besieging Philippsburg and occupying towns along the Rhine River. As the war began to widen, Louis XIV ordered French troops to systematically devastate the Palatinate in 1688–89, burning Mannheim, Heidelberg, and dozens of other cities in the region. According to the marquis de Chamlay, who helped plan this elaborate campaign of destruction, Mannheim was leveled "like a field."[38] Louis XIV and his military advisors had hoped that the devastation of the Palatinate would intimidate German princes and create a barrier to protect France from enemy armies for the next year. Shocking news of the massive destruction in the Palatinate instead galvanized anti-French sentiment in the Holy Roman Empire, prompting the formation of a broad European alliance against Louis XIV and greatly widening the scope of the war. French military planners assumed that Louis XIV could gain diplomatic benefits from a strategy of intimidation while avoiding a general European war, as they had during the *réunion* campaigns to annex certain German cities in 1683–84.

However, Louis XIV and his advisors miscalculated terribly in employing such brutality in 1689, making the Palatinate a *cause célèbre* in contemporary European popular culture and a lasting example of atrocity against civilians in European historical memory. A pamphlet written at the time bellowed: "It only remains for us to serve for all eternity as witnesses of French brutality and to cry, to all Europe, where we have been driven into exile: Vengeance! Vengeance!"[39]

Meanwhile, William III, Prince of Orange had taken advantage of the chaotic political situation in England, where the unpopular James II had sought to secure the succession of his newborn Catholic son. William embarked a Dutch army in 284 naval transports and crossed the English Channel, invading England in the autumn of 1688. William's army joined with the Protestant opposition forces and advanced on London. Stuart dynastic rule suddenly collapsed as the English army dissolved and James II fled into exile, allowing William to seize control of the English monarchy as William III in the so-called Glorious Revolution of 1688. Despite a French naval victory at Beachy Head in July 1690, William III succeeded in defeating the deposed James II's army in Ireland at the battle of the Boyne the same month.[40]

William III rapidly reorganized the Anglo-Dutch army and established his dynastic rule in England, calling for a Grand Alliance against Louis XIV. Protestant German princes and Huguenot adventurers joined in the alliance, seeing it as a crusade against Catholic France. Imperial, Spanish, and Savoyard troops soon joined the English and Dutch forces – opposing Louis XIV for political and dynastic motives.

The war expanded well beyond its initial theaters in the Rhine valley and England. The maréchal de Luxembourg led a French army into the Spanish Netherlands in 1690, destroying an Allied army at the battle of Fleurus in July. The war in the Netherlands soon settled into intense positional warfare, with major sieges at Mons, Namur, Charleroi, and other cities. The epic 1692 siege of Namur pitted the two most famous military engineers of the seventeenth century against each other. Vauban personally directed the French approach and bombardment of the fortifications of Namur, while Menno van Coehoorn organized the city's impressive defenses. Louis XIV visited his besieging forces and personally observed the capitulation of Namur in July 1692.

Despite these French successes, the armies of the Grand Alliance were able to continue fighting positional warfare in the Netherlands, while organizing offensives in Germany, Italy, and Spain. Each of the states involved in the war raised increasingly large state-commission armies. By 1695, Louis XIV's armies had adopted a defensive strategy along fortified lines, leading to more sieges and attritional warfare.[41] The Nine Years War tested the new techniques of war finance that had been developed by fiscal-military administrations. In June 1697, Vauban orchestrated the "perfect" siege of Ath, a city that he had previously fortified. French batteries used Vauban's new technique of *ricochet* fire, which involved making cannonballs bounce along destructively, to dismantle one of Ath's bastions and breech the walls.[42]

Although the Nine Years War started as a European territorial dispute, the conflict developed global dimensions. Naval forces and privateers fought engagements in the Mediterranean, the Atlantic, the Caribbean, and the Indian Ocean. French and English colonial troops fought in North America during what was locally known as King William's War. Dutch forces seized the French port city of Pondicherry in 1693, taking advantage of the French concentration on land defense within Europe. The English EIC suffered losses to the Mughals in India during the conflict, in part because of the costs of waging territorial warfare in Europe. The Nine Years War came to an end with the peace of Ryswick in autumn 1697, as Louis XIV recognized William III and the belligerents all agreed to territorial concessions and colonial exchanges.

Conclusion

States that could afford to invest in permanent armies and administrative institutions incorporated various fiscal-military techniques.

David B. Ralston demonstrates that European military engineers, officers, and technical experts served states willing to pay for their services, producing a global exportation of the techniques of military professionalization.[43] Unfortunately, such interpretations tend to consider the diffusion of military techniques as a unidirectional process, extending from Europe to the rest of the world. Fiscal-military administrative techniques and organizations actually developed simultaneously in state development processes that sometimes displayed convergences and parallels.

The Moroccan state of Mulay Isma'il illustrates well some of the patterns of territorial warfare and imperial expansion that produced new state development processes in the late seventeenth century. Sultan Mulay Isma'il (1672–1727) unified Morocco and strengthened the Moroccan royal state through military and administrative reforms. Morocco had previously been divided into two kingdoms based in Fez and in Marrakech, but Mulay Isma'il gained the allegiance of the inhabitants of both regions, in part by building a new capital at Meknes. Three of Mulay Isma'il's brothers raised a rebellion in 1678–79, but a royal army suppressed it. Mulay Isma'il controversially enslaved free black men in Morocco to create new military slave forces. Moroccan armies employing contingents of slave warriors and renegades resisted European imperial encroachments, seizing Spanish fortresses and *factorías* at La Mamora, Larache, and Arzila.[44] New governing institutions and military policies enhanced Morocco's territorial power in North Africa and allowed the kingdom to maintain diplomatic relationships with Louis XIV and other distant rulers. Mulay Isma'il had created an effective Moroccan royal state that would have a lasting presence in North Africa and the Mediterranean.[45]

Conclusion: c.1700

This book has stressed sweeping changes in the relationships between war, culture, and society in the early modern world, while at the same time identifying a number of significant long-term continuities. Military innovations, global encounters, imperial structures, trans-oceanic connections, and state development processes together transformed organized armed violence around the world.

Innovative military technologies and technical practices redefined warfare on land and sea during the early modern period. Sailing warships, artillery fortresses, firearms, and infantry drill spread worldwide, yet often in unexpected ways. A global diffusion of firearms and gunpowder technologies occurred, allowing infantry units in most armies to adopt arquebuses and muskets. Cannon founding techniques also spread, allowing diverse military systems to construct artillery. Military historians have too often focused exclusively on technological developments as motors of changes in warfare. Arguments in the Military Revolution debate have often concentrated overwhelmingly on the diffusion of military technologies and techniques from Europe to the rest of the world. This book has instead argued that the technological developments were not exclusively European in nature, nor were technology transfers unidirectional.

Artillery fortresses proliferated worldwide by the early eighteenth century, providing some of the most visible traces of new military technologies. Only dynastic rulers and wealthy city-states could afford the high costs of artillery founding and fortification building, however. The Mughal and Ottoman Empires improved their existing city fortification systems with new artillery fortresses in the late seventeenth century. The Qing Empire intensified fortifications along the Great

Wall and major cities in China. European states constructed bastioned fortifications to protect their urban centers, trading factories, ports, and strategic sites in far-flung colonies. Even small ports or isolated forts might have impressive artillery defenses by the late seventeenth century. As a result, positional warfare involving the prolonged battery of bastioned artillery defenses became a normal aspect of conflicts around the globe.

Maritime expeditions utilizing new navigational techniques and cartographical information rapidly expanded global connectivity during the early modern period. Warships and armed merchant ships forged dense commercial and transportation networks linking the Americas with Eurasia and Africa in the Atlantic World. The Indian Ocean World became more closely connected, but also more violent as Portuguese, Ottoman, Dutch, English, and French forces battled for control of spice production and distribution in India and Southeast Asia. The Caribbean Sea, the Melaka Straits, and other waters became chaotic, as warships, pirates, and privateers raided and plundered merchant ships and vulnerable coastal settlements. By the early eighteenth century, even the Pacific Ocean was becoming more closely connected, as Manila galleons linked the Philippines with Acapulco, Spanish ships plied the western coastline of the Americas, and Dutch ships operated throughout Southeast Asia. Riverine and canal traffic connected many inland cities with broader maritime transportation and trading networks. By 1700, only remote islands and interior highland regions remained isolated from the economic, political, and military forces of globalization.

Long-distance overland communication networks continued to thrive alongside the growing maritime connections, especially in areas such as West Africa and Central Asia. Large territorial empires competed to dominate borderlands and steppes regions in the late seventeenth century. The Ottoman and Mughal Empires faced serious challenges, even as the Russian and Chinese Empires expanded into Central Asia. Russia emerged as a powerful Eurasian empire as Peter the Great's armies advanced into Siberia and expelled the Ottomans from Azov in the 1690s. Russian and Chinese forces competed over mineral resources and mining sites in Central Asia in the late seventeenth century. At the turn of the eighteenth century, Sweden and Russia entered into the Great Northern War (1700–21), with Russian military and naval forces demonstrating their ability to contest Swedish dominance in the Baltic Sea. Russia was now so integrated into European diplomatic networks that it arguably could be considered a European state, yet it simultaneously developed an expansive Eurasian empire across the steppes. East Asian, Central Asian, and

African empires greatly influenced warfare and society in the early modern period, not just as "gunpowder empires," but also as mercantile empires with sophisticated taxation and war finance systems.

Mercantile warfare developed its own dynamics, which involved colonial competition and economic motives. States and their mercantile companies exported, imported, and blended aspects of military organization from other military systems. G.V. Scammel argues that "the first imperial age, far from freeing Europe from internecine strife by providing an outlet for aggressive energies, saw colonies, colonial trade and control of distant waters become yet further matters for conflict between the states of the continent."[1] This insight may also be applied to non-European states, as mercantile warfare drove Chinese, Russian, Ottoman, and Mughal imperial expansion in this period.

Dynastic states continued to predominate in most parts of the world in 1700. Princely rulers and their ministers formulated military policies for monarchies and empires, deciding on the terms of war and peace. Conflicting dynastic claims between the Habsburgs and Bourbons produced the War of the Spanish Succession (1701–14), which engulfed most of Europe. Nobles and other social elites played important roles as military and administrative officers in dynastic states throughout the early modern period. Despite claims for the rise of "absolutist" states, nobles remained incredibly powerful in most societies, closely integrated with the armed forces and fiscal-military administrations of their rulers. Royal states and territorial empires organized warfare using coordinated units employing artillery and firearms, often manufactured within their own societies. The expanding global population and the growing sizes of permanent state-commission armies during the seventeenth century created enormous demands for information and logistical services.

Early modern dynastic states and empires never established effective monopolies on violence, however, as Max Weber theorized.[2] Noble violence, vendettas, and dueling continued to trouble societies, although their forms altered over time. Peasant protests and tax revolts continued around the world throughout the early modern period, as subsistence crises and famines regularly occurred. Dynastic states and their growing armies imposed massive tax burdens on farmers, prompting protests and revolts. Rural living conditions worsened in some areas, as Japanese and Chinese empires tightened peasant obligations and Eastern European states implemented a "second serfdom." Banditry and rural violence proliferated in forests and along highways during prolonged wars and civil conflicts. Nonetheless, the Little Ice Age finally ended toward the end of the seventeenth century, improving global climate conditions and lessening the intensity of subsistence crises worldwide.

Many smaller states and indigenous peoples in the Atlantic and Indian Ocean Worlds were still able to wage raiding warfare and defend themselves effectively against imperial powers in the early eighteenth century. African kingdoms could effectively resist European imperial incursions beyond their coastal trading posts. The Marathas resisted the Mughal Empire in South Asia, while maintaining commerce with European trading companies. Chinese and Japanese empires attempted to limit contact with European merchants and missionaries after recognizing the potentially disruptive influence of global trade. Colonial warfare increasingly shaped ethnic identities and racial categories, as states stressed ethno-national linguistic identities and moved toward the creation of nation-states. Religion remained vital to many ethnic and national identities, but religious motives for warfare seem to have declined in the late seventeenth century as legal, educational, and scientific institutions increasingly questioned apocalyptical and messianic movements.

The production of military knowledge changed radically during the early modern period, as printed media circulated war news and technical information. Bellicose literature and chronicles of rulers' exploits were supplanted by siege narratives, news pamphlets, histories, war memoirs, and military treatises. Information about warfare and military practices traveled along trading and communication networks that employed printed, manuscript, and oral media. These developments in the perceptions of early modern war and conflict would have long-reaching consequences.

This book has argued that warfare became increasingly globalized from 1500 to 1700 as increasing trans-oceanic contacts, commercial networks, and empires transformed many dimensions of war and society. Cross-cultural exchanges encouraged common military practices and shared understandings of warfare, as well as competing war aims. By 1700, global dimensions of warfare were embedded in the diverse processes of globalization that were transforming economies and societies around the world.

Notes

Preface

1 John Keegan, *The Face of Battle* (New York, 1976).
2 John Whiteclay Chambers II, "The New Military History: Myth and Reality," *Journal of Military History* 55 (July 1991): 395–406.
3 Robert M. Citino, "Military Histories Old and New: A Reintroduction," *American Historical Review* 112 (October 2007): 1070–1090.
4 Elaine Scarry, *The Body in Pain: The Making and Unmaking of the World* (Oxford, 1985).

Introduction

1 Théodore de Bry, "Franciscus Monteio Lucatanae provinciae praefici-tur. Quidam ex Cacicis, foedus cum illo contrahere velle simulans, tragula illum conficere conatur," in *Americae pars quinta nobilis & admiratione plena Hieronymi Bezoni Mediolanesis secundae setionis Hispanorum* (Frankfurt am Main, 1595).
2 Henry Keazor, "Theodore de Bry's Images for America," *Print Quarterly* 15: 2 (June 1998): 131–149.
3 Girolamo Benzoni, *History of the New World*, trans. W.H. Smyth (London, 1857), 142–144.
4 Inga Clendinnen, *Ambivalent Conquests: Maya and Spaniard in Yucatan, 1517–1570* (Cambridge, 1987), 20–37.
5 Benjamin Schmidt, *Innocence Abroad: The Dutch Imagination and the New World, 1570–1670* (Cambridge, 2001); Tom Conley, "De Bry's Las Casas," in *Amerindian Images and the Legacy of Columbus*, ed. René Jara and Nicholas Spadaccini (Minneapolis, MN, 1992), 103–131.
6 Carl von Clausewitz, *On War*, trans. Michael Howard and Peter Paret (Princeton, NJ, 1976), 87–88.

7 The lecture is best known in its revised version, published in 1967 and reprinted as Michael Roberts, "The Military Revolution, 1560–1660," in *The Military Revolution Debate: Readings on the Military Transformation of Early Modern Europe*, ed. Clifford J. Rogers (Boulder, CO, 1995), 13–35.

8 J.R. Hale, *War and Society in Renaissance Europe, 1450–1620* (Baltimore, MD, 1985); George N. Clark, *War and Society in the Seventeenth Century* (Cambridge, 1958).

9 Geoffrey Parker, *The Army of Flanders and the Spanish Road, 1567–1659: The Logistics of Spanish Victory and Defeat in the Low Countries' Wars* (Cambridge, 1972); Geoffrey Parker, "The 'Military Revolution, 1560–1660' – A Myth," in *The Military Revolution Debate: Readings on the Military Transformation of Early Modern Europe*, ed. Clifford J. Rogers (Boulder, CO, 1995), 37–54.

10 Geoffrey Parker, *The Military Revolution: Military Innovation and the Rise of the West, 1500–1800*, 2nd edn (Cambridge, 1996; 1st edn 1988).

11 Parker, *The Military Revolution*, 176.

12 Jeremy Black, *Beyond the Military Revolution: War in the Seventeenth-Century World* (Basingstoke, 2011); Jeremy Black, *A Military Revolution? Military Change and European Society, 1550–1800* (Atlantic Highlands, NJ, 1991).

13 Clifford J. Rogers, ed., *The Military Revolution Debate: Readings on the Military Transformation of Early Modern Europe* (Boulder, CO, 1995).

14 Carlo M. Cipolla, *Guns, Sails, and Empires: Technological Innovation and the Early Phases of European Expansion, 1400–1700* (New York, 1965); William H. McNeill, *The Rise of the West: A History of the Human Community* (Chicago, IL, 1963).

15 William H. McNeill, *The Pursuit of Power: Technology, Armed Force, and Society since AD 1000* (Chicago, IL, 1982).

16 Jeremy Black, ed., *War in the Early Modern World. 1450–1815* (Boulder, CO, 1999), xi.

17 David B. Ralston, *Importing the European Army: The Introduction of European Military Techniques and Institutions into the Extra-European World, 1600–1914* (Chicago, IL, 1990).

18 Alfred W. Crosby, *The Columbian Exchange: Biological and Cultural Consequences of 1492*, 30th anniversary edn (Westport, CT, 2003).

19 Crosby, *The Columbian Exchange*, 3.

20 John Robert McNeill, *Mosquito Empires: Ecology and War in the Greater Caribbean, 1620–1914* (New York, 2010).

21 Anthony Pagden, *European Encounters with the New World: From Renaissance to Romanticism* (New Haven, CT, 1993).

22 Geoffrey Parker, *Global Crisis: War, Climate Change and Catastrophe in the Seventeenth Century* (New Haven, CT, 2013).

23 Brian Sandberg, "Beyond Encounters: Religion, Ethnicity, and Violence in the Early Modern Atlantic World, 1450–1700," *Journal of World History* 17 (March 2006): 1–25.

24 Alfred W. Crosby, *Ecological Imperialism: The Biological Expansion of Europe, 900–1900* (Cambridge, 1986); Crosby, *The Columbian Exchange*.

25 Wayne E. Lee, ed., *Empires and Indigenes: Intercultural Alliance, Imperial Expansion, and Warfare in the Early Modern World* (New York, 2011), 1.

26 Timothy Brook, *Vermeer's Hat: The Seventeenth Century and the Dawn of the Global World* (New York, 2008).

27 J.M. Blaut, *The Colonizer's Model of the World: Geographical Diffusionism and Eurocentric History* (New York, 1993), 10.

28 Immanuel Maurice Wallerstein, *World-Systems Analysis: An Introduction* (Durham, NC, 2004).

29 Jane Burbank and Frederick Cooper, *Empires in World History: Power and the Politics of Difference* (Princeton, NJ, 2010), 8.

30 Eric Wolf, *Europe and the People without History* (Berkeley, CA, 1982).

31 László Kontler, Antonella Romano, Silvia Sebastiani, and Borbála Zsuzsanna Török, eds., *Negotiating Knowledge in Early-Modern Empires: A Decentered View* (Basingstoke, 2014), 1–22.

32 Burbank and Cooper, *Empires in World History*; Jeremy Black, *War in the World: A Comparative History, 1450–1600* (Basingstoke, 2011).

33 J.H. Elliott, *Empires of the Atlantic World: Britain and Spain in America, 1492–1830* (New Haven, CT, 2006).

34 Victor B. Lieberman, ed., *Beyond Binary Histories: Re-Imagining Eurasia to c.1830* (Ann Arbor, MI, 1999), 1–18; Sanjay Subrahmanyam, "Connected Histories: Notes towards a Reconfiguration of Early Modern Eurasia," *Modern Asian Studies* 31 (July 1997): 735–762.

35 Richard White, *The Middle Ground: Indians, Empires, and Republics in the Great Lakes Region, 1650–1815* (Cambridge, 1991), x.

36 R. Brian Ferguson and Neil L. Whitehead, "The Violent Edge of Empire," in *War in the Tribal Zone: Expanding States and Indigenous Warfare*, ed. R. Brian Ferguson and Neil L. Whitehead (Santa Fe, NM, 1992), 1–30.

37 John K. Thornton, *A Cultural History of the Atlantic World, 1250–1820* (Cambridge, 2012).

38 Wayne E. Lee, *Barbarians and Brothers: Anglo-American Warfare, 1500–1865* (Oxford, 2011).

39 Jerry H. Bentley, "Cross-Cultural Interaction and Periodization in World History," *American Historical Review* 101 (June 1996): 749–770; Patrick Manning, "The Problem of Interactions in World History," *American Historical Review* 101 (June 1996): 771–782; Gale Stokes, "The Fates of Human Societies: A Review of Recent Macrohistories," *American Historical Review* 106 (April 2001): 508–525.

40 John K. Thornton, *Africa and Africans in the Making of the Atlantic World, 1400–1800*, 2nd edn (Cambridge, 1998), 13–42.

41 Julius Ruff, *Violence in Early Modern Europe, 1500–1800* (Cambridge, 2001).

42 Charles Tilly, "Reflections on the History of European State-making," in *The Formation of National States in Western Europe*, ed. Charles Tilly

(Princeton, NJ, 1975), 42. This argument is expanded in Charles Tilly, *Coercion, Capital, and European States, AD 990–1992*, rev. edn (Oxford, 1992).

43 Max Weber, "The Profession and Vocation of Politics," in *Weber: Political Writings*, ed. Peter Lasman and Ronald Speirs (Cambridge, 1994), 310–311; emphasis in original.

44 Norbert Elias, *The Civilizing Process: Sociogenetic and Psychogenetic Investigations*, trans. Edmund Jephcott, rev. edn (Malden, MA, 2000).

45 John A. Lynn, *Giant of the* Grand Siècle*: The French Army, 1610–1715* (Cambridge, 1997).

46 Tilly, *Coercion, Capital, and European States*.

47 William Beik, "The Absolutism of Louis XIV as Social Collaboration," *Past and Present* 188 (2005): 195–224.

48 J.H. Elliott, "The Cultural and Political Construction of Europe: A Europe of Composite Monarchies," *Past and Present* 137 (1992): 48–71.

49 B. Ann Tlusty, *The Martial Ethic in Early Modern Germany: Civic Duty and the Right of Arms* (New York, 2011).

50 David Parrott, *The Business of War: Military Enterprise and Military Revolution in Early Modern Europe* (Cambridge, 2012).

51 Jack Goody, *Renaissances: The One or the Many?* (Cambridge, 2010).

52 Charles Tilly, *European Revolutions, 1492–1992* (Oxford, 1993), 1–20.

53 Jack A. Goldstone, *Revolution and Rebellion in the Early Modern World* (Berkeley, CA, 1991), 10.

54 Stathis N. Kalyvas, *The Logic of Violence in Civil War* (Cambridge, 2006).

55 Penny Roberts, *Peace and Authority During the French Religious Wars, c.1560–1600* (Basingstoke, 2013); Jean-Pierre Kintz and Georges Livet, *350e anniversaire des Traités de Westphalie, 1648–1998. Une Genèse de l'Europe, une société à reconstruire* (Strasbourg, 1999); Olivier Christin, *La Paix de religion. L'autonomisation de la raison politique au XVIe siècle* (Paris, 1997).

56 Wolf, *Europe and the People without History*, 3.

57 Lieberman, *Beyond Binary Histories*, 1–18.

58 Black, ed., *War in the Early Modern World*, xi.

59 Black, *War in the World*.

60 Lee, *Empires and Indigenes*. See also Routledge's *Modern Wars in Perspective* book series.

61 Wayne E. Lee, ed., *Warfare and Culture in World History* (New York, 2011); Stephen Morillo, Jeremy Black, and Paul Lococo, *War in World History: Society, Technology, and War from Ancient Times to the Present*, 2 vols (Boston, MA, 2009); Azar Gat, *War in Human Civilization* (Oxford, 2006); Christon I. Archer, John R. Ferris, Holger H. Herwig, and Timothy H.E. Travers, *World History of Warfare* (Lincoln, NE, 2002).

Chapter 1   Innovative Warfare, 1450s–1520s

1 George Sphrantzes, *The Fall of the Byzantine Empire: A Chronicle*, trans. Marios Philippides (Amherst, MA, 1980), 103.

2   Kelly DeVries, "Gunpowder Weapons at the Siege of Constantinople, 1453," in *War and Society in the Eastern Mediterranean, 7th–15th Centuries*, ed. Yaacov Lev (Leiden, 1997), 342–362.

3   Niccolò Barbaro paraphrased and Byzantine historian Doukas quoted in Ebru Boyar and Kate Fleet, *A Social History of Ottoman Istanbul* (Cambridge, 2010), 6–11.

4   Bert S. Hall, *Weapons and Warfare in Renaissance Europe: Gunpowder, Technology, and Tactics* (Baltimore, MD, 1997), 55–66.

5   Maurizio Arfaioli, *The Black Bands of Giovanni: Infantry and Diplomacy during the Italian Wars (1526–1528)* (Pisa, 2005), 4–9.

6   J.R. Hale, *War and Society in Renaissance Europe, 1450–1620* (Baltimore, MD, 1985), 53–56.

7   John K. Thornton, *Warfare in Atlantic Africa, 1500–1800* (London, 1999), 19–40.

8   John A. Lynn, "The Evolution of Army Style in the Modern West, 800–2000," *International History Review* 18 (August 1996): 505–756.

9   Lynn, "The Evolution of Army Style in the Modern West," 505–756.

10   László Veszprémy, "The State and Military Affairs in East-Central Europe, 1380–c.1520s," in *European Warfare, 1350–1750*, ed. Frank Tallett and D.J.B. Trim (Cambridge, 2010), 96–109.

11   Richard Hellie, *Enserfment and Military Change in Muscovy* (Chicago, 1971).

12   Peter C. Perdue, *China Marches West: The Qing Conquest of Central Eurasia* (Cambridge, MA, 2005), 57–63.

13   Peter Allan Lorge, *War, Politics and Society in Early Modern China, 900–1795* (London, 2005), 119–128.

14   Edward Farmer, "The Hierarchy of Ming City Walls," in *City Walls: The Urban Enceinte in Global Perspective*, ed. James Tracy (New York, 2000), 461–487.

15   Denis Crispin Twitchett and Frederick W. Mote, eds., *The Cambridge History of China*, vol. 7: *The Ming Dynasty, 1368–1644, Part 1* (Cambridge, 1988), 323–376.

16   Weston F. Cook, Jr., "The Cannon Conquest of Nasrid Spain and the End of the Reconquista," *Journal of Military History* 57 (January 1993): 43–70.

17   Fernando del Pulgar, quoted in Hall, *Weapons and Warfare in Renaissance Europe*, 125–126.

18   Alonso de Palencia, quoted in Cook, "The Cannon Conquest of Nasrid Spain and the End of the Reconquista," 62.

19   Cook, "The Cannon Conquest of Nasrid Spain and the End of the Reconquista," 70.

20   David Coleman, *Society and Religious Culture in an Old-World Frontier City, 1492–1600* (Ithaca, NY, 2003), 13–31.

21   Francesco Guicciardini, *The History of Italy*, trans. Sidney Alexander (Princeton, NJ, 1969), 49–52.

22   Henry Kamen, *Empire: How Spain became a World Power, 1492–1763* (New York, 2003), 23–27.

23 Guicciardini, *The History of Italy*, 341.
24 Guicciardini, *The History of Italy*, 202–203.
25 Filippo Camerota "L'arte militare," in *Nel Segno di Masaccio: L'Invenzione della Prospettiva* (Florence, 2001), 207–217.
26 Martha D. Pollak, *Cities at War in Early Modern Europe* (Cambridge, 2010).
27 Simon Pepper, "Ottoman Military Architecture in the Early Gunpowder Era: A Reassessment," in *City Walls: The Urban Enceinte in Global Perspective*, ed. James D. Tracy (Cambridge, 2000), 288–293.
28 Giosi Amirante, "Origine e Dismissione di Due Fortezze Napoletane: Castel dell'Ovo e Castel Nuovo," in *L'Architettura degli Ingegneri: Fortificatzioni in Italia tra '500 e '600*, ed. Angela Marino (Rome, 2005), 165–194.
29 Martin M. Elbl, "Portuguese Urban Fortifications in Morocco: Borrowing, Adaptation, and Innovation along a Military Frontier," in *City Walls: The Urban Enceinte in Global Perspective*, ed. James D. Tracy (Cambridge, 2000), 349–385.
30 Pietro C. Marani, ed., *Disegni di fortificazioni da Leonardo a Michelangelo* (Florence, 1984).
31 Andrea Bruno, "Federico Ghislieri Soldato, Trattista, Inventore nei Documenti dell'Archivio di Stato di Torino," in *L'Architettura degli Ingegneri: Fortificatzioni in Italia tra '500 e '600*, ed. Angela Marino (Rome, 2005), 43–52.
32 Andrew Pettegree, *The Book in the Renaissance* (New Haven, CT, 2010), 141–142.
33 Veszprémy, "The State and Military Affairs in East-Central Europe," 96–109.
34 J.R. Hale, *Artists and Warfare in the Renaissance* (New Haven, CT, 1990), 137–148, 184–192.
35 John W. Dardess, *Ming China, 1368–1644: A Concise History of a Resilient Empire* (Landham, MD, 2012), 65–66.
36 Albrecht Dürer, *The Triumphal Arch*, 1515, reproduced in Giulia Bartrum, *Albrecht Dürer and His Legacy: The Graphic Work of a Renaissance Artist* (London, 2002), 194–197.
37 Remy du Puys, *La tryumphante et solemnelle entree faicte sur le nouuel et ioyeux aduenement de treshault trespuissant et tresexcellent prince monsieur Charles prince des Hespaignes archiduc daustrice duc de Bourgongne conte de Flandres, en sa ville de Bruges* (Paris, 1515).
38 Keith Moxey, *Peasants, Warriors, and Wives: Popular Imagery in the Reformation* (Chicago, IL, 1989), 67–100.
39 Anthony Reid, *Southeast Asia in the Age of Commerce, 1450–1680. Volume Two: Expansion and Crisis* (New Haven, CT, 1993), 10–16.
40 Palmira Brummett, *Ottoman Seapower and Levantine Diplomacy in the Age of Discovery* (Albany, 1994), 89–93.
41 Nicolò Cillacio, quoted in Thomas Benjamin, *The Atlantic World: European, Africans, Indians and Their Shared History, 1400–1900* (Cambridge, 2009), 80.
42 Hale, *War and Society in Renaissance Europe*, 56–58.

Chapter 2   Maritime Conflict and Colonial Expansion, 1490s–1530s

1   Nicholás Wey Gómez, *The Tropics of Empire: Why Columbus Sailed South to the Indies* (Cambridge, MA, 2008), 12–13, 341–344.
2   Wey Gómez, *The Tropics of Empire*, 367–369.
3   Christopher Columbus, "First Voyage," in Felipe Fernández-Armesto, *Columbus on Himself* (Indianapolis, IN, 2010), 52–53.
4   Wey Gómez, *The Tropics of Empire*, 401.
5   Christopher Columbus, "The Account of the Third Voyage Made by the Admiral Don Cristóbal Colón ,...," in Felipe Fernández-Armesto, *Columbus on Himself* (Indianapolis, IN, 2010), 164–165.
6   Samuel Eliot Morison, *Admiral of the Ocean Sea: A Life of Christopher Columbus* (Boston, MA, 1942).
7   Gaspar Correia, quoted in John F. Guilmartin, Jr., *Galleons and Galleys* (London, 2002), 82.
8   Michael Pearson, *The Indian Ocean* (New York, 2003), 121.
9   Girolamo Priuli, quoted in Sanjay Subrahmanyam, "The Birth-Pangs of Portuguese Asia: Revisiting the Fateful 'Long Decade' 1498–1506," *Journal of Global History* 2 (2007): 273.
10   Vincenzo Quirini, quoted in Subrahmanyam, "The Birth-Pangs of Portuguese Asia," 265.
11   Duarte Pereira Pacheco, quoted in Geoffrey Parker, "In Defense of *The Military Revolution*," in *The Military Revolution Debate: Readings on the Military Transformation of Early Modern Europe*, ed. Clifford J. Rogers (Boulder, CO, 1995), 342.
12   Geoffrey Parker, "The Artillery Fortress as an Engine of European Overseas Expansion, 1480–1750," in *City Walls: The Urban Enceinte in Global Perspective*, ed. James D. Tracy (Cambridge, 2000), 416.
13   Palmira Brummett, *Ottoman Seapower and Levantine Diplomacy in the Age of Discovery* (Albany, 1994), 118–119.
14   Giancarlo Casale, *The Ottoman Age of Exploration* (Oxford, 2010), 52.
15   Brummett, *Ottoman Seapower and Levantine Diplomacy in the Age of Discovery*, 172–173.
16   Ross Hassig, "War, Politics and the Conquest of Mexico," in *War in the Early Modern World*, ed. Jeremy Black (Boulder, CO, 1999), 222.
17   Alfred W. Crosby, *The Columbian Exchange: Biological and Cultural Consequences of 1492*, 30th anniversary edn (Westport, CT, 2003), 31.
18   Toribio Motolinía, quoted in Crosby, *The Columbian Exchange*, 52.
19   Pedro Pizarro, quoted in Crosby, *The Columbian Exchange*, 55.
20   Alfred W. Crosby, *Ecological Imperialism: The Biological Expansion of Europe, 900–1900* (Cambridge, 1986).
21   Diego Velásquez de Cuéllar, quoted in Crosby, *The Columbian Exchange*, 76.
22   Antonio de Mendoza, quoted in Crosby, *The Columbian Exchange*, 99.

23 Crosby, *The Columbian Exchange*, 73.
24 Walter D. Mignolo, *The Darker Side of the Renaissance: Literacy, Territoriality, and Colonization* (Ann Arbor, MI, 1995), 313.
25 Denis Cosgrove, "Mapping New Worlds: Culture and Cartography in Sixteenth-Century Venice," *Imago Mundi* 44 (1992): 65–89.
26 David M. Whitford, *The Curse of Ham in the Early Modern Era: The Bible and the Justifications for Slavery* (Farnham, 2009).
27 Philip D. Curtin, *The Rise and Fall of the Plantation Complex: Essays in Atlantic History*, 2nd edn (Cambridge, 1998), 45.

Chapter 3   Schism and Social Conflict, 1510s–1560s

1   Sanjay Subrahmanyam, "Connected Histories: Notes towards a Reconfiguration of Early Modern Eurasia," *Modern Asian Studies* 31 (1997): 735–762.
2   Samuel P. Huntington, *The Clash of Civilizations and the Remaking of World Order* (New York, 1996).
3   Moojan Momen, *An Introduction to Shi'i Islam* (New Haven, CT, 1985), 165–171.
4   Dean Phillip Bell, *Jews in the Early Modern World* (Lanham, MD, 2008), 143–190.
5   Daniel T. Reff, "Sympathy for the Devil: Devil Sickness and Lore among the Tohono O'odham," *Journal of the Southwest* 50 (Winter 2008): 355–376.
6   Andrew J. Newman, *Safavid Iran: Rebirth of a Persian Empire* (London, 2006), 13–25.
7   John Renard, *Friends of God: Islamic Images of Piety, Commitment, and Servanthood* (Berkeley, CA, 2008), 205–206.
8   Pinar Emiraolioglu, *Geographical Knowledge and Imperial Culture in the Early Modern Ottoman Empire* (Farnham, 2014), 13–56.
9   Gábor Ágoston, "Firearms and Military Adaptation: The Ottomans and the European Military Revolution, 1450–1800," *Journal of World History* 25 (March 2014): 85–124.
10 Ágoston, "Firearms and Military Adaptation," 85–124.
11 Naim R. Farooqi, "Moguls, Ottomans, and Pilgrims: Protecting the Routes to Mecca in the Sixteenth and Seventeenth Centuries," *International History Review* 10 (May 1988): 198–220.
12 Giancarlo Casale, *The Ottoman Age of Exploration* (Oxford, 2010), 82.
13 Casale, *The Ottoman Age of Exploration*, 30–31.
14 Tijana Krstić, *Contested Conversions to Islam: Narratives of Religious Change in the Early Modern Ottoman Empire* (Stanford, 2011), 12–13.
15 Caroline Finkel, *Osman's Dream: The Story of the Ottoman Empire, 1300–1923* (New York, 2005), 125–126.
16 Stephen F. Dale, *The Muslim Empires of the Ottomans, Safavids, and Mughals* (Cambridge, 2010), 87–96.

17 Martin Luther, *Ninety-Five Theses* (1517), repr. in Michael G. Baylor, *The German Reformation and the Peasants' War: A Brief History with Documents* (Boston, MA, 2012), 43–46.

18 Martin Luther, *To the Christian Nobility of the German Nation* (1520), repr. in Michael G. Baylor, *The German Reformation and the Peasants' War: A Brief History with Documents* (Boston, MA, 2012), 50–54.

19 James M. Stayer, *The German Peasants' War and Anabaptist Community of Goods* (Montreal, 1991).

20 Peter Blickle, *The Revolution of 1525: The German Peasants' War from a New Perspective*, trans. Thomas A. Brady, Jr. and H.C. Erik Midlefort (Baltimore, MD, 1985); James M. Stayer, *The German Peasants' War and Anabaptist Community of Goods* (Montreal, 1991).

21 Thomas Müntzer, quoted in *The German Peasants' War: A History in Documents*, ed. and trans. Tom Scott and Bob Scribner (New York, 1991), 238

22 Martin Luther, quoted in Heiko Oberman, *Luther: Man between God and the Devil*, trans. Eileen Walliser-Schwarzbart (New York, 1992), 289.

23 Hermann Mühlpfort, quoted in *The German Peasants' War: A History in Documents*, ed. and trans. Tom Scott and Bob Scribner (New York, 1991), 322.

24 André Chastel, *The Sack of Rome, 1527* (Princeton, NJ, 1983).

25 Spanish source, quoted in Paul Flemer, "Clement VII and the Crisis of the Sack of Rome," in *Society and Individual in Renaissance Florence*, ed. William J. Connell (Berkeley, CA, 2002), 409.

26 John L. Esposito, Darrell J. Fasching, and Todd Lewis, *Religion and Globalization: World Religions in Historical Perspective* (Oxford, 2008), 402–408.

27 Carol Richmond Tsang, *War and Faith: Ikko Ikki in Late Muromachi Japan* (Cambridge, 2007), 229.

28 Anthony Reid, *Southeast Asia in the Age of Commerce, 1450–1680. Volume Two: Expansion and Crisis* (New Haven, CT, 1993), 132–136.

29 Pauline Moffitt Watts, "Prophesy and Discovery: On the Spiritual Origins of Christopher Columbus's 'Enterprise of the Indies,'" *American Historical Review* 90 (February 1985): 73–102; James Axtell, "Columbian Encounters: 1992–1995," *The William and Mary Quarterly* 52 (October 1995), 651–655.

30 Andrew Keitt, "Religious Enthusiasm, the Spanish Inquisition, and the Disenchantment of the World," *Journal of the History of Ideas* (2004): 231–250.

31 Luc Giard and Louis de Vaucelles, eds., *Les Jésuites à l'âge baroque (1540–1640)* (Grenoble, 1996); Christian Sorrel and Frédéric Meyer, eds., *Les Missions intérieurs en France et en Italie du XVIe au XXe siècle* (Chambéry, 2001).

32 Megan C. Armstrong, *The Politics of Piety: Franciscan Preachers During the Wars of Religion, 1560–1600* (Rochester, NY, 2004), 170.

33 J.H. Elliott, "The Mental World of Hernán Cortés," in *Spain and its World, 1500–1700: Selected Essays* (New Haven, CT, 1989), 38–40.

34 John K. Thornton, *A Cultural History of the Atlantic World, 1250–1820* (Cambridge, 2012), 412.

35 Geoffrey C. Gunn, *First Globalization: The Eurasian Exchange, 1500–1800* (Lanham, MD, 2003), 85–94.
36 Mary Elizabeth Berry, *Hideyoshi* (Cambridge, MA, 1982), 87–89; R. Po-Chia Hsia, *The World of Catholic Renewal, 1540–1770* (Cambridge, 1998), 180–184.
37 Liam Matthew Brockey, *Journey to the East: The Jesuit Mission to China, 1579–1724* (Cambridge, MA, 2007).
38 The term "religions of the oppressed" is Vittorio Lanternari's. Bruce Lincoln has proposed the term "religions of resistance" instead. Bruce Lincoln, *Holy Terrors: Thinking About Religion after September 11* (Chicago, IL, 2003), 77–79.
39 Patricia Lopes Don, *Bonfires of Culture: Franciscans, Indigenous Leaders, and the Inquisition in Early Mexico, 1524–1540* (Norman, OK, 2010).
40 Edward W. Osowski, *Indigenous Miracles: Nahua Authority in Colonial Mexico* (Tucson, AZ, 2010), 1–4.
41 Cristóbal de Molina, quoted in Jeremy Mumford, "The Taki Onqoy and the Andean Nation: Sources and Interpretations," *Latin American Research Review* 33 (1998): 150–165.
42 John K. Thornton, *Africa and Africans in the Making of the Atlantic World, 1400–1800*, 2nd edn (Cambridge, 1998), 235–253.
43 Helen Vella Bonavita, "Key to Christendom: The 1565 Siege of Malta, Its Histories, and Their Use in Reformation," *Sixteenth Century Journal* 33 (Winter 2002): 1021–1043.
44 Rhoads Murphey, *Ottoman Warfare, 1500–1700* (New Brunswick, 1999), 149.
45 Nevill Barbour, "North West Africa from the 15th to 19th Centuries," in *The Muslim World, Part III: The Last Great Muslim Empires* (Leiden, 1969), 97–152; Richard L. Smith, *Ahmad al-Mansur: Islamic Visionary* (London, 2006), 51–53.
46 Ahmad al-Mansur to Elizabeth I, Marrakech, mid-Rabi II 1000/c. January 30, 1592, in *Letters from Barbary, 1576–1774: Arabic Documents in the Public Records Office*, trans. J.F.P. Hopkins (Oxford, 1982), 5–6.
47 Henry Kamen, "The Mediterranean and the Expulsion of Spanish Jews in 1492," *Past and Present* 119 (May 1988): 30–55.
48 Henry Kamen, *The Spanish Inquisition: An Historical Revision* (London, 1997), 320.
49 Bell, *Jews in the Early Modern World*, 74–76.
50 Molly Greene, *A Shared World: Christians and Muslims in the Early Modern Mediterranean* (Princeton, NJ, 2000).

Chapter 4   Dynastic War and State Development, 1520s–1580s

1 Stephen F. Dale, *The Muslim Empires of the Ottomans, Safavids, and Mughals* (Cambridge, 2010), 70–74.

2   Karin Friedrich, *Brandenburg-Prussia, 1466–1806* (Houndmills, 2012).
3   Michael Roberts, *The Early Vasas: A History of Sweden, 1523–1611* (Cambridge, 1968).
4   David Robinson, *Muslim Societies in African History* (Cambridge, 2004), 32–40.
5   Anthony Reid, *Southeast Asia in the Age of Commerce, 1450–1680. Volume Two: Expansion and Crisis* (New Haven, CT, 1993), 202–219.
6   Matthew Vester, *Renaissance Dynasticism and Apanage Politics: Jacques de Savoie-Nemours, 1531–1585* (Kirksville, MO, 2012), 168.
7   John W. Dardess, *Ming China, 1368–1644: A Concise History of a Resilient Empire* (Landham, MD, 2012), 30–31, 52–53.
8   Leslie P. Peirce, *The Imperial Harem: Women and Sovereignty in the Ottoman Empire* (Oxford, 1993), 21–22.
9   Munis D. Faruqui, *The Princes of the Mughal Empire, 1504–1719* (Cambridge, 2012), 24–45.
10 Paula Sutter Fichtner, *Protestantism and Primogeniture in Early Modern Germany* (New Haven, CT, 1989), 11–14.
11 John Knox, *The First Blast of the Trumpet against the Monstrous Regiment of Women* (1558).
12 William Monter, *The Rise of Female Kings in Europe, 1300–1800* (New Haven, CT, 2012), 36–41.
13 Jonathan Spangler, *The Society of Princes: The Lorraine-Guise and the Conservation of Power and Wealth in Seventeenth-Century France* (Farnham, 2009).
14 Vester, *Renaissance Dynasticism and Apanage Politics*, 16.
15 John Skelton, quoted in Roger Lockyer, *Tudor and Stuart Britain, 1471–1714*, 2nd edn (Burnt Mill, 1985), 16.
16 Robert J. Knecht, *Renaissance Warrior and Patron: The Reign of Francis I* (Cambridge, 1994), 41–49.
17 Robert J. Knecht, *The French Renaissance Court, 1483–1589* (New Haven, CT, 2008), 94–106.
18 Hugo Soly, ed., *Charles V and His Time, 1500–1558* (Antwerp, 1999).
19 Ernst Hartwig Kantorowicz, *The King's Two Bodies: A Study in Mediaeval Political Theology* (Princeton, NJ, 1957).
20 John L.H. Keep, *Soldiers of the Tsar: Army and Society in Russia, 1462–1874* (Oxford, 1985).
21 John K. Thornton, *Warfare in Atlantic Africa, 1500–1800* (London, 1999), 16.
22 Charles V, quoted in Mia J. Rodríguez-Salgado, "Charles V and the Dynasty," in *Charles V and His Time, 1500–1558*, ed. Hugo Soly (Antwerp, 1999), 21.
23 Monter, *The Rise of Female Kings in Europe*, 95.
24 Eric Dursteler, *Venetians in Constantinople: Nation, Identity, and Coexistence in the Early Modern Mediterranean* (Baltimore, MD, 2006), 23–40.
25 John K. Thornton, "Firearms, Diplomacy, and Conquest in Angola: Cooperation and Alliance in West Central Africa, 1491–1671," in

Empires and Indigenes: Intercultural Alliance, Imperial Expansion, and Warfare in the Early Modern World, ed. Wayne E. Lee (New York, 2011), 164–191.

26 Thornton, *Warfare in Atlantic Africa*, 99–102.

27 Martin du Bellay, quoted in David Potter, *Renaissance France at War: Armies, Culture and Society, c.1480–1560* (Woodbridge, 2008), 22.

28 Maurizio Arfaioli, *The Black Bands of Giovanni: Infantry and Diplomacy during the Italian Wars (1526–1528)* (Pisa, 2005).

29 Eric Cochrane, *Florence in the Forgotten Centuries, 1527–1800* (Chicago, IL, 1973), 10.

30 Daniel Goffman, *The Ottoman Empire and Early Modern Europe* (Cambridge, 2002), 107–108.

31 Gábor Ágoston, "Information, Ideology, and the Limits of Imperial Policy: Ottoman Grand Strategy in the Context of Ottoman–Habsburg Rivalry," in *The Early Modern Ottomans: Remapping the Empire*, ed. Virginia H. Aksan and Daniel Goffman (Cambridge, 2007), 75–103.

32 Frances E. Dolan, *Marriage and Violence: The Early Modern Legacy* (Philadelphia, PA, 2008), 9.

33 Peirce, *The Imperial Harem*.

34 Dardess, *Ming China*, 65–66.

35 Peirce, *The Imperial Harem*, 15.

36 Thornton, *Warfare in Atlantic Africa*, 99–102.

37 Arfaioli, *The Black Bands of Giovanni*, 12–15.

38 Potter, *Renaissance France at War*, 11–12.

39 Potter, *Renaissance France at War*, 332–334.

Chapter 5   Noble Violence, 1520s–1620s

1 Hillay Zmora, *State and Nobility in Early Modern Germany: The Knightly Feud in Franconia, 1440–1567* (Cambridge, 1997).

2 Friedrich IV Margrave of Brandenburg, quoted in Zmora, *State and Nobility in Early Modern Germany*, 93.

3 Stuart Carroll, *Blood and Violence in Early Modern France* (Oxford, 2006), 5–10.

4 R.J. Barendse, "The Feudal Mutation: Military and Economic Transformations of the Ethnosphere in the Tenth to Thirteenth Centuries," *Journal of World History* 14 (December 2003): 503–529; Steven Morrillo, "A 'Feudal Mutation'? Conceptual Tools and Historical Patterns in World History," *Journal of World History* 14 (December 2003): 531–550.

5 Michel Nassiet, *Parenté, noblesse et états dynastiques: XVe–XVIe siècles* (Paris, 2000).

6 Lawrence Stone, *The Crisis of the Aristocracy, 1558–1641* (Oxford, 1965); Davis Bitton, *The French Nobility in Crisis, 1560–1640* (Stanford, CA, 1969); Samuel Clark, *State and Status: The Rise of the State and Aristocratic Power in Western Europe* (Montreal, 1995).

7   R. Brian Ferguson and Neil L. Whitehead, "The Violent Edge of Empire," in *War in the Tribal Zone: Expanding States and Indigenous Warfare*, ed. R. Brian Ferguson and Neil L. Whitehead (Santa Fe, NM, 1992), 1–30.

8   Pradeep Barua, *The State at War in South Asia* (Lincoln, NE, 2005), 29–36.

9   Sanjay Subrahmanyam, "Iranians Abroad: Intra-Asian Elite Migration and Early Modern State Formation," *Journal of Asian Studies* 51 (May 1992): 340–363.

10   John F. Richards, *The Mughal Empire* (Cambridge, 1993), 24–25, 64–67.

11   Jonathan Dewald, *The European Nobility, 1400–1800* (Cambridge, 1996), 15–27.

12   Brian Sandberg, *Warrior Pursuits: Noble Culture and Civil Conflict in Early Modern France* (Baltimore, MD, 2010).

13   Herluf Trolle, quoted in Knud J.V. Jespersen, "The Rise and Fall of the Danish Nobility, 1600–1800," in *The European Nobilities in the Seventeenth and Eighteenth Centuries. II: Northern, Central and Eastern Europe*, ed. H.M. Scott (London, 1995), 41–70.

14   Robert I. Frost, "The Nobility of Poland-Lithuania, 1569–1795," in *The European Nobilities in the Seventeenth and Eighteenth Centuries. II: Northern, Central and Eastern Europe*, ed. H.M. Scott (London, 1995), 183–222.

15   László Veszprémy, "The State and Military Affairs in East-Central Europe, 1380–c.1520s," in *European Warfare, 1350–1750*, ed. Frank Tallett and D.J.B. Trim (Cambridge, 2010), 96–109; Peter Schimert, "The Hungarian Nobility in the Seventeenth and Eighteenth Centuries," in *The European Nobilities in the Seventeenth and Eighteenth Centuries. II: Northern, Central and Eastern Europe*, ed. H.M. Scott (London, 1995), 144–182.

16   Heinz-Werner Lewerken, "The Dresden Armory in the New Stable," in *Princely Splendor: The Dresden Court, 1580–1620*, ed. Dirk Syndram and Antje Scherner (Milan, 2004), 70–79.

17   Jean-Marie Constant, "Un groupe socio-politique stratégique dans la France de la première moitié du XVIIe siècle: La noblesse seconde," in *L'Etat et les aristocraties (France, Angleterre, Ecosse), XIIe–XVIIe siècles*, ed. Philippe Contamine (Paris, 1989), 279–304; J.H.M. Salmon, "A Second Look at the Noblesse Seconde: The Key to Noble Clientage and Power in Early Modern France?" *French Historical Studies* 25 (Autumn 2002): 575–593.

18   Roland Mousnier, "Les concepts d''ordres', d''états', de 'fidélité' et de 'monarchie absolue' en France de la fin du XVIe siècle à la fin du XVIIIe," *Revue Historique* 247 (1972): 289–312.

19   Sharon Kettering, *Patrons, Brokers, and Clients in Seventeenth-Century France* (Oxford, 1986), 4.

20   Kristen B. Neuschel, *Word of Honor: Interpreting Noble Culture in Sixteenth-Century France* (Ithaca, NY, 1989).

21   William Ian Miller, *Bloodtaking and Peacemaking: Feud, Law, and Society in Saga Iceland* (Chicago, IL, 1990), 179–220.

22 Keith M. Brown, *Bloodfeud in Scotland, 1573–1625: Violence, Justice, and Politics in an Early Modern Society* (Edinburgh, 1986).
23 James J. Reid, *Studies in Safavid Mind, Society, and Culture* (Costa Mesa, CA, 2000), 287, 292–300.
24 Richards, *The Mughal Empire*, 129–130.
25 Edward Muir, *Mad Blood Stirring: Vendetta and Factions in Friuli During the Renaissance* (Baltimore, MD, 1993).
26 William Shakespeare, *Romeo and Juliet*, ed. Peter Holland (London, 2000), 3.
27 Eric Dursteler, *Venetians in Constantinople: Nation, Identity, and Coexistence in the Early Modern Mediterranean* (Baltimore, MD, 2006), 63–72.
28 Pascal Brioist, Hervé Drévillon, and Pierre Serna, *Croiser le fer. Violence et culture de l'épée dans la France moderne (XVIe–XVIIIe siècle)* (Seyssel, 2002).
29 Brioist, Drévillon, and Serna, *Croiser le fer*, 71–128.
30 François Billacois, *Le Duel dans la société française des XVIe–XVIIe siècles: essai de psychosociologie historique* (Paris, 1986), 7–10.
31 Scott Taylor, "Credit, Debt, and Honor in Castile, 1600–1650," *Journal of Early Modern History* 7 (2003): 8–27; Brioist, Drévillon, and Serna, *Croiser le fer*, 7.
32 Hinatsu Shigetaka, quoted in John M. Rogers, "Arts of War in Times of Peace: Swordsmanship in Honcho Bugei Shoden, Chapter 6," *Monumenta Nipponica* 46 (Summer 1991): 191.
33 Amanda J. Weidman, "Beyond Honor and Shame: Performing Gender in the Mediterranean," *Anthropological Quarterly* 76 (Summer 2003): 519–530.
34 Markuu Peltonen, *The Duel in Early Modern England: Civility, Politeness and Honour* (Cambridge, 2003).
35 Linda A. Pollock, "Honor, Gender, and Reconciliation in Elite Culture, 1570–1700," *Journal of British Studies* 46 (January 2007): 3–29.
36 Nancy Shields Kollmann, *By Honor Bound: State and Society in Early Modern Russia* (Ithaca, NY, 1999).
37 Arlette Jouanna, *Le Devoir de révolte: la noblesse française et la gestation de l'état moderne, 1559–1661* (Paris, 1989).
38 Sandberg, *Warrior Pursuits*, xxi.
39 I.A.A. Thompson, "The Nobility in Spain, 1600–1800," in *The European Nobilities in the Seventeenth and Eighteenth Centuries. I: Western Europe*, ed. H.M. Scott (London, 1995), 174–236.
40 Gábor Ágoston, "Empires and Warfare in East-Central Europe, 1550–1750: The Ottoman–Habsburg Rivalry and Military Transformation," in *European Warfare, 1350–1750*, ed. Frank Tallett and D.J.B. Trim (Cambridge, 2010), 110–134; Rhoads Murphey, *Ottoman Warfare, 1500–1700* (New Brunswick, 1999); Sam White, *The Climate of Rebellion in the Early Modern Ottoman Empire* (Cambridge, 2011), 150–152.
41 Jonathan Spangler, *The Society of Princes: The Lorraine-Guise and the Conservation of Power and Wealth in Seventeenth-Century France* (Farnham, 2009), 35.

42   Richards, *The Mughal Empire*, 10–11.
43   Paul Varley, "Warfare in Japan 1467–1600," in *War In The Early Modern World, 1450–1815*, ed. Jeremy Black (Boulder, CO, 1999), 53–86.
44   Mary Elizabeth Berry, *Hideyoshi* (Cambridge, MA, 1989).
45   Norbert Elias, *The Civilizing Process: Sociogenetic and Psychogenetic Investigations*, trans. Edmund Jephcott (Malden, MA, 2000), xi–xvii, 465–475.
46   Ellery Schalk, *From Valor to Pedigree: Ideas of Nobility in France in the Sixteenth and Seventeenth Centuries* (Princeton, NJ, 1986).
47   Carroll, *Blood and Violence in Early Modern France*; Sandberg, *Warrior Pursuits*, xxiiii–xxvii.
48   Kate Van Orden, *Music, Discipline, and Arms in Early Modern France* (Chicago, IL, 2005).
49   Nicolas Faret, *L'Honneste-homme*, 15–17, trans. in Jonathan Dewald, *Aristocratic Experience and the Origins of Modern Culture* (Berkeley, CA, 1993), 45.
50   Antoine de Pluvinel, *Instruction du roy, en l'exercice de monter à cheval* (Amsterdam: Jean Schipper, 1666); Mark Edward Motley, *Becoming a French Aristocrat* (Princeton, NJ, 1990), 98–153.
51   David Quint, "Duelling and Civility in Sixteenth-Century Italy," *I Tatti Studies: Essays in the Renaissance* 7 (1997): 258–263.
52   Gregory Hanlon, *The Twilight of a Military Tradition: Italian Aristocrats and European Conflicts, 1560–1800* (New York, 1998).
53   Richard Cust and Andrew Hopper, "Duelling and the Court of Chivalry in Early Stuart England," in *Cultures of Violence: Interpersonal Violence in Historical Perspective*, ed. Stuart Carroll (Houndmills, 2007), 156.
54   A.F. Upton, "The Swedish Nobility, 1600–1772," in *The European Nobilities in the Seventeenth and Eighteenth Centuries. II: Northern, Central and Eastern Europe*, ed. H.M. Scott (London, 1995), 11–40.
55   B. Ann Tlusty, *The Martial Ethic in Early Modern Germany: Civic Duty and the Right of Arms* (New York, 2011), 234–243.
56   Brioist, Drévillon, and Serna, *Croiser le fer*, 479–490.

Chapter 6   Sectarian Violence and Religious Warfare, 1560s–1640s

1   James B. Wood, *The King's Army: Warfare, Soldiers, and Society during the Wars of Religion in France, 1561–1576* (Cambridge, 1996).
2   Barbara B. Diefendorf, *Beneath the Cross: Catholics and Huguenots in Sixteenth-Century Paris* (Oxford, 1991).
3   Jean Crespin, quoted in Diefendorf, *Beneath the Cross*, 102.
4   Wood, *The King's Army*, 4–5, 246–274.
5   Mack P. Holt, *The Duke of Anjou and the Politique Struggle during the Wars of Religion* (Cambridge, 1986).
6   Nicolas Le Roux, *Un Régicide au nom de Dieu: l'assassinat d'Henri III, 1er août 1589* (Paris, 2006).

7   Michael Wolfe, *The Conversion of Henri IV: Politics, Power, and Religious Belief in Early Modern France* (Cambridge, 1993).

8   Brian Sandberg, "'To Deliver a Greatly Persecuted Church': Resituating the Edict of Nantes within the History of *Laïcité*," *Storica* 38 (2007): 33–64.

9   Brian Sandberg, "'Re-establishing the True Worship of God': Divinity and Religious Violence in France after the Edict of Nantes," *Renaissance and Reformation/Renaissance et Réforme* 29 (2005): 139–182.

10 Brian Sandberg, *Warrior Pursuits: Noble Culture and Civil Conflict in Early Modern France* (Baltimore, MD, 2010).

11 Andrew Pettegree, *Emden and the Dutch Revolt: Exile and the Development of Reformed Protestantism* (Oxford, 1992).

12 *Tyranny of Alva*, reproduced in Graham Darby, ed., *The Origins and Development of the Dutch Revolt* (London, 2001); *A Defence and True Declaration of the Things lately Done in the Low Country …*, in *The Dutch Revolt*, ed. and trans. Martin van Gelderen (Cambridge, 1993), 58.

13 Spanish captain, quoted in Henry Kamen, *The Duke of Alba* (New Haven, CT, 2004), 114–115.

14 Peter Arnade, *Beggars, Iconoclasts, and Civic Patriots: The Political Culture of the Dutch Revolt* (Ithaca, NY, 2008), 212–259.

15 James D. Tracy, "Keeping the Wheels of War Turning: Revenues of the Province of Holland, 1572–1619," in Graham Darby, ed., *The Origins and Development of the Dutch Revolt* (London, 2001), 133–150.

16 Andrew Pettegree, "Religion and the Revolt," in Graham Darby, ed., *The Origins and Development of the Dutch Revolt* (London, 2001), 67–83.

17 Paul C. Allen, *Philip III and the Pax Hispanica, 1598–1621* (New Haven, CT, 2000).

18 Mary Elizabeth Berry, *Hideyoshi* (Cambridge, MA, 1982).

19 Toyotomi Hideyoshi to the Viceroy of the Indies, in *Religious Transformations in the Early Modern World: A Brief History with Documents*, ed. Merry E. Wiesner-Hanks (Boston, MA, 2009), 155–157.

20 Asao Naohiro, "The Sixteenth-Century Unification," in *The Cambridge History of Japan*. Volume 4: *Early Modern Japan*, ed. John Whitney Hall (Cambridge, 1991), 40–95.

21 John Whitney Hall, "The *bakuhan* System," in *Warrior Rule in Japan*, ed. Marius B. Jansen (Cambridge, 1995), 147–201.

22 Conrad Totman, *Early Modern Japan* (Berkeley, CA, 1993), 152–153.

23 Geoffrey Parker, *Global Crisis: War, Climate Change and Catastrophe in the Seventeenth Century* (New Haven, CT, 2013), 485–486.

24 Timothy Brook, *The Troubled Empire: China in the Yuan and Ming Dynasties* (Cambridge, MA, 2010), 119–126, 171–172.

25 Timothy Brook, *The Chinese State in Ming Society* (London, 2005), 146–162.

26 Anthony Reid, *Southeast Asia in the Age of Commerce, 1450–1680. Volume Two: Expansion and Crisis* (New Haven, CT, 1993), 187–188, 210–211, 219–233.

27 Reid, *Southeast Asia in the Age of Commerce, 1450–1680. Volume Two*, 192–201.

28 Anthony Reid, *Southeast Asia in the Age of Commerce, 1450–1680. Volume One: The Lands below the Winds* (New Haven, CT, 1988), 124, 191.

29 Yoneo Ishii, "Religious Patterns and Economic Change in Siam in the Sixteenth and Seventeenth Centuries," in *Southeast Asia in the Early Modern Era: Trade, Power, and Belief*, ed. Anthony Reid (Ithaca, NY, 1993), 180–194.

30 Lansiné Kaba, "Archers, Musketeers, and Mosquitoes: The Moroccan Invasion of the Sudan and the Songhay Resistance (1591–1612)," *Journal of African History* 22, 4 (1981): 457–475.

31 Stephen F. Dale, *The Muslim Empires of the Ottomans, Safavids, and Mughals* (Cambridge, 2010), 87–96.

32 Jos Gommans, *Mughal Warfare: Indian Frontiers and High Roads to Empire, 1500–1700* (London, 2002), 39–56.

33 Daniel Goffman, *The Ottoman Empire and Early Modern Europe* (Cambridge, 2002), 73–75.

34 Goffman, *The Ottoman Empire and Early Modern Europe*, 117–119.

35 Marco van der Hoeven, ed., *Exercise of Arms: Warfare in the Netherlands, 1568–1648* (Leiden, 1997).

36 Michael Roberts, *Gustavus Adolphus*, 2nd edn (Harlow, 1992), 90–108.

37 Michael Roberts, "The Military Revolution, 1560–1660," in *The Military Revolution Debate: Readings on the Military Transformation of Early Modern Europe* (Boulder, CO, 1995), 13–36.

38 Geoffrey Parker, *The Army of Flanders and the Spanish Road, 1567–1659: The Logistics of Spanish Victory and Defeat in the Low Countries' Wars* (Cambridge, 1972).

39 Gráinne Henry, *The Irish Military Community in Spanish Flanders, 1586–1621* (Dublin, 1992), 146.

40 Olivier Christin, *Confesser sa foi. Conflits confessionnels et identités religieuses dans l'Europe moderne (XVIe–XVIIe siècles)* (Seyssel, 2009), 162–179.

41 Geoffrey Parker, ed., *The Thirty Years' War*, 2nd edn (London, 1997), 20–26.

42 Quoted in Parker, ed., *The Thirty Years' War*, 47.

43 Howard Louthan, *Converting Bohemia: Force and Persuasion in the Catholic Reformation* (Cambridge, 2009).

44 Peter Wilson, *The Thirty Years War: Europe's Tragedy* (Cambridge, MA, 2009), 314–361.

45 Parker, ed., *The Thirty Years' War*, 66–72, 97.

46 Wilson, *The Thirty Years War*, 467–470.

47 Wilson, *The Thirty Years War*, 9–10.

48 Robert Bireley, *The Jesuits and the Thirty Years War: Kings, Courts, and Confessors* (Cambridge, 2003), 61–62.

49 Tryntje Helfferich, *The Iron Princess: Amalia Elisabeth and the Thirty Years War* (Cambridge, 2013), 124.

50   Parker, ed., *The Thirty Years' War*, 112, plate 23.
51   Derek Croxton, *Peacemaking in Early Modern Europe: Cardinal Mazarin and the Congress of Westphalia, 1643–1648* (Selinsgrove, NJ, 1999).
52   Wilson, *The Thirty Years War*, 779–821.
53   Benjamin J. Kaplan, *Divided by Faith: Religious Conflict and the Practice of Toleration in Early Modern Europe* (Cambridge, MA, 2007).

Chapter 7   Raiding Warfare, 1580s–1640s

1   Armstrong Starkey, *European and Native American Warfare, 1675–1815* (Norman, OK, 1998), 34.
2   Lawrence H. Keeley, *War before Civilization: The Myth of the Peaceful Savage* (Oxford, 1996).
3   Harry Holbert Turney-High, *Primitive War: Its Practice and Concepts* (Columbia, SC, 1949).
4   R. Brian Ferguson and Neil L. Whitehead, eds., *War in the Tribal Zone: Expanding States and Indigenous Warfare* (Santa Fe, NM, 1992).
5   Keeley, *War before Civilization*, 127–141.
6   Wendy Bracewell, *The Uskoks of Senj: Piracy, Banditry, and Holy War in the Sixteenth-Century Adriatic* (Ithaca, NY, 1992).
7   Molly Greene, *A Shared World: Christians and Muslims in the Early Modern Mediterranean* (Princeton, NJ, 2000).
8   John Francis Guilmartin, *Gunpowder and Galleys: Changing Technology and Mediterranean Warfare at Sea in the Sixteenth Century* (Cambridge, 1974).
9   Robert C. Davis, *Christian Slaves, Muslim Masters: White Slavery in the Mediterranean, the Barbary Coast, and Italy, 1500–1800* (Houndmills, 2003).
10   James McDermott, *England and the Spanish Armada: The Necessary Quarrel* (New Haven, CT, 2005), 24.
11   McDermott, *England and the Spanish Armada*, 327–328.
12   Jan Glete, *War and the State in Early Modern Europe: Spain, the Dutch Republic and Sweden as Fiscal-Military States, 1500–1660* (London, 2002), 174–189.
13   Carla Rahn Phillips, *Six Galleons for the King of Spain: Imperial Defense in the Early Seventeenth Century* (Baltimore, MD, 1986), 3–5.
14   Sanjay Subrahmanyam, "Of Imarat and Tijarat: Asian Merchants and State Power in the Western Indian Ocean, 1400 to 1750," *Comparative Studies in Society and History* 37 (October 1995): 750–780.
15   Adam Clulow, "From Global Entrepôt to Early Modern Domain: Hirado, 1609–1641," *Monumenta Nipponica* 65 (Spring 2010): 1–35; Peter D. Shapinsky, "Predators, Protectors, and Purveyors: Pirates and Commerce in Late Medieval Japan," *Monumenta Nipponica* 64 (Autumn 2009): 273–313.
16   Tonio Andrade, *Lost Colony: The Untold Story of China's First Great Victory over the West* (Princeton, NJ, 2011).

17　Tonio Andrade, "The Company's Chinese Pirates: How the Dutch East India Company Tried to Lead a Coalition of Pirates to War against China, 1621–1662," *Journal of World History* 15 (December 2004): 443.

18　Lauren Benton, *A Search for Sovereignty: Law Geography in European Empires, 1400–1900* (Cambridge, 2010), 151–156.

19　Benton, *A Search for Sovereignty*, 112–120, 149–152.

20　Benton, *A Search for Sovereignty*, 104–161.

21　R. Brian Ferguson and Neil L. Whitehead, "The Violent Edge of Empire," in *War in the Tribal Zone: Expanding States and Indigenous Warfare*, ed. R. Brian Ferguson and Neil L. Whitehead (Santa Fe, NM, 1992), 3.

22　Richard White, *The Middle Ground: Indians, Empires, and Republics in the Great Lakes Region, 1650–1815* (Cambridge, 1991), x.

23　*Annals of the Four Masters*, quoted in Patricia Palmer, "At the Sign of the Head: The Currency of Beheading in Early Modern Ireland," in *Cultures of Violence: Interpersonal Violence in Historical Perspective*, ed. Stuart Carroll (Houndmills, 2007), 136.

24　John F. Richards, *The Unending Frontier: An Environmental History of the Early Modern World* (Berkeley, CA, 2003), 397.

25　Richards, *The Unending Frontier*, 534–537.

26　Sam White, *The Climate of Rebellion in the Early Modern Ottoman Empire* (Cambridge, 2011), 229–248.

27　John K. Thornton, *Warfare in Atlantic Africa, 1500–1800* (London, 1999).

28　Michael N. Pearson, *Port Cities and Intruders: The Swahili Coast, India, and Portugal in the Early Modern Era* (Baltimore, MD, 1998), 129–154.

29　Richards, *The Unending Frontier*, 283–296.

30　James C. Scott, *The Art of Not Being Governed: An Anarchist History of Upland Southeast Asia* (New Haven, CT, 2010).

31　Martin Van Creveld, *Supplying War: Logistics from Wallenstein to Patton* (Cambridge, 1977).

32　John A. Lynn, "The History of Logistics and *Supplying War*," in *Feeding Mars: Logistics in Western Warfare from the Middle Ages to the Present*, ed. John A. Lynn (Boulder, CO, 1993), 9–27.

33　John A. Lynn, "How War Fed War: The Tax of Violence and Contributions During the *Grand Siècle*," *Journal of Modern History* 65, 2 (1993): 286–310.

34　Myron P. Gutmann, *War and Rural Life in the Early Modern Low Countries* (Princeton, NJ, 1980).

35　Katie Hornstein, "Just Violence: Jacques Callot's *Grandes Misères et Malheurs de la Guerre*," *Bulletin of the University of Michigan Museums of Art and Archaeology* 16 (2005).

36　Rhoads Murphey, *Ottoman Warfare, 1500–1700* (New Brunswick, 1999), 85–103.

37　Griet Vermeesch, "War and Garrison Towns in the Dutch Republic: The Cases of Gorinchem and Doesburg (c.1570–c.1660)," *Urban History* 36, 1 (2009): 3–23.

38   Geoffrey Parker, "The Artillery Fortress as an Engine of European Overseas Expansion, 1480–1750," in *City Walls: The Urban Enceinte in Global Perspective*, ed. James D. Tracy (Cambridge, 2000), 416.
39   *La Requeste des trois Estats présentée à messieurs du Parlement*, quoted in John A. Lynn, *Giant of the* Grand Siècle: *The French Army, 1610–1715* (Cambridge, 1997), 603.
40   Maréchal de Turenne, quoted in Lynn, *Giant of the* Grand Siècle, 212.
41   Anthony Reid, *Southeast Asia in the Age of Commerce, 1450–1680. Volume Two: Expansion and Crisis* (New Haven, CT, 1993), 208–233.
42   Pierre-Yves, Manguin, "*Lancaran, Ghurba,* and *Ghali*: Mediterranean Impact on War Vessels in Early Modern Southeast Asia," in *Anthony Reid and the Study of the Southeast Asian Past*, ed. Geoff Wade and Li Tana (Singapore, 2012), 146–182; Anthony Reid, "The Pre-Modern Sultanate's View of its Place in the World," in *Verandah of Violence: The Background to the Aceh Problem*, ed. Anthony Reid (Singapore, 2006), 52–71; Pierre-Yves Manguin, "The Vanishing Jong: Insular Southeast Asian Fleets in Trade and War (Fifteenth to Seventeenth Centuries)," in *Southeast Asia in the Early Modern Era: Trade, Power, and Belief* (Ithaca, NY, 1993), 197–21.

Chapter 8   Peasant Revolt and Rural Conflict, 1590s–1650s

1   Chester S.L. Dunning, *Russia's First Civil War: The Time of Troubles and the Founding of the Romanov Dynasty* (University Park, PA, 2001), 90–108.
2   John L.H. Keep, *Soldiers of the Tsar: Army and Society in Russia, 1462–1874* (Oxford, 1985), 19.
3   George F.E. Rudé, *The Crowd in History; A Study of Popular Disturbances in France and England, 1730–1848* (New York, 1964).
4   For a typology of peasant revolts, see Yves-Marie Bercé, *History of Peasant Revolts: The Social Origins of Rebellion in Early Modern France*, trans. Amanda Whitmore (Ithaca, NY, 1990).
5   Emmanuel Le Roy Ladurie, *Les Paysans de Languedoc*, 2 vols (Paris, 1966).
6   Steven L. Kaplan, *The Famine Plot Persuasion in Eighteenth-Century France* (Philadelphia, PA, 1982), 62–63.
7   Mikhail Bakhtin, *Rabelais and His World*, trans. Hélène Iswolsky (Bloomington, IN, 1984).
8   Samuel Kinser, "Presentation and Representation: Carnival at Nuremberg, 1450–1550," *Representations* 13 (Winter, 1986): 1–41.
9   Anthony Reid, *Southeast Asia in the Age of Commerce, 1450–1680. Volume One: The Lands below the Winds* (New Haven, CT, 1988), 173–192.
10   Emmanuel Le Roy Ladurie, *Le Carnaval de Romans* (Paris, 1979).
11   E.P. Thompson, "The Moral Economy of the English Crowd in the Eighteenth Century," *Past and Present* 50 (1971): 77–136.

12   Andrew Cunningham and Ole Peter Grell, *The Four Horsemen of the Apocalypse: Religion, War, Famine and Death in Reformation Europe* (Cambridge, 2000), 200–209.

13   Peregrine Horden and Nicholas Purcell, *The Corrupting Sea: A Study of Mediterranean History* (Oxford, 2000), 123–172.

14   John H. Munro, "Money, Prices, Wages, and 'Profit Inflation' in Spain, the Southern Netherlands, and England during the Price Revolution Era, ca.1520–ca.1650," *História e Economia Revista Interdisciplinar* 4, 1 (2008): 13–71.

15   Kenneth Pomeranz, *The Great Divergence: China, Europe, and the Making of the Modern World Economy* (Princeton, NJ, 2000).

16   Stephen Broadberry and Bishnupriya Gupta, "The Early Modern Great Divergence: Wages, Prices and Economic Development in Europe and Asia, 1500–1800," *Economic History Review* 59, 1 (2006): 2–31.

17   Geoffrey Parker, *Global Crisis: War, Climate Change and Catastrophe in the Seventeenth Century* (New Haven, CT, 2013).

18   Francis Bacon, quoted in Geoffrey Parker, "Crisis and Catastrophe: The Global Crisis of the Seventeenth Century Reconsidered," *AHR* 113 (October 2008): 1063.

19   William S. Atwell, "Volcanism and Short-Term Climatic Change in East Asian and World History, c.1200–1699," *Journal of World History* 12 (Spring 2001): 29–98.

20   Parker, *Global Crisis*, 3–8.

21   James B. Collins, *The State in Early Modern France* (Cambridge, 1995), 150–153.

22   Parker, *Global Crisis*, 115–151, 484–506.

23   Parker, *Global Crisis*, 445–446, 468–477.

24   Parker, *Global Crisis*, 446–460.

25   Fernand Braudel, *The Mediterranean and the Mediterranean World in the Age of Philip II*, trans. Siân Reynolds (Berkley, CA, 1995), I: 85–102.

26   R.J. Barendse, "Trade and State in the Arabian Seas: A Survey from the Fifteenth to the Eighteenth Century," *Journal of World History* 11 (Fall 2000): 173–225.

27   Ken Albala, *Food in Early Modern Europe* (Westport, CT, 2003), 1–20.

28   Christopher Hill, *The World Turned Upside Down: Radical Ideas during the English Revolution* (London, 1975), 52.

29   Emmanuel Le Roy Ladurie, *The Peasants of Languedoc*, trans. John Day (Urbana, 1974), 55.

30   Karl Appuhn, *A Forest on the Sea: Environmental Expertise in Renaissance Venice* (Baltimore, MD, 2009).

31   John F. Richards, *The Unending Frontier: An Environmental History of the Early Modern World* (Berkeley, CA, 2003), 214.

32   Jan de Vries and A.M. van der Woude, *The First Modern Economy: Success, Failure, and Perseverance of the Dutch Economy, 1500–1815* (Cambridge, 1997), 27–31.

33   Collins, *The State in Early Modern France*, 16–21.

34   Dirk H. A. Kolff, *Naukar, Rajput, and Sepoy: The Ethnohistory of the Military Labour Market in Hindustan, 1450–1850* (Cambridge, 1990), 3–17.

35   William Beik, *A Social and Cultural History of Early Modern France* (Cambridge, 2009), 56.

36   Parker, *Global Crisis*, 484–506.

37   Yves-Marie Bercé, *Croquants et nu-pieds: les soulèvements paysans en France du XVIe au XIXe siècle* (Paris, 1974); Parker, *Global Crisis*, 509–533.

38   James Tong, *Disorder Under Heaven: Collective Violence in the Ming Dynasty* (Stanford, CA, 1991).

39   Parker, *Global Crisis*, 509–533.

40   Beik, *A Social and Cultural History of Early Modern France*, 248.

41   Beik, *A Social and Cultural History of Early Modern France*, 248–252.

42   Emmanuel Le Roy Ladurie, *The French Peasantry, 1450–1660* (Berkeley, CA, 1987), 387–391.

43   Thomas Willard Robisheaux, *Rural Society and the Search for Order in Early Modern Germany* (Cambridge, 1989), 216–220.

44   Sam White, *The Climate of Rebellion in the Early Modern Ottoman Empire* (Cambridge, 2011), 163–186.

45   Parker, *Global Crisis*, 185–210; White, *The Climate of Rebellion in the Early Modern Ottoman Empire*, 229–236.

46   Suraiya Faroqhi, "Political Activity among Ottoman Taxpayers and the Problem of Sultanic Legitimation (1570–1650)," *Journal of the Economic and Social History of the Orient* 35 (1992): 1–39.

47   White, *The Climate of Rebellion in the Early Modern Ottoman Empire*, 163–186.

48   Zhang Dai, quoted in Jonathan D. Spence, *Return to Dragon Mountain: Memories of a Late Ming Man* (New York: Viking, 2007), 196.

49   Wang Jiazhen, quoted in Sucheta Mazumdar, "The Impact of New World Food Crops on the Diet and Economy of China and India, 1600–1900," in *Food in Global History*, ed. Raymond Grew (Boulder, CO, 1999), 65.

50   He lineage genealogy, quoted in Helen F. Siu and Liu Zhimwi, "Lineage, Market, Pirate, and Dan: Ethnicity in the Pearl River Delta of South China," in *Empire at the Margins: Culture, Ethnicity, and Frontier in Early Modern China*, ed. Pamela Kyle Crossley, Helen F. Siu, and Donald S. Sutton (Berkeley, CA, 2006), 300.

Chapter 9   Ethnic Conflict, 1620s–1660s

1   Melanie Perreault, "'To Fear and to Love Us': Intercultural Violence in the English Atlantic," *Journal of World History* 17 (March 2006): 71–93.

2 Alden T. Vaughan, "'Expulsion of the Salvages': English Policy and the Virginia Massacre of 1622," *William and Mary Quarterly*, 3rd series, 35 (January 1978): 57–84.

3 John Smith, *The Generall Historie of Virginia, New-England and the Summer Isles* (London, 1624), 286.

4 Geoffrey Parker, "The Artillery Fortress as an Engine of European Overseas Expansion, 1480–1750," in *City Walls: The Urban Enceinte in Global Perspective*, ed. James D. Tracy (Cambridge, 2000), 386–416.

5 Bert S. Hall, *Weapons and Warfare in Renaissance Europe: Gunpowder, Technology, and Tactics* (Baltimore, MD, 1997), 125.

6 David Coleman, *Creating Christian Granada: Society & Religious Culture in an Old-World Frontier City, 1492–1600* (Ithaca, NY, 2003).

7 Cynthia Radding, *Wandering Peoples: Colonialism, Ethnic Spaces, and Ecological Frontiers in Northwestern Mexico, 1700–1850* (Durham, NC, 1997).

8 Neil L. Whitehead, "Tribes Make States and States Make Tribes: Warfare and the Creation of Colonial Tribes and States in Northeastern South America," in *War in the Tribal Zone: Expanding States and Indigenous Warfare*, ed. R. Brian Ferguson and Neil L. Whitehead (Santa Fe, NM, 1992), 127–150.

9 Elaine Scarry, "Injury and the Structure of War," *Representations* 10 (Spring 1985): 1–51.

10 Arthur Kleinman, Veena Das, and Margaret Lock, "Introduction," in *Social Suffering*, ed. Arthur Kleinman, Veena Das, and Margaret Lock (Berkeley, CA, 1997), ix–xxvii.

11 Abbé Guyon, *Histoire des Amazones anciennes et modernes, enrichie de médailles* (Paris, 1740).

12 Claude Lévi-Strauss, *Tristes Tropiques*, trans. John Weightman and Doreen Weightman (New York, 1975), 81–88, 326, 335, 351–353, 383–393.

13 Frank Lestringant, *Mapping the Renaissance World: The Geographical Imagination in the Age of Discovery*, trans. David Fausett (Berkeley, CA, 1994).

14 Stephen Greenblatt, "Foreword," in Lestringant, *Mapping the Renaissance World*, vii–xv.

15 Michel de Certeau, *The Writing of History*, trans. Tom Conley (New York, 1988), 209–243; Robert M. Kingdon, *Myths About the St. Bartholomew's Day Massacres, 1572–1576* (Cambridge, 1988), 58–62.

16 Andrew Cunningham and Ole Peter Grell, *The Four Horsemen of the Apocalypse: Religion, War, Famine and Death in Reformation Europe* (Cambridge, 2000), 200–246.

17 René Girard, *Violence and the Sacred*, trans. Patrick Gregory (Paris, 1977), 145–149, 274–308.

18 H.E. Martel, "Hans Staden's Captive Soul: Identity, Imperialism, and Rumors of Cannibalism in Sixteenth-Century Brazil," *Journal of World History* 17 (March 2006): 51–69.

19 Gananath Obeyesekere, *The Apotheosis of Captain Cook: European Mythmaking in the Pacific* (Princeton, NJ, 1992), 16–18.

20 Daniel K. Richter, "War and Culture: The Iroquois Experience," *William and Mary Quarterly*, 3rd series, 40 (October 1983): 537–544; Anthony F.C. Wallace, *The Death and Rebirth of the Seneca* (New York, 1972), 76–107.

21 James Axtell and William C. Sturtevant, "The Unkindest Cut, or Who Invented Scalping," *William and Mary Quarterly*, 3rd series, 37 (July 1980): 451–472; Armstrong Starkey, "European–Amerindian Warfare in North America, 1513–1815," in *War in the Early Modern Period, 1450–1815*, ed. Jeremy Black (Boulder, CO, 1999), 248–249.

22 Patricia Lopes Don, "Franciscans, Indian Sorcerers, and the Inquisition in New Spain, 1536–1543," *Journal of World History* 17 (March 2006): 27–49.

23 Lisa Silverman, *Tortured Subjects: Pain, Truth, and the Body in Early Modern France* (Chicago, IL, 2001), 8–9.

24 Robin Law, "Warfare on the West African Slave Coast, 1650–1850," in *War in the Tribal Zone: Expanding States and Indigenous Warfare*, ed. R. Brian Ferguson and Neil L. Whitehead (Santa Fe, NM, 1992), 103–126.

25 John Thornton, *Africa and Africans in the Making of the Atlantic World, 1400–1800*, 2nd edn (Cambridge, 1998), 98–125.

26 David Eltis et al., *The Transatlantic Slave Trade, 1562–1867: A Database CD-Rom* (Cambridge, 1998); Herbert S. Klein, *The Atlantic Slave Trade*, 2nd edn (Cambridge, 2010), 130–160.

27 Bartolomé de Las Casas, *A Short Account of the Destruction of the Indies*, trans. Nigel Griffin (London, 1992).

28 Richard L. Kagan, "Prescott's Paradigm: American Historical Scholarship and the Decline of Spain," in *Imagined Histories: American Historians Interpret the Past*, ed. Anthony Molho and Gordon S. Wood (Princeton, NJ, 1998), 324–348.

29 Mark Grimsley and Clifford J. Rogers, eds., *Civilians in the Path of War* (Lincoln, NE, 2002).

30 Michael Howard, George J. Andreopoulos, and Mark R. Shulman, eds., *The Laws of War: Constraints on Warfare in the Western World* (New Haven, CT, 1994); Michael Walzer, *Just and Unjust Wars* (New York, 1977).

31 Don Higginbotham, "The Military Institutions of Colonial America: The Rhetoric and the Reality," in *Tools of War: Instruments, Ideas, and Institutions of Warfare, 1445–1871*, ed. John A. Lynn (Urbana, IL, 1990), 131–153.

32 Mark Juergensmeyer, *Terror in the Mind of God: The Global Rise of Religious Violence*, 3rd edn (Berkeley, 2003), 148–165, 190–218.

33 John Smith, quoted in Vaughan, "'Expulsion of the Salvages': English Policy and the Virginia Massacre of 1622," 62–63.

34 John S. Nolan, "The Militarization of the Elizabethan State," *Journal of Military History* 58 (July 1994): 391–420.

35 Nicholas P. Canny, "The Ideology of English Colonization: From Ireland to America," *William and Mary Quarterly*, 3rd series, 30 (October 1973): 596–597.

36 Robin Clifton, "'An Indiscriminate Blackness'? Massacre, Counter-Massacre, and Ethnic Cleansing in Ireland, 1640–1660," in *The Massacre in History*, ed. Mark Levene and Penny Roberts (New York, 1999), 107–126.

37 Barbara Donagan, "Atrocity, War Crime, and Treason in the English Civil War," *American Historical Review* 99 (October 1994): 1137–1166.

38 Nicholas P. Canny, *Kingdom and Colony: Ireland in the Atlantic World, 1560–1800* (Baltimore, MD, 1988); Harold E. Selesky, "Colonial America," in *The Laws of War: Constraints on Warfare in the Western World*, ed. Michael Howard, George J. Andreopoulos, and Mark R. Shulman (New Haven, CT, 1994), 60–62.

39 Markus Vink, "'The World's Oldest Trade': Dutch Slavery and Slave Trade in the Indian Ocean in the Seventeenth Century," *Journal of World History* 14 (June 2003): 131–177.

40 Nicholas Canny, ed., *Europeans on the Move: Studies on European Migration, 1500–1800* (Oxford, 1994).

41 Herbert S. Klein, *The Atlantic Slave Trade*, 2nd edn (Cambridge, 2010), 162–172.

42 Philip D. Curtin, *The Rise and Fall of the Plantation Complex: Essays in Atlantic History*, 2nd edn (Cambridge, 1998), 73–85, 100–102; Sidney W. Mintz, "Pleasure, Profit, and Satiation," in *Seeds of Change: A Quincentennial Commemoration*, ed. Herman J. Viola and Carolyn Margolis (Washington, DC, 1991), 112–129; David Barry Gaspar, "Antigua Slaves and Their Struggle to Survive," in *Seeds of Change*, ed. Viola and Margolis, 130–138.

43 David Eltis, "Europeans and the Rise and Fall of Slavery in the Americas: An Interpretation," *American Historical Review* 98 (December 1993): 1399–1423; Robert C. Davis, *Christian Slaves, Muslim Masters: White Slavery in the Mediterranean, the Barbary Coast, and Italy, 1500–1800* (Houndmills, 2003), 190–193.

44 Donald Harman Akenson, *If the Irish Ran the World: Montserrat, 1630–1730* (Liverpool, 1997); Jane Ohlmeyer, "Seventeenth-Century Ireland and the New British and Atlantic Histories," *American Historical Review* 104 (April 1999): 457–462.

45 Curtin, *The Rise and Fall of the Plantation Complex*, 52.

46 J.R. McNeil, *Mosquito Empires: Ecology and War in the Greater Caribbean, 1620–1914* (Cambridge, 2010), 23–32.

47 Philip P. Boucher, *France and the American Tropics to 1700: Tropics of Discontent?* (Baltimore, MD, 2008), 231–232.

48 James Pritchard, *In Search of Empire: The French in the Americas, 1670–1730* (Cambridge, 2004), 90–91.

49 Tzvetan Todorov, *The Conquest of America: The Question of the Other*, trans. Richard Howard (New York, 1984).

50 Martel, "Hans Staden's Captive Soul," 51–69.

51 Alfred A. Cave, "Who Killed John Stone? A Note on the Origins of the Pequot War," *William and Mary Quarterly*, 3rd series, 49 (July 1992): 509–521; Alfred A. Cave, *The Pequot War* (Amherst, MA, 1996).

52 Perreault, "'To Fear and to Love Us,'" 71–93.

53 Patrick M. Malone, *The Skulking Way of War: Technology and Tactics among the New England Indians* (Lanham, MD, 1991); Wayne E. Lee, "Fortify, Fight, or Flee: Tuscarora and Cherokee Defensive Warfare and Military Culture Adaptation," *Journal of Military History* 68 (July 2004): 713–770.

54 John Foran, *Fragile Resistance: Social Transformation in Iran from 1500 to the Revolution* (Boulder, CO, 1993), 19–50.

55 Rudi Matthee, "Unwalled Cities and Restless Nomads: Firearms and Artillery in Safavid Iran," in *Safavid Persia: The History and Politics of an Islamic Society*, ed. Charles Melville (London, 1996), 389–416.

56 Pradeep Barua, *The State at War in South Asia* (Lincoln, NE, 2005), 38–39.

57 Jos Gommans, *Mughal Warfare: Indian Frontiers and High Roads to Empire, 1500–1700* (London, 2002), 13.

58 Jorge Cañizares Esguerra, "New World, New Stars: Patriotic Astrology and the Invention of Indian and Creole Bodies in Colonial Spanish America, 1600–1650," *American Historical Review* 104 (February 1999), 33–68.

59 Juergensmeyer, *Terror in the Mind of God*, 148–165.

60 Cunningham and Grell, *The Four Horsemen of the Apocalypse*, 79–82.

61 Antoine d'Arnauld, *Presentation de Monsieur de Montmorency en l'office d'Admiral de France. 1612* (Paris: Denys du Val, 1612), Bibliothèque Nationale de France, 8° Ln^{27} 14695.

62 Anthony Reid, *Southeast Asia in the Age of Commerce, 1450–1680. Volume Two: Expansion and Crisis* (New Haven, CT, 1993), 132–136.

63 Marc David Baer, *Honored by the Glory of Islam: Conversion and Conquest in Ottoman Europe* (Oxford, 2008).

64 John F. Richards, *The Mughal Empire* (Cambridge, 1995).

65 Gommans, *Mughal Warfare*, 60–61, 77–81, 187–199.

66 George A. De Vos, "Ethnic Pluralism: Conflict and Accommodation," in *Ethnic Identity: Creation, Conflict, and Accommodation*, ed. Lola Romanucci-Ross and George A. De Vos (Walnut Creek, 1995), 15–47.

67 Thomas S. Abler, "Beavers and Muskets: Iroquois Military Fortunes in the Face of European Colonization," in *War in the Tribal Zone: Expanding States and Warfare*, ed. R. Brian Ferguson and Neil L. Whitehead (Santa Fe, NM, 1992), 151–174; Richard R. Johnson, "The Search for a Usable Indian: An Aspect of the Defense of Colonial New England," *Journal of American History* 64 (December 1977): 623–651.

68 Neil L. Whitehead, "Carib Ethnic Soldiering in Venezuela, the Guianas, and the Antilles, 1492–1820," *Ethnohistory* 37 (Autumn 1990): 357–385.

69   Richter, "War and Culture: The Iroquois Experience," 537–544; Thomas D. Hall, *Social Change in the Southwest, 1350–1880* (Lawrence, KS), 70–86.
70   Malone, *The Skulking Way of War*, 89–90, 96–98.
71   Vink, "'The World's Oldest Trade,'" 131–177.
72   Massimo Livi-Bacci, "Return to Hispaniola: Reassessing a Demographic Catastrophe," *Hispanic American Historical Review* 83 (February 2003): 3–51.
73   Stuart B. Schwartz, "Indian Labor and New World Plantations: European Demands and Indian Responses in Northeastern Brazil," *American Historical Review* 83 (February 1978): 43–79.
74   Miguel Angel de Bunes Ibarra, *La Imagen de Los Musulmanes y del Norte de Africa en la España de los Siglos XVI y XVII: Los Caracteres de una Hostilidad* (Madrid, 1989).
75   Arlette Jouanna, *L'Idée de race en France au XVIe siècle et au début du XVIIe*, édition revue, 2 vols (Montpellier, 1981).
76   Boucher, *France and the American Tropics to 1700*; Kenneth J. Banks, *Chasing Empire Across the Sea: Communications and the State in the French Atlantic, 1713–1763* (Montreal, 2003).
77   John Hale, *The Civilization of Europe in the Renaissance* (London, 1993), 3–50.
78   Michael Wintle, *The Image of Europe: Visualizing Europe in Cartography and Iconography Throughout the Ages* (Cambridge, 2009).
79   Dirk Van der Cruysse, *Louis XIV et le Siam* (Paris, 1991); Ronald S. Love, "Monarchs, Merchants, and Missionaries in Early Modern Asia: The *Missions Étrangères* in Siam, 1662–1684," *International History Review* 21 (March 1999): 1–27.

Chapter 10   Rebellion and Civil Warfare, 1630s–1660s

1   Geoffrey Parker, *Global Crisis: War, Climate Change and Catastrophe in the Seventeenth Century* (New Haven, CT, 2013), 254–290.
2   Jeroen Duindam, *Myths of Power: Norbert Elias and the Early Modern European Court* (Amsterdam, 1994), 1–12.
3   Daniel Goffman, *The Ottoman Empire and Early Modern Europe* (Cambridge, 2002), 60–64.
4   Sam White, *The Climate of Rebellion in the Early Modern Ottoman Empire* (Cambridge, 2011), 191.
5   Parker, *Global Crisis*, 152–184.
6   Arlette Jouanna, *Le Devoir de révolte: la noblesse française et la gestation de l'Etat moderne, 1559–1661* (Paris, 1989).
7   Brian Sandberg, *Warrior Pursuits: Noble Culture and Civil Conflict in Early Modern France* (Baltimore, MD, 2010), xxi–xxii; Brian Sandberg, " 'Se couvrant toujours…du nom du roi'. Perceptions nobiliaires de la révolte dans le sud-ouest de la France, 1610–1635," *Histoire, Économie et Société* 17, 3 (1998): 423–440.

8 Geoffrey Parker, "Early Modern Europe," in *The Laws of War: Constraints on Warfare in the Western World*, ed. Michael Howard, George J. Andreopoulous, and Mark R. Shulman (New Haven, CT, 1994), 40–58.

9 Francois Hotman, *Francogallia*, trans. J.H.M. Salmon (Cambridge, 1972); Kathleen Ann Parrow, *From Defense to Resistance: Justification of Violence During the French Wars of Religion* (Philadelphia, PA, 1993).

10 John F. Richards, *The Mughal Empire* (Cambridge, 1993), 151–164.

11 Richards, *The Mughal Empire*, 162.

12 William Beik, *Urban Protest in Seventeenth-Century France: The Culture of Retribution* (Cambridge, 1997).

13 Beik, *Urban Protest in Seventeenth-Century France*, 49–72, 116–144.

14 Sharon Kettering, "Patronage and Politics during the Fronde," *French Historical Studies* 14 (Spring 1986): 409–441.

15 B. Ann Tlusty, *The Martial Ethic in Early Modern Germany: Civic Duty and the Right of Arms* (New York, 2011), 137–141.

16 Stuart B. Schwartz, "Panic in the Indies: The Portuguese Threat to the Spanish Empire, 1640–1650," *Colonial Latin American Review* 2 (1993): 165–187.

17 Parker, *Global Crisis*, 461–462.

18 Parker, *Global Crisis*, 421–444.

19 A 1642 pamphlet, quoted in John Kenyon and Jane Ohlmeyer, "Background to the Civil Wars in the Stuart Kingdoms," in *The Civil Wars: A Military History of England, Scotland, and Ireland, 1638–1660*, ed. John Kenyon and Jane Ohlmeyer (Oxford, 1998), 28–31.

20 Ian Gentles, "The Civil Wars in England, in *The Civil Wars: A Military History of England, Scotland, and Ireland, 1638–1660*, ed. John Kenyon and Jane Ohlmeyer (Oxford, 1998), 103–154.

21 Ian Gentles, "The Civil Wars in England," 103–154.

22 Barbara Donagan, *War in England, 1642–1649* (Oxford, 2008), 312–388.

23 Jane Ohlmeyer, "The Civil Wars in Ireland," in *The Civil Wars: A Military History of England, Scotland, and Ireland, 1638–1660*, ed. John Kenyon and Jane Ohlmeyer (Oxford, 1998), 73–102.

24 Eamon Duffy, *The Stripping of the Altars: Traditional Religion in England, c.1400–c.1580* (New Haven, CT, 1992); Christopher Hill, *The World Turned Upside Down; Radical Ideas During the English Revolution* (New York, 1972).

25 Orest Ranum, *The Fronde: A French Revolution* (New York, 1993), 303.

26 Sharon Kettering, "Patronage and Politics during the Fronde," *French Historical Studies* 14 (Spring 1986): 409–441.

27 William M. Reger IV, "European Mercenary Officers and the Reception of Military Reform in the Seventeenth-Century Russian Army," in *Modernizing Muscovy: Reform and Social Change in Seventeenth-Century Russia*, ed. Jarmo Kotilaine and Marshall Poe (London, 2004), 214–237.

28 Robert I. Frost, *The Northern Wars: War, State and Society in Northeastern Europe, 1558–1721* (Harlow, 2000), 156–187.

29   Jan K. Ostrowski, ed., *Land of the Winged Horsemen: Art in Poland, 1572–1764* (Alexandria, VA, 1999).
30   Richard Hellie, *Enserfment and Military Change in Muscovy* (Chicago, IL, 1971), 246.
31   John K. Thornton, *Warfare in Atlantic Africa, 1500–1800* (London, 1999).
32   Philip D. Curtin, *The Rise and Fall of the Plantation Complex: Essays in Atlantic History*, 2nd edn (Cambridge, 1998), 104–106.
33   Parker, *Global Crisis*, 530.
34   Hilary McD. Beckles, "A 'Riotous and Unruly Lot': Irish Indentured Servants and Freemen in the English West Indies, 1644–1713," *William and Mary Quarterly*, 3rd series, 47 (October 1990): 503–522.
35   Olivier Pétré-Grenouilleau, "Maritime Powers, Colonial Powers: The Role of Migration (c.1492–1792)," in *Migration, Trade, and Slavery in an Expanding World: Essays in Honor of Pieter Emmer*, ed. Wim Klooster (Leiden, 2009), 48.
36   Femme S. Gaastra, "Soldiers and Merchants: Aspects of Migration from Europe to Asia in the Dutch East India Company in the Eighteenth Century," in *Migration, Trade, and Slavery in an Expanding World: Essays in Honor of Pieter Emmer*, ed. Wim Klooster (Leiden, 2009), 99–118.
37   Myriam Yardeni, *Enquêtes sur l'identité de la nation France: de la Renaissance aux Lumières* (Seyssel, 2005).
38   John Childs, *The British Army of William III, 1689–1702* (Manchester, 1987), 132–137.
39   Steve Murdoch and A. Mackillop, eds., *Fighting for Identity: Scottish Military Experience c.1550–1900* (Leiden, 2002).
40   Parker, *Global Crisis*, xxii.
41   Peter Lorge, "War and Warfare in China, 1450–1815," in *War in the Early Modern World, 1450–1815*, ed. Jeremy Black (Boulder, CO, 1999), 99.

Chapter 11   Mercantile War, 1630s–1690s

1   P.A. Leupe and Mac Hacobian, "The Siege and Capture of Malacca from the Portuguese in 1640–1641," *Journal of the Malayan Branch of the Royal Asiatic Society* 14 (1936): i–iii, 1–178.
2   Governor Arent Gardenijs, quoted in Wil O. Dijk, *Seventeenth-century Burma and the Dutch East India Company, 1634–1680* (Singapore, 2006), 152–153.
3   Londa Schiebinger, "Prospecting for Drugs: European Naturalists in the West Indies," in *Colonial Botany: Science, Commerce, and Politics in the Early Modern World*, ed. Londa Schiebinger and Claudia Swan (Philadelphia, PA, 2005), 119–133.
4   Julie Berger Hochstrasser, "The Conquest of Spice and the Dutch Colonial Imaginary: Seen and Unseen in the Visual Culture of Trade," in *Colonial Botany: Science, Commerce, and Politics in the Early Modern World*, ed. Londa Schiebinger and Claudia Swan (Philadelphia, PA, 2005), 169–186.

5   Regina Grafe, *Distant Tyranny: Markets, Power, and Backwardness in Spain, 1650–1800* (Princeton, NJ, 2012).

6   Timothy Brook, *Vermeer's Hat: The Seventeenth Century and the Dawn of the Global World* (New York, 2008), 117–151.

7   Özkan Bardakçi and François Pugnière, *La Dernière Croisade. Les français et la guerre de Candie 1669* (Rennes, 2008).

8   Susan Pinkard, *A Revolution in Taste: The Rise of French Cuisine* (Cambridge, 2009), 211–230.

9   Robert Finlay, *The Pilgrim Art: Cultures of Porcelain in World History* (Berkeley, CA, 2010); Brook, *Vermeer's Hat*, 54–83.

10 Brook, *Vermeer's Hat*, 26–53.

11 H. Ph. Vogel, "The Republic as Exporter of Arms 1600–1650," in *The Arsenal of the World: The Dutch Arms Trade in the Seventeenth Century*, ed. Jan Piet Puype and Marco van der Hoeven (Amsterdam, 1996), 13–21.

12 Vogel, "The Republic as Exporter of Arms 1600–1650," 13–21.

13 James D. Tracy, *A Financial Revolution in the Habsburg Netherlands: Renten and Renteniers in the County of Holland, 1515–1565* (Berkeley, CA, 1985).

14 Larry Neal, *The Rise of Financial Capitalism: International Capital Markets in the Age of Reason* (Cambridge, 1990), 17.

15 Anne Goldgar, *Tulipmania: Money, Honor, and Knowledge in the Dutch Golden Age* (Chicago, IL, 2007), 1–2, 31, 40, 202–204, 217–223.

16 Goldgar, *Tulipmania*, 1–2, 199, 228–232, 247–249, 253–304.

17 Goldgar, *Tulipmania*, 318–319.

18 Harold J. Cook, *Matters of Exchange: Commerce, Medicine, and Science in the Dutch Golden Age* (New Haven, CT, 2007), 188–191.

19 Jonathan I. Israel, *The Dutch Republic and the Hispanic World, 1606–1661* (Oxford, 1982), 271–281.

20 Cook, *Matters of Exchange*, 189.

21 Jan Glete, *Warfare at Sea, 1500–1650: Maritime Conflicts and the Transformation of Europe* (London, 2002).

22 Bruce P. Lenman, "The Transition to European Military Ascendancy in India, 1600–1800," in *Tools of War: Instruments, Ideas, and Institutions of Warfare, 1445–1871* (Urbana, IL, 1990), 100–130.

23 Suraiya Faroqhi, *Artisans of Empire: Crafts and Craftspeople Under the Ottomans* (London, 2009), 13–15, 23–44, 46–47.

24 Daniel Goffman, *The Ottoman Empire and Early Modern Europe* (Cambridge, 2002), 18.

25 Herbert S. Klein, *The Atlantic Slave Trade*, 2nd edn (Cambridge, 2010).

26 Robert Harms, *The Diligent: A Voyage through the Worlds of the Slave Trade* (New York, 2002).

27 José Jobson de Andrade Arruda, "Colonies as Mercantile Investments: The Luso-Brazilian Empire, 1500–1808," in *The Political Economy of Merchant Empires*, ed. James D. Tracy (Cambridge, 1991), 360–420.

28 James Pritchard, *In Search of Empire: The French in the Americas, 1670–1730* (Cambridge, 2004), 254–260.

29   Benjamin Worsley, *The Advocate* (1651), quoted in Robert Brenner, *Merchants and Revolution: Commercial Change, Political Conflict, and London's Overseas Traders, 1550–1653* (Princeton, NJ, 1993), 627.
30   Jean Peter, *Les Manufactures de la marine sous Louis XIV. La naissance d'une industrie de l'armement* (Paris, 1997).
31   Maarten Prak, *The Dutch Republic in the Seventeenth Century* (Cambridge, 2005), 252–255.
32   Chandra Mukerji, *Impossible Engineering: Technology and Territoriality on the Canal Du Midi* (Princeton, NJ, 2009).
33   Jan Glete, *War and the State in Early Modern Europe: Spain, the Dutch Republic and Sweden as Fiscal-Military States, 1500–1660* (London, 2002), 36–37, 200–201.
34   Alfred Thayer Mahan, *The Influence of Sea Power Upon History, 1660–1783* (1890; Reprint, Cambridge, 2010).
35   Glete, *War and the State in Early Modern Europe*, 36–37, 170–171; J.R. Jones, *The Anglo-Dutch Wars of the Seventeenth Century* (London, 1996).
36   Colbert, quoted in Roger Mettam, ed., *Government and Society in Louis XIV's France* (London, 1977), 174–175.
37   Daniel Dessert, *La Royale. Vaisseaux et marins du Roi-Soleil* (Paris, 1996).
38   Bardakçi and Pugnière, *La Dernière Croisade*.
39   Contemporary account quoted in Molly Greene, *A Shared World: Christians and Muslims in the Early Modern Mediterranean* (Princeton, NJ, 2000), 18.
40   Greene, *A Shared World*, 13–18, 29–30, 33–44, 78–109.

Chapter 12   Territorial War, 1660s–1700s

1   John A. Lynn, *The Wars of Louis XIV, 1667–1714* (London, 1999), 118–120.
2   John A. Lynn, *Giant of the Grand Siècle: The French Army, 1610–1715* (Cambridge, 1997), 575–578.
3   Lauren Benton, *A Search for Sovereignty: Law and Geography in European Empires, 1400–1900* (Cambridge, 2010), 2.
4   John A. Lynn, "The Evolution of Army Style in the Modern West, 800–2000," *International History Review* 18 (August 1996): 518.
5   Lynn, *Giant of the* Grand Siècle, 158–160.
6   Derek McKay, *The Great Elector* (London, 2001), 169–178.
7   Karin Friedrich, *Brandenburg-Prussia, 1466–1806* (Houndmills, 2012), 79–83.
8   Paul Sonnino, *Louis XIV and the Origins of the Dutch War* (Cambridge, 1988).
9   Lynn, *The Wars of Louis XIV*, 367–376.
10   Turenne, quoted in Lynn, *The Wars of Louis XIV*, 128.
11   Lynn, *The Wars of Louis XIV*, 71–82.

12   Christopher Duffy, *The Fortress in the Age of Vauban and Frederick the Great, 1660–1789* (London, 1985), 63–71.

13   George Steinmetz, "Introduction: Culture and the State," in *State/Culture: State-Formation after the Cultural Turn*, ed. George Steinmetz (Ithaca, NY, 1999), 8–9.

14   Jan Glete, *War and the State in Early Modern Europe: Spain, the Dutch Republic and Sweden as Fiscal-Military States, 1500–1660* (London, 2002), 1–66.

15   David Parrott, *The Business of War: Military Enterprise and Military Revolution in Early Modern Europe* (Cambridge, 2012), 307–327.

16   John Brewer, *The Sinews of Power: War, Money and the English State, 1688–1783* (London, 1989), 137–138.

17   John Childs, *The Nine Years War and the British Army, 1688–1697: The Operations in the Low Countries* (Manchester, 1991), 51–58.

18   Darryl Dee, *Expansion and Crisis in Louis XIV's France: Franche-Comté and Absolute Monarchy, 1674–1715* (Rochester, NY, 2009), 50–57, 84.

19   Charles Tilly, *The Contentious French: Four Centuries of Popular Struggle* (Cambridge, MA, 1989), 148–149.

20   Chandra Mukerji, *Territorial Ambitions and the Gardens of Versailles* (Cambridge, 1997).

21   Gábor Ágoston, "Information, Ideology, and the Limits of Imperial Policy: Ottoman Grand Strategy in the Context of Ottoman-Habsburg Rivalry," in *The Early Modern Ottomans: Remapping the Empire*, ed. Virginia H. Aksan and Daniel Goffman (Cambridge, 2007), 75–103.

22   Gábor Ágoston, "Firearms and Military Adaptation: The Ottomans and the European Military Revolution, 1450–1800," *Journal of World History* 25 (March 2014): 85–124.

23   Charles Tilly, *Coercion, Capital and European States, AD 990–1992* (Oxford, 1992), 2.

24   Conrad Totman, *Early Modern Japan* (Berkeley, CA, 1993), 152–153.

25   Linda Colley, *Britons: Forging the Nation, 1707–1837* (New Haven, CT, 2005), 3–4.

26   Steve Murdoch and A. Mackillop, eds., *Fighting for Identity: Scottish Military Experience c.1550–1900* (Leiden, 2002).

27   Elizabeth Mancke, "Empire and State," in *The British Atlantic World, 1500–1800*, ed. David Armitage and Michaael J. Braddick, 2nd edn (Houndmills, 2009), 193–213.

28   Jahyun Kim Haboush, "Dead Bodies in the Postwar Discourse of Identity in Seventeenth-Century Korea: Subversion and Literary Production in the Private Sector," *Journal of Asian Studies* 62 (May 2003): 415–442.

29   David A. Bell, *The Cult of the Nation in France: Inventing Nationalism, 1680–1800* (Cambridge, MA, 2003), 1–9.

30   Carol B. Stevens, "Modernizing the Military: Peter the Great and Military Reform," in *Modernizing Muscovy: Reform and Social Change in Seventeenth-Century Russia*, ed. Jarmo Kotilaine and Marshall Poe (London, 2004), 238–253.

31　Peter C. Perdue, *China Marches West: The Qing Conquest of Central Eurasia* (Cambridge, MA, 2005), 134–208.
32　Pradeep Barua, *The State at War in South Asia* (Lincoln, NE, 2005), 39–51.
33　Stephen F. Dale, *The Muslim Empires of the Ottomans, Safavids, and Mughals* (Cambridge, 2010), 187–195, 249–256.
34　George Satterfield, *Princes, Posts, and Partisans: The Army of Louis XIV and Partisan Warfare in the Netherlands (1673–1678)* (Leiden, 2003).
35　Gábor Ágoston, "Empires and Warfare in East-Central Europe, 1550–1750: The Ottoman-Habsburg Rivalry and Military Transformation," in *European Warfare, 1350–1750*, ed. Frank Tallett and D. J. B. Trim (Cambridge, 2010), 110–134.
36　Micahel Hochedlinger, *Austria's Wars of Emergence, 1683–1797* (London, 2003), 153–166, 187–192.
37　Jill Lepore, *The Name of War: King Philip's War and the Origins of American Identity* (New York, 1998), 72–73, 166–167.
38　Jules-Louis Bolé, marquis de Chamlay, quoted in Lynn, "A Brutal Necessity? The Devastation of the Palatinate, 1688–1689," in *Civilians in the Path of War*, ed. Mark Grimsley and Clifford J. Rogers (Lincoln, NE, 2002), 85.
39　*Concusus creditorum* (1689), quoted in Lynn, "A Brutal Necessity?" 87–88.
40　John Childs, *The British Army of William III, 1689–1702* (Manchester, 1987).
41　Lynn, *The Wars of Louis XIV*, 191–265.
42　Jamel Ostwald, *Vauban Under Siege: Engineering Efficiency and Martial Vigor in the War of the Spanish Succession* (Leiden, 2007), 21–45.
43　David B. Ralston, *Importing the European Army: The Introduction of European Military Techniques and Institutions into the Extra-European World, 1600–1914* (Chicago, IL, 1990).
44　Chouki El Hamel, *Black Morocco: A History of Slavery, Race, and Islam* (Cambridge, 2012), 155–184.
45　Younès Nekrouf, *Une Amitié orageuse. Moulay Ismaïl et Louis XIV* (Paris, 1987).

Conclusion: c.1700

1　G.V. Scammel, *The First Imperial Age: European Overseas Expansion c.1400–1715* (London, 1989), 247.
2　Max Weber, "Politics as a Vocation," repr. in *From Max Weber*, ed. Hans Gerth and C. Wright Mills (New York, 1958), 77–128.

Index